DeepSeek in Practice

From basics to fine-tuning, distillation, agent design, and prompt engineering of open source LLM

Andy Peng

Alex Strick van Linschoten

Duarte O.Carmo

DeepSeek in Practice

Portfolio Director: Gebin George
Relationship Lead: Sonia Chauhan
Project Manager: Prajakta Naik
Technical Editor: Aditya Bharadwaj and Rahul Limbachiya
Copy Editor: Safis Editing
Indexer: Manju Arasan
Proofreader: Safis Editing
Production Designer: Jyoti Kadam

First published: November 2025

Production reference: 2021225

Published by Packt Publishing Ltd.
Grosvenor House
11 St Paul's Square
Birmingham
B3 1RB, UK.

ISBN 978-1-80602-085-0
`www.packtpub.com`

Contributors

About the authors

Andy Peng, a builder with curiosity, is motivated by research and product innovation. He specializes in large language model inference optimization and evaluation for state-of-the-art models like DeepSeek, Qwen, and Claude. His work spans AWS Bedrock, SageMaker, Amazon S3, AWS Fargate, AWS App Runner, Alexa Health & Wellness, and fintech. A NeurIPS 2025 Chair and program committee member for ICML, ICLR, and KDD, he contributes to CNCF and the Linux Foundation, mentors at the University of Washington, and serves as Resident Expert at the AI2 Incubator.

I would like to express my gratitude to my family for their support and for understanding that I needed to work long hours on this book. My sincere thanks go to my manager, Rakesh Ramakrishnan, and my colleagues, Raj Vippagunta and Siddharth Shah, for their valuable input and support.

I would also like to thank Gebin George for reaching out with the opportunity to write this book, which has been a truly unique experience. Special thanks to my co-authors, Alex and Duarte, and to the entire Packt team—including Vandita Grover, Prajakta, Gebin, and everyone else—for their unwavering support throughout the writing process. I first connected with Packt in 2022, and it is a pleasure to see the successful delivery of our first new book.

Alex Strick van Linschoten is a Machine Learning Engineer at ZenML. His work focuses on bridging the gap between machine learning research and production deployment, particularly within the LLMOps space. He leads and maintains the LLMOps Database, a comprehensive collection of over 1,000 case studies examining LLMOps and GenAI implementations in production environments. He transitioned to software engineering after earning a PhD in History and spending 15 years living and working as a historian and researcher in Afghanistan. He has authored, edited, and translated several books based on his historical research and is currently based in Delft, the Netherlands.

I'd like to thank Saba, Aria, and Blupus for their patience as I took many weekends off to work on the chapters of this book. I'd also like to thank Hamza and the rest of the ZenML team for their support in thinking through how best to present the ideas introduced below. Of course, much appreciation goes to the Packt team as well for their support in getting this out into the world!

Duarte O. Carmo is a technologist from Lisbon, Portugal, now based in Copenhagen, Denmark. For the past decade, he's worked at the intersection of machine learning, artificial intelligence, software, data, and people. He has helped solve problems for both global corporations and small startups across industries such as healthcare, finance, agriculture, and advertising. His approach to solving tough problems always starts with the same thing: people. For the past five years, he's been running his one-man consulting company, working with clients of all sizes and across industries. He's also a regular speaker in the Python and machine learning communities and an active writer.

*I'd like to thank my family, who have always encouraged me to follow my passion. In particular, I want to thank **Vittoria**. Writing a book is no easy task. Following your passion is no easy task. Leaving the dinner table because a client has a problem is no easy task. Hiding in the attic to write about an open-source LLM while the rest of you are on holiday is no easy task. Your unconditional support and love inspire me every day to keep going. As you once told me: **"There are a lot of fun things out there to do—go do them!"***

About the reviewer

Franck Benichou is a Senior AI Engineer with over six years of experience in machine learning and large language model (LLM) engineering. He currently works at Carta, the leading platform for private-market equity and fund data management. Following Carta's acquisition of Accelex, Franck drives advancements in AI-powered document intelligence, applying Generative AI to transform complex financial data into structured insights. Before joining Carta, Franck worked at Deloitte (2024–2025) as an in-house Generative AI Developer, creating enterprise AI solutions and contributing to the firm's internal AI strategy. From 2022 to 2024, he led Generative AI initiatives at EY (Ernst & Young), developing retrieval-augmented and content automation systems. Earlier, at Intact Financial Corporation's R&D Data Lab (2020–2022), he specialized in usage-based insurance modeling and analytics, supporting telematics-driven pricing innovation. Franck combines strong technical depth with a product-focused mindset, building scalable and interpretable AI systems that bring automation, intelligence, and measurable value to data-driven organizations.

Table of Contents

Chapter 2: Deep Dive into DeepSeek 39

Chapter 5: Building with DeepSeek 199

Chapter 6: Agents with DeepSeek 249

Part 3: Distilling and Deploying DeepSeek 291

Chapter 7: DeepSeek-Driven Fine-Tuning of Gemma 3 for Legal Reasoning 293

Chapter 9: Epilogue 389

Chapter 10: Appendix 391

Preface

The space of large language models (LLMs) is evolving at a ludicrous pace. As we write this, the DeepSeek team has just released a new paper showing how to compress an LLM's context using computer vision techniques. The sheer level of activity in the field of artificial intelligence is impressive and shows no signs of slowing down.

As authors of this book, we thought, *What can we possibly write about DeepSeek that wouldn't make this book instantly outdated?* Our answer is simple: we believe that the future of AI technology is open, and the pioneer of that movement is DeepSeek.

DeepSeek has not stopped surprising the world of artificial intelligence, from releasing incredibly powerful models to publishing breakthrough research focused on LLMs. Given these developments, it was clear to us that we needed to write a book about what was happening.

The goal of this book is to give you - dear reader - the necessary tools to master DeepSeek. We want it to serve as your guide to mastering open-source language models.

In this book, we cover nearly everything you might encounter while working with DeepSeek models - from understanding what sets DeepSeek models apart to how you can use them for practical applications. We also cover how to master prompting DeepSeek models, so you can become an expert at interacting with this family of models. Finally, we dive deep into the practical side of things, with examples of how to design, build, and deploy agentic and non-agentic applications powered by DeepSeek models.

In this book, we start with an introduction to DeepSeek, where we explore its foundations and understand what sets it apart from the rest (*Chapters 1* and *2*). Once you understand what DeepSeek can do, it's time to learn how to use it effectively. We have an entire chapter dedicated to the art of prompting reasoning models, where we show you how *less is more* (*Chapter 3*).

We then move into practical applications, demonstrating how to use it to produce consultant-grade analysis of complex problems (*Chapter 4*). From there, we build a complete end-to-end application where you'll go from a simple API all the way to a fully containerized service running on Amazon Web Services (*Chapter 5*).

In the final part of this book, we explore the edge of LLM and AI technologies. You'll learn how to use DeepSeek models as backbones for agentic applications (*Chapter 6*). We also walk you through a more complex MLOps use case where you'll use a more powerful DeepSeek model to distill knowledge into a smaller one (*Chapter 7*). In the last chapter of this book, we cover the deployment of DeepSeek models, with their many trade-offs, so you can choose the best deployment methodology for your use case (*Chapter 8*).

To conclude this book we have an *Epilogue* to walk you through the key takeaways. The book also provides an *Appendix* that guides you through various ways to use DeepSeek.

Who this book is for

This book is aimed at anyone who wants to learn how DeepSeek models work. Whether you are an AI Engineer, a Software Developer, a Machine Learning Engineer, or a Researcher - as long as you are familiar with Python - you'll be able to benefit from this book. If you have experience with Data Science, APIs, and some Machine Learning concepts, you'll be able to benefit even more!

What this book covers

Chapter 1, What is DeepSeek, introduces DeepSeek, an open-source large language model, exploring its breakthroughs, evolution, comparisons with other LLMs, and impact on the global AI landscape today.

Chapter 2, Deep Dive into DeepSeek, dives into DeepSeek's architecture, reasoning mechanics, advanced capabilities, offering a practical understanding of its unique strengths and emerging controversies.

Chapter 3, Prompting DeepSeek, shows you how to effectively craft prompts for DeepSeek models, making sure to showcase the difference between how this should be done for the V- and R-series models.

Chapter 4, Using DeepSeek: Case Studies, showcases real-world DeepSeek case studies, revealing how industry leaders apply it to boost productivity, improve development, and implement AI-assisted workflows using practical methodologies.

Chapter 5, Building with DeepSeek, takes you through creating a real-world application backed by DeepSeek models, how to iteratively improve it, and how to deploy DeepSeek models to AWS as an isolated service.

Chapter 6, Agents with DeepSeek, shows you how to start building agents with DeepSeek models, the different agentic patterns that exist, and a quick introduction to MCP.

Chapter 7, DeepSeek-Driven Fine-Tuning of Gemma 3 for Legal Reasoning, covers the distillation of DeepSeek's R1 down into a fine-tuned Gemma 3 model. We explore a legal use case and how this would be evaluated in production scenarios.

Chapter 8, Deploying DeepSeek Models, showcases how to deploy DeepSeek models for production use cases. We show you how to spin up the full-scale models on cloud infrastructure and guide you on how to manage these as part of your production stack.

Chapter 9, Epilogue, reflects on the journey you took to understand the internals of DeepSeek, how to use it effectively, from application to deployment.

Chapter 10, Appendix, contains a DeepSeek Cheat Sheet which shows you how to get started quickly.

To get the most out of this book

- Hands-on experience with Python, APIs, and tools like Ollama or llama.cpp
- Experience with tools and platforms like `uv` and Docker
- A solid understanding of machine learning concepts

Declaration

The authors acknowledge the use of cutting-edge AI, such as ChatGPT, with the sole aim of enhancing the language and clarity within the book, thereby ensuring a smooth reading experience for readers.

Download the example code files

The code bundle for the book is hosted on GitHub at `https://github.com/PacktPublishing/DeepSeek-in-Practice`. We also have other code bundles from our rich catalog of books and videos available at `https://github.com/PacktPublishing`. Check them out!

Download the color images

We also provide a PDF file that has color images of the screenshots/diagrams used in this book. You can download it here: `https://packt.link/gbp/9781806020850`.

Conventions used

There are a number of text conventions used throughout this book.

`CodeInText`: Indicates code words in text, database table names, folder names, filenames, file extensions, pathnames, dummy URLs, user input, and Twitter handles. For example: "Execute the `python-garminconnect` command:"

A block of code is set as follows:

```
# We get the values as environmental variables
GARMIN_EMAIL = os.getenv("GARMIN_EMAIL") # your email
GARMIN_PASSWORD = os.getenv("GARMIN_PASSWORD") # your password
```

When we wish to draw your attention to a particular part of a code block, the relevant lines or items are set in bold:

```
tools = [{
    "type": "function",
    "function": {
        "name": "analyze_sentiment",
        "description": "Analyze the sentiment of text",
        "parameters": {
            "type": "object",
            "properties": {
                "text": {"type": "string"},
                "confidence": {"type": "number",
                               "minimum": 0, "maximum": 1}
            },
            "required": ["text", "confidence"]
        }
    }
}]
```

Any command-line input or output is written as follows:

```
git clone https://github.com/PacktPublishing/DeepSeek-in-Practice.git
cd Chapter03
pip install -r requirements.txt
```

Bold: Indicates a new term, an important word, or words that you see on the screen. For instance, words in menus or dialog boxes appear in the text like this. For example: "Access the Cursor model configuration through the **Settings** menu."

Warnings or important notes appear like this.

Tips and tricks appear like this.

Get in touch

Feedback from our readers is always welcome.

General feedback: If you have questions about any aspect of this book or have any general feedback, please email us at `customercare@packt.com` and mention the book's title in the subject of your message.

Errata: Although we have taken every care to ensure the accuracy of our content, mistakes do happen. If you have found a mistake in this book, we would be grateful if you reported this to us. Please visit `http://www.packt.com/submit-errata`, click **Submit Errata**, and fill in the form.

Piracy: If you come across any illegal copies of our works in any form on the internet, we would be grateful if you would provide us with the location address or website name. Please contact us at `copyright@packt.com` with a link to the material.

If you are interested in becoming an author: If there is a topic that you have expertise in and you are interested in either writing or contributing to a book, please visit `http://authors.packt.com/`.

Share your thoughts

Once you've read *DeepSeek in Practice*, we'd love to hear your thoughts! Scan the QR code below to go straight to the Amazon review page for this book and share your feedback.

https://packt.link/r/180602084X

Your review is important to us and the tech community and will help us make sure we're delivering excellent quality content.

Free Benefits with Your Book

This book comes with free benefits to support your learning. Activate them now for instant access (see the "*How to Unlock*" section for instructions).

Here's a quick overview of what you can instantly unlock with your purchase:

PDF and ePub Copies

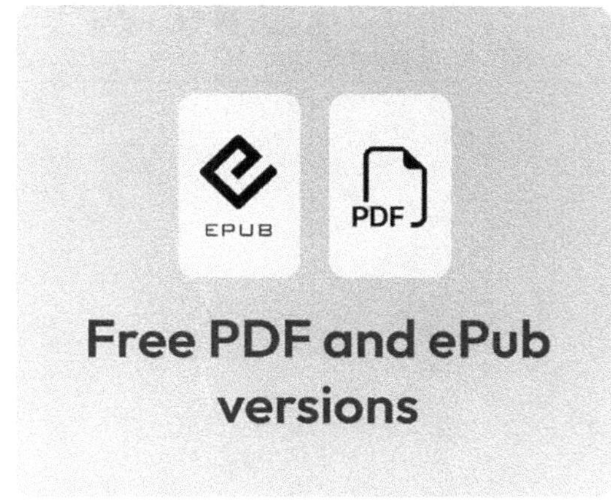

- Access a DRM-free PDF copy of this book to read anywhere, on any device.
- Use a DRM-free ePub version with your favorite e-reader.

Next-Gen Web-Based Reader

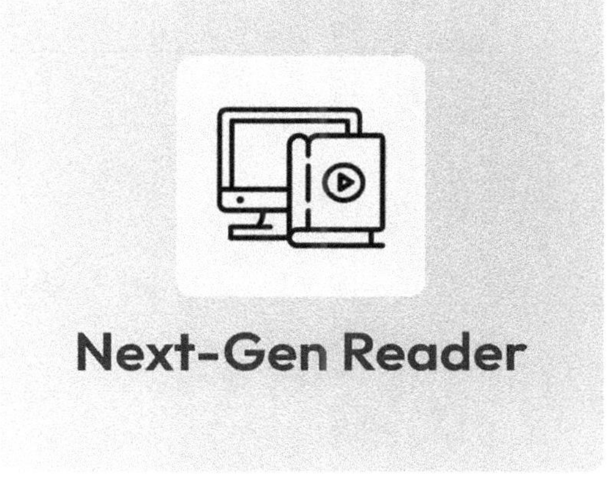

- **Multi-device progress sync**: Pick up where you left off, on any device.
- **Highlighting and notetaking**: Capture ideas and turn reading into lasting knowledge.
- **Bookmarking:** Save and revisit key sections whenever you need them.
- **Dark mode**: Reduce eye strain by switching to dark or sepia themes.

How to Unlock

UNLOCK NOW

Scan the QR code (or go to `packtpub.com/unlock`). Search for this book by name, confirm the edition, and then follow the steps on the page.

Note: *Keep your invoice handy. Purchases made directly from Packt don't require one.*

Stay tuned

To keep up with the latest developments in the fields of Generative AI and LLMs, subscribe to our weekly newsletter, *AI_Distilled*, at `https://packt.link/8Oz6Y`.

Join our communities on Discord and Reddit

Have questions about the book or want to contribute to discussions on Generative AI and LLMs?

Join our Discord server at `https://packt.link/4Bbd9` and our Reddit channel at `https://packt.link/wcYOQ` to connect, share, and collaborate with like-minded enthusiasts.

Part 1

Understanding and Exploring DeepSeek

In the first part of this book, we'll build a strong foundation for understanding DeepSeek and its role in the rapidly evolving world of AI. We begin by introducing DeepSeek as an open-source large language model and exploring why it has gained global attention. Next, we take a deep dive into its internal architecture, reasoning mechanics, and advanced capabilities to uncover what truly sets it apart. We'll also explore effective prompting strategies to help you get the most out of DeepSeek models.

By the end of this part, you'll have the context, technical understanding, and practical insights needed to confidently leverage DeepSeek in modern AI workflows.

This part of the book includes the following chapters:

- *Chapter 1, What is DeepSeek*
- *Chapter 2, Deep Dive into DeepSeek*
- *Chapter 3, Prompting DeepSeek*

Stay tuned

To keep up with the latest developments in the fields of Generative AI and LLMs, subscribe to our weekly newsletter, *AI_Distilled*, at `https://packt.link/80z6Y`.

Join our communities on Discord and Reddit

Have questions about the book or want to contribute to discussions on Generative AI and LLMs?

Join our Discord server at `https://packt.link/4Bbd9` and our Reddit channel at `https://packt.link/wcYOQ` to connect, share, and collaborate with like-minded enthusiasts.

1

What Is DeepSeek?

Artificial intelligence (**AI**) is rapidly evolving, and with it comes a suite of tools that allow developers, researchers, and innovators to build smarter, more adaptive systems. One such emerging tool is **DeepSeek**: a powerful, open-source **large language model** (**LLM**) designed to rival the capabilities of major LLMs such as GPT-4 and LLaMA. But what exactly is DeepSeek, and why should you care?

In this chapter, we're going to dive into what DeepSeek is, how it fits into the broader AI landscape, and why it's generating interest across the tech industry. You'll gain an understanding of DeepSeek's unique features and how it compares to other models in terms of training data, efficiency, and performance benchmarks.

By the end of this chapter, you'll be equipped to understand the development of DeepSeek and key contributors to its success.

In this chapter, we're going to cover the following main topics:

- Introducing DeepSeek
- Understanding the technical breakthroughs of DeepSeek
- Impact on the global AI ecosystem
- Exploring the versions and evolution of DeepSeek

Free Benefits with Your Book

Your purchase includes a free PDF copy of this book along with other exclusive benefits. Check the *Free Benefits with Your Book* section in the Preface to unlock them instantly and maximize your learning experience.

Introducing DeepSeek

DeepSeek is an open-source language model that aims to democratize and make advanced AI accessible. The first version, DeepSeek-R1, appeared on 20 January 2025, just before the Chinese New Year. Instead of shipping only a closed binary, the team published the weights, training scripts, and inference code, so anyone can examine or rebuild the system.

Released under the MIT license, the model carries no usage fees or strict terms. Anyone may run it locally or adapt it for new tasks. This freedom drew developers, researchers, teachers, and small firms worldwide. They apply DeepSeek-R1 in support bots, classroom aids, lab studies, and writing tools.

Benchmarks show DeepSeek-R1, competing with OpenAI-o3 and Gemini-2.5-Pro. It handles math, code, many languages, and complex prompts. The results suggest strong models need not be closed and underscores China's growing role in frontier AI. The release also revived debates on open access and safety, and improving global research cooperation. On September 17, 2025, another milestone was reached as the DeepSeek-AI team published their research on the model DeepSeek-R1 in ***Nature*** and made it to the cover of that issue (`https://www.nature.com/articles/s41586-025-09422-z`).

From an architectural standpoint, DeepSeek leaned heavily on innovations in transformer-based models, while adding its own spin in later versions (explored in depth in the section, *Versions and evolution of DeepSeek*). But what made it truly stand out was its usability. DeepSeek could be deployed in a wide range of environments, from cloud servers to edge devices, and even laptops using lightweight versions.

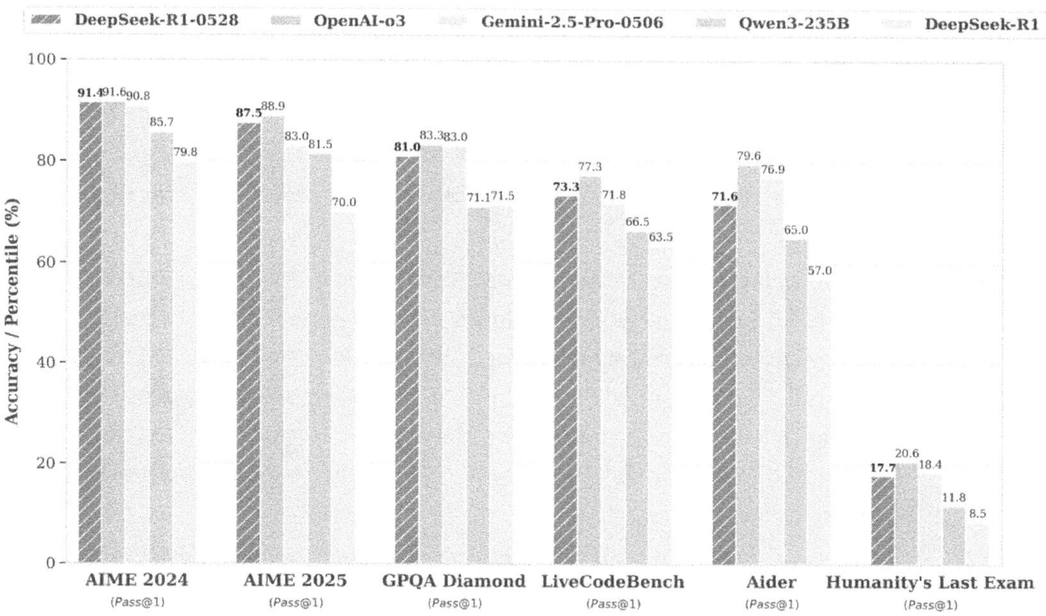

Figure 1.1: Benchmark performance of DeepSeek-R1 (0528) (source: `https://api-docs.deepseek.com/news/news250528`*)*

Let's talk about the various factors that contributed to the sudden rise and popularity of DeepSeek:

- **Open source architecture and training details**: DeepSeek-R1 was released with a detailed research paper (`https://arxiv.org/abs/2501.12948`) outlining its architecture and training approach, benchmark scores across reasoning, math, and programming tasks (`https://artificialanalysis.ai/providers/deepseek`). This release was supported by full model weights, configuration files, and training scripts, along with six smaller ***distilled variants*** suited for local or low-resource environments (`https://api-docs.deepseek.com/news/news250120`) and immediate API availability (`https://api-docs.deepseek.com/guides/reasoning_model`) for developers wanting hosted access.
- **Timing**: Part of its popularity was due to timing, as global organizations, scientists, and developers began exploring the new release. Additionally, the MIT license provided complete freedom for commercial use – an increasingly rare trait among performant models. The release also sparked excitement because it was not a research-only artifact; it was practical. Developers were able to fine-tune it, deploy it in production environments, and integrate it into existing AI workflows. The combination of power and usability became an instant draw.

- **Initial technical highlights**: The most notable aspects of DeepSeek-R1 at launch included the following:
    - **Reasoning**: It outperformed or matched leading models on key benchmarks involving mathematics, code, and logical reasoning.
    - **Efficiency**: It provided performance close to GPT-4-level systems at significantly lower inference costs.
    - **Reinforcement-first training**: Unlike conventional fine-tuning workflows that depend on supervised human-annotated data, DeepSeek skipped straight to **reinforcement learning from human feedback** (**RLHF**) or similar paradigms – though with minimal human labeling. The change sped up reasoning scores, lowered human-labeling costs, and allowed the model to tackle diverse tasks, such as math problems, zero-shot code, and so on, without needing narrow task-specific instructions.
    - **Custom architecture**: While based on the transformer framework, DeepSeek-R1 incorporated innovations optimized for training stability and long-context understanding.

  These elements together enabled the model to punch well above its weight, especially in multi-step reasoning and problem solving.

- **Real-world readiness**: DeepSeek demonstrated real-world readiness from the outset, standing apart from many state-of-the-art models that excel in benchmarks but struggle in deployment. Unlike others that require extensive setup or closed infrastructure, DeepSeek was immediately usable in practical settings. It offered production-ready access via its API, local deployment with open weights and inference code, and customization through LoRA fine-tuning or prompt engineering. Integration with enterprise platforms such as Trae and Windsurf further streamlined orchestration. These capabilities, rarely combined so seamlessly in other models at launch, underscored DeepSeek's commitment to practical utility beyond academic performance.

- **Community interest**: DeepSeek-R1's release sparked intense community activity. GitHub quickly overflowed with plug-ins, adapters, and fine-tuned spin-offs, while thousands of Hugging Face forks powered tools for contract review, tutoring, research aid, summarization, and coding support. Online forums shared benchmarks and hardware guides, and universities adopted the model for courses and lab projects. Forums such as Reddit, Zhihu, and Stack Overflow buzzed with shared experiments, performance tests, and guides for fine-tuning DeepSeek on local hardware. The accessibility of the model turned casual enthusiasts into researchers and developers into entrepreneurs. Today, DeepSeek also fuels educational initiatives. Several MOOCs and university labs have begun teaching LLM theory and experimentation using DeepSeek as the base model due to its openness and clarity.
- **Philosophical vision**: DeepSeek's vision aligns with a broader movement to build AI ***not as a gatekept asset***, but as a ***shared global resource***. Much like how Linux reshaped the software industry, DeepSeek aims to reshape AI development by putting tools in the hands of anyone curious or capable enough to use them. Its strategy is not just to compete with OpenAI or Google but to focus on accessibility and collaborative innovation.

DeepSeek-R1's success is attributed to three factors: RLHF training, open source commitment, and its competitive performance across benchmarks.

Together, these elements laid the groundwork for DeepSeek not just as a model, but as an ecosystem. The remainder of this chapter will explore the reception of DeepSeek-R1 and the motivations behind its open philosophy, what technical breakthroughs powered it, and how it is evolving into a full-scale ecosystem.

Understanding the technical breakthroughs of DeepSeek

What truly sets DeepSeek-R1 apart are the *technical innovations* embedded in its architecture and training process. These innovations enabled it to outperform many contemporary models and helped redefine how future LLMs might be built.

The training process

Before we begin with DeepSeek's training process, let's first take a look at the development process of leading LLMs, which usually consists of the following:

1. **Pretraining on massive corpora using self-supervised learning**: In this stage, models are exposed to large-scale, diverse datasets such as books, websites, and code. The goal is to learn general language patterns without explicit labels. Common pretraining strategies include the following:
    a. **Autoregressive modeling** (e.g., GPT): The model predicts the next word in a sequence.
    b. **Masked language modeling** (e.g., BERT): The model predicts missing (masked) words.
    c. **Permutation-based modeling** (e.g., XLNet): The model learns over multiple possible word orders.
2. **Transformer architecture**: Most LLMs use the **transformer architecture** (*Figure 1.2*), known for its scalability and performance in **Natural Language Processing (NLP)** tasks. They usually employ **self-attention** to determine contextual relationships between words. Some of the variants are as follows:
    a. **Encoder-only** (e.g., BERT) for classification or understanding.
    b. **Decoder-only** (e.g., GPT) for generation.
    c. **Encoder-decoder** (e.g., T5) for tasks such as translation and summarization.

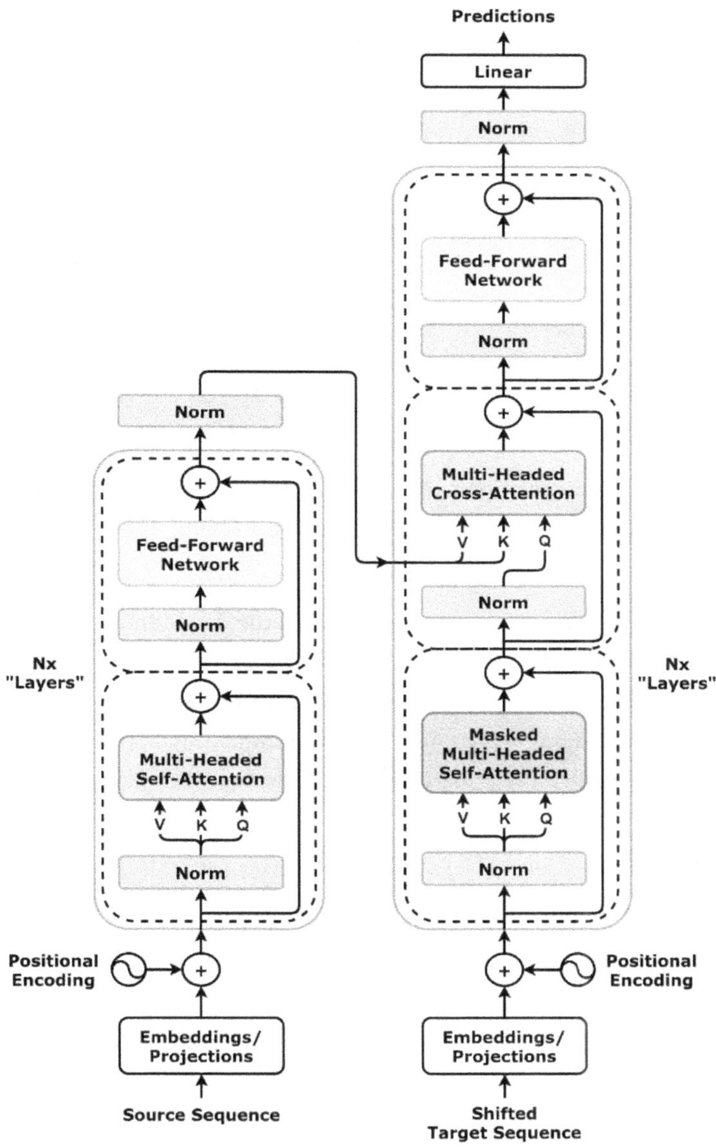

Figure 1.2: Transformer architecture (Attention Is All You Need, Vaswani et al., `https://arxiv.org/pdf/1706.03762`*)*

3. **Supervised fine-tuning on curated instruction-following datasets**: After pretraining, the model is fine-tuned on high-quality, labeled datasets where it learns to follow specific instructions and perform useful tasks. These datasets typically consist of human-written prompts and ideal responses, helping the model learn how to interact more directly and purposefully.
4. **RLHF**: To better align model outputs with human preferences, RLHF is applied:
    a. Human reviewers evaluate and rank multiple model responses.
    b. A **reward model** is trained to predict these rankings.
    c. The LLM is then fine-tuned using reinforcement learning algorithms (commonly Proximal Policy Optimization (PPO)) to generate outputs that maximize the reward model's score, thus better aligning with human values and expectations.

DeepSeek-R1 broke this convention by ***bypassing supervised fine-tuning entirely***. Instead, it jumped directly from pretraining to reinforcement learning, helping it learn strong reasoning skills on its own.

Avoiding **supervised fine-tuning (SFT)** eliminates the dependency on expensive, manually annotated datasets. Instead, DeepSeek adopts **rule-based reward mechanisms**, such as automatically validating correct answers or checking output formats. This approach is more scalable and cost-efficient, and helps overcome the limitations of human data curation. Additionally, the use of explicit, rule-driven rewards, such as verifying answers within designated structures or confirming code functionality, mitigates reward hacking, a common issue with less predictable neural reward models.

Figure 1.3 shows the workflow diagram of DeepSeek's model training.

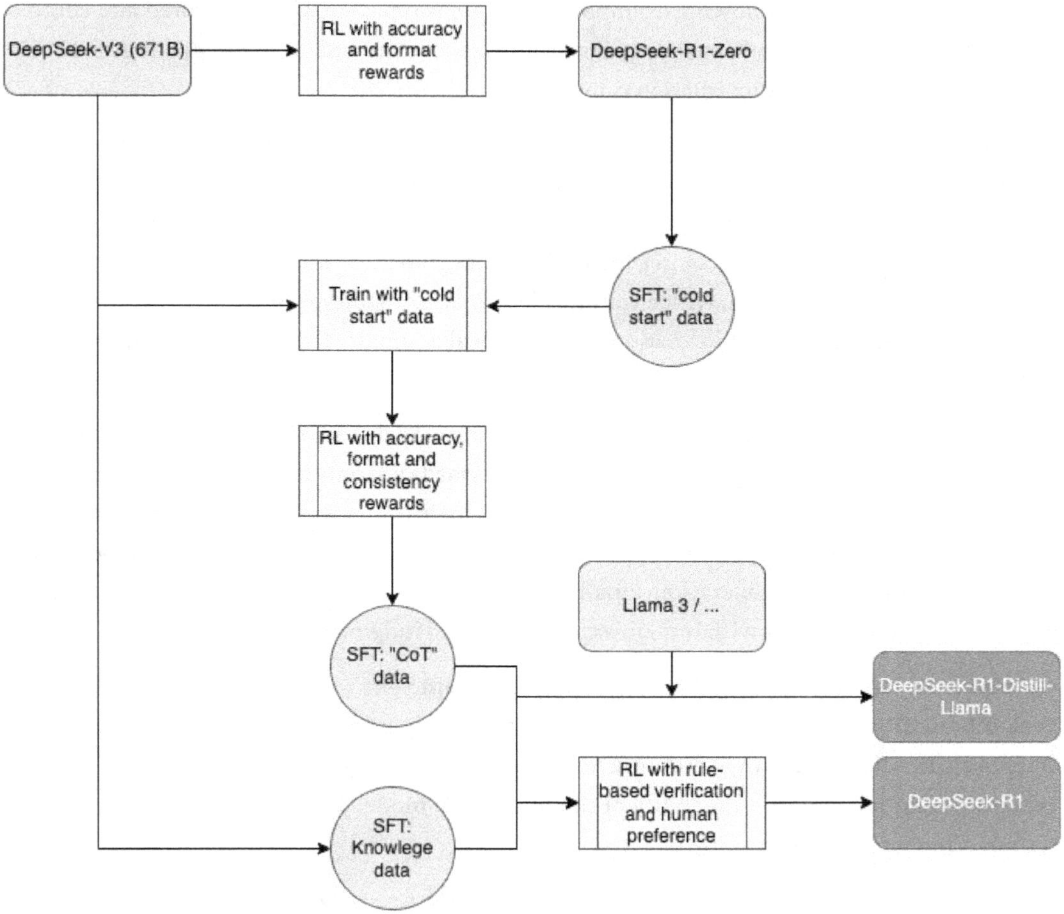

Figure 1.3: DeepSeek-R1 model training

The training pipeline for DeepSeek-R1 begins with **DeepSeek-V3**, a large 671B-parameter base model. This foundational model undergoes **reinforcement learning** (**RL**) using rewards focused on accuracy and output formatting, resulting in an intermediate model called **DeepSeek-R1-Zero**. This model serves as a crucial transition point, enabling more task-specific training in the following stages.

Next, DeepSeek-R1-Zero is fine-tuned using **cold start data**, which refers to a broad and diverse collection of instruction-following examples. This data is typically well-structured and curated to give the model a basic understanding of various task formats and domains, making it suitable for initial general-purpose instruction tuning.

Following this phase, additional rounds of SFT are applied using two specialized datasets. The first is **chain-of-thought (CoT) data**, which emphasizes multi-step reasoning. This data helps the model learn how to solve complex problems by breaking them down into intermediate steps – essential for mathematical reasoning, logical inference, and multi-hop question answering. The second set is **knowledge data**, which contains fact-rich, domain-specific content such as scientific literature, encyclopedic information, and technical manuals. This helps the model improve factual accuracy and domain coverage.

Once these fine-tuning stages are complete, the resulting model, DeepSeek-R1, is further enhanced through advanced RL techniques. It is trained with **rewards** not only for accuracy and formatting, but also for consistency, ensuring that its outputs are logically coherent and self-consistent. Furthermore, **rule-based verification** is applied to automatically validate responses in domains such as mathematics and code generation. Finally, **human preference fine-tuning** is incorporated to align the model's behavior with human expectations and judgments of quality.

DeepSeek-R1 has been distilled into smaller, more efficient variants. These include **DeepSeek-R1-Distill-Qwen**, which uses Qwen 2.5 models ranging from 1.5B to 32B parameters, and **DeepSeek-R1-Distill-LLaMA**, which utilizes LLaMA 3 models in 8B and 70B sizes. These distilled versions retain much of the capability of the original R1 model but are optimized for different resource and latency constraints.

Overall, the DeepSeek-R1 pipeline represents a multi-phase strategy combining supervised learning, reward-based tuning, and targeted model distillation to deliver a family of instruction-following language models optimized for performance, generalization, and deployment flexibility.

As a result, the training process becomes more stable and efficient, benefiting from simplified, reliable reward signals that reduce noise and ambiguity.

DeepSeek's training approach helped in the following aspects:

- **Reduced human labor cost**: No need to manually annotate or rank thousands of instructions.
- **Faster development cycle**: The training timeline was streamlined significantly.
- **Greater generalization**: The model learned to generalize instruction-following through trial-and-error interactions rather than fixed templates.

Despite lacking traditional supervised instruction datasets, DeepSeek-R1 demonstrated *robust instruction-following capabilities*, competitive with models that underwent fine-tuning. This suggested that RL alone – when well-designed – can endow a model with a deep understanding of instructions and intent.

Let's take a look at DeepSeek's **inference pipeline**, as depicted in *Figure 1.4*.

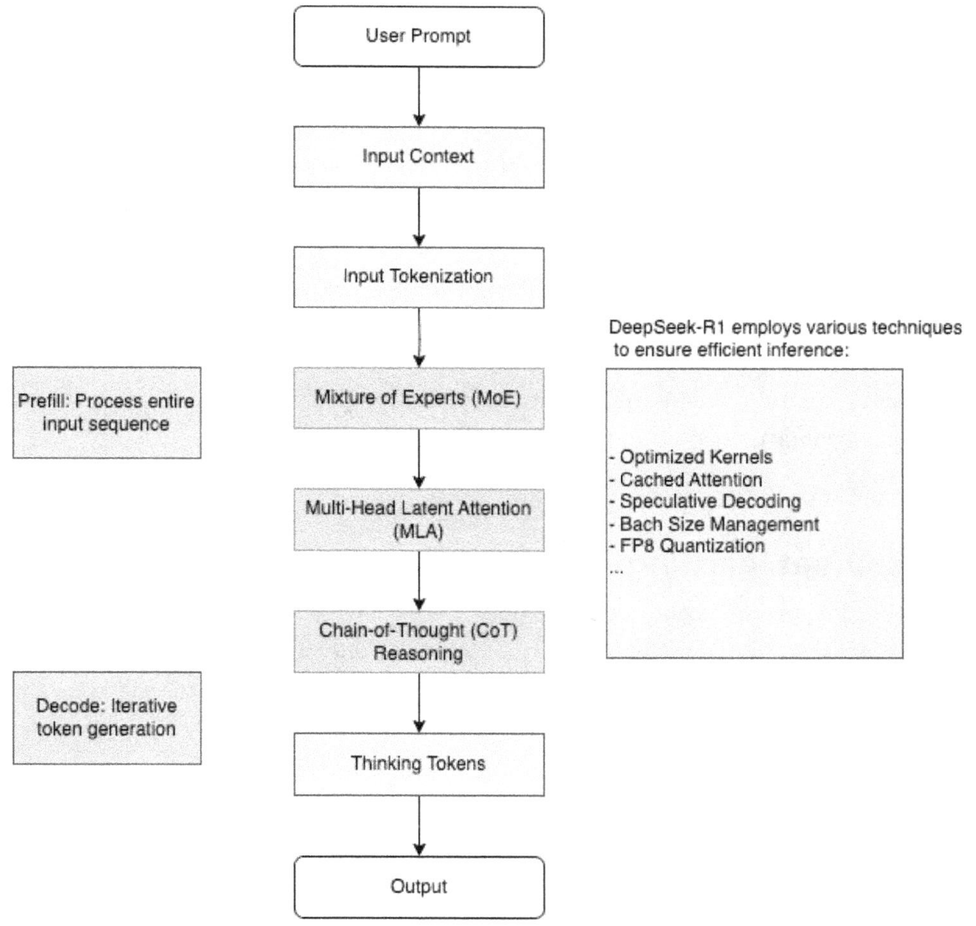

Figure 1.4: DeepSeek-R1 model inference

The inference pipeline of DeepSeek-R1 is designed to prioritize structured, verifiable outputs through a combination of **rule-aware decoding** and **prompt optimization**. During inference, DeepSeek-R1 leverages **formatting-aware generation mechanisms**, where the model is encouraged, often via prompt design and internal alignment, to produce well-structured, interpretable responses, especially for tasks involving code, math, or CoT reasoning. It is optimized not only for fluency but also for factual and logical coherence, frequently incorporating intermediate steps (CoT) in its answers, even without explicit prompting. This enables DeepSeek-R1 to deliver step-by-step solutions and structured outputs in JSON, Markdown, or code blocks, increasing reliability for downstream applications.

What sets DeepSeek-R1 apart from other state-of-the-art LLMs is its rule-based, **reward-aligned inference behavior**. Many leading LLMs rely primarily on end-to-end training with human preference fine-tuning, whereas DeepSeek-R1 integrates **rule-based verification** techniques directly into the RL loop. This has downstream effects at inference time: DeepSeek-R1 is more likely to generate outputs that are compatible with formal validators or downstream evaluators (e.g., test cases for code, equations for math). As a result, it shows stronger performance in domains where precision, structure, and interpretability are critical, while slightly trading off open-ended conversational flexibility.

Next up is DeepSeek's RL approach.

Reinforcement learning

DeepSeek-R1's RL approach is notable for its distinctive design choices, which we will explore in depth in *Chapter 2*. Unlike many models that apply RL only in the final stages of training, DeepSeek-R1 introduced **alignment techniques**. Alignment techniques are the methods aimed at steering the model's outputs to be more helpful, honest, and harmless – early in its training process. This early alignment contributes to more consistent and desirable behavior throughout the model's development.

It also replaced large-scale human annotation with an automated reward model, significantly improving scalability and reducing reliance on manual labeling. Another defining feature was its use of self-play and **iterative refinement**, enabling the model to generate, evaluate, and improve its own outputs. This approach helped DeepSeek-R1 internalize advanced reasoning patterns and strategic decision-making, making it particularly effective at multi-turn reasoning, code explanation and completion, and solving complex mathematical problems.

Moreover, RL training helped ***mitigate hallucinations*** by reinforcing factual accuracy through self-generated success metrics.

For readers unfamiliar with alignment in the context of AI, it generally refers to techniques that ensure a model's behavior aligns with human intent and values. A helpful introduction to these concepts can be found in OpenAI's alignment overview (`https://openai.com/index/our-approach-to-alignment-research/`) or in the Alignment Newsletter (`https://www.alignmentforum.org/s/dT7CKGXwq9vt76CeX`).

Apart from this, DeepSeek made some modifications to the transformer architecture. Let's find out.

Architecture modifications

DeepSeek-R1 builds on the widely adopted transformer architecture, which forms the foundation for most modern LLMs. At its core, the transformer uses a **self-attention mechanism** that allows each token in an input sequence to weigh the importance of every other token, regardless of position. This enables the model to capture long-range dependencies and contextual relationships more effectively than traditional recurrent models.

However, standard attention becomes computationally expensive as input length increases. To address this, DeepSeek-R1 introduces **adaptive attention routing**, a major architectural evolution. Unlike traditional transformers that apply fixed full attention across all tokens, this mechanism allows the model to ***selectively attend to the most relevant tokens*** based on learned **relevance scores** computed during training. These scores are typically derived from internal attention weights or auxiliary **gating mechanism**s, which prioritize tokens that contribute most to minimizing the training loss. By focusing computational resources on high-impact tokens, especially in long sequences, adaptive attention routing enables DeepSeek-R1 to handle inputs of up to ***32,000 tokens*** more efficiently. This not only enhances the model's ability to comprehend and summarize large documents but also reduces computational overhead by avoiding redundant attention over less informative tokens.

Figure 1.5 compares the traditional transformer attention and DeepSeek's adaptive attention routing.

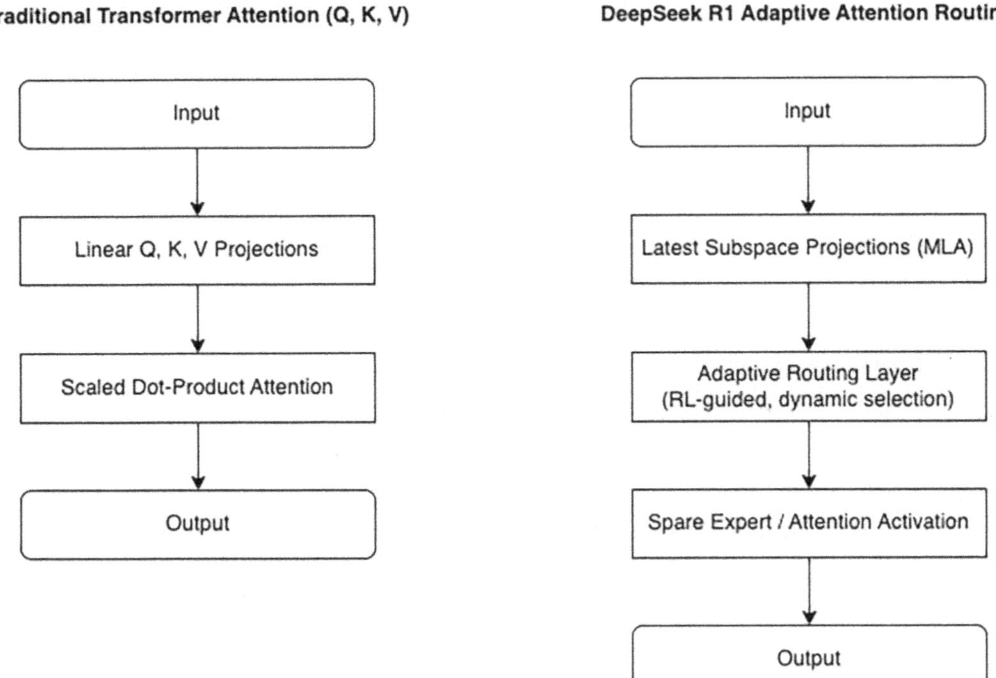

Figure 1.5: Traditional transformer attention versus DeepSeek-R1 adaptive attention routing

In addition, DeepSeek-R1 employs **mixed-precision optimization**, combining **FP16 (half-precision)** and **INT8 (quantized)** arithmetic to improve training and inference efficiency. This approach reduces memory usage and accelerates computation while maintaining competitive model performance in terms of accuracy and perplexity. Typically, FP16 is used throughout most of the model for general computation, while INT8 quantization is selectively applied to inference-time matrix multiplications, often in attention and feed-forward layers, where precision can be reduced without significantly impacting output quality. By carefully choosing which layers to quantize, DeepSeek-R1 achieves a favorable trade-off between efficiency and performance. This approach significantly accelerates inference and training while maintaining output quality, making it ideal for deployment at scale.

The model also benefits from efficient parallelization strategies. It leverages tensor parallelism and activation checkpointing to reduce memory usage during training, allowing it to be trained on multi-GPU systems more effectively.

Together, these enhancements make DeepSeek-R1 an evolution of the transformer, one that is not only more scalable and context-aware but also more cost-efficient in both training and inference.

Let's now turn our focus to how the DeepSeek architecture compares to the architecture of other LLMs.

Comparison of major LLM architectures (2025)

As the field of LLMs evolves, different architectures and training paradigms have emerged. This comparison focuses (*Table 1.1*) on key differentiators, particularly the use of **Mixture-of-Experts** (**MoE**) architectures and RL among some of the most impactful models in recent years.

Model	**MoE ?**	**Key architecture highlights**	**RLHF**	**Open source?**
DeepSeek-R1	Yes. Sparse MoE	671 B params; MoE + Multi-Head Latent Attention; reasoning-centric	No RLHF, uses pure reinforcement learning (GRPO)	Yes (MIT)
Claude 4	No	Dense transformer; built with Anthropic's Constitutional AI and **Direct Preference Optimization** (**DPO**)	Yes, advanced RLHF + DPO	No
Gemini 2.5 Pro	Yes. Sparse MoE	Multimodal sparse MoE transformer; 1 M token context (2 M soon)	Yes. RLHF + ongoing alignment	No
GPT-4.5	No	Released Feb 27, 2025; OpenAI's largest non-CoT model (**Orion**)	Yes. RLHF + SFT	No

Model	MoE ?	Key architecture highlights	RLHF	Open source?
o3	Unknown (likely dense)	Optimized for personalized assistant tasks; improved grounding and memory modules	Yes, advanced RLHF	No
Grok 3.5	No evidence of MoE	Dense transformer; enhanced reasoning from Grok 3; advanced "Think" mode; still proprietary	Yes. RL-based training + RLHF fine-tuning	No
Gemma 3	No, dense	Lightweight MoE; instruction-tuned with long-context	Yes. RLHF	Yes (Apache 2.0)
LLaMA 4	No	Dense transformer; advanced memory and modular layers	Yes. RLHF and safety fine-tuning	Yes

Table 1.1: Comparison of LLM architectures

Leading language models are increasingly diverging in their architectural strategies, particularly around the use of MoE. Models such as Gemini 2.5 Pro and DeepSeek-R1 adopt sparse MoE architectures, enabling large parameter scales while maintaining efficient compute usage. GPT-4.1 is widely believed to incorporate some form of MoE or sparse expert routing, based on its strong performance and low-latency characteristics, though exact details remain undisclosed.

Sitting between these approaches, Grok 3.5 retains a dense transformer architecture, optimized for real-time responsiveness and integrated reasoning. It avoids MoE entirely, focusing instead on RL techniques and iterative refinement using live feedback data.

In contrast, Claude 4 and LLaMA 4 continue with fully dense designs, prioritizing simplicity, alignment stability, and predictable behavior over raw parameter scaling.

Now that we have introduced you to the DeepSeek's technical innovation, we will dive deeper into the MoE design of DeepSeek.

MoE architecture

A major architectural breakthrough in DeepSeek-R1 is the integration of the MoE design.

MoE is a modular neural network design where only a subset of parameters (called **experts**) is activated for any given input. Rather than using the full parameter space for every prediction, MoE selectively activates a few experts dynamically.

How DeepSeek implements MoE

DeepSeek employs a sparse **MoE architecture**, in which a gating network dynamically selects two out of N expert networks at each layer to process a given input. Selecting two experts strikes a balance between computational efficiency and model expressiveness. It allows the model to leverage diverse expertise without incurring the full cost of activating all experts. This approach enables specialization across experts while keeping inference latency and resource usage manageable. These experts are not manually assigned to specific tasks such as math or code; instead, specialization emerges during training. The gating mechanism learns, through optimization, to route inputs to the most effective experts based on contextual cues. Over time, certain experts become more activated for specific domains (e.g., language, reasoning, and coding) as a result of this learned routing, effectively developing functional specialization.

Figure 1.6 provides an overview of this architecture.

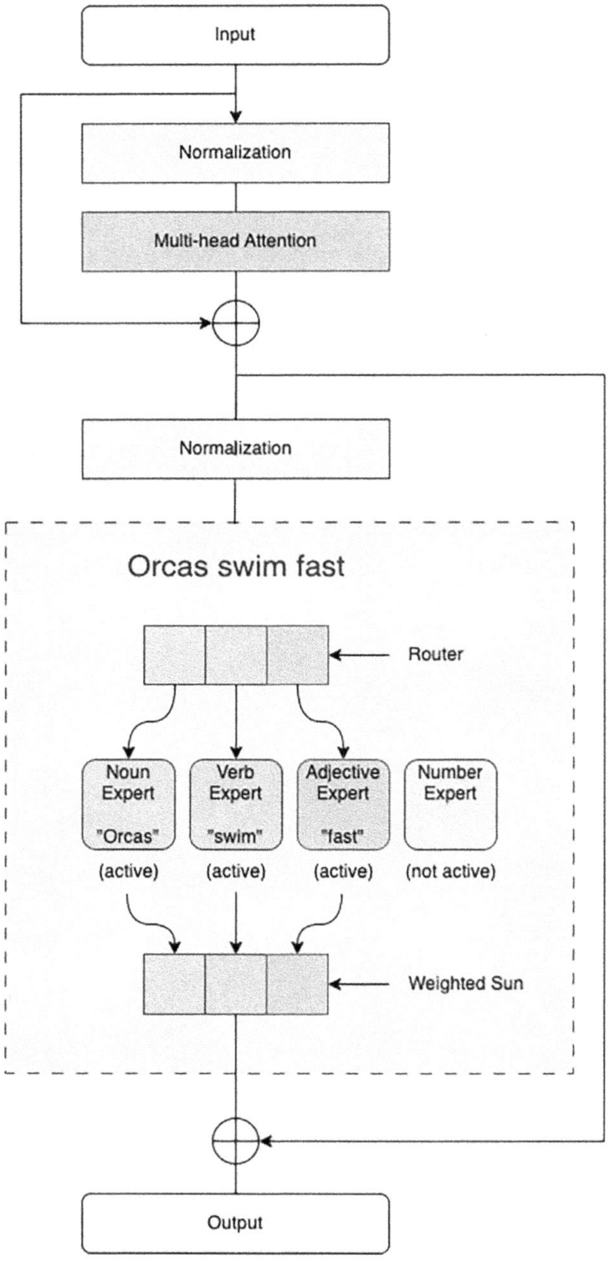

Figure 1.6: Conceptual view of MoE architecture

Each expert processes the same type of input representations but may learn to emphasize different aspects depending on the patterns it receives. Their ***role*** is shaped by the data they are most often routed for, which, in turn, guides their parameter updates. This allows experts to take on distinct roles organically, without needing different input formats or encodings. The model contains a large pool of expert subnetworks (each a small feed-forward network), but only a small subset – typically two – is activated per input token. A gating network evaluates the context and dynamically decides which experts to activate, allowing the model to adaptively route information where it's most effectively processed.

This structure yields several key benefits:

- **Scalability**: Since only a few experts are active at any time, the model can maintain a large number of total parameters while consuming less compute per token than a dense model of equivalent size. This enables DeepSeek to scale up without linear increases in computational cost.
- **Modularity**: Experts can be trained, frozen, updated, or even swapped independently. This modularity allows for efficient continual learning, domain adaptation, or task-specific fine-tuning without retraining the entire model.
- **Specialization**: As the gating network learns to route different inputs to different experts, these subnetworks begin to specialize; some become more attuned to code, others to mathematical reasoning, natural language, or dialogue. This reduces the risk of overfitting and enhances the model's ability to generalize across diverse tasks.

Through this architecture, DeepSeek-R1 essentially behaves like an ensemble of domain-specific models, but without duplicating resources or incurring the latency overhead typically associated with running multiple systems in parallel.

Apart from DeepSeek, many **state-of-the-art (SOTA)** LLMs also employ MoE architecture, the details of which are provided in the following table:

Model	Parameter count	Active experts per token	Total experts	Routing type	Use case strengths
DeepSeek-R1	~130B total / ~30B active	2	~64	Sparse + Gating	Math, reasoning, code, and multilingual understanding
Gemini 2.5 Pro	Estimated 1T+ (MoE config)	Unspecified (Likely 2–4)	Dozens	Proprietary Sparse	Multimodal apps, coding, and retrieval-augmented reasoning

Model	**Parameter count**	**Active experts per token**	**Total experts**	**Routing type**	**Use case strengths**
Grok-3	Estimated 400B+ total (MoE)	2–4 (adaptive)	Unspecified (20+)	Advanced Dynamic MoE	Enhanced reasoning, DeepSearch, vision + code + chat, and long context
Grok-1.5	Estimated 300B total	2–4 (adaptive)	16+	Dynamic Routing	Real-time interaction, multimodal learning, and large-scale context tracking
Mixtral 8x7B	56B total / 12.9B active	2	8	Top-2 Gated MoE	General-purpose reasoning, fast inference, and multilingual
Switch Transformer	1.6T total / ~15B active	1	2,048	Top-1 Routing	Scalability benchmark; pioneered MoE at trillion-scale
GLaM	1.2T total / 93B active	2	64	Top-2 Routing	NLP understanding, code, and scientific tasks

Table 1.2: Comparison of MoE models

With MoE architecture gaining traction, Mixtral 8×7B showed how open source models could gain strong reasoning with limited compute, while newer systems such as Grok and Gemini 2.5 add adaptive or proprietary routing and multimodal pretraining. Google's Switch Transformer and GLaM, both trillion-parameter prototypes, first confirmed that MoE could scale reliably. Together, these projects show how MoE lets very large models grow while keeping inference fast enough for real-time, high-performance tasks.

Another foundational aspect of building an LLM is the data on which it is trained. Let's see how DeepSeek utilized its training dataset.

Training dataset and philosophy

In the paper *DeepSeek-R1: Incentivizing Reasoning Capability in LLMs via Reinforcement Learning* (`https://arxiv.org/abs/2501.12948`), the authors state that DeepSeek-R1 was trained on a large, diverse, and domain-rich multilingual dataset intended to support reasoning, coding, and cross-lingual understanding.

While the precise composition of this dataset is not publicly disclosed, the paper outlines the use of carefully curated cold-start data and approximately 800,000 SFT samples, integrated into a multi-stage RL framework to develop the model.

The data selection strategy emphasized high-quality sources across several key domains:

- The model was heavily trained on programming languages such as Python, JavaScript, and Rust, using curated code from repositories such as GitHub and developer Q&A platforms such as Stack Overflow.
- To strengthen mathematical and logical reasoning, the dataset incorporated formal logic corpora, symbolic mathematics benchmarks, and collections of competitive math problems (e.g., MATH, GSM8K, and ProofWriter).
- Scientific understanding was bolstered through pretraining on academic publications and technical manuals, drawing from sources such as arXiv, and open-access research datasets.
- The multilingual component of the dataset was anchored in both Chinese and English, with additional coverage of major global languages sourced from datasets such as CCMatrix and OPUS.

This diverse training foundation reflects DeepSeek-R1's objective: to combine high-level reasoning with robust multilingual and domain-specific capabilities.

In the same paper, the authors describe adopting a low-filtering strategy in curating their training data, contrasting with the more aggressive data filtering pipelines used by many other LLM developers. This design choice was made to preserve the natural complexity and diversity of language, enabling the model to better capture informal expressions, culturally specific idioms, emotionally charged language, and edge-case scenarios. According to the authors, such linguistic variety supports more expressive, creative, and contextually fluent model behavior. However, the paper does not specify exactly what types of content, if any, were filtered out. Without transparency into the dataset composition or filtering criteria, it remains unclear whether the training corpus included potentially harmful content such as hate speech, misinformation, or offensive material. While this low-filtering approach may enhance the model's ability to generalize across diverse linguistic and cultural contexts, it also introduces the risk that undesirable content could be learned and reproduced. These trade-offs underscore the importance of downstream safeguards and responsible use, particularly when deploying the model in real-world settings.

DeepSeek-R1's architecture and training strategy resulted in a model particularly well-suited for open-ended tasks. It demonstrates strong capabilities in brainstorming, idea generation, and exploratory dialogue – areas that benefit from flexibility and minimal preconception. The model also performs well in nuanced translation and multilingual reasoning, aided by its diverse language training. Additionally, DeepSeek-R1 is noted for its adaptability to user tone and conversational style, which many users find useful in creative and collaborative contexts.

Well, there have been several versions of DeepSeek, and we expect newer releases as the race toward artificial general intelligence heats up.

In the next section, we will talk about how the DeepSeek ecosystem has evolved since the release of R1.

Versions and evolution of DeepSeek

The story of DeepSeek is not just about a single model launch. It's about a continuously evolving ecosystem. Each iteration of DeepSeek introduces significant upgrades in reasoning, usability, safety, and integration across platforms. Understanding the evolution of DeepSeek is critical to appreciating its long-term vision and potential.

DeepSeek's evolving ecosystem

Since its debut, DeepSeek has made significant strides across multiple domains, including language understanding, mathematical reasoning, code generation, and multimodal capabilities. Each version introduces meaningful enhancements, underscoring DeepSeek's goal of democratizing high-performance language models without compromising on quality.

Understanding DeepSeek's evolution provides critical insight into its growth trajectory, vision, and how it continues to disrupt both proprietary and open AI ecosystems. In the following table, we chronologically explore the key milestones, model variants, and product layers that now form the DeepSeek suite.

Version	Release date	Key features
DeepSeek LLM	Jan 2025	Foundational model; multilingual, open weights
DeepSeek-R1	Jan 20, 2025	Full MIT-licensed release, strong reasoning, multilingual, chat + code
DeepSeek V2	Early 2025	Refined alignment, better factual grounding
DeepSeek Coder	Feb 2025	Specialized coding model with top-tier performance in Python and JS
DeepSeek VL	Mar 2025	Vision-language model (image+text), multimodal groundwork
DeepSeek Math	Apr 2025	Focused on algebra, logic, and multi-step reasoning
DeepSeek V3	May 2025	Upgraded generalist model with better long-context and planning
DeepSeek-R1-0528	May 2025	Latest refinement: stronger factuality, 32k token context, improved alignment
DeepSeek Coder V2	Jun 2025	Massive improvement in code synthesis and inline documentation
DeepSeek V3.1	Aug 2025	Hybrid inference, fast thinking, and stronger agent skills
DeepSeek V3.2-Exp	Sep 2025	DeepSeek Sparse Attention (DSA) for faster, more efficient, and inference on long context.

Table 1.3: DeepSeek model evolution

Each of these models targets specific use cases, from general-purpose chatbot functions to highly focused coding and math tasks. Let's talk about them in detail.

Deep dive: Feature comparison of each model

The DeepSeek ecosystem has rapidly evolved into a suite of specialized models, each designed to address different use cases in reasoning, coding, vision, and general-purpose AI. While all variants build on a shared architectural backbone and training philosophy, each model iteration introduces new capabilities, performance trade-offs, and domain optimizations. Here is an overview of the key models within the DeepSeek family and how they compare in terms of specialization and utility:

- **DeepSeek LLM** (`https://github.com/deepseek-ai/DeepSeek-LLM`): The original backbone of the DeepSeek family, the DeepSeek LLM laid the foundation for all future iterations. While it lacked some specialized capabilities, it established multilingual competence and solid reasoning as core priorities.

- **DeepSeek Math** (`https://github.com/deepseek-ai/DeepSeek-Math`): Tailored for students, researchers, and technical professionals, DeepSeek Math focuses on multi-step reasoning problems in algebra, calculus, geometry, and symbolic logic. It serves as a viable open source alternative to Wolfram Alpha-like reasoning systems.
- **DeepSeek Coder** (`https://github.com/deepseek-ai/DeepSeek-Coder`) and **Coder V2** (`https://github.com/deepseek-ai/DeepSeek-Coder-V2`): The first Coder model introduced competitive performance in Python and JavaScript, integrated with development environments such as VS Code and GitHub Copilot. Coder V2 (June 2025) significantly raised the bar, approaching Claude 3.5 in inline function synthesis, docstring generation, and type inference.
- **DeepSeek VL** (`https://github.com/deepseek-ai/DeepSeek-VL`): A pivotal release for multimodal applications, VL supports both image and text inputs, opening the door for applications in visual question answering, optical character recognition, document summarization, and more. While it still lags behind GPT-4-V or Gemini 1.5 Pro in vision capabilities, it's rapidly improving.
- **DeepSeek V2** (`https://github.com/deepseek-ai/DeepSeek-V2`) and **V3** (`https://github.com/deepseek-ai/DeepSeek-V3`): The V2 update prioritized prompt alignment, minimizing hallucinations and expanding support for longer contexts. V3 followed up with better long-term memory support, faster inference, and internal planning modules that enabled early-stage agentic behavior.
- **DeepSeek-R1** (`https://github.com/deepseek-ai/DeepSeek-R1`): This was the launch version that started it all. Released on January 20, 2025, it quickly became the top-performing open source model across a wide array of benchmarks. Key highlights include a fully open source, MIT-licensed release that provides model weights, a tokenizer, and the entire training pipeline. DeepSeek-R1 delivers strong logical reasoning capabilities, surpassing most open models and rivaling some proprietary systems, along with robust multilingual performance in both English and Chinese. As already discussed, the release also features a set of smaller, distilled variants under 20B parameters, enabling efficient use in local or edge environments. Practical applications range from API-based chatbot integration and Copilot-style coding assistance to lightweight deployments via platforms such as Ollama and VS Code extensions.

- **DeepSeek-R1-0528** (`https://github.com/marketplace/models/azureml-deepseek/DeepSeek-R1-0528`): This update solidified DeepSeek's position at the top of the open source pyramid. The May 28 version refined the core model, making it more aligned, accurate, and efficient. The new features and enhancements include the following:
    - **Substantial reduction in hallucinations**: Notably in scientific and historical facts.
    - **Improved coding fluency**: Achieved parity with GPT-4-turbo in many Python tasks.
    - **Mathematics performance**: Enhanced accuracy in multi-step algebra, geometry, and logic problems.
    - **Updated prompt alignment**: Better adherence to user instructions, even in ambiguous prompts.
    - **Multimodal readiness**: Architecture adapted for future image/text fusion.

  In benchmark evaluations, the May release of DeepSeek-R1-0528 showed a 7% improvement in mathematical reasoning tasks compared to the January version. Code generation performance, measured on HumanEval-style benchmarks, increased by 9%. Additionally, the model demonstrated effective long-context reasoning, handling inputs up to 32,000 tokens with minimal performance degradation.

  The release of DeepSeek-R1-0528 underscored that the pace of DeepSeek's development remained strong and consistent. Its improved performance and open accessibility led many developers to begin migrating entire workflows from GPT-based systems to DeepSeek APIs. This shift was further supported by a surge in ecosystem integrations, including Visual Studio Code plugins, Ollama compatibility, and Dockerized deployment options, signaling growing adoption across both individual and enterprise-level users.

- **DeepSeek-V3.1** (August 2025) (`https://huggingface.co/deepseek-ai/DeepSeek-V3.1`): DeepSeek V3.1 is a cutting-edge hybrid reasoning model featuring both *thinking* and *non-thinking* modes, advanced agent and tool use capabilities, a massive 685-billion-parameter architecture, and an extended 128,000-token context window for long-document understanding. The model is engineered for fast, structured, multi-step reasoning and supports code generation, search, and agentic workflows, with enhanced efficiency from MoE architecture and optimized inference, matching or surpassing previous DeepSeek benchmarks while maintaining low latency. DeepSeek V3.1 also boasts strong multilingual support, open source availability for research, and specialized training for reliable external tool integration and reduction of hallucinations, making it suitable for diverse enterprise and developer applications.

Apart from various models, DeepSeek has created many products for streamlined adoption and use. Let's take a look.

DeepSeek product ecosystem

Beyond the models themselves, DeepSeek has developed a growing suite of user-facing products and developer tools that make adoption frictionless:

- **DeepSeek app**: A mobile-first AI assistant app available for Android and iOS, offering real-time interaction with DeepSeek-R1 and Math/Coder variants. Key features include voice input, code cell execution, note-taking, and multilingual support.
- **DeepSeek web app**: Accessible at `deepseek.com/chat`, this offers a clean and responsive interface for real-time interaction with various DeepSeek model variants. It includes conversation memory, allowing users to maintain context across multiple exchanges for more coherent dialogues. Prompt templates are available to streamline repetitive tasks or structured inputs, making it easier to prototype or test specific behaviors. Additionally, users can export entire chat sessions in Markdown or PDF formats, which is particularly useful for documentation, collaboration, or offline review.
- **DeepSeek developer platform** (`https://platform.deepseek.com/`): Offers a flexible and open environment for building and deploying AI-powered applications. Developers can fine-tune models to create custom endpoints tailored to specific tasks or domains. The platform supports seamless model selection across the DeepSeek family, including general-purpose (R1), coding-focused (Coder), and multimodal (VL) variants. With support for context-aware API calls up to 32,000 tokens, it enables sophisticated multi-turn reasoning and long-form content processing. A beta feature for role and function calling is also available, allowing developers to define structured interactions and extend model capabilities for tools, agents, or workflow automation.

DeepSeek's value proposition lies in its accessible model weights, strong reasoning capabilities, and low cost. This combination makes DeepSeek-R1 an attractive choice for educational use, research and development, and start-ups seeking advanced AI tools without restrictive licensing or high costs.

Now, let's take a look at the integration and deployment support DeepSeek offers.

Platform integrations and deployment ecosystem

DeepSeek's accessibility is one of its defining strengths, thanks to a wide range of integration and deployment options across local, cloud, and web environments. Here is a high-level overview of where and how DeepSeek can be used:

- For local and edge deployment, DeepSeek runs seamlessly on platforms such as Ollama (`https://ollama.com/library/deepseek-r1 – ollama run deepseek`), Docker Hub (`https://hub.docker.com/r/devlinrocha/ollama-deepseek-r1-7b/tags`), and through VS Code extensions (`https://github.com/enesbasbug/deepseek-vscode-extension`) for code completion and inline assistance. It also supports private cloud and on-premises deployments via Kubernetes, Docker Compose, or direct GPU cluster setups.
- In the cloud, DeepSeek is integrated with Amazon Bedrock (`https://aws.amazon.com/bedrock/deepseek`), Amazon SageMaker (`https://aws.amazon.com/blogs/machine-learning/deploy-deepseek-r1-distilled-models-on-amazon-sagemaker-using-a-large-model-inference-container/`), Azure ML (`https://azure.microsoft.com/en-us/blog/deepseek-r1-is-now-available-on-azure-ai-foundry-and-github/`), and Google Cloud Vertex AI (`https://cloud.google.com/vertex-ai/generative-ai/docs/maas/deepseek`), enabling scalable inference via Hugging Face or custom containers.
- Hosted APIs are available via providers such as Fireworks.ai (`https://fireworks.ai/`), Together.ai (`https://www.together.ai/`), Replicate (`https://replicate.com/`), and Modal (`https://modal.com/`), offering both rapid prototyping and production-ready workflows.
- For lightweight and browser-based access, users can try models on `deepseek.com/chat`, Hugging Face Spaces, or through ready-to-run notebooks on Google Colab and Kaggle.

If you wish to explore these deployment options, we have created an *Appendix* toward the end of the book for you to explore.

DeepSeek also integrates with popular orchestration frameworks such as LangChain, Haystack, and LlamaIndex for **retrieval-augmented generation** (**RAG**), as well as no-code tools such as Turing, Trae, and Windsurf for structured agent workflows.

DeepSeek's upcoming roadmap outlines an ambitious expansion of its model capabilities and deployment strategies. Planned developments include multimodal training that incorporates image and audio understanding, as well as the creation of autonomous agents equipped with memory, planning, and tool-use functions for complex workflows. The team is also working on smaller, task-specific variants tailored to domains such as medical question answering, legal analysis, and STEM education. In addition, DeepSeek is investing in privacy-focused deployments through federated training methods and secure, on-premises LLMs. Following the success of the R1 series, anticipation is building for a potential DeepSeek-R2 release in late 2025. While unconfirmed, early reports suggest it may offer structured reasoning capabilities that rival GPT-5, while maintaining a fully open source framework.

But with all the hype comes skepticism, too. The next section will examine how DeepSeek's choices have influenced the broader AI ecosystem, including pricing models, competition, and global policy dynamics. We will also talk about some concerns and risks that are being commonly discussed in the community.

DeepSeek's impact on the global AI ecosystem

The release of DeepSeek-R1 wasn't just a technical milestone; it was a *strategic turning point* for the global AI industry. Its unique combination of open source accessibility and top-tier performance sent shockwaves through research labs, start-ups, and policy circles alike. The implications have spanned economic competition, academic acceleration, ethical discourse, and geopolitical realignment.

Market disruption and price wars

Before DeepSeek-R1, frontier-level LLMs were typically expensive, restricted to API-only access, or bound by licenses that limited commercial use. The release of DeepSeek-R1, with freely available model weights, inference code, and permissive licensing, marked a significant shift, making high-performing language models far more accessible.

DeepSeek-R1 made a notable impact on the AI landscape by introducing free, full access to a high-performing reasoning model. It demonstrated competitive accuracy across domains such as mathematics, programming, and formal logic – areas traditionally dominated by proprietary systems. By making these capabilities openly available, DeepSeek offered a viable alternative to closed source platforms for both researchers and commercial developers.

Perhaps the most significant consequence of this release was the market pressure it generated. By lowering the economic barrier to advanced AI experimentation, DeepSeek-R1 challenged prevailing assumptions about access and affordability in the field. Its open availability pushed several proprietary labs to accelerate their own open source strategies in response. Moreover, the move sparked broader conversations about AI equity, competition, and global governance, highlighting the growing tension between innovation, accessibility, and responsible deployment. Its open release created ripples far beyond China, inspiring labs in Europe, India, and even Silicon Valley start-ups to explore more transparent models.

DeepSeek-R1's release triggered a notable shift in AI pricing and market positioning. In response, OpenAI introduced more affordable options, such as discounted access to GPT-3.5 Turbo, while keeping premium GPT-4.1 plans priced at around USD 200 per month for those needing top-tier performance. Anthropic and Cohere also reacted by launching smaller, lower-cost chat models aimed at maintaining their appeal to budget-conscious users. Meanwhile, Meta reaffirmed its commitment to its LLaMA roadmap, signaling expanded licensing options and underscoring a pivot toward broader accessibility in model deployment.

Open source suddenly wasn't a niche, with DeepSeek becoming a ***serious economic threat*** to closed-model business models. Enterprises, particularly cost-sensitive ones, began evaluating DeepSeek for customer support bots, embedded agents, and enterprise knowledge bases, replacing more expensive APIs.

Sparking the next wave of open source AI

DeepSeek's open release emboldened the global open source movement. Developers and researchers who had previously felt locked out of meaningful LLM contributions found new momentum. DeepSeek demonstrated that you didn't need a billion-dollar infrastructure to create something truly impactful.

This led to the following:

- **Academic labs** fine-tuning DeepSeek for specialized domains (biomedicine, law, and STEM education).
- **Start-ups** building SaaS tools using DeepSeek as a backend.
- **Governments** investigating use cases for public-sector LLM deployment.

Open source development surged globally following DeepSeek-R1's release, with new models emerging in regions such as India, South Korea, the EU, and Latin America. On Hugging Face, one notable Indian-based project, `Deepdive404/Deepseek-fork`, released distilled versions of R1 across multiple parameter sizes: 1.5B, 7B, 8B, 14B, 32B, and 70B. You can find it here: `https://huggingface.co/Deepdive404/Deepseek-fork` Meanwhile, the original `deepseek-ai/DeepSeek-R1` repository provides the core R1 and R1-Zero models at `https://huggingface.co/deepseek-ai/DeepSeek-R1`, along with its distilled variants.

These community-driven forks incorporate local languages, regional usage patterns, and various export formats, evidenced by quantized and optimized versions such as `gghfez/DeepSeek-R1-11446-Q2_K` at `https://huggingface.co/gghfez/DeepSeek-R1-11446-Q2_K`, which is tailored for efficient GPU inference. Within just months, Hugging Face recorded hundreds of forks and integrations inspired by DeepSeek, spotlighting localized models, quantization, and community-led improvements.

The model also inspired collaboration across borders. Researchers began publishing cross-lab benchmark studies using DeepSeek as a baseline, and community-maintained evaluation leaderboards gave the model credibility well beyond its original launch hype (`https://artificialanalysis.ai/models/deepseek-r1`, `https://www.statista.com/statistics/1552824/deepseek-performance-of-deepseek-r1-compared-to-open-ai-by-benchmark/`, and `https://pubmed.ncbi.nlm.nih.gov/40267969/`).

A symbol of the technological maturity of China

DeepSeek-R1 marked a milestone as one of the first open source model from China to achieve competitive performance on globally recognized benchmarks. Its strong results in reasoning-intensive tasks and rapid international adoption challenged the perception of Western dominance in frontier AI. The model's reception highlighted the growing importance of open collaboration and cross-border evaluation in legitimizing AI innovation worldwide.

Benchmarks from independent labs confirmed that DeepSeek-R1-0528 was rivaling OpenAI's O3 and Google's Gemini 2.5 Pro. For an open source model, this was unprecedented.

It proved two critical things:

- DeepSeek was not a one-hit wonder – it was a growing ecosystem.
- Open source development could keep pace with proprietary labs when supported by community collaboration and smart engineering.

The release of DeepSeek-R1-0528 on May 28, 2025, delivered enhanced performance in mathematical reasoning, code generation, and factual retrieval. It also demonstrated reduced hallucination rates in factual question-answering benchmarks and introduced improved long-context handling, now supporting input lengths of up to 32,000 tokens – thus, making it more effective for complex, multi-turn tasks and extended document analysis, and reaffirming continuous model improvement with this new release.

The release of DeepSeek-R1 has also prompted critical questions and ongoing debates. Let's talk about some of the controversies surrounding DeepSeek.

Controversies surrounding DeepSeek

As with any major development in AI, DeepSeek has not emerged without controversy. While it is widely celebrated for its technical sophistication, open source stance, and trailblazing approach to reasoning, its ascent has stirred debate in areas ranging from research ethics and safety to geopolitical strategy and intellectual property. This section explores the multifaceted controversies that have accompanied DeepSeek's rise, acknowledging the tension between technological progress and responsible innovation.

Potential for bias and misuse

One area of concern stems from DeepSeek's decision to rely on RL alone for alignment, without the conventional SFT or RLHF. Critics argue this could leave the model vulnerable to alignment drift or unpredictable behaviors over time. Others have questioned whether the open-access nature of the model, while consistent with the team's stated goals of transparency and collaboration, increases the potential for misuse. There have also been public discussions about whether the model suppresses or softens responses to politically sensitive topics, raising questions about transparency in content moderation and training data choices.

DeepSeek's team has published several papers, such as *DeepSeekR1* (`https://arxiv.org/abs/2501.12948`) and news docs (`https://api-docs.deepseek.com/news/news250120`) that describe evaluation methodologies for community, researchers, and critics alike. DeepSeek has also released smaller variants for deployment in sensitive, more conservative, or resource-constrained settings. Some of these models are DeepSeek-R1-Zero and several distilled 1.5B–70B models; these are available via the official GitHub repositories at `deepseek-ai/DeepSeek-R1`(`https://github.com/deepseek-ai/DeepSeek-R1`) and Hugging Face `deepseek-ai/DeepSeek-R1`(`https://huggingface.co/deepseek-ai/DeepSeek-R1`).

While these measures have helped reassure many in the developer and research communities, they do not fully resolve the tension between openness and control. Underscoring the reality, balancing powerful general-purpose AI with responsible deployment remains an unresolved and evolving challenge.

DeepSeek's radical transparency reignited the AI community's debates on **access versus control**:

- Was it responsible to release a powerful model with minimal guardrails?
- Could it be misused to generate disinformation or harmful content?
- Was community red-teaming enough to ensure safety?

Supporters argued that this openness enabled academic research into LLM alignment and trustworthiness in ways no closed model could. Critics insisted more should be done to prevent misuse. Nonetheless, DeepSeek showed that the conversation around safety didn't have to be confined to corporate hallways. It could be open, collaborative, and community-governed.

For the curious reader, a high-level assessment of the DeepSeek-R1 model's trustworthiness, summarizing its risk levels across dimensions such as security, privacy, hallucination, toxicity, stereotypes, ethics, performance, and robustness, along with general recommendations for mitigating these risks, is available in *Trust Report: Vijil DeepSeek-R1 Trust Report* (`https://www.vijil.ai/blog/deepseek-trust-report`).

Openness and national security concerns

One of the most polarizing aspects of DeepSeek is its radical openness. While celebrated by academic and open-source communities, the model's full weight releases, training recipes, and RL protocols have drawn criticism from national security analysts and policy think-tanks. Some argue that the sophistication of DeepSeek-V3 and R1 rivals or exceeds many proprietary models and could be misused in ways that amplify the capabilities of bad actors.

For example, intelligence analysts have expressed concern over DeepSeek's potential application in automated propaganda generation, cyber-intrusion planning, and synthetic misinformation campaigns, especially given its RAG and code-writing prowess. The ability to simulate reasoning, explain complex concepts, and even manipulate dialogue patterns through CoT scaffolding makes DeepSeek powerful in the wrong hands.

This debate echoes broader tensions in AI: How much openness is too much? Should models capable of autonomous reasoning be released without constraints? While DeepSeek has implemented content filters and RL-based ethical instruction, the absence of API gatekeeping (as seen in OpenAI or Anthropic) means fewer restrictions on end use. The model's utility for good is clear, but so too is the risk of abuse.

Still, supporters argue that censoring open science in the name of security may backfire. They contend that transparency enables greater research collaboration on alignment and safety, decentralizes innovation, and builds public trust. As of mid-2025, DeepSeek's team has maintained their position that controlled openness – combined with robust documentation and red-teaming – remains the best path forward for responsible AI.

Cultural and political perceptions

Given DeepSeek's origins in China and bilingual training in both English and Chinese, it has become a lightning rod for geopolitical scrutiny. Some Western commentators have accused DeepSeek of being a strategic tool for soft power projection – an effort to establish AI dominance not just through capability, but through influence over global open source ecosystems. While such claims are speculative and often politically charged, they reflect real anxieties about AI leadership in a multipolar world. Open source software, once considered neutral ground, is increasingly viewed as a geopolitical asset. DeepSeek's success in outperforming Western models on key reasoning benchmarks has intensified this narrative.

However, within the global AI community, DeepSeek's dual-language foundation is often viewed more charitably – as a sign of pluralism and linguistic inclusivity. By publishing its models and reasoning data in multiple languages, DeepSeek has arguably done more than most to support cross-cultural research collaboration. It has also enabled more diverse participation in AI benchmarking, training, and evaluation – key ingredients for scientific equity.

That said, critics have questioned the model's internal content moderation standards. While the model includes guardrails against sensitive or violent outputs, regional norms and political sensitivities inevitably shape training data and reward functions. This raises questions about value alignment across cultures, whose norms are encoded in the model's reasoning scaffolds? And should open models be required to disclose ideological biases explicitly?

Academic and industrial pushback

Another point of tension arises from DeepSeek's disruption of traditional research hierarchies. In democratizing access to world-class LLMs, DeepSeek has inadvertently challenged the academic-industrial complex that has long governed AI progress. Some large labs and commercial players have criticized DeepSeek for eroding the competitive advantage that proprietary models enjoy.

Academics have also raised concerns about reproducibility, despite DeepSeek's transparent releases. Some worry that without shared benchmark governance or citation conventions, the proliferation of DeepSeek derivatives could muddy scientific attribution and disrupt standardization efforts. Additionally, there's unease that DeepSeek's rapid publication cadence may incentivize volume over peer review, leading to a *release-first, refine-later* culture that undermines the rigor of academic research.

Others, however, see DeepSeek as a necessary counterweight to gatekeeping. Its model weights and training protocols offer students, independent researchers, and non-Western institutions a way to participate in top-tier research on their own terms. Rather than collapsing academic standards, they argue, DeepSeek offers a complementary path that integrates open engineering with scholarly goals.

Ethical debates around RL methods

DeepSeek's R1-Zero approach, which uses sparse **binary rewards** for CoT scaffolding, has ignited debate in the alignment community. While celebrated for its simplicity and elegance, critics argue that it lacks nuance in ethical edge cases. Binary correctness may not capture subtleties in moral reasoning, social fairness, or user-centric alignment.

For example, by scoring only based on structural format and correctness, R1-Zero may overlook tone, ambiguity, or unintended implications in its output. Compared to multi-signal preference modeling in Claude or the nuanced style-weighted reward systems in GPT-4o, DeepSeek's RL strategy may appear blunt.

However, defenders highlight that R1-Zero is not a final destination but a starting point. By showing that CoT reasoning can emerge from sparse signals, DeepSeek challenges the field to rethink how alignment can be achieved efficiently and scalably. It raises a compelling question: Is a *think clearly, answer correctly* paradigm sufficient for safe AI interaction? Or must alignment always involve intricate preference networks?

What's clear is that DeepSeek's alignment choices – both in what it rewards and what it omits – will shape how future models reason. The community's engagement with these methods, through critique or replication, will help determine their evolution.

Discourse as a feature, not a flaw

DeepSeek's controversies are not signs of dysfunction but indicators of relevance. They reflect the model's central position in ongoing conversations about openness, safety, equity, and governance in AI. While no model is beyond reproach, DeepSeek's willingness to publish, iterate, and engage in public discourse positions it uniquely in the ecosystem.

Whether one sees DeepSeek as a democratizing force or a disruptive wildcard, its impact is undeniable. By provoking new questions and challenging old assumptions, DeepSeek does not merely participate in the AI debate – it helps shape it.

Summary

In this chapter, we explored the foundations of DeepSeek, a powerful open source language model series that is shaping the next wave of AI innovation. We began by understanding what DeepSeek is and why it stands out in the growing field of LLMs. We took a closer look at the technical breakthroughs that power DeepSeek, from its training methodology and architecture to its impressive performance on key benchmarks. We also examined the broader impact DeepSeek is having on the global AI ecosystem, especially in terms of open source access, innovation democratization, and regional development. Finally, the last section provided an overview of the different versions of DeepSeek, illustrating its rapid evolution and ongoing improvements in capabilities. You should now be able to clearly articulate what DeepSeek is, what makes it technically significant, how it's influencing the global AI landscape, and how its different versions reflect strategic design choices over time. These foundational insights will serve as your lens for evaluating and working with DeepSeek in practice.

In the next chapter, we'll go deeper into the model's inner workings, examining how DeepSeek reasons, its approach to multimodality, and the broader implications and limitations of the system. This exploration will equip you to critically assess not just what DeepSeek can do, but how and why it does it.

2

Deep Dive into DeepSeek

In this chapter, we will take a comprehensive look under the hood of DeepSeek. This chapter will equip you with a practical understanding of what makes DeepSeek unique and how it fits into the evolving landscape of AI models. We will begin with DeepSeek's technical architecture, components, and training datasets. Then, we will walk you through how these components come together to form DeepSeek's reasoning mechanisms. You will also learn about DeepSeek's emerging multimodal features and where DeepSeek stands in the multimodal landscape.

In this chapter, we're going to cover the following topics:

- Key architectural components of DeepSeek
- Understanding the reasoning mechanics of DeepSeek
- Advanced capabilities of DeepSeek

Key architectural components of DeepSeek

As you may recall from *Chapter 1*, DeepSeek builds on the foundational transformer architecture introduced by Vaswani et al. (2017), using its core components as a baseline for subsequent innovations. We will first discuss the key architectural components.

The key architectural components of DeepSeek include the **decoder, multi-head latent attention (MLA)**, and **mixture-of-experts (MoE)**, as illustrated in *Figure 2.1*.

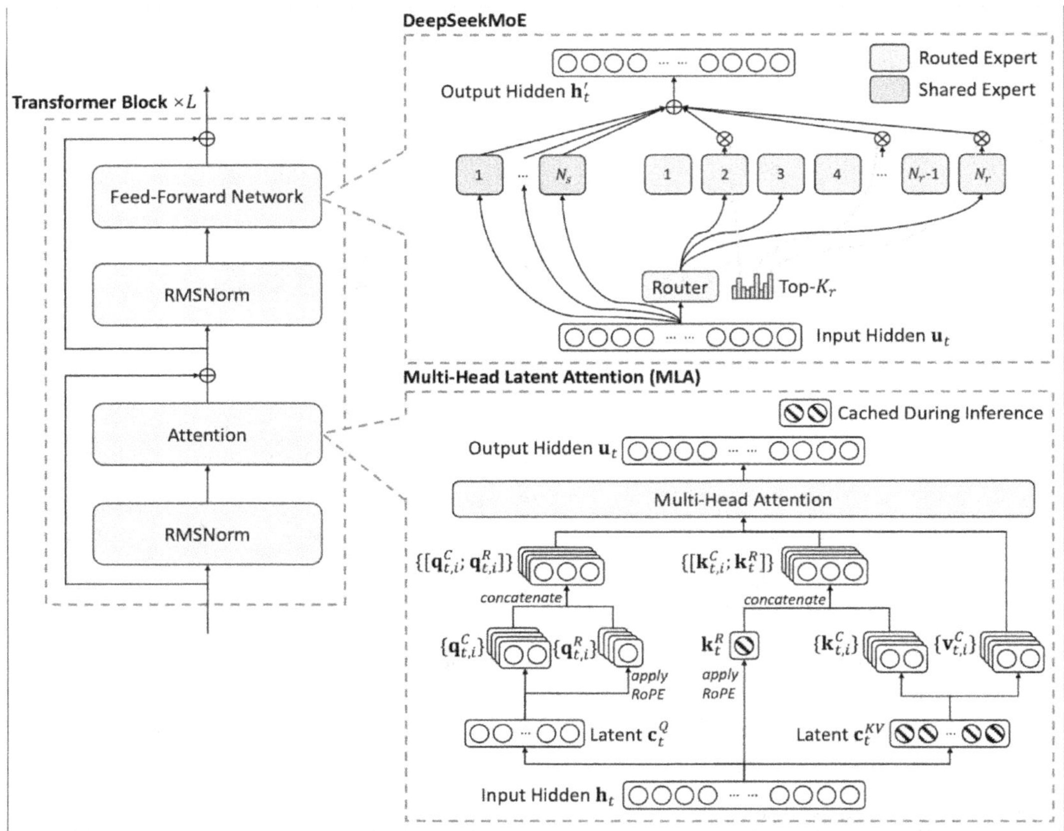

Figure 2.1: DeepSeek V3/R1 architecture

The architecture and training pipeline support modularity and specialization in ways that directly enhance reasoning. Instead of relying on a single, monolithic transformer, DeepSeek routes the prompt through specialized components.

Let us talk about **prompt routing** first.

Prompt routing in DeepSeek

Take a look at the following figure, which illustrates how DeepSeek routes the prompt through its components.

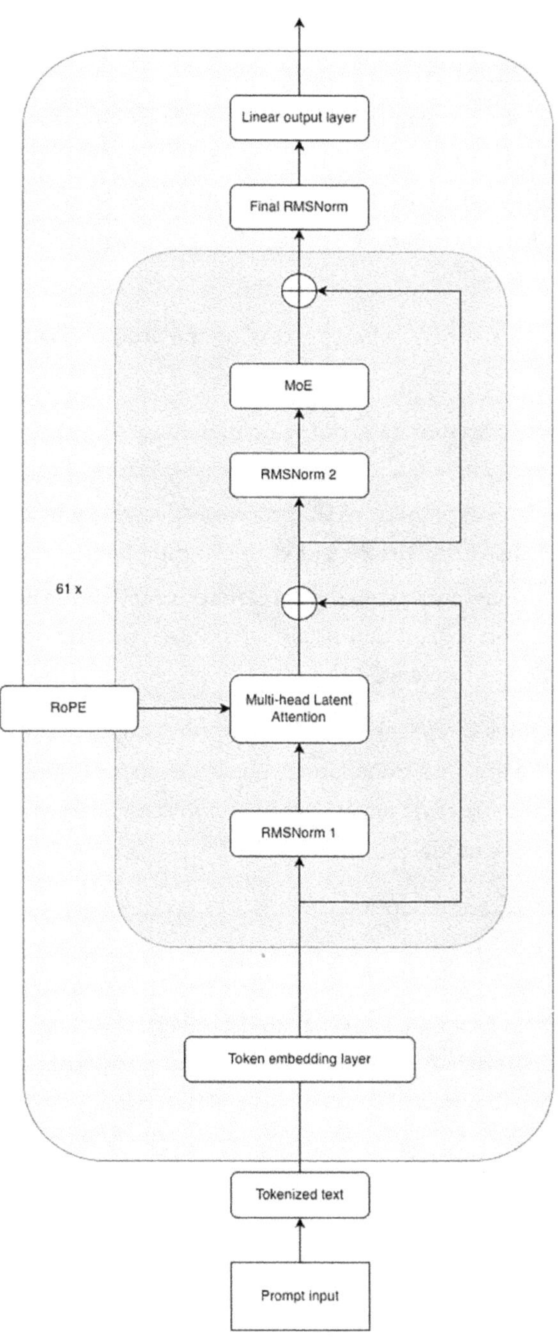

Figure 2.2: Prompt routing in DeepSeek

Here is what happens once the prompt is input and tokenized:

1. **Retrieval modules** fetch relevant knowledge.
2. Next, **reranker modules** evaluate and refine retrieved information to prioritize the most logically pertinent content.
3. The **lightweight decoder** then incrementally builds the response, leveraging the MoE to dynamically activate sub-networks specialized in mathematical reasoning and logical inference.

For example, let's see what happens when processing the prompt `Sum of the odd numbers is even`:

1. DeepSeek first retrieves foundational principles about odd and even sums from its knowledge base (here odd and even numbers and arithmetic properties).
2. The reranker elevates explanations that correctly describe why an odd plus an odd equals an even number, discarding irrelevant or misleading facts.
3. The decoder then generates a stepwise explanation, activating experts that focus on arithmetic properties and logical deduction, ultimately producing a coherent justification before stating the final answer.

This modular process allows DeepSeek to adapt reasoning depth and pathway dynamically, ensuring precise, context-aware, and transparent outputs even for topics requiring layered understanding. This flexible infrastructure paves the way for much more nuanced reasoning than seen in traditional autoregressive models.

Let's now talk about the decoder module.

Decoder

With **DeepSeek-R1** (`https://arxiv.org/abs/2501.12948`), DeepSeek employs a **decoder-only autoregressive transformer** that generates rationales and explanations as part of its output. *Figure 2.3* shows the block diagram of the DeepSeek-R1 decoder.

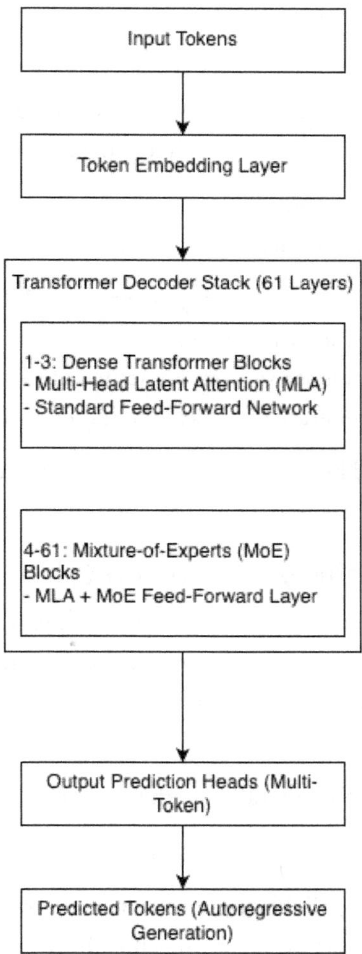

Figure 2.3: DeepSeek-R1 decoder block diagram

The decoder block of DeepSeek consists of the following:

- **Embedding layer**: This converts input tokens into vector representations.
- **Layers 1–3**: The first three layers use the following:
    - MLA for efficient attention and **rotary positional embedding** (**RoPE**) for extended sequence handling.
    - Standard dense **feed-forward networks** (**FFNs**).

- **Layers 4–61**: These layers use the following:
    - Each block contains MLA as previously.
    - Feed-forward is replaced with a MoE layer: a routing mechanism selects a subset of specialized FFN ***experts*** for each token, improving both capacity and efficiency.
- **Prediction heads**: Final output goes to one or more heads to support next-token and multi-token prediction, a technique for more reliable generation.

When the tokens enter the embedding layer, they are processed through a stack of 61 transformer decoder blocks. The initial blocks are fully dense, while blocks 4–61 employ a MoE architecture, each utilizing MLA to achieve a response from an activated expert. This output is then passed through prediction heads that generate the next token(s) in an autoregressive manner.

Okay, then, now you understand how the prompt and tokens flow through the decoder. And we know now you are itching to understand what is happening behind the scenes. Let's dive right in.

Internal mechanics of the decoder module

DeepSeek-R1's decoder module consists of 61 transformer layers, where the first three are dense, and the remaining 58 employ a MoE structure. Within each MoE layer, there is a combination of one **shared expert**, which is always active, and 256 routed experts for a total of 14,906 experts distributed throughout the model.

Let's look at all the components that work through the tokens.

Token processing and generation with router

For every input or generated token, a lightweight **router** evaluates which specialized sub-networks (the routed experts) should process that token. Specifically, the router dynamically chooses 8 out of 256 routed experts in each layer, together with the always-on shared expert. This selection isn't random; it's determined for each token by considering the token's context and matching its features to the *affinity* or specialization of each expert. Which experts are activated depends on the nature of the prompt and the type of token being generated. For example, when generating a rationale that involves a mathematical argument or code, the model will preferentially activate those experts that are specialized in mathematical reasoning or programming. Similarly, for reasoning or refusal behaviors, analyses using **functional token resonance imaging (fTRI)** have shown that certain identifiable experts are consistently activated, depending on the category of response required.

Finally, the retrieval candidates are generated.

In DeepSeek-R1, reranking plays a central role in transforming retrieval candidates into high-quality, human-readable justifications. Typically, the model follows the process as shown in the following figure.

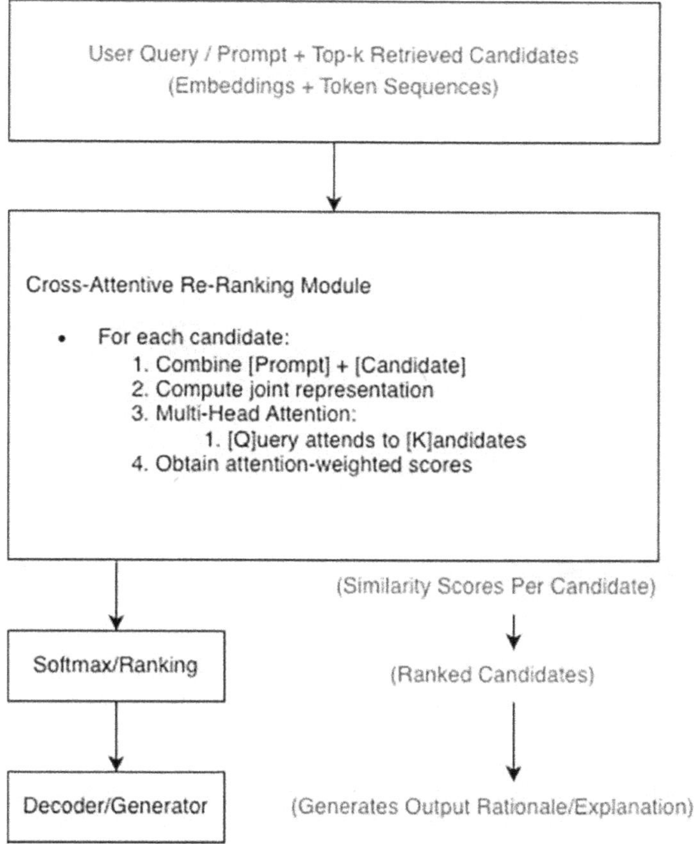

Figure 2.4: Cross-attentive reranking module

Here is how it works for your prompt:

1. **Top-k retrieval**: Given a prompt (e.g., a user query or reasoning task), an initial retriever selects the *k* most relevant candidate passages or answers using fast, often vector-based similarity (such as cosine or dot-product in embedding space).

2. **Cross-attentive reranking**: These candidates, their embeddings, and the original prompt are input into a specialized transformer block. This module uses cross-attention – attending jointly to both the query and each candidate – to compute refined similarity scores and produce reranked outputs that inform the next generation step.
3. **Final justification generation**: The aligned, reranked candidates (plus intermediate scoring vectors) are then processed in the decoder, which generates a rationale or explanation as part of its output.

Consider, for example, the following prompt:

```
"What is the capital of France?"
```

Assuming *k*= *3*, the top 3 retrieved passages are as follows:

```
["Paris is a major European city.", "Berlin is the capital of Germany.",
"Paris has many museums."]
```

The cross-attentive reranker, via attention to both query and answer, scores `Paris as a major European city`, the highest, since `Paris` and `capital` align strongly.

After top-k retrieval and cross-attentive ranking, the model consumes the aligned embeddings and token sequences to generate human-readable justifications through its standard generation process.

Consequently, as DeepSeek-R1 generates tokens for a rationale or explanation step by step, the exact subset of experts activated can shift dynamically from one token to the next.

For each token, the following happens:

1. The router takes the hidden state corresponding to that token and rapidly computes similarity scores with each expert's centroid representation.
2. It then selects the top-k (say *k*= *8*) experts with the highest scores and routes that token to be processed only by those experts, alongside the always-active shared expert, for that layer.
3. Across a sequence of tokens and diverse prompt types, a wide variety of expert subsets become active, enabling DeepSeek-R1 to marshal highly specialized capabilities, such as complex logical reasoning or domain-specific knowledge, while maintaining computational efficiency by not activating all experts at once.

This MoE-based architecture ensures that DeepSeek-R1 can construct detailed, step-by-step explanations or rationales.

Each token in the generated output can benefit from both the context (previous tokens) and the unique expertise of a dynamically selected set of expert networks at every layer, allowing for nuanced, efficient, and highly specialized reasoning throughout the response.

Autoregressive transformer

DeepSeek-R1 uses the autoregressive transformer, where the model produces one token at a time, with each new token being generated based on all previously generated tokens. This design choice is called ***autoregressive*** because, at every generation step, the model's next token prediction is conditioned explicitly on the entire sequence constructed so far, not on the future context, enabling the model to build coherent, contextually relevant outputs step by step.

Once the initial input or prompt is set, the following happens:

1. The sequence is processed through attentive and feed-forward components in the transformer stack.
2. The model then predicts the most likely next token, appends it to the sequence, and repeats the process for the following token – always conditioning exclusively on what has already been generated:

    - **Autoregressive generation** works by generating only a single token per forward pass, not a batch or series of tokens simultaneously.
    - However, through repeated forward passes, the model constructs a growing sequence, one token at a time, until a stopping condition is met (such as an end-of-sequence token).

    This stepwise process is crucial for structured tasks such as logical explanations or code, where the meaning of each next token often tightly depends on the context set by all previous outputs.

3. As for the possible tokens generated at each step, the model considers its entire vocabulary, potentially tens of thousands of tokens.
4. For every new position, the decoder outputs a probability distribution over the full vocabulary. Probable candidates include syntactically and semantically plausible tokens based on the current context. For example, after the phrase `The answer is`, likely next tokens might be numbers, a colon, or words expressing a solution. If generating source code, probable tokens could include keywords such as `def`, data types, or variable names, guided by the prompt and semantic coherence.

Multi-head attention

DeepSeek-R1 also uses a **multi-head self-attention** design, specifically an optimized variant called MLA. This allows the model to analyze relationships between tokens effectively. DeepSeek-R1's multi-head attention does not mean each head focuses on a single token. Instead, multiple heads operate in parallel, each learning to attend to different parts of the input sequence simultaneously.

Although the exact number of heads in DeepSeek-R1's transformer layers isn't explicitly stated in available sources, typical large transformer models use dozens of heads (e.g., 64 or more), balancing the total available heads with the number of tokens. It is indeed possible to have a trade-off – more heads can provide finer-grained attention at the cost of more computation, while fewer heads reduce complexity but may capture less diverse relationships.

The core function of multi-head attention is to capture different types of relationships between tokens in the input sequence. Each head computes **queries**, **keys**, and **values** (**Q**, **K**, and **V**) that interact to generate attention scores, which highlight how much one token should consider others when forming its internal representation.

- **Queries**: In a transformer, the query is a vector representing what information or context the model is looking for in the input data.
- **Keys**: The key is a vector representing the characteristics or features of each element in the input that the query is compared against to find relevant information.
- **Values**: The value is a vector containing the content or information associated with each key, which is weighted and aggregated based on similarity to the query to produce the output.
- More information can be found at `https://en.wikipedia.org/wiki/Attention_(machine_learning)`.

Through this, attention identifies pairwise relationships not just between the existing input tokens but also takes into account previously generated tokens during autoregressive generation, since the model attends over the entire prefix.

To better handle the large sequence lengths DeepSeek-R1 supports (up to 128K tokens), it employs ***RoPE***. RoPE injects positional information so the model knows the relative positions of tokens, which is crucial for meaningful attention over long contexts.

Suppose the input tokens so far include the phrase `The answer is` during autoregressive generation. Multi-head attention enables some heads to focus on the phrase `The answer` while others attend to the latest token, `is`, combining these perspectives to predict plausible next tokens, such as numbers or words, forming a solution. As the model generates new tokens, these tokens get appended to the sequence, and the attention mechanism extends over this growing sequence, dynamically adapting which tokens are most relevant, all processed in parallel by multiple heads.

Moreover, DeepSeek-R1 integrates an efficiency optimization with MLA. Here, instead of separately storing full key and value matrices for each head, the model factorizes them into latent vectors, reducing memory consumption without sacrificing the quality of attention.

Layer normalization

Layer normalization is applied to the hidden representations (also called **activations**) of tokens at specific points within each transformer layer to improve training stability, convergence speed, and overall model performance. More precisely, the normalization operates on the token embedding vectors; these vectors represent the tokens' current states as they are processed through the network.

Activations in an LLM transformer refer to the specific scalar values in the hidden states of the model during its layer-by-layer computations; these activations represent the transformed input features at various stages and play a critical role in how the model processes and generates language.

The **key transformations** where layer normalization is applied include critical components inside each transformer layer: the multi-head self-attention module and the FFN (also called the **position-wise network**). Here is how this works:

1. Before entering the attention mechanism, the token embeddings are normalized by computing their mean and variance across the embedding dimensions and then scaling and shifting these values to have consistent statistical properties. This **pre-attention normalization** ensures that the inputs to the attention computations have stable distributions, which helps the model learn more effectively.
2. After the attention output is added (via residual connections) back to the tokens, another normalization step is often applied to keep the activations well-conditioned as they move into the FFN.
3. Similarly, **pre-** and **post-normalization** also occur around the feed-forward layers, ensuring that the transformations – which involve linear projection, nonlinear activations (such as GELU), and another linear projection – maintain stable activation statistics.

For example, consider the `Calculate the sum` prompt tokens:

1. As these tokens enter a transformer layer, their embeddings are normalized before self-attention calculates how much each token should attend to itself and others in the prompt.
2. The attention module produces updated embeddings, after which layer normalization again stabilizes these new vectors before passing them into the FFN.
3. This FFN then applies linear weights, a nonlinearity, and another linear transformation – key transformations where normalization supports smooth gradient flow and mitigates internal covariate shift.
4. Following this, a final normalization step prepares the output embeddings to enter the next transformer layer or the output head.
5. Layer normalization in DeepSeek-R1 normalizes the token embeddings before and after the key internal transformations – multi-head self-attention and feedforward layers – within each transformer block. This layered normalization keeps the token representations consistent and stable throughout the stepwise, autoregressive generation process, thereby enhancing training reliability and model accuracy over very long sequences.

The use of MoE and attention optimizations such as **grouped-query attention** (**GQA**) enables the model to scale without excessive resource demands.

GQA is an optimized attention mechanism in transformer models that divides query heads into groups, where each group shares a single key and value projection, balancing computational efficiency and model performance by interpolating between multi-head attention and multi-query attention.

Through its structured reasoning capabilities, DeepSeek-R1 can not only generate answers but also produce explanations, verifications, and arguments, critical abilities for domains such as theorem proving, law, and structured reasoning. The decoder module in DeepSeek-R1 refers to a stack of transformer decoder blocks (61 layers in total) that form the core of its autoregressive language modeling capabilities.

We will now show you how this works for our sample prompt.

Working example

Suppose the user inputs the following:

```
Prove that the sum of two even numbers is even.
```

This prompt goes through the following steps:

1. **Tokenization**: The input is split into tokens and embedded as vectors for processing. Typical tokens might be (in plain text) the following:

   `Prove`, `that`, `the`, `sum`, `of`, `two`, `even`, `numbers`, `is`, `even`, `.`

2. **Sequential processing**: The embedded tokens flow through the decoder stack. In each layer of DeepSeek-R1's decoder, self-attention enables each token to consider earlier tokens in the sequence using **key** (K), **query** (Q), and **value** (V) representations. For example, suppose token t_2 wants to attend to t_1 and t_0; it generates Q_2, compares it to K_1 and K_0, and uses the resulting attention scores to weight V_1 and V_0. This operation allows t_2 to aggregate relevant contextual information from preceding tokens.
3. **Causal masking** enforces the autoregressive property by blocking each token from attending to future tokens, ensuring that predictions only depend on previously seen inputs and preserving the left-to-right generation structure. As output is generated, the model selects the most relevant prior token activations according to the attention scores, building understanding with each forward step.

   It is important to distinguish that this self-attention operates within a single sequence, the tokens of the input prompt or generated response, allowing the model to capture internal dependencies. In contrast, cross-attention is used in separate, specialized modules (such as cross-attentive reranking), where the model allows tokens from one sequence (e.g., the prompt) to attend to tokens from another sequence (e.g., retrieved candidates) to refine similarity scores before entering the decoder. Thus, the decoder itself relies on self-attention for in-sequence reasoning, while cross-attention is applied earlier during retrieval and ranking.

4. **Autoregressive token generation**: After each pass through the decoder, the model predicts the next token by scoring multiple possible candidates. For example, after generating the prefix `<think> Let the two even numbers be 2a and 2b, where a and b are integers`, the model considers several top candidates for the next token. Suppose the top-k options are as follows:

   - `Their` (score: 0.34)
   - `The` (score: 0.21)
   - `Sum` (score: 0.18)
   - `Difference` (score: 0.16)
   - `Product` (score: 0.11)

Using cross ranking, `Their` receives the highest score, so it is selected as the next token:

```
<think> Let the two even numbers be 2a and 2b, where a and b are
integers.
<think> Their sum is 2a + 2b = 2(a + b)
<answer> Since a + b is an integer, 2(a + b) is even.
<answer> Therefore, the sum of two even numbers is even.
```

At each generation step, the decoder weighs its top candidates and picks the token with the highest score, constructing the output token by token, guided by context and autoregressive constraints.

Phew! That was quite something. Well, there is more. Let's now move to the next component, the MoE.

Mixture of experts

As outlined in *Chapter 1*, MoE routing improved parameter efficiency by selectively activating specialized submodules for each token. Throughout all stages, advancements in projection and pooling methods contributed to stabilizing embedding norms, which enhanced retrieval performance. Furthermore, metadata-aware cross-attention allowed DeepSeek's encoders to incorporate contextual document features such as titles and categories.

In DeepSeek-R1, the MoE architecture selectively activates specialized expert sub-networks dynamically for each token during generation, enabling efficient use of vast model capacity. When processing a prompt, the model's router evaluates the token's contextual embedding and compares it with learned centroids representing each expert's specialization. Based on this similarity, it activates a small subset of experts, typically 8 out of 256 routed experts plus one shared expert per MoE layer, tailoring computation to the token's semantic and functional needs.

If you are wondering how this expert selection happens, keep reading.

How are experts initialized and configured?

DeepSeek-R1's architecture defines hundreds of routed experts (e.g., a noun expert, number expert, web expert, etc.) for each MoE layer, distinguished by learnable centroid vectors. These centroids begin as random vectors and, throughout pretraining, are shaped to specialize in distinct linguistic or semantic domains – such as recognizing numbers, identifying named entities, or interpreting reasoning cues – depending on patterns encountered in the training data. Experts such as the number expert or web expert are not hardcoded; instead, these specializations emerge as different experts are repeatedly activated for certain token types or contexts during training.

For example, consider the following partial prompt token sequence: `Prove that the sum of two even numbers is even.` During autoregressive generation, when the model encounters tokens related to mathematical reasoning (such as `even numbers`, `sum`, or `prove`), experts specialized in mathematical operations and stepwise logic are strongly activated.

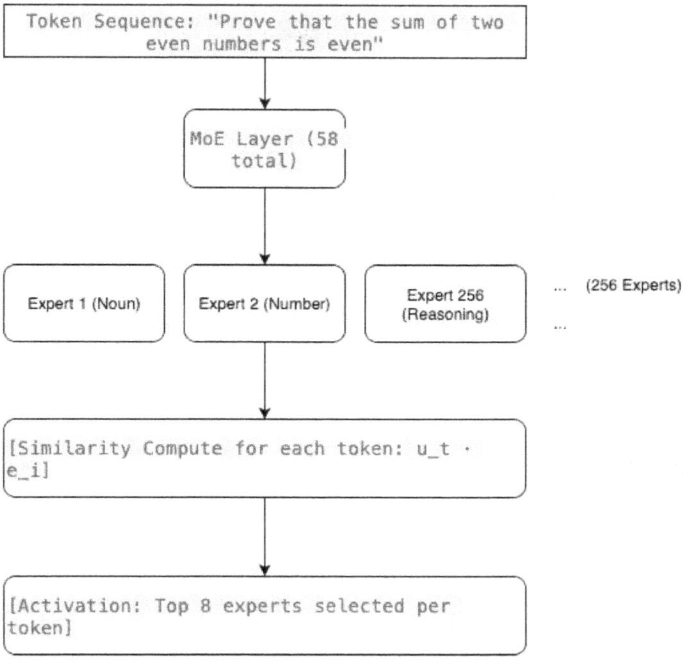

Figure 2.5: MoE routing in DeepSeek-R1

The router selects those experts whose specialization best matches the role of each token: mathematical experts handle numeric manipulations and proof steps, while reasoning experts are chosen for tokens that demand justification or logical explanation.

If the prompt shifts to programming, such as outputting `def` or specific variable names, the router would preferentially activate experts trained in code generation. In this way, **context-sensitive routing** ensures that the model leverages the knowledge of those experts most relevant to the current task.

How does gating compute which experts to activate?

When a prompt such as `Prove that the sum of two even numbers is even` is tokenized and fed into the model, each token's embedding (its hidden state) is processed by the **MoE gating network** at every MoE layer it passes through. For each token at each layer, the following happens:

1. The token's embedding is compared to every expert's centroid vector (pre-learned) using a dot product, producing **affinity scores** that measure how closely the token's features align with each expert's specialization.
2. These affinity scores pass through a normalized gating function. DeepSeek-R1 typically uses a sigmoid-based mechanism with potential bias adjustments for balancing expert usage, rather than a simple softmax.
3. The **gating function** selects the top-K experts (e.g., $K=8$) with the highest affinity scores for that token, plus one shared expert that is always activated.
4. Only the selected experts process the token; their outputs are weighted by the gating scores and combined to form the output representation for that token at the layer.

How are experts activated?

We will now go back to our sample prompt to see how the experts get activated.

Consider the token `even` within the prompt `Prove that the sum of two even numbers is even`. At an MoE layer, the router compares the embedding of `even` to the centroids of all experts:

- If `even` aligns closely with the ***mathematical reasoning*** expert's centroid, that expert's affinity score will be high, making it one of the top-K experts selected.
- Tokens such as `sum` and `prove`, associated with logical reasoning and proof construction, may activate ***reasoning*** or ***proof-logic*** experts.
- If the prompt context included programming syntax or variable names, ***programming*** experts would be preferentially routed instead, but for this mathematical proof, such experts are less relevant.
- Even connective tokens such as `that`, `of`, or `two` undergo this gating independently, leading to a dynamic, token-specific expert routing pathway throughout the prompt.

This **token-by-token gating mechanism** generates a unique activation pathway through the expert network tailored to each input and generated token. It efficiently leverages specialized expert knowledge exactly when needed, minimizing computational overhead. This **dynamic routing** also supports DeepSeek-R1's ability to produce clear, stepwise explanations and reasoned outputs by activating the most relevant experts precisely at the right time.

On the other hand, the traditional state-of-the-art (SOTA) LLMs (such as GPT-4o or Claude) mostly use dense architectures, meaning all parameters are used on every input, leading to high resource use. DeepSeek achieves SOTA-level performance but with much lower effective active parameter count, making it much more efficient. Additionally, metadata-aware cross-attention layers incorporate contextual features such as document titles or categories, enriching the representations that influence expert routing and enhancing retrieval and relevance. Instead of routing input through every neuron in every layer, each layer contains multiple *expert* subnetworks, but only a few specialists (e.g., 8 out of 64 experts) are activated per token. This drastically lowers computational load while maintaining capacity.

The following equation shows how the experts get activated:

$$\text{Output} = \sum_{k=1}^{K} G_k(x) \cdot \text{Expert}_k(x)$$

where gating functions $G_k(x)$ select which experts to use (K is the total number of experts; often only the top two are activated).

Next up, we will move our focus to MLA.

Multi-head latent attention: Memory-efficient attention for long contexts

MLA was first operationalized in DeepSeek-V2 and later refined in DeepSeek-V3 to reduce memory usage during inference without compromising output quality.

Standard transformers (and many SOTA models such as LlaMa 3 and GPT-4o) use **multi-head attention** with full **key-value (KV)** caches for each token, leading to high memory requirements for long contexts. DeepSeek-V2, V3, and R1 introduce MLA, compressing the KV cache into a compact latent for each head, reducing inference memory by over 90% while preserving or improving quality.

MLA replaces the standard multi-head attention mechanism by introducing a form of low-rank compression to the KV cache. Instead of storing a large set of key and value memory tensors for every token during inference, leading to immense memory usage, especially with long sequences, MLA absorbs these representations into a smaller set of learned latent vectors. At each layer, attention computations are performed not directly over the full cache, but through these compressed latents, which maintain sufficient contextual information for high-quality generation.

Additional enhancements include selective application of rotary positional embeddings and advanced weight absorption techniques, allowing this mechanism to match or exceed the model's original reasoning quality while often reducing inference cache size by over 90%. This innovation is a key reason behind DeepSeek-R1's ability to efficiently handle long-context tasks and to offer economical large language model inference at scale.

Let's take a look at how this works.

In MLA, instead of storing $O(N)$ keys/values (where N is sequence length), KV for each head is projected into a much smaller latent space:

$$\mathrm{KV}_{\mathrm{latent}} = f(\{K_i, V_i\}_{i=1}^{N})$$

During attention, queries attend to this latent rather than the full sequence – a major speed and memory gain.

LLaMa 3 and many GPT models use GQA to reduce KV cache size, but MLA empirically delivers better modeling performance and higher efficiency, as attested by benchmarks and publications.

For the prompt `Prove that the sum of two even numbers is even`, MLA enhances the model's understanding by incorporating external context, such as document titles or category information, into the attention mechanism. This external context provides additional signals that help the model better interpret and specialize its response based on relevant metadata. Within one attention head, the key and value vectors are first computed from the input token embeddings. Each of these vectors, originally high-dimensional (e.g., 1,024 dimensions), is then projected into a smaller latent space (for example, 64 dimensions) using learned projection matrices. This dimensionality reduction allows for more efficient computation and focuses attention on the most relevant features. The projected keys represent the contextual features used to match against the query (**Q**), while the projected values carry the enriched information that is aggregated. MLA achieves this by attending to both the token sequence and the injected metadata simultaneously across multiple latent subspaces, allowing the model to weigh and integrate relevant external knowledge dynamically as it generates the proof. This process enables more accurate, context-aware reasoning for claims like the sum of two even numbers being even.

There are other key aspects that make DeepSeek one of the most competitive models. Hang in there.

DeepSeek features for efficient and context-aware responses

Apart from the architectural innovations mentioned, DeepSeek employed several other techniques to ensure efficiency and context-aware responses. Let's talk about them.

FP8 training and precision control

DeepSeek-R1 is among the first LLMs to implement a true, large-scale **FP8 (8-bit floating point)** mixed-precision strategy for both pretraining and inference. FP8 is one of the key factors behind DeepSeek's breakthrough in speed and memory efficiency over earlier formats such as FP16 or BF16. However, the successful deployment of FP8 required a deliberately engineered approach to address the well-known risks of numerical instability and degraded convergence that commonly arise with such low-precision arithmetic.

The careful design lies in DeepSeek's mixed-precision training framework, where the majority of computation-heavy operations, such as linear transformations (matrix multiplications, or **general matrix multiply** (GEMM) operations) involved in both forward and backward passes, are executed in FP8 precision. For each linear operator (whether for the forward pass, gradient backpropagation, or weight update), model weights and activations are quantized and processed in FP8, doubling computational throughput relative to BF16 and slashing memory usage by half.

Critically, to preserve accuracy, the actual accumulation of products (sums) is performed in FP32. Activations and gradients are cached in BF16 for memory efficiency and stability.

What distinguishes DeepSeek-R1 is its selective application of FP8. Through a detailed empirical study, the team identified specific modules where further reduction in precision would undermine model stability or learning dynamics. For example, they retain higher (BF16 or FP32) precision for embedding layers, the sequence output head, MoE gating modules, layer normalization, and the attention operators, all of which are sensitive to quantization noise and demand more numerical robustness. Only the dense core (GEMM) and certain memory-intensive pathways are safely quantized to FP8. This selective approach ensures that while the vast bulk of the network benefits from the efficiency of FP8 (and thus enables scaling to much larger models within the same compute envelope), key computations always retain the precision needed for model convergence and high-fidelity output. The optimizer states, master weights, and weight gradients are all stored in BF16 or FP32, with sophisticated sharding and parallelism techniques (such as DualPipe pipeline parallelism) further reducing memory and communication overhead.

During DeepSeek-R1's pretraining, matrix multiplications for token transformations and intermediate computations, such as those in mathematical prompts, for example, `Prove that the sum of two even numbers is even`, are performed using FP8 precision to maximize computational efficiency. Meanwhile, critical operations, including the MoE gating logic, layer normalization, and final output generation, utilize higher precision to ensure accuracy and stability as the sequence lengthens. This targeted, module-specific precision approach balances efficiency with reliability, enabling DeepSeek-R1 to train multi-trillion-parameter models at scale in a single run without compromising output quality or training stability. This explanation highlights the practical trade-offs and design decisions important for understanding how the model achieves efficient and stable training at unprecedented scale.

Multi-token prediction for strategic decoding

Most transformer language models are trained as autoregressive models, maximizing the likelihood of the next token given the sequence so far:

$$\max \sum_{t=1}^{T} \log P(x_{t+1} \mid x_{\leq t})$$

This means the model learns to predict just one token at a time, always conditioning on all previous tokens.

At inference time, the model generates text one token after another (token-by-token), sampling or greedily picking the most likely next token.

DeepSeek's V3 model introduces **multi-token prediction** (**MTP**), inspired by **speculative decoding**. Here, the model learns to predict not just the next token, but several future tokens in parallel. Here is the MTP joint likelihood objective DeepSeek employs:

$$\max \sum_{i=1}^{k} \log P(x_{t+i} \mid x_{\leq t})$$

Instead of focusing only on the immediate next token, MTP jointly optimizes for *k* tokens ahead.

This aligns the training objective with more efficient decoding and better captures long-range dependencies.

Some of the benefits of MTP include the following:

- **Parallelizes training**: By predicting multiple tokens together, training can be faster and more efficient.
- **Enhances context modeling**: The model learns to anticipate broader patterns and plan ahead, encouraging globally coherent and consistent reasoning.
- **Accelerates inference**: At generation time, the model can validate or propose multiple tokens per forward pass, drastically increasing throughput.

DeepSeek-R1's **group relative policy optimization** (**GRPO**) represents a major step beyond standard RLHF by enabling much more precise and context-aware reward assignment during fine-tuning. Let's explore this in detail.

GRPO and advanced RLHF

In the custom GRPO system of DeepSeek, during training, the policy model generates multiple responses per prompt – typically, a fixed number such as 4 to 8 samples, though this number can vary depending on the training phase or prompt complexity. Each sampled output is assigned a **binary reward** (acceptable or not) based on strict rule-based criteria. Even if some responses in the group are incorrect and receive zero reward, they are still included in the group to compute an average reward. This means that the presence of incorrect outputs lowers the group's average reward baseline, effectively penalizing poorer quality responses relative to better ones. In practice, a scalar reward is computed from rule-based checks (e.g., correctness and a simple formatting constraint), which often reduces to an effectively binary signal; GRPO uses this scalar after centering by the group mean to push up higher-scoring samples and push down lower-scoring ones.

The model's advantage for each response is then calculated by comparing its binary reward against this group average (and normalizing by the group's standard deviation), guiding policy updates toward responses that outperform the group mean. This relative scoring mechanism encourages consistent improvement while accounting for varied output quality across all samples for the same prompt.

With GRPO, when the prompt `Prove that the sum of two even numbers is even` is presented, the model generates a group of candidate responses in parallel. For example, suppose the candidates and their rewards are as follows:

- **Candidate A**: `Let the two even numbers be 2a and 2b. Their sum is 2(a + b), which is even.` (Reward: 0.85).

- **Candidate B:** `Two even numbers added together result in an even number because even plus even equals even.` (Reward: 0.75).
- **Candidate C:** `Since even numbers are multiples of 2, their sum is divisible by 2, so it's even.` (Reward: 0.80).

GRPO first calculates the mean reward of the group:

Mean reward = (0.85 + 0.75 + 0.80) / 3 = 0.80

Then, for each candidate, it computes the advantage by subtracting this mean reward from its reward, and optionally normalizes by the group's standard deviation to balance scale differences, as shown here:

- Advantage A = 0.85 - 0.80 = +0.05
- Advantage B = 0.75 - 0.80 = -0.05
- Advantage C = 0.80 - 0.80 = 0.00

By optimizing based on these relative advantages rather than absolute rewards alone, the model learns to prefer responses that stand out positively within the realistic set of candidates, improving overall generation quality and relevance for complex prompts like this proof.

Rewards in DeepSeek-R1 can be based on multiple criteria: logical correctness, coherence, faithfulness to the prompt, completeness, or even adherence to mathematical principles or style – in short, any property that can be evaluated by a rule, heuristics, or through **outcome-based scoring**. For instance, when fine-tuning a reasoning task, rewards may be higher for outputs that provide a logical **chain of thought (CoT)** or precise intermediate steps, not merely for producing the final correct answer.

By using each group's average reward as a context-specific baseline, GRPO reduces reward hacking and noise, encouraging the policy to favor relatively better responses in each situation. DeepSeek-R1 also adds a **KL-divergence** penalty (`https://hanj.cs.illinois.edu/cs412/bk3/KL-divergence.pdf`) to the loss to stabilize updates and maintain desired behavior. This granular, group-relative approach enables precise control over learning, improving clarity, factual accuracy, and alignment with user intent – especially for complex, multi-step reasoning tasks. GRPO underpins DeepSeek-R1's strong performance in producing detailed, interpretable, and user-aligned outputs.

Chain-of-thought reasoning: CoT and long CoT

DeepSeek's training, especially with specialized prompts (`<think>`, `<answer>`), is optimized for stepwise, interpretable reasoning. It is particularly strong at long CoT tasks – demonstrated by winning in the 2025 US Math Olympiad LLM challenges.

Consider this prompt, for example:

```
Explain why the sum of two odd numbers is even?
```

Here is DeepSeek's response:

```
<think> Let the numbers be 2a+12a+1 and 2b+12b+1.
<think> Their sum is 2a+1+2b+1=2(a+b+1)2a+1+2b+1=2(a+b+1), which is even.
```

Other SOTA LLMs can produce CoT outputs, but DeepSeek excels due to its architectural and training bias toward structured explanations (more on this in the next section and *Chapter 4*), often outperforming in competitive benchmarks.

Choice of datasets

Recall from *Chapter 1* that DeepSeek's dataset curation spans a rich and diverse set of sources, thoughtfully selected to cover reasoning, coding, science, and general world knowledge. For programming tasks, DeepSeek leverages large-scale, open source code from repositories such as the official GitHub dataset, as well as curated forums and libraries found in data collections such as *The Stack* (`bigcode/the-stack`) and *CodeContests* (`https://huggingface.co/datasets/deepmind/code_contests`). For mathematical and scientific reasoning, the model is trained on benchmark math datasets (such as GSM8K and MATH), scientific paper corpora (such as arXiv and PubMed Central), and collections of logic puzzles and textbook problems.

Crucially, DeepSeek's training diets include explicit CoT datasets, notably using CoT-annotated examples from resources such as the *CoT Collection* (`https://github.com/kaistAI/CoT-Collection`), MathQA (`https://math-qa.github.io/`), and curated human rationales. Instructional and narrative diversity is provided via synthetic datasets inspired by prompts from *Flan Collection* (`https://github.com/google-research/FLAN`), Alpaca (`https://github.com/gururise/AlpacaDataCleaned`), and datasets released for self-instruction or dialogue supervision. For robust multilingual and domain-general competence, DeepSeek includes substantial portions of Wikipedia (`https://www.wikipedia.org/`), Common Crawl – filtered for quality – (`https://commoncrawl.org/`), Project Gutenberg (`https://www.gutenberg.org/`), and domain-specific corpora ranging from legal documents (e.g., Pile-CC's legal section at `https://pile.eleuther.ai/`) to medical literature, such as PMC-PubMed (`https://pmc.ncbi.nlm.nih.gov/`) and MedQA (`https://huggingface.co/datasets/bigbio/med_qa`).

Test-time scaling

DeepSeek-R1 applies **test-time scaling** by allocating extra computational resources during inference, enabling step-by-step deep reasoning over input prompts to produce higher-quality outputs. Instead of generating a single direct answer, the model performs chains of inference passes, similar to *The Human System 2* (deliberate, effortful reasoning) logical reasoning, iteratively evaluating possible solutions before finalizing a response. This approach is supported by its MoE architecture, which routes each token to multiple experts in parallel and leverages advanced hardware acceleration to deliver rapid multi-expert evaluation.

At runtime, the model's output quality improves as more compute is devoted to inference, especially for complex tasks in math, coding, and logical analysis. Real-time answers from DeepSeek-R1, which scales up to thousands of tokens per second on modern GPU clusters, require tightly connected high-performance infrastructure to maximize token throughput and expert communication. This scaling mechanism effectively extends the model's ability to *think longer*, check and refine its reasoning, and boost benchmark performance on tasks demanding extended computation and precise logic.

Together, this broad, carefully curated mix equips DeepSeek with the breadth and depth needed to reason, code, answer multi-step questions, and generalize across languages and domains. For more detailed breakdowns or pointers to documentation of each dataset, you may refer to the associated repositories or academic dataset leaderboards.

Whoa! That's too much to digest. We suggest you take a breather and come back to see how all these concepts come together to form the reasoning mechanics of DeepSeek.

Understanding the reasoning mechanics of DeepSeek

What makes DeepSeek more than just another transformer is its focus on reasoning. **Reasoning** in language models refers to the ability to solve multi-step problems, understand cause and effect, perform symbolic manipulation, or derive answers based on implicit context.

Rather than offering isolated performance gains, DeepSeek's architectural innovations organize internal representations, maintain extended context within a prompt, and structure its responses in a more deliberate and context-aware manner – leading to faster, more reliable reasoning across diverse domains.

DeepSeek's approach to prompt engineering, training design, and model alignment underlines a deliberate shift toward explicit, **structured reasoning**. Rather than relying solely on the model to infer a logical chain behind the scenes, DeepSeek encourages intermediate reasoning steps by introducing structured prompting formats, such as explicit `<think>` and `<answer>` tokens or instruction-tuned templates that guide the model to *show its work*. This is not the same as using a **system prompt** in the conversational sense. This approach relies on carefully designed, task-specific prompt formats that are explicitly embedded into the model's training and fine-tuning datasets.

During data preparation, examples are structured with dedicated tokens such as `<think>` to mark intermediate reasoning steps and `<answer>` to signal the final conclusion. These tokens serve as clear semantic cues that instruct the model to generate detailed, stepwise explanations rather than immediate final answers.

This involves the following steps:

1. The training corpus includes large quantities of annotated data where human-written or model-augmented rationales accompany final responses, broken down into logical inference steps.
2. The model is then trained not only to predict the correct final token sequence but also to reproduce the intermediate reasoning steps within the output sequence.
3. Loss functions are applied over the entire token sequence, including these reasoning steps, to encourage faithful reproduction of structured thought.
4. Moreover, during fine-tuning and reinforcement learning phases (such as using GRPO), evaluation metrics explicitly reward outputs for clarity, coherence, factual alignment, and completeness of reasoning, not just answer correctness. This encourages the model to value interpretability and internal consistency of its *chain of thought*, reinforcing behaviors that make the reasoning process transparent and verifiable.

As a result, DeepSeek's training pipeline instills an operational paradigm where structured prompts with embedded reasoning markers become integral to both the learning objective and output evaluation. This end-to-end design ensures that the model reliably *shows its work* through explicit intermediate steps, producing outputs that users can inspect for logical validity and trustworthiness rather than opaque final answers alone.

So, how does DeepSeek think? Let's zoom in right away.

DeepSeek's thinking

One notable aspect of DeepSeek's development was observed during the training of DeepSeek-R1-Zero, a variant trained solely with RL and without any supervised fine-tuning data. During this process, the model began to demonstrate emergent reasoning abilities that were not explicitly programmed, highlighting new insights into how language models can develop reasoning skills through RL alone.

The training setup for R1-Zero was straightforward. Engineers at DeepSeek designed a fixed prompt structure during training and alignment that encourages the model to reason through problems explicitly before providing an answer.

There are three key factors at play here: the think and answer blocks, GRPO, and RLHF on training samples. Let's talk about them.

The think and answer blocks

While the exact system prompt remains proprietary, available tokens and training artifacts suggest that prompts were consistently framed to include a `<think>` token preceding an `<answer>` token, guiding the model to generate structured, intermediate reasoning steps before arriving at a final response. This explicit delineation between thinking and answering – whether embedded directly in system instructions or demonstrated across supervised examples – acts like a latent system-level directive, conditioning the model to treat reasoning as an integral first-class step rather than an optional behavior.

DeepSeek models (particularly in the R1 series) show strong performance in multi-step tasks such as mathematical problem solving and legal argumentation, where breaking down the question into logical steps is essential for accuracy and transparency. Each model response was expected to follow a two-stage structure, consisting of a `<think>` block that contains intermediate reasoning steps and an `<answer>` block with the final conclusion. This format, introduced during training and evaluation, reinforces explicit reasoning before decision-making, especially for tasks that demand step-by-step logic. The boundary between the two is defined by special tokens, such as `<think>` and `<answer>`, which act as delimiter cues for both formatting and behavior.

This explicit prompt structure helps make the model's reasoning transparent, verifiable, and extensible, particularly for complex domains such as mathematics, law, and multi-turn decision tasks. We will discuss prompt formats in detail in *Chapter 3*.

Consider the following prompt, for example:

```
"Is the sum of two even numbers always even? Explain why."
```

The model responds as follows:

```
<think>
Let the two even numbers be represented as 2a and 2b, where a and b are
integers.
Their sum is 2a + 2b = 2(a + b), which is divisible by 2 and therefore
even.
</think>
<answer>
Yes, the sum of two even numbers is always even.
</answer>
```

Let's look at the structure of the response generated by the model. The `<think>` section is where the model is encouraged to lay out the step-by-step reasoning, while the `<answer>` section delivers the final response succinctly.

Now, the GRPO mechanism comes into play for the model response, which we discuss next.

Evaluating response quality with GRPO

During training and alignment with GRPO, the quality of the `<think>` section is evaluated through a **group-relative reward mechanism** that fosters granular control over intermediate reasoning steps. Instead of assigning an absolute reward to each model output, GRPO compares multiple candidate responses generated for the same prompt as a group:

- For each response, including its `<think>` intermediate reasoning block, the reward assigned is relative to the performance of other candidates in that group. This relative advantage is computed by subtracting the group's average reward and normalizing by its standard deviation. This setup allows explicit evaluation of the `<think>` section quality based on criteria such as logical coherence, consistency, factual correctness, formatting, and interpretability, independently of just the final answer correctness.
- By rewarding outputs that contain clear, stepwise, and well-structured reasoning, the model learns not merely to guess answers but to construct them logically and transparently. Concretely, during GRPO fine-tuning, the model generates multiple candidate explanations per prompt.

- A **scoring function**, typically a weighted combination of heuristics and learned reward models, assigns scores for attributes such as the clarity and correctness of the `<think>` block.
- The learned reward models often include neural rankers or reward predictors trained on human preference data to evaluate reasoning quality, factual accuracy, and coherence within the generated explanations.

GRPO uses the scores (outlined in the preceding list) to compute group-relative advantages, which guide policy updates, aligning the model toward producing better intermediate reasoning aligned explicitly with human-aligned quality standards.

Here is how the reward functions work:

- The **accuracy reward** $R_{accuracy}$remained a binary signal, assigned as `1` if the final answer was correct and properly formatted (e.g., including `<think>` and `<answer>` blocks), and `0` otherwise. This evaluation leveraged automatic checks and, where necessary, manual validation against ground-truth answers as established in earlier stages.
- The **consistency reward** $R_{consistency}$was designed to quantify how uniformly the model maintained a single language style and logical coherence throughout the reasoning steps, preventing mixing of languages or incoherent phrasing within a single response. Conceptually, this reward can be expressed as a scalar function.

  The consistency reward, denoted as $R_{consistency}$, is defined as a function $f_{consistency}$applied to the model's response:

  $$R_{consistency} = f_{consistency}(Response)$$

  The value of $R_{consistency}$ lies within a certain range (e.g., from `0` up to a maximum value of `10`), where the function $f_{consistency}$evaluates the internal linguistic uniformity and coherence of the response text. For instance, $f_{consistency}$might perform the following:

  1. Calculate the proportion of tokens or sentences in the dominant language compared to any other languages present.
  2. Penalize abrupt changes in stylistic tone or phrasing.
  3. Apply coherence metrics across the chain of reasoning to ensure logical flow.

  The combined reward that guides policy optimization in RL is then computed as the sum of the accuracy reward and a weighted consistency reward:

  $$R_{final} = R_{accuracy} + \lambda \times R_{consistency}$$

Here, $R_{accuracy}$is a binary or scalar reward measuring the correctness of the final response, and λ is a weighting coefficient that balances the effect of the consistency reward relative to the accuracy reward.

This combined reward R_{final} is used within the GRPO framework. GRPO calculates relative advantages by comparing the total reward of each sampled response to the group average reward, encouraging the model to generate outputs that are not only accurate and well-structured but also linguistically consistent and logically coherent throughout their reasoning process.

While this sampling and comparison process increases the compute workload during training – since several candidate completions must be generated and evaluated per prompt – the impact is confined strictly to the training stage and does not affect inference speed once deployment begins. During inference (serving real user requests), only a single model rollout per prompt is needed, just like any conventional LLM. As a result, DeepSeek achieves strong reasoning alignment and sample efficiency during training, but delivers responses at standard, highly efficient inference speeds in production, without incurring overhead from GRPO's training-time multi-sampling methods. GRPO did not require auxiliary value networks or rollouts, making it fast, stable, and accessible.

Rule-based RLHF

The range of example questions used during training and evaluation spanned a variety of domains, from simple arithmetic and symbolic logic to code generation and physics, demonstrating the model's versatility across different reasoning challenges.

DeepSeek's rule-based RLHF signals were applied in a relatively straightforward manner, where each response or reasoning step was marked as acceptable or not based on fixed, predefined logical criteria rather than learned via a complex reward model. According to technical descriptions, this process was not entirely manual annotation in the traditional sense but relied on rule-based heuristics that automatically evaluated outputs against set logic for correctness and format. This approach reduced the need for time-consuming manual labeling of each sample or step by humans, making it more scalable and less resource-intensive than typical RLHF involving learned reward models or human rankings.

However, some initial manual effort was still required to define the precise logical rules and thresholds that constituted *acceptable* steps, which is a significant upfront design task. The simplicity of binary, rule-based feedback also means fewer annotators or less annotation effort per data point is needed during training, since the evaluation is automated and less subjective. This contrasts with standard RLHF workflows, where human annotators must spend significant time comparing multiple responses or assigning scalar reward scores, which can be costly and slow.

DeepSeek's method balanced between manual and automated tasks: manual logic design upfront to create rule-based evaluators, combined with automated binary labeling of the model outputs during training, thus obtaining clear accept/reject signals without heavy manual annotation burden or the use of complex learned reward functions. This made the alignment process more efficient and scalable while preserving meaningful feedback for reinforcing correct reasoning steps. It also made the feedback pipeline much more scalable and efficient, even if it sometimes lacked the fine-grained alignment possible with advanced learned reward models. The system evaluated outputs for correctness and format compliance.

How DeepSeek handles complex scenarios

Consider a scenario where you want DeepSeek to identify a bug in your code.

In such a scenario, where a code snippet compiles correctly but produces an incorrect result, DeepSeek employs multiple training and alignment strategies to identify and rectify errors. For instance, consider the task of implementing a function to sum two numbers. The model might initially generate the following code, which compiles but returns the product instead of the sum:

```
def sum_two_numbers(a, b):
    # Incorrect implementation: returns product instead of sum
    return a * b

# Testing the function
result = sum_two_numbers(8, 6)
print("Initial output (incorrect):", result)  # Outputs 48 instead of 14
```

During training, DeepSeek's feedback mechanisms detect the logical discrepancy between the expected output and the actual result. Leveraging these signals, the model iteratively refines its output, leading to the corrected implementation:

```
def sum_two_numbers(a, b):
    # Correct implementation: returns the sum of two numbers
    return a + b
```

```
# Testing the corrected function
corrected_result = sum_two_numbers(8, 6)
print("Corrected output:", corrected_result)  # Outputs 14 as expected
```

This correction process is supported by targeted reward models and error diagnostics that guide the model to recognize and amend mistakes. As a result, DeepSeek produces code that is not only syntactically valid but also functionally accurate and reliable.

The reasoning mechanics are also driven by how DeepSeek was trained. Let's check it out.

DeepSeek training

DeepSeek's sparse but well-defined rule-based feedback was applied selectively on training samples identified through a data-driven prioritization strategy. Samples were chosen based on criteria such as prompt complexity, presence of multi-step reasoning, factual or logical difficulty, or decision-critical context where alignment and correctness were paramount.

For instance, prompts involving multi-step mathematical proofs, code generation with correctness checks, or intricate legal reasoning were flagged for receiving explicit rule-based evaluation signals. In contrast, simpler or more routine prompts, such as straightforward fact retrieval or common conversational queries, were often skipped or assigned coarser, indirect rewards, reducing unnecessary computational load. Once these reward signals guide updates to the model's parameters through policy optimization (e.g., via GRPO), the learning is encoded directly into the model weights, meaning the model generalizes what it learned across similar prompts, even if feedback wasn't explicitly provided for every case.

Throughout training, as R1-Zero iterated through complex reasoning tasks, an emergent behavior was observed: the model increasingly generated longer and more detailed intermediate reasoning steps. This was not explicitly incentivized by rewards tied to response length; rather, the underlying GRPO framework naturally favored reasoning paths that improved correctness. Mathematically, longer stepwise reasoning sequences tended to receive higher relative rewards because they more reliably demonstrated logical coherence and correctness across intermediate steps. These rewards are influenced by weighted components within the reward model that prioritize factors such as accuracy, completeness, and clarity, assigning greater weight to sustained logical consistency throughout the reasoning chain.

In essence, by producing extended CoTs, the model maximized its expected reward signal computed under GRPO's group-relative scoring function, defined as the normalized **advantage**:

$$Advantage_i = \frac{(R_i - \mu_R)}{\sigma_R}$$

Here, Ri is the reward of candidate i, μ_R is the mean reward across the candidate group, and σ_R is the standard deviation. This formal, optimization-based framework explains the increase in reasoning detail – DeepSeek effectively *learned* to elaborate its internal thought process when doing so increased the relative reward advantage and improved the likelihood of the correct final answer. Therefore, the model's longer reasoning outputs emerge as a strategic response to the reward structure rather than a random or unexplained behavior.

The model did not receive explicit supervised CoT labels during training. Instead, its outputs were assessed based on both the correctness of the final answer and adherence to a prescribed structured format containing intermediate reasoning steps (e.g., `<think>` and `<answer>` blocks).

Since the model was exposed to examples where intermediate reasoning steps correlated causally with receiving a reward, it began favoring generation paths where thought preceded answer, leading to a form of self-organized internal reasoning strategy. Importantly, this behavior was not present in earlier DeepSeek models trained with standard supervised fine-tuning alone. Those versions might reach correct answers, but their outputs lacked explainability, struggled with multistep tasks, and did not generalize well to harder benchmarks such as ***AIME***, ***MATH***, and ***GPQA***. In contrast, R1-Zero, without using any supervised CoT data, began outperforming these earlier models simply by being aligned through this reward-only approach.

This was the real *A-ha moment* that a model could discover interpretable and effective reasoning patterns, not because it mimicked labeled explanations, but because it was incentivized to generate structured outputs that worked *consistently*. It challenged the belief that hand-crafted rationales were necessary for learning to reason, and laid the foundation for the fully realized DeepSeek-R1 model.

Cold start data for training

DeepSeek's team invested heavily in generating high-quality, structured reasoning data – not by manually labeling thousands of CoT examples, but by leveraging R1-Zero's unsupervised reasoning ability. Once R1-Zero began generating outputs that adhered to the CoT format and were largely accurate, a large set of these model-generated responses was collected to serve as **cold start supervised training data**.

The correctness of these outputs was validated automatically whenever possible by comparing generated final answers against known ground truths using programmatic checks, test cases, or logical verification rules. In cases where automated validation was insufficient or ambiguous, human reviewers performed selective manual verification to ensure quality and correctness. While the manual checks required additional time and effort, the majority of validation leveraged automated procedures, making the overall process more efficient and scalable than fully manual annotation. This **hybrid validation strategy** enabled the researchers to efficiently bootstrap high-quality CoT-labeled data from the model's own outputs without incurring prohibitive annotation costs. Though this data was model-generated, it effectively became labeled: each sample contained the original prompt (implicit question), a `<think>` block with reasoning steps, and an `<answer>` block with the final response.

Consider, for example, the following prompt:

```
"What is the square of the sum of 3 and 2?"
```

The model output is as follows:

```
<think>
3 + 2 = 5.
5² = 25.
</think>
<answer>
25
</answer>
```

This structured dataset seeded the next phase: using the R1-Zero-generated corpus to fine-tune a checkpoint of DeepSeek-V3, thereby transferring R1-Zero's emergent reasoning into the larger backbone. Here, R1-Zero functioned as both a student and a teacher – initially learning through simple, rule-based reward signals during reinforcement learning, and subsequently guiding its own training by generating distilled examples. While this process shares similarities with GRPO's reward-driven optimization, R1-Zero's approach focuses specifically on reinforcing behaviors aligned with logical reasoning and correctness rather than just maximizing a group-relative advantage.

Unlike traditional **knowledge distillation** that uses supervised loss to match teacher outputs, DeepSeek leveraged reward signals to explicitly optimize for structured, stepwise reasoning quality and adherence to output format, which standard distillation losses alone struggle to capture. Employing reinforcement learning in this way helped the model dynamically explore and refine reasoning strategies, discovering outputs that maximize clarity and correctness. These outputs then served as reliable ***teacher examples*** for subsequent supervised fine-tuning, effectively bootstrapping improved performance while complementing GRPO's group-relative reward framework.

Here is what happens during training:

1. DeepSeek-R1's training begins with pretraining to establish foundational language understanding and expert specializations.
2. Following this, the model is further trained on the CoT data, where the RL process is enhanced by an additional consistency reward alongside the original binary correctness and format rewards.
3. While the original reward function primarily assigned binary accept/reject signals based on the correctness of the final answer and adherence to the `<think> + <answer>` output structure, the consistency reward encourages language consistency and coherence across the model's generated responses. These two rewards are combined by simple summation to form the final reward used in policy optimization.
4. The **consistency reward** is computed per response and does not explicitly store or compare against previous responses generated for the same prompt. Instead, it evaluates the internal coherence of each individual output using a combination of rule-based heuristics and learned models, typically analyzing factors such as language uniformity and stylistic consistency to assign a consistency reward. For example, if the prompt is in English, responses are rewarded for maintaining English without introducing other languages or inconsistent phrasing.

   This reward was introduced after observing issues with mixed-language outputs in earlier models (such as DeepSeek-R1-Zero). Ablation studies showed that while the consistency reward sometimes slightly reduced raw task performance, it greatly improved human-readability and user experience by encouraging outputs that are linguistically coherent.

   This additional signal ensured that the model's reasoning style remained coherent across all steps – not just logically sound, but also stylistically aligned and linguistically fluid.

5. The consistency reward function combines a binary signal with language-based metrics to evaluate internal coherence within each output. Formally, it can be expressed as follows:

   $$R_{consistency} = \alpha \cdot R_{binary} + (1 - \alpha) \cdot R_{language}$$

Let's break this down:

- R_{binary} is a rule-based binary signal indicating the presence or absence of key consistency criteria (e.g., adherence to formatting rules or logical constraints), valued as 0 or 1
- $R_{language}$ is a continuous score derived from language models measuring stylistic uniformity, fluency, and semantic coherence
- $\alpha \in [0,1]$ is a weighting factor balancing the contribution of the binary and language-based signals

By integrating these components, the model effectively rewards outputs that both meet explicit rule-based standards and demonstrate natural, consistent language flow, enhancing overall reasoning clarity and coherence.

This process wasn't a one-off; it was iterative and self-reinforcing, running through multiple cycles (typically 3–5 iterations) where each iteration used the latest distilled examples and updated reward signals to progressively enhance the model's reasoning ability and output quality, creating what we describe as a looped strategy. Improved reasoning led to higher-quality CoT examples, which in turn trained better models – which then produced even stronger outputs, fueling the next cycle of generation and refinement.

The final DeepSeek-R1 model resulted from a multi-stage process combining efficient architecture, adaptive training rewards, and a data-driven approach that encouraged clear reasoning and used top outputs to improve future training.

Now, let's see how all that we have learnt comes together in the training pipeline.

The training pipeline of R1

The training pipeline of DeepSeek involved the following steps:

Figure 2.6: The training pipeline of DeepSeek-R1

Let's walk you through these stages:

1. **Cold start SFT with R1-Zero outputs:** The cold start data served as a bootstrapping corpus for a new model checkpoint built upon the DeepSeek-V3 base.

This stage served two purposes:

- First, it transferred the emerging reasoning behavior from R1-Zero into a new model through supervised learning
- Second, it allowed the team to evaluate how well the DeepSeek-V3 base could generalize from R1-Zero's reasoning traces.

The results were promising. Even without additional reinforcement learning at this point, the model trained with cold start **supervised fine-tuning** (**SFT**) data began showing measurable improvements in structured reasoning compared to V3 alone. This was reflected in evaluation metrics such as the accuracy on multi-step reasoning benchmarks, where the cold-start SFT model achieved an improvement of approximately 10–15% over V3 – for example, going from around 65% accuracy to 75–80% correctness on complex math and logic tasks. Additionally, metrics assessing reasoning coherence and adherence to the expected `<think> + <answer>` format showed significant gains, indicating that the model was not only more accurate but also produced better-organized and transparent reasoning paths.

2. **Reinforcement learning with consistency reward**: The next step in the pipeline involved training this new checkpoint via a second round of RL. This time, the training included not only the original reward signals based on accuracy of the response, which was measured by comparing each model output against the expected, known correct answers following the criteria established in the cold start phase, but also a newly introduced metric: linguistic consistency.
3. **Final SFT with general knowledge CoT fusion**: Although the original pipeline envisioned a distinct final SFT round to integrate common-sense and world knowledge into CoT-style reasoning, this stage was ultimately bypassed. Instead, training proceeded directly from large-scale pretraining to supervised fine-tuning using the distilled CoT datasets. This approach effectively combined the model's broad general knowledge with structured reasoning examples within a single fine-tuning phase, without requiring an additional dedicated fusion round. The rationale was straightforward: a reasoning model cannot thrive in the real world if it can only solve equations and puzzles. It must also handle everyday queries, facts, and human-interpretable logic.

   DeepSeek fuses CoT reasoning with broad pretrained knowledge through fine-tuning on a mixed dataset combining unsupervised text and supervised, stepwise CoT examples. This trains the model to generate coherent, fact-based explanations by integrating structured reasoning traces with its extensive knowledge base.

Multi-task objectives and consistency constraints further refine this integration, enabling DeepSeek to produce transparent, logically sound outputs across diverse domains while amplifying patterns linked to accurate, interpretable answers.

4. **Final RLHF**: The final stage in R1's training involved RLHF, where the model's outputs were optimized using explicit reward functions based on human preferences. This phase also involved preference comparison pairs, where human annotators ranked multiple responses to the same prompt. These signals were used to fine-tune a reward model that then guided a final RL loop.

   To capture and enforce these preferences, the RL phase used explicit reward functions designed to evolve the model's behavior iteratively:

   - **User expectation definition**: A panel of domain experts and annotators developed detailed guidelines describing desirable model responses. These guidelines emphasized avoiding ambiguity, minimizing unnecessary verbosity, maintaining precision in factual and logical statements, and prioritizing helpfulness in context.
   - **Rule-based checks**: Automated rule-based evaluation scripts parsed each generated response to check for compliance with these guidelines, as in these examples:
     - Ambiguity was detected by scanning for vague words or contradictory statements.
     - Verbosity was measured by comparing token counts against expected length ranges for similar prompt types.
     - Helpfulness was partially evaluated through heuristic indicators such as the presence of relevant explanations, stepwise reasoning, and actionable conclusions.
     - Precision was assessed by comparing model outputs against ground-truth answers or reference solutions, primarily using binary correctness labels.
   - **Score computation**: Each response was assigned a composite reward score combining multiple factors:

     $$R_{total} = w_{accuracy}.R_{accuracy} + w_{clarity}.R_{clarity} + w_{verbosity}.R_{verbosity} + w_{helpfulness}.R_{helpfulness}$$

     - $R_{accuracy}$is `1` if the final answer is correct and corresponds to the known truth, else `0`.
     - $R_{clarity}$ is a scalar reward based on the absence of ambiguous phrases.

- $R_{verbosity}$ penalizes overly long or redundant responses (lower values for excessive length).
- $R_{helpfulness}$rewards the presence of detailed, relevant reasoning and explanations.
- The weights { w_i }were tuned to balance these aspects according to human preference studies.

For the `Prove that the sum of two even numbers is even` prompt, DeepSeek's reward functions combine multiple components weighted to balance logical correctness, clarity, and consistency.

- **Rule-based check heuristics**: The following are performed:
  - Verification that all key mathematical terms (e.g., `even`, `sum`, `2a`, `2b`) appear in the proof.
  - Structural checking to ensure the proof follows an expected logical format: definition, substitution, and conclusion.
  - Formatting rules, such as correct use of symbols and stepwise argument separation.
- **Weight choices for reward components**: The reward components include the following:
  - Logical correctness (rule-based checks) weighted heavily at around `0.5` due to its critical role.
  - Clarity and language consistency (language model-derived signals) weighted at `0.3` to reward fluent, understandable explanations.
  - Internal coherence and adherence to the reasoning format weighted at `0.2` to encourage stepwise structure.
- **Human preference data collection**: Human annotators were presented with multiple candidate proofs generated for the prompt and asked to rank them based on correctness, clarity, and completeness. These rankings were used to train reward predictors that estimate human preferences, guiding the model to prioritize reasoning quality over superficial attributes. This data-driven supervision helped calibrate reward weights and shape heuristic rules, aligning automated scoring with human judgment.

Together, these methods ensured that DeepSeek produced mathematically sound, clear, and well-structured proofs, such as the example demonstrating that the sum of two even numbers is even.

After finalizing the main R1 model, DeepSeek performed distillation experiments to transfer its advanced reasoning abilities to smaller, more efficient models.

Distillation and distribution

Distillation is important because it enables compact models to learn complex behaviors by training on high-quality outputs from larger models, improving accessibility and deployment flexibility. In this process, the distribution of R1's detailed CoT outputs serves as the training data distribution, guiding smaller models such as DeepSeek-R1-Distill-Qwen and DeepSeek-R1-Distill-Llama to generalize sophisticated reasoning even without RL.

The implications were significant in demonstrating that reasoning capabilities could be effectively transferred through knowledge distillation. Instead of retraining large models via costly RL cycles, the **CoT traces** generated by DeepSeek-R1 served as high-quality ***teacher*** data for training smaller, more efficient student models.

During distillation, a combined loss function was used to balance the student's imitation of the teacher's soft output distributions and adherence to ground-truth labels. Specifically, the loss L was formulated as follows:

$$L = \alpha \cdot L_{KD}(T) + (1 - \alpha) \cdot L_{CE}$$

Let's break this down:

- $L_{KD}(T)$ is the **knowledge distillation loss**, computed as the Kullback-Leibler divergence between the softened probability distributions of the teacher and student models.
- L_{CE} is the standard **cross-entropy loss** with the ground-truth labels.
- α is a weighting hyperparameter controlling the balance between distillation and supervised learning.
- **Temperature** T is applied to soften the teacher's logits before calculating L_{KD}, typically set to T=2 or T=4 to provide richer gradient signals.

DeepSeek's distillation process balanced knowledge transfer and supervised learning by tuning hyperparameters such as α (commonly set to `0.7`) and temperature T (often `T=3`) to optimize learning signals. These settings led to substantial reductions in model size and inference latency while closely matching the teacher model's reasoning accuracy. For further details on distillation loss and hyperparameter choices, you can refer to the DeepSeek research paper at `https://arxiv.org/abs/2501.12948`.

This distillation strategy effectively compressed the large-scale reasoning competence of R1 into lighter models by leveraging CoT instructional material as a rich supervisory signal. It demonstrated that large-scale reasoning need not be restricted to hefty architectures or repeated RL training, enabling scalable deployment of strong, explainable reasoning assistants.

Emergent patterns in self-teaching

One of the most fascinating aspects of this pipeline was its self-reinforcing structure. R1-Zero created an iterative cycle:

Figure 2.7: DeepSeek's self-teaching iterative cycle

This iterative cycle continued for a fixed number of rounds (typically 3–5 iterations) until performance gains plateaued and further improvements became marginal (please refer to *Figure 2.7* for a quick recap).

This controlled loop allowed the model to progressively bootstrap stronger reasoning abilities without running indefinitely, balancing training efficiency with quality improvements. At each stage, the model was learning not just from external feedback, but from its own historical best efforts.

Well, well! Who said it was so easy to build an LLM!

Next, we turn to how DeepSeek's engineering pushed the boundaries of efficiency without sacrificing intelligence.

Advanced capabilities of DeepSeek

DeepSeek's evolution from a powerful text reasoning model into a general-purpose AI agent continues in its multimodal and real-world extensions. In this section, we explore DeepSeek's foray into multimodal reasoning, its emerging agent framework, and how these innovations will pave the way for real-world deployment across education, science, enterprise, and daily life.

Vision capabilities of DeepSeek

DeepSeek's architecture (originally designed for language tasks) has evolved to support multimodal capabilities, particularly through models such as DeepSeek-VL. These models integrate text and visual inputs, enabling the system to understand and reason about images jointly with language. While DeepSeek is currently multimodal in the sense that it supports text and vision, there is no official support yet for additional modalities such as audio or video in publicly released versions.

Architectural changes for vision-language integration

To enable image understanding, DeepSeek-VL extends its language foundation with a vision encoder, typically a modified **vision transformer** (**ViT**) or **convolutional neural network** (**CNN**).

The system is composed of three main components: a hybrid vision encoder, a vision-language adapter, and a language model.

The following figure shows how the vision-language adapter works:

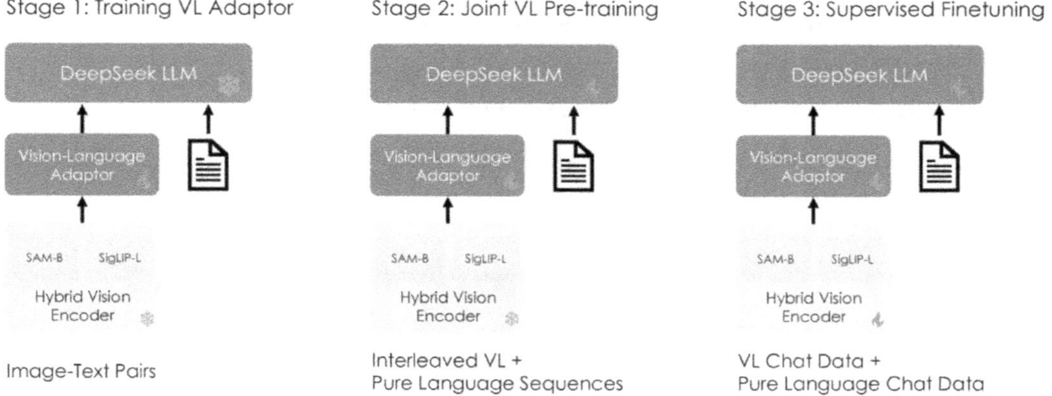

Figure 2.8: DeepSeek's vision adapter (source: `https://arxiv.org/html/2403.05525v2`*)*

DeepSeek utilizes a two-layer hybrid MLP to effectively connect the vision encoder with the LLM. Initially, separate single-layer MLPs are used to process high-resolution and low-resolution visual features independently. These processed features are then concatenated and passed through an additional MLP layer, which maps them into the input space of the LLM. Specifically, the DeepSeek-VL-1B model is built upon DeepSeek-LLM-1B, which was trained on approximately 500 billion text tokens. Similarly, the DeepSeek-VL-7B model is based on DeepSeek-LLM-7B, trained on roughly 2 trillion text tokens.

When a user includes an image in the input, the model first processes it using a vision encoder (typically a CNN or ViT) that converts the image into fixed-size patch embeddings, each represented as a vector in a shared latent space (commonly 768 or 1,024 dimensions). These patch-level embeddings capture local visual features and are then fed into cross-modal attention layers alongside tokenized text embeddings of the same dimension.

The model identifies relevant image regions by dividing the image into uniform patches (e.g., 16x16 pixels), which serve as the units of attention. Through cross-modal attention within each transformer block, text tokens (processed via a standard tokenizer) learn to focus selectively on these visual patches. For example, when processing the word `graph`, the model attends to specific patches containing visual elements of the graph, effectively aligning linguistic context with spatial features.

This multimodal fusion allows the model to build a joint representation incorporating both the semantic content of text and the spatial hierarchy of images, enabling coherent reasoning and generation across modalities. This explanation balances technical detail and clarity, making it accessible for our target audience while highlighting how patch-based attention drives visual grounding.

Suppose a user inputs the following, along with the image:

```
Refer to the attached chart and explain if the growth pattern in Q2 seems
normal compared to Q1 and Q3.
```

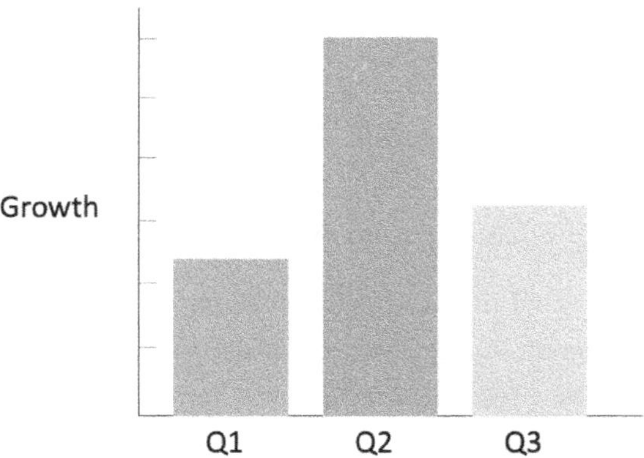

Figure 2.9: An example image input for DeepSeek

Here is how DeepSeek-VL-7B processes this:

1. **Visual encoding**: The image (e.g., a chart) in the prompt is divided into patches and passed through a vision encoder. This step captures details such as bar heights, axis labels, and overall layout.
2. **Text encoding**: The question is tokenized and fed into the language backbone, which creates a representation of the user's intent (for example, `growth pattern in Q2`).
3. **Cross-modal alignment**: The model uses attention to link words or phrases in the question to the most relevant visual regions. For instance, `Q2` activates attention over the part of the chart labeled *Q2*, while `growth` links to the corresponding bar's height.
4. **Response generation**: By combining these aligned representations, the model generates an answer, such as `The growth in Q2 is noticeably higher than Q1 and Q3, suggesting a likely one-time event or seasonal spike.`

The ability to reason simultaneously over text and imagery enables DeepSeek-VL-7B to solve problems that neither modality could address alone, such as interpreting a diagram with accompanying questions or reading and correcting handwritten equations. In education, this supports intelligent tutoring systems that can interpret scanned notebooks; in enterprise settings, it enables systems to extract structure and meaning from invoices, tables, or schematics.

DeepSeek extends its use of MoE and MLA into the multimodal regime. This means that even when handling visual data, the system activates only a subset of its parameters, ensuring efficient computation. Visual reasoning does not dramatically increase the inference cost thanks to this dynamic specialization approach.

Agentic reasoning and tool integration

Although this chapter primarily discusses reasoning mechanisms, it is important to acknowledge that DeepSeek also includes foundational components that support broader agentic capabilities. These include the ability to interact with external tools, perform multi-step task planning, and dynamically adapt its actions based on feedback. Some of these features are elaborated in detail in *Chapter 6*.

DeepSeek models, especially DeepSeek-R1, serve as powerful reasoning engines within AI agents by enabling them to break down complex problems into explicit, verifiable reasoning chains through CoT techniques. This structured reasoning underpins DeepSeek's proficiency in multi-step problem solving, logical inference, and contextual decision-making.

In applied workflows, DeepSeek can act as an autonomous agent by doing the following:

- Executing sequential actions informed by intermediate outputs and environmental feedback.
- Integrating external tools and data sources dynamically to augment its decision-making process.
- Handling dependencies and error recovery through context-aware planning.
- Coordinating multi-agent workflows for complex task execution.

These agentic reasoning capabilities make DeepSeek suitable for real-world applications requiring adaptive, goal-directed behavior beyond static question-answering.

We will now focus on how DeepSeek compares with other LLMs and some of the shortcomings.

DeepSeek in the global LLM landscape

The global LLM landscape is bustling with new models and techniques, with a competitive race to achieve reasoning capabilities and, ultimately, **artificial general intelligence (AGI)**. LLMs form the necessary first step toward AGI.

Take a look at how different LLMs compare against each other (as of mid-2025):

Parameter	DeepSeek (V3, R1, CoderV2/V3)	OpenAI GPT-4o	Anthropic Claude 4 Sonnet	Google Gemini 2.5 Pro
Technique used	Sparse MoE, FP8 low-precision, RL CoT, single-pass training	Dense transformer, speculative decoding, vision-augmented layers	Dense transformer, advanced RLHF, long-context, improved multimodal	Dense transformer, multimodal fusion, advanced RLHF, long-context, video capabilities
Architecture	670B total params: 37B active per inference, 2 experts/layer from 256 experts, MLA, MoE routing	~175B params (rumored ~1T planned), dense, multimodal vision layers	~400–600B dense params, all activated per input	~600–800B dense params, dense activation per input

Parameter	DeepSeek (V3, R1, CoderV2/V3)	OpenAI GPT-4o	Anthropic Claude 4 Sonnet	Google Gemini 2.5 Pro
Tasks and capabilities	State-of-the-art structured reasoning, math, symbolic logic, code-generation, retrieval-augmented Q&A, interpretable CoT output, scalable context	Leading Q&A, multimodal (vision-language), summarization, math, advanced code, high robustness	Excellent general Q&A, advanced summarization, strong math/programming, long-context reasoning, robust vision-language synergy	Cutting-edge multimodal, video understanding, long context, advanced reasoning, generative workflows
Cost (training)	~$5.6M (2,000 H800 GPUs), open source recipes, efficient via FP8 and MoE	Rumored $100–300M, dense, proprietary	Estimated $100M+, proprietary, dense, high GPU requirements	Estimated $150M+ scale, proprietary, extensive multimodal training costs
Performance	SOTA/better on math (AIME, MATH, GPQA), code (pass@1, pass@5), transparent stepwise reasoning	SOTA in vision, general AI, multimodal tasks, code/math competitive	SOTA on long-text, strong on math, code, and vision-to-text, robust reasoning, and summarization	Leading performance in multimodal video generation, long context reasoning
Parameters active	37B (MoE) per inference out of 670B total	100% model activated per step	100% model activated per step	100% model activated per step

Parameter	DeepSeek (V3, R1, CoderV2/V3)	OpenAI GPT-4o	Anthropic Claude 4 Sonnet	Google Gemini 2.5 Pro
Metrics	pass@1/pass@5 (HumanEval++, Codeforces, LeetCode), MATH/GPQA/ AIME accuracy, interpretability, retrieval benchmarks	Similar standard benchmarks, detailed scores not public	Benchmark metrics (MATH, GPQA, code), limited public availability	Proprietary benchmark results, showing cutting-edge multimodal capabilities
Inference time/latency	Approximately 5x faster than dense models at a similar scale; typical latency ~100–150ms per token on optimized hardware for 32–64k token context	Moderate to high latency, around 500–700ms per token depending on input length and hardware; optimized for batch inference	Slightly higher latency than GPT-4o, approx. 700–900ms per token due to complex dense activations and long-context processing	Comparable or slightly higher latency than Anthropic, with additional overhead for multimodal and video processing
Reasoning traceability	Explicit "think/ answer" format, public CoT tools/data, interpretable intermediate reasoning steps	Limited transparency; mostly black-box internal logic	Some interpretability emphasis, less exposed intermediate representations than DeepSeek	Some interpretability, but focus on multimodal fusion and certain black-box components
Transparency and openness	100% open source (weights, data, recipes, RL protocols)	Closed source, minimal model details released	Closed source, sparse technical disclosures	Closed source, released via commercial API and partnerships

Table 2.1: Comparative table of DeepSeek versus leading LLMs (mid-2025)

DeepSeek delivers strong cost-to-performance efficiency through sparse routing, interpretable reasoning outputs, and full open source transparency, excelling in math, code, and CoT tasks. GPT-4o stands out in multimodal and vision capabilities but comes with high computational costs and limited transparency. Claude 4 Sonnet offers a competitive proprietary alternative with improved efficiency and long-context handling over previous Claude models, performing well in long text, math, and code tasks, though it remains less open and constrained by dense inference bottlenecks.

DeepSeek's limitations and how they compare to other models

While DeepSeek has pushed the envelope in reasoning, openness, and architectural innovation, it is by no means without limitations. Like all language models, it grapples with trade-offs between scale and interpretability, latency and capability, openness and performance.

This section aims to provide a balanced view of DeepSeek's current boundaries, how they stack up against its peers such as GPT-4o, Claude 3.5/4, Gemini 1.5, and Mistral, and how these challenges might be addressed in future iterations.

Scaling challenges and sparse expertise limitations

DeepSeek-V3's 670B parameters – while efficient via MoE – still make training and serving the model a non-trivial task. Even with sparse activation (37B active params per inference), deploying DeepSeek at scale requires high-throughput GPUs and bandwidth-optimized environments. This means that for many smaller institutions, full model usage remains aspirational, despite the release of distilled variants.

Moreover, MoE introduces its own set of constraints. Routing instability across experts, token-drop issues, and expert under-utilization remain areas of active research. DeepSeek's use of shared experts and FFN pre-routing helps mitigate some of these issues, but performance degradation at tail token distributions still occurs. In contrast, dense models such as Claude 4 or GPT-4o, while more compute-heavy, maintain more stable token flow across all layers.

Sparse models also suffer from limited representation sharing across unrelated inputs, meaning generalization in certain zero-shot scenarios may lag behind dense counterparts. This trade-off between efficiency and universality is not unique to DeepSeek, but its manifestation is accentuated at DeepSeek's unprecedented scale.

Inference latency and real-time interaction trade-offs

Although MoE and FP8 training help speed up inference per token, DeepSeek still faces latency challenges in real-time settings, especially when paired with search modules or multi-document rerankers. While CoT reasoning improves output quality, it often results in longer responses, which increases perceived latency.

Claude 4 and GPT-4o, with their highly optimized decoding and caching strategies, often outperform DeepSeek in real-time generation benchmarks. GPT-4o, in particular, benefits from tight model-server integration and aggressive speculative decoding, yielding response times comparable to GPT-3.5 with GPT-4 level reasoning.

DeepSeek's **multi-token prediction** (**MTP**) and KV compression (via MLA) help alleviate this somewhat, but user-facing applications requiring millisecond-level responsiveness, such as chat agents or embedded devices, may find Claude or GPT variants better optimized today.

Interpretability and alignment risks

Ironically, while DeepSeek pioneered structured reasoning with *think/answer* formatting, this strength can also become a bottleneck. The enforcement of CoT outputs means models can hallucinate rationales that appear structured but are subtly flawed, leading to false confidence. Because the model is trained to produce coherent logic, even wrong answers may be wrapped in convincing language, creating alignment and safety risks.

This issue isn't unique to DeepSeek. GPT-4 and Claude 4 also face similar concerns around hallucination in multi-step reasoning. However, their models often include adversarial preference modeling and multi-signal safety protocols – techniques still being developed for DeepSeek. The lack of a **preference ranking model** (**PRM**)-based training step in DeepSeek means alignment relies on simpler reward heuristics, potentially missing nuance in ethical or edge-case scenarios.

Context length and compression ceiling

Although DeepSeek uses MLA to reduce context footprint, it still trails Claude 4 and Gemini 1.5 in ultra-long context tasks. Claude's 200k context window and Gemini's sparse attention tricks make them more capable of absorbing entire books, legal documents, or multi-session dialogues. DeepSeek caps more realistically at 64k tokens for usable performance.

Additionally, while MLA compression helps, it requires trade-offs in retrieval fidelity, particularly in multi-document QA or hybrid retrieval/ranking setups. In contrast, Claude's context prioritization and GPT-4o's selective attention offer more intelligent context utilization at scale.

Dataset and cultural scope gaps

Despite its multilingual focus, DeepSeek remains comparatively undertrained on certain cultural datasets and niche domain corpora. GPT-4 and Claude 4, which benefit from broad corpus ingestion and fine-grained domain tuning, demonstrate superior nuance in fields such as finance, law, and niche scientific domains. DeepSeek, due to its cost-aware pretraining, takes a more generalist route, occasionally at the cost of narrow-domain depth.

However, this is also where DeepSeek's open infrastructure shines: its modular retriever, reranker, and decoder setup allows researchers to fine-tune for missing knowledge areas, a flexibility that proprietary models do not offer.

Outlook on limitations

DeepSeek's limitations are real but surmountable. As the community around it grows, many of these challenges – especially those related to routing, real-time decoding, safety tuning, and context optimization – are likely to be addressed by research contributions. Unlike proprietary models, DeepSeek's transparent ecosystem allows for shared learning and iterative correction.

In many ways, the very act of exposing limitations becomes an invitation for others to refine, adapt, and challenge the model itself. That's the promise of open science – not perfection, but participation.

Summary

In this chapter, we delved into the core research and technical evolution behind DeepSeek, tracing its trajectory. We examined how DeepSeek's development splits into two powerful threads: the construction of foundational models and the advancement of reasoning capabilities. Each successive version of DeepSeek added a new layer of innovation, from scaling dense architectures to pioneering efficient MoE models, and, ultimately, refining multi-step reasoning through rule-based reinforcement learning.

We explored how the adoption of MoE techniques led to significant performance gains at lower compute costs, and how innovations such as MLA, MTP, and GRPO addressed key challenges in training stability, inference efficiency, and reasoning reliability. The chapter also highlighted DeepSeek's specialized efforts in areas such as code intelligence, mathematics, and formal logic, illustrating its versatile application across domains.

The release of DeepSeek-R1 represents the culmination of these developments, demonstrating that a powerful, efficient, and reasoning-capable LLM can emerge from the integration of sparse architectures and minimal, rule-driven reinforcement learning. You should now have a clear understanding of how DeepSeek evolved through iterative innovation and the technical breakthroughs that drive its performance.

In the next chapter, we will discuss various techniques for prompting DeepSeek.

3

Prompting DeepSeek

If you've ever moved from writing imperative code, manually telling the **Domain Object Model** (**DOM**) how to update a web page step-by-step, to a declarative framework such as React, you know the required mental shift. You stop giving meticulous instructions and start describing the desired outcome, trusting the system to figure out the how. The same principle applies when moving from traditional LLMs such as Mistral 7B or Llama 3.3 8B to DeepSeek's reasoning engines. The muscle memory you've developed for carefully guiding a model's thought process might actually work against you with an engine that's built to reason on its own.

This chapter is all about navigating those differences, from the headline-grabbing quirks (such as R1's allergy to system prompts) to the subtle behavioral shifts that can make or break your results. Whether you're migrating an existing prompt library or starting fresh with DeepSeek, consider this chapter as your field guide to a fundamentally different paradigm in language models.

It's important to remember that we are in the early days of understanding these powerful new models. At this point, the DeepSeek models are almost a year old. The guidance in this chapter is a synthesis of the best information currently available: official documentation from the DeepSeek team, usage reports from industry pioneers, and the first wave of academic papers exploring these systems. Think of this as a living document: a snapshot of our collective understanding today. The best practices will undoubtedly evolve as the community learns more, but what follows is our best map of the terrain so far.

Most of this chapter focuses on the R1 series: DeepSeek's reasoning-first models that flip conventional prompt engineering wisdom on its head. These models don't just process differently; they were trained differently, using reinforcement learning techniques that created a model with its own internal **Chain-of-Thought (CoT)** process. It's like the difference between giving turn-by-turn directions to a human driver versus simply telling a self-driving car the destination. The R1 models already know how to navigate the reasoning journey.

The implications ripple through every aspect of prompt design:

Few-shot examples? They'll actually make your results worse (a 15% accuracy drop, as mentioned in the original DeepSeek paper (`https://arxiv.org/html/2501.12948v1`).

Think step -by step instructions? Redundant. R1 already does that internally.

Rich system prompts? The model might ignore them entirely.

Complex, verbose instructions? Less effective than clear, minimal directives.

Meanwhile, the V-series models behave more like the LLMs you're used to, but even they have their quirks. For example, temperature mappings differ from OpenAI's defaults, and there is a preference for structured formatting that goes beyond typical markdown.

This chapter dissects the DeepSeek prompting paradigm piece by piece. We'll explore the core mental models that explain why these differences exist (hint: it's all about that reinforcement learning), provide concrete dos and don'ts backed by official documentation and community testing, and equip you with templates and troubleshooting strategies for both R-series and V-series models.

By the end, you'll understand not just what to do differently, but why DeepSeek's unique training approach demands we rethink prompt engineering from first principles. Think of it as learning a new programming paradigm. Once you grasp the underlying philosophy, the specific techniques fall naturally into place.

In this chapter, we will cover the following main topics:

- Core mental models and principles of DeepSeek
- General tips and advice for prompting DeepSeek
- Working with the structured output
- Unique prompting techniques for the V series
- Troubleshooting
- Prompt migration guide

Technical requirements

You will need the following for this chapter:

- Start with the project repository and install the dependencies:

```
git clone https://github.com/PacktPublishing/DeepSeek-in-Practice.
git
cd Chapter03
pip install -r requirements.txt
```

  The requirements file includes OpenAI and Instructor for sending prompts and getting structured output, and `Pydantic` for helping to create structures we can pass to our models.

- API Keys and environment variables: You will need API keys for accessing OpenRouter models (like DeepSeek and any others you want).
- OpenRouter provides access to DeepSeek models for generating baseline comparisons during evaluation. Sign up at `openrouter.ai` and obtain your API key from the dashboard. We will use a free model to access the base DeepSeek-R1 model, but you need an API key to access it (via `litellm`). If you do not have an OpenRouter API key, you can create one at `https://openrouter.ai/docs/api-reference/api-keys/get-api-key`.

Core mental models and principles of DeepSeek

Before we dive into the technical weeds, let's recalibrate your mental model of what DeepSeek models, especially the R-series models, actually are. Forget everything you know about coaxing ChatGPT into the right response with elaborate system prompts.

Here are three things you need to be careful about when you structure your prompts for the DeepSeek-R1 series.

- **DeepSeek models work more like theorem provers and less like chatbots**: Think of R1 less like a conversational partner and more like a mathematical proof assistant that happens to speak English. When you submit a prompt to R1, you're not starting a dialogue. You're submitting a formal problem specification to a reasoning engine.

This isn't just rhetoric. The R1 models were trained with reinforcement learning to prioritize getting the right answer on verifiable tasks (e.g., math/coding), and they do substantial internal deliberation before replying. Concretely, the model first generates a hidden reasoning scratchpad (the *<think>* block) and only then emits the final answer (see *Chapter 2* for a refresher on hidden *thinking* tokens).

What this means in practice:

- Your prompt is a problem statement, not a conversation starter.
- Expect the model to internally sketch a plan/scratchpad and then produce a single solution. (By *internal plan*, we simply mean the model's hidden CoT/scratchpad; there is no separate compilation phase.)
- You usually get back a solution – not a chatty back-and-forth.

- **Structure your prompt like a research request**: Imagine you're commissioning a research paper from a brilliant but literal-minded graduate student. You wouldn't give them a rambling email with examples of other papers. You'd provide a clear problem statement, constraints, and expected output format. Good DeepSeek prompt structure mirrors academic problem specification. In other words, if you create a prompt in this order and format, DeepSeek generally will give you better results. It's not something specified as official guidance, though:

```
Context: [What background information is essential?]
Task: [What specific problem needs solving?]
Constraints: [What limitations or requirements exist?]
Output: [What format should the solution take?]
```

This isn't about being formal or stuffy – it's about clarity. The model performs best when it can parse your intent without ambiguity.

For example, if I were interested in understanding the philosophical implications of deploying a new triage model for an emergency department, I might use a prompt such as this with a *traditional* LLM like Mistral Medium 3.1:

```
Is it ethically OK for a hospital to use a black-box AI triage
system in the ER if it's more accurate than doctors? Please discuss
pros and cons and conclude with what you'd recommend.
```

You can see we get a response like this from a Mistral model (Medium 3.1), for example:

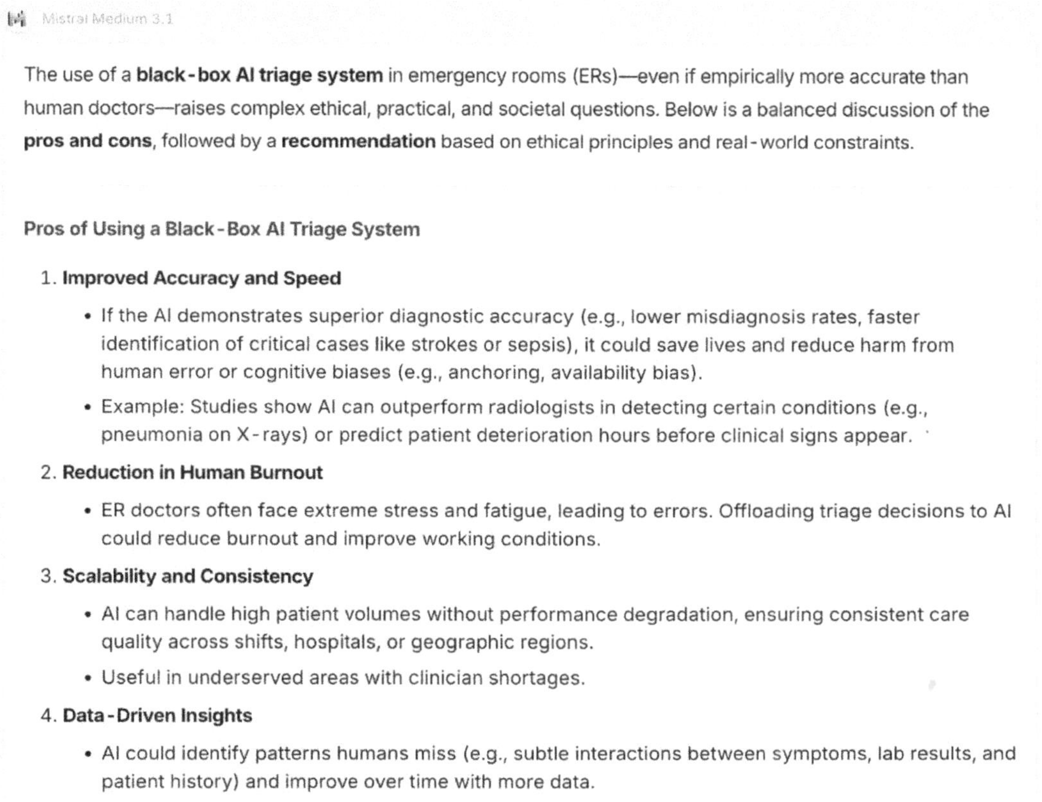

Mistral Medium 3.1

The use of a **black-box AI triage system** in emergency rooms (ERs)—even if empirically more accurate than human doctors—raises complex ethical, practical, and societal questions. Below is a balanced discussion of the **pros and cons**, followed by a **recommendation** based on ethical principles and real-world constraints.

Pros of Using a Black-Box AI Triage System

1. **Improved Accuracy and Speed**
   - If the AI demonstrates superior diagnostic accuracy (e.g., lower misdiagnosis rates, faster identification of critical cases like strokes or sepsis), it could save lives and reduce harm from human error or cognitive biases (e.g., anchoring, availability bias).
   - Example: Studies show AI can outperform radiologists in detecting certain conditions (e.g., pneumonia on X-rays) or predict patient deterioration hours before clinical signs appear.
2. **Reduction in Human Burnout**
   - ER doctors often face extreme stress and fatigue, leading to errors. Offloading triage decisions to AI could reduce burnout and improve working conditions.
3. **Scalability and Consistency**
   - AI can handle high patient volumes without performance degradation, ensuring consistent care quality across shifts, hospitals, or geographic regions.
   - Useful in underserved areas with clinician shortages.
4. **Data-Driven Insights**
   - AI could identify patterns humans miss (e.g., subtle interactions between symptoms, lab results, and patient history) and improve over time with more data.

Figure 3.1: Response from a traditional LLM – Mistral Medium 3.1

You can check out `eg1.py` in the book's GitHub repository for full responses (`https://github.com/PacktPublishing/DeepSeek-in-Practice/blob/main/Chapter03/eg1.py`). But a structured prompt that follows the preceding specification might look like this (see `eg2.py` `https://github.com/PacktPublishing/DeepSeek-in-Practice/blob/main/Chapter03/eg2.py`):

```
## Context:
You are analyzing an ethical policy choice in clinical triage. The
model is more accurate on retrospective data than clinicians but its
internal logic is not interpretable.
## Task:
Evaluate whether the hospital should deploy the model and under what
conditions.
```

```
## Constraints:
- Evaluate explicitly under: (1) Utilitarianism, (2) Deontology
(Kantian duties), (3) Virtue ethics, (4) Ethics of care.
- For each lens: state a verdict {permit|forbid|conditional} with a
1-2 sentence justification.
- Address: fairness, accountability, transparency, harm mitigation,
informed consent/assent, oversight.
- Include one strong counterargument that could overturn your
conclusion and how you'd test it.
- Do NOT reveal chain-of-thought; provide only final labeled
reasoning.
- Keep each field ≤ 60 words.
## Output:
Return ONLY JSON with this shape:
{
  "per_lens": {
    "utilitarianism": {"verdict": "permit|forbid|conditional",
"rationale": "..."},
    "deontology": {"verdict": "...", "rationale": "..."},
    "virtue_ethics": {"verdict": "...", "rationale": "..."},
    "care_ethics": {"verdict": "...", "rationale": "..."}
  },
  "deployment_recommendation": {"verdict":
"permit|forbid|conditional", "conditions": ["...","..."]},
  "oversight_plan": ["metric_audits","bias_monitoring","appeals_
process","A/B_safety_guardrails"],
  "counterargument": {"claim": "...", "test": "..."},
  "residual_risks": ["...","..."],
  "confidence": 0.0
}
```

This prompt resulted in a long *thinking* output by DeepSeek-R1 and then the following JSON response (as requested):

```
{
  "per_lens": {
    "utilitarianism": {"verdict": "permit", "rationale": "Superior
accuracy maximizes overall patient outcomes and welfare, fulfilling
the utilitarian goal of the greatest good for the greatest
number."},
```

```
    "deontology": {"verdict": "forbid", "rationale": "The opaque
logic treats patients as mere means to an end, violating the
duty to respect persons by making unexplainable, non-autonomous
decisions."},
    "virtue_ethics": {"verdict": "conditional", "rationale":
"Permit only if it supports, not replaces, clinician prudence and
compassion. Deployment must foster trust and collaboration, not
undermine professional virtues."},
    "care_ethics": {"verdict": "conditional", "rationale": "Permit
only as a supportive tool. The model lacks empathy and context;
final decisions must remain with human caregivers to preserve
relational care."}
  },
  "deployment_recommendation": {"verdict": "conditional",
"conditions": ["Use only as a decision-support tool for clinicians,
not autonomous triage", "Implement robust, continuous bias auditing
on protected classes", "Secure informed consent/assent from patients
disclosing AI involvement"]},
  "oversight_plan": ["metric_audits", "bias_monitoring", "appeals_
process", "A/B_safety_guardrails"],
  "counterargument": {"claim": "The model's superior retrospective
accuracy may not translate to real-world performance due to hidden
confounding variables or data drift, causing net harm.", "test":
"Run a rigorous prospective A/B trial comparing model-assisted vs.
standard care, with an independent DSMB monitoring for significant
outcome differences and safety."},
  "residual_risks": ["Automation bias leading clinicians to over-
rely on the model", "Model performance degradation over time due to
data drift"],
  "confidence": 0.8
}
```

- **The minimalist mindset (or how I learned to stop worrying and trust the model):** Here's where seasoned prompt engineers often struggle. With DeepSeek, less really is more. Those carefully crafted few-shot examples you've been collecting? They're not just unnecessary. They're actively harmful. That detailed step-by-step breakdown you usually provide? You're micromanaging a system that already knows how to think. It's like the difference between teaching someone to drive by explaining every micro-movement versus just telling them the destination. DeepSeek models, especially R1, already have the *how to think* part down. They just need to know what to think about.

Here are some guidelines to get you started with the minimalist prompts for DeepSeek:

- Stating the problem clearly and getting out of the way.
- Resisting the urge to over-explain or provide examples
- Accepting that the model's internal reasoning might be better than your external guidance.

This minimalist approach can feel uncomfortable at first, especially if you're used to the *prompt engineering as creative writing* approach that works well with other models. But once you embrace it, you'll find that DeepSeek's responses are often more thorough and accurate precisely because you didn't constrain its reasoning process.

In a practical sense, a minimalist prompt template derived from the preceding suggestion could look like this:

```
Task: [what to decide/compute; 1-2 sentences]
Constraints: [numbered rules or lenses; keep to essentials]
Output: [tight schema or bullet template; short fields only; no
chain-of-thought]
```

See `eg3.py` in the repository (`https://github.com/PacktPublishing/DeepSeek-in-Practice/blob/main/Chapter03/eg3.py`) for an example of this principle in action. `eg3.py` runs a controlled comparison of three prompting styles – zero-shot minimal, few-shot with examples, and verbose step-by-step – on the same ethical triage task, using DeepSeek via OpenRouter's OpenAI-compatible client. It constructs message payloads for each style, requests a JSON-only answer with a tight **schema**, and validates the response by checking required keys, allowed verdicts, word limits, and types (with minor tolerance for capitalization). Each run is timed, token usage is captured when available, and outputs are printed with PASS/FAIL validation feedback. This example highlights how minimalist prompts often comply better and cost less.

Schema: Here, ***schema*** means the explicit specification of the model's expected output – the shape and constraints of the answer. A schema defines field names, data types, allowed values/enums, required versus optional fields, nesting, and limits (for example, word or range constraints). We express it in the prompt or via API features (JSON mode, function/tool parameters, Pydantic) so the model knows what to return, and we can validate it reliably. In short: the prompt describes the task; the schema is the output contract the response must satisfy (e.g., `{"verdict": "approve|deny|escalate", "rationale": "string, <=50 words"}`).

Now that you have a broad understanding of the kind of prompts that work with DeepSeek, let's find out why they work.

Why structured, minimal prompts "click" with the R series (what's happening under the hood)

If the ***research brief → JSON (or single-shot)*** answer style feels unusually effective with R1, that's because it is aligned to how the model was trained to win. R1 wasn't optimized to produce eloquent chat; it was optimized to produce verifiable, format-compliant answers after hidden reasoning.

Recall from *Chapter 2,* that, during post-training, DeepSeek used reinforcement learning where each candidate response was graded by rule-based checkers: math answers were checked for the right value in a specified final-answer slot; code was compiled and tested; and a format reward enforced a separation between an internal reasoning region and a clean final answer region (originally expressed with `<think> … </think>` and `<answer> … </answer>` in the training template). Give the model a tight output contract, and it recognizes the game it was trained to play. That's why a clear problem statement plus a strict schema routinely beats ornate role-play or example dumps.

R1 trains with **Group Relative Policy Optimization** (**GRPO**): for each prompt, the policy samples K responses (typically 4–8), deterministic rule based graders compute a single scalar reward per sample (usually correctness, plus a small formatting check), rewards are centered by the group average, and the policy is updated so above-average samples gain probability mass while below-average ones lose it. In R1-Zero, there is no learned reward model – only these deterministic graders.

During training the model also learns **test-time scaling**: for harder problems, it *thinks* longer internally before responding – so you don't need to instruct *think step-by-step*. Your job is to define the target and the format; the model plans privately.

Test-time scaling: R1 adaptively allocates more internal reasoning to difficult inputs and less to easy ones at inference time. This emergent behavior lets accuracy improve by *thinking longer* about hard problems without any special *step-by-step* prompting.

This training recipe also explains two practical quirks you saw earlier:

- **Few-shot hurts**: In R1 evaluations, adding demonstrations consistently degraded performance; the authors recommend zero-shot with an explicit output format. Examples bias the internal planner toward your exemplar trail rather than the strategy RL already rewarded.
- **System prompts**: Early R1 runs effectively down-weighted system role instructions in practice, hence the *put everything in the user message* advice. With the R1-0528 refresh, a system prompt is now supported – but it is still best kept minimal (identity, date, global policy), with task-specific constraints and schemas living in the user content.

A natural question that may come to your mind at this point is, why don't the traditional chat-based LLMs have these quirks? Let's answer this for you, dear readers.

Why don't other LLMs behave like this?

Most *chat* LLMs (e.g., V series, GPT-4o, Claude 3.x) were tuned primarily via supervised fine-tuning and preference/RLHF, so they often benefit from few-shot exemplars and CoT demonstrations – the classic GPT-3 and CoT results. The traditional LLMs weren't broadly trained with rule-based verifiers that grade a single, rule-checked final answer per prompt, so schemas help for parsing, but demonstrations still tend to teach the distribution. Reasoning-first models (R1, OpenAI o1) flipped the objective: reward verifiable correctness and format after internal deliberation, so zero-shot and schema becomes the safer default.

Here are some advantages and trade-offs DeepSeek possesses as compared to traditional LLMs:

- **Pros**: A higher ceiling on verifiable tasks (math, code, scientific QA); less reliance on demos; stronger reliability when you pin outputs to a single slot or strict JSON (what the RL loop reinforced).
- **Cons**: More internal *thinking* means latency/cost trade-offs; over-prompting (few-shot CoT, role-play) can degrade results; on open-ended, style-heavy tasks without checkers, the advantage narrows and a classic chat model with good exemplars may equal or beat R1 at a lower cost.

So, keep in mind this mental model when you prompt DeepSeek: you're not *teaching a chatbot*. You're giving a verifier-graded specification to a planner. The more unambiguous the spec and the tighter the output contract, the more you let the RL-trained behaviors do their work.

Ready to see how this mental model translates into concrete techniques? Let's get specific.

General tips and advice for prompting DeepSeek

With the foundational principles established, we will lay down some prompt guidelines to help you achieve accurate and reliable results with DeepSeek. As we discussed in the previous section, many of these recommendations directly contradict established practices for other leading models. This adjustment is a necessary consequence of DeepSeek's unique architecture and training methodology.

First up, we will talk about how few-shot prompting, otherwise popular, may in fact be detrimental to DeepSeek's responses.

The few-shot fallacy

The most significant departure from conventional prompt engineering is DeepSeek's handling of few-shot examples. While this technique is a cornerstone for improving performance on models such as OpenAI's GPT-4o, providing examples to DeepSeek-R1 is actively detrimental. The official documentation is unequivocal on this point: *Do not provide examples in the prompt, as this consistently degrades model performance.*

In controlled experiments, accuracy dropped from 79.8% to ~70% when few-shot examples were added (`https://www.linkedin.com/pulse/zero-shot-few-rag-benchmaking-deep-seek-sandeep-k-gil1c/`).

This performance degradation occurs because providing examples interferes with the model's native reasoning process. R1 was trained using reinforcement learning to develop its own internal problem-solving methodologies, which manifest as a hidden CoT process. When examples are included in the prompt, they attempt to force a specific reasoning path, overriding the model's more robust, internally optimized strategy.

Instead of examples, provide the following:

- Clear task descriptions.
- Explicit output format requirements.
- Schema definitions (for structured output).

You may want to take a look at `eg3.py` (`https://github.com/PacktPublishing/DeepSeek-in-Practice/blob/main/Chapter03/eg3.py`) to check out some zero-shot prompt samples.

Next, we will talk about why system prompts are not a popular approach to follow with DeepSeek.

System prompts

It's common to use a system prompt to set an assistant's role and global constraints. With the original DeepSeek-R1 releases, however, system prompts were largely ignored in practice; the official guidance was to avoid them and place all actionable instructions in the user message. This reflects how early R1 was trained and evaluated: the chat template emphasized a user→assistant exchange where the model first *thinks* internally and then answers, rather than attending strongly to a separate system role.

In May 2025, the R1-0528 refresh added support for system prompts. DeepSeek's own apps use a deliberately minimal system message (identify the assistant; include the current date). Even so, the practical rule of thumb still stands: keep the system message for high-level, global constraints (identity, policy, formatting preferences) and put task-specific instructions in the user message. You no longer need to seed `<think>`; the model will reason without it.

For the V series (V3/V3.1), system prompts do work and the official chat templates include a system slot, but they aren't essential for good results. In line with DeepSeek's examples, prefer short, declarative system text and focus your effort on making the user instruction clear and specific. In short: with DeepSeek, simple, explicit user prompts do the heavy lifting.

With DeepSeek, simple and clear prompts do the job just right. Let's talk about this in detail next.

The verbose prompt trap

If you're used to writing prompts that read like Victorian novels, it's time to channel your inner Hemingway. DeepSeek's official guidance emphasizes: *Complex, lengthy prompts often lead to less effective results. Focus on clarity over complexity.*

This isn't about being terse for its own sake. It's about signal-to-noise ratio. Every extra word is another opportunity for the model to misinterpret your intent. Remember, R1 is going to generate potentially thousands of tokens of internal reasoning. It doesn't need your help overthinking things.

Here is an example of a good prompt for R1:

```
Analyze the security vulnerabilities in this code snippet.
Focus on SQL injection and authentication bypass.
Code: [your code here]
```

One example of a bad prompt could be the following:

```
You are an expert security researcher with 20 years of experience.
I want you to carefully examine the following code, thinking about
all possible security issues. Consider things like SQL injection,
XSS, authentication problems, and any other vulnerabilities...
[several more paragraphs of instructions]
```

To see an illustration of this example, check out `eg4.py` (`https://github.com/PacktPublishing/DeepSeek-in-Practice/blob/main/Chapter03/eg4.py`), which runs the same vulnerable Flask snippet through two prompts – a concise *good* prompt that focuses explicitly on SQL injection and authentication bypass.

Here is the response for the good prompt:

```
Security Vulnerabilities Analysis
1. SQL Injection
Vulnerability: The code uses direct string interpolation for SQL queries:
query = f"SELECT id, password_hash FROM users WHERE username =
'{username}'"
Risk: Attackers can inject malicious SQL by manipulating the username
input. For example:
' OR 1=1 -- would return the first user in the database, bypassing
authentication.
'; DROP TABLE users; -- could delete tables.
Why It's Critical: Direct string interpolation allows arbitrary SQL
execution, compromising data confidentiality, integrity, and availability.
2. Authentication Bypass via Weak Hash Comparison
...
3. Admin Privilege Escalation
...
4. Insecure Password Hashing
...
7. Database Connection Management
...
Exploit Scenarios
SQL Injection + Auth Bypass:
...
Fix Recommendations
Prevent SQL Injection:
```

```
query = "SELECT id, password_hash FROM users WHERE username = ?"
...
Fixed Code Snippet
...
```

On the other hand, you will observe that a verbose, *bad* prompt invites topic drift.

Check out a snippet of the prompt response here:

```
Security Analysis of the Provided Flask Login Code
1. SQL Injection (Critical - CVSS 9.8)
Issue
query = f"SELECT id, password_hash FROM users WHERE username =
'{username}'"
...
Mitigation
Use parameterized queries:
query = "SELECT id, password_hash, is_admin FROM users WHERE username = ?"
cur.execute(query, (username,))
Reference: OWASP SQL Injection Prevention Cheat Sheet
2. Weak Password Hashing (Critical - CVSS 9.8)
...
8. Database Connection Management (Low - CVSS 3.7)
Issue: No connection pooling or error handling.
Mitigation: Use context managers (with sqlite3.connect()).
...
Broader Architectural Concerns
No rate limiting → susceptible to brute force.
Missing login attempt logging and monitoring.
Weak credential storage practices.
Database not isolated securely.
Dependencies not pinned → supply-chain risks.
Severity Summary
...
Corrected Code (Secure Example)
...
Additional Recommendations
References
...
```

Here, as you can see, the response could have been more focused.

Using the same DeepSeek model via OpenRouter at a low temperature, the script prints both outputs and computes simple focus heuristics (mentions of SQLi/auth bypass, off-topic hits like XSS/CSRF, a `focus_score`, sentence-level signal-to-noise ratio, and word count).

The `eg4.py` script also summarizes which prompt produced the tighter, more on-target answer:

```
Summary: focus_winner=Good shorter_output=Good | good_focus_score=17 bad_
focus_score=9 | good_words=380 bad_words=872
```

Let's now talk about additional factors that may impact DeepSeek's response generation.

Other factors impacting DeepSeek's response to prompts

Apart from prompting techniques, there are other factors that may impact how DeepSeek processes and responds to prompts. Let's find out.

- **Temperature**: The official docs (`https://api-docs.deepseek.com/`) land on temperature ≈ 0.6 as the sweet spot for R1. Too low, and you risk repetition loops (the model gets stuck in local optima). Too high, and the careful reasoning process starts to hallucinate.

  For V3, there's an additional quirk: the API maps temperature=1.0 to an effective 0.3, so you might want to set it even lower for factual tasks.

  Recommended settings for R1 are `temperature=0.6`, `top_p=0.95`. For V3, use `temperature=0.3-0.5` for factual tasks, up to `0.7` for creative work.

- **Persona hints**: While elaborate role-playing is out, subtle persona cues can dramatically improve results. Community testing shows that simple audience-level hints such as `I'm new to finance` cause R1 to adjust explanation depth without compromising accuracy.

  This works because you're providing context about the ***output requirements***, not trying to change the model's reasoning process. It's the difference between saying `pretend you're a teacher` (role-play) and `explain this for a high school student` (output specification).

  Here are some examples of effective persona hints:

  ```
  I'm a software engineer familiar with Python.
  Writing for a general audience blog post.
  Technical documentation for API developers.
  ```

A reliable way to write persona hints is to keep them to one sentence that specifies audience, deliverable, and depth – nothing about *acting as* anything. Phrase it as an output requirement, not a role: who it's for, what you want back, and how deep to go.

A useful template is `For [audience], produce [format] that [purpose]; assume [background] and [depth constraints].`

For example, consider this prompt:

```
For a non-technical CFO, produce a 150-word briefing that informs a
buy/no-buy decision; assume no ML background and define acronyms,
or For API engineers, provide a runnable Python 3.12 snippet with
a docstring; avoid external deps and keep the explanation under 5
lines.
```

This prompt is targeted and specifies one audience, one output, and one depth. If the result is still off, iterate by adjusting those three dials rather than adding role-play.

There are a few more techniques worth applying for DeepSeek prompting:

- **Structured formatting**: Use XML tags or markdown headers to organize complex prompts. R1 parses these beautifully. Here is how you can structure the prompt with XML tags, for example:

  ```
  <context>Background information here</context>
  <task>Specific problem to solve</task>
  <constraints>Any limitations or requirements</constraints>
  <output>Expected format</output>
  ```

  You may recall from *Chapter 1* that R1 exhibits formatting-aware generation (i.e., a consistent structure that acts as signposts the decoder can follow). In *Chapter 2*, we showed how structured prompts encourage private intermediate reasoning (e.g., implicit think → answer).

  We can now operationalize these learnings: use a light, flat structure to specify inputs and outputs, then let the model do the planning internally. You're not *making R1 an XML parser*; you're giving it a stable layout it can align to.

- **Explicit output formats**: For math problems, always specify an explicit output format for final answers. For code, specify the language and any style requirements upfront.
    - You may remember from our previous discussions in *Chapter 1* and *Chapter 2* that R1 is reinforced with rule-based validators that check final answers and format conformance. Therefore, the safest way to boost reliability is to define an output contract that a machine could grade.
    - In practice, give the model exactly one slot for the final result, specify units and precision, and forbid extra prose. Here are a few tips and tricks you could try:
- For math, require a single `<answer>` field (or final answer: line) with explicit rounding rules and units – do not ask for step-by-step.
- For code, require one fenced block with the language and version (e.g., Python `3.12`), an entry-point signature, and any constraints (stdlib-only, no network, time/memory limits).
- If you need metadata (confidence, method), put it in separate fields – never mix with the final answer.
    - Keep the contract stable across tasks; validators reward consistency more than cleverness. For example, using tags for a math problem, you could use something like this:

````
### Output
Return only:
<answer units="m/s^2" rounding="3dp">…</answer>
Or for code you could use something like this:
### Output
Return exactly one fenced code block:
```python
# Python 3.12, stdlib only
def normalize(v: list[float]) -> list[float]:
    ...
if __name__ == "__main__":
    ...
````
````

`eg5.py` (`https://github.com/PacktPublishing/DeepSeek-in-Practice/blob/main/Chapter03/eg5.py`) demonstrates how to pair explicit output contracts with lightweight, machine-checkable validators. The script sends three prompts to DeepSeek: two math problems that require returning only a single `<answer>` tag with specified units and decimal precision, and one programming task that must be returned as exactly one fenced Python 3.12 code block with a particular entry-point signature and a main guard.

Some of the prompt excerpts used in `eg5.py` (truncated) are as follows:

```
Math prompt 1
### Task
A car accelerates from rest to 20 m/s in 8 s. Compute the
constant acceleration.
### Constraints
- Do not show steps or intermediate numbers.
- Do not include any text outside the required tag.
### Output
Return only:
<answer units="m/s^2" rounding="3dp">…</answer>

Math prompt 2
### Task
Compute the area of a circle with radius r = 3.2 m. Use π ≈
3.141592653589793.
### Constraints
- Do not show steps or intermediate numbers.
- Do not include any text outside the required tag.
### Output
Return only:
<answer units="m^2" rounding="2dp">…</answer>

Code prompt
### Task
Implement a vector normalization function.
### Requirements
- Language: Python 3.12
```

````
- Libraries: stdlib only (no third-party imports)
- Style: Type hints; PEP 8 friendly; include a minimal main
guard demo
- Entry point signature must be exactly:
  def normalize(v: list[float]) -> list[float]:
### Output
Return exactly one fenced code block:
```python
# Python 3.12, stdlib only
def normalize(v: list[float]) -> list[float]:
    ...
if __name__ == "__main__":
    ...
````

You will notice the following from these prompts:

- There are no extra prose, explanations, or additional code fences: The validators check that math answers have exactly one `&lt;answer&gt;` tag with the correct units, rounding, and value; and that the code response is exactly one Python code fence with the header line, the normalize `(v: list[float]) -> list[float]` function, a main guard, and no non-`stdlib` imports.
- For each response, `eg5.py` prints the raw model output and runs simple validators: A tag parser verifies units, rounding, and numeric correctness for the math items, while a code checker ensures there is exactly one Python code fence, the `Python 3.12, stdlib only` header, the normalize `(v: list[float]) -> list[float]` function, a main guard, and no non-`stdlib` imports. This shows how clear contracts plus automatic checks can raise reliability without needing to inspect CoT or intermediate steps.
- You can check out the response here: `https://app.warp.dev/block/SmWy7R2GE1nsLIGoFNYwUg`.

- **Chain-of-Draft**: For token efficiency, you can ask R1 to `keep only a minimum draft for each thinking step`. This reduces token usage by 80% while maintaining accuracy. **Chain-of-Draft (CoD)** is not the same as CoT. CoT asks the model to externalize full step-by-step reasoning (often verbose). CoD is a compression policy for intermediate notes: you tell the model to keep only minimal, checkpoint-style drafts per step (e.g., 3–7 words) and return a clean final answer field.
````

- With R1, those drafts typically live in the hidden `<think>` space – you're not asking for visible reasoning, you're constraining how much scratchpad it uses. Because R1 is rewarded on final-answer correctness and format adherence, compressing the draft often preserves accuracy while cutting tokens substantially (reports range from ~40% to ~80% fewer tokens, task-dependent). Use CoD when you care about latency/cost but still want robust reasoning; use CoT only when you truly need a readable derivation.
- Here's an example of what that might look like in a prompt:

```
### Constraints
- Reasoning: think step by step, but keep only a minimal
draft
  (≤5 words per step, ≤4 steps). If stuck, expand to 8 words.
- Do not print the draft; return only the final field below.

### Output
<answer rounding="2dp" units="m/s^2">…</answer>
```

Here are a few more tips for CoD prompting:

- If answers degrade, raise the per-step word cap (5→8→12) or allow one extra step.
- For proofs/long derivations, prefer a higher cap or skip CoD.
- Keep the final-answer slot stable across prompts; validators reward consistency.

Let's take a look at a quick checklist of dos and don'ts for prompting DeepSeek (*Table 3.1*).

Technique	Do	Don't	Why
Examples	Describe the task clearly	Provide few-shot examples	Examples degrade R1 performance by 5-15%
System Prompts	Put everything in user message (R1)	Use system role for instructions	R1 ignores system prompts entirely
Prompt Length	Be concise and structured	Write verbose explanations	Clarity beats complexity for reasoning models
Temperature	Use 0.6 for R1, 0.3-0.5 for V3	Go below 0.5 or above 0.7 (R1)	Prevents repetition loops and hallucinations
Personas	Give audience-level hints	Heavy role-playing instructions	Context helps without constraining reasoning

Technique	Do	Don't	Why
Formatting	Use XML/markdown structure	Dump unstructured text	Clear parsing improves compliance
Output Specs	Define format explicitly	Assume model knows your needs	Ensures consistent, usable outputs
Reasoning	Trust internal process	Add *think step by step*	R1 already does CoT internally

Table 3.1: Dos and don'ts of prompting DeepSeek

Remember, these aren't just arbitrary preferences. Each recommendation stems from how DeepSeek models were trained and what they've learned to expect.

Once you have a grip of the fundamentals to prompt DeepSeek, you'll be ready for the model-specific techniques that we'll explore next.

Advanced techniques and tooling for structured output

A primary challenge in productionizing language models is ensuring their outputs are in a reliable, machine-readable format. While many models require extensive post-processing to parse unstructured text, DeepSeek provides dedicated features for generating structured data like JSON. However, DeepSeek's implementation has unique characteristics and requirements that differ from other models, and understanding them is key to successful integration.

The capabilities for structured output in DeepSeek models improved significantly with the R1-0528 release in May 2025 (`https://huggingface.co/deepseek-ai/DeepSeek-R1-0528`). This update introduced native JSON mode and function-calling capabilities, aligning DeepSeek more closely with the feature sets of other prominent models.

A notable characteristic of DeepSeek's implementation, however, is that even when using the dedicated JSON mode, performance is more reliable when the prompt also explicitly requests a JSON output. This prompting requirement is a crucial detail for ensuring consistent results.

Here's the *why* and *when* before we get into the *how*. Structured output (JSON, function calls, or typed models) isn't just for building chat UIs; it's for any place where model output will be consumed by code rather than eyeballs.

Imagine you need to implement the following for your application:

- Routing a support ticket to the right queue.
- Writing extracted entities into a database row.
- Triggering a downstream tool with typed parameters.
- Running evaluation harnesses that assert on fields.
- Emitting telemetry that your observability stack can parse.

In these situations, you don't want prose that a human can interpret – you want a predictable schema your program can validate, retry, and `diff` in tests.

In a typical product, end users almost never see JSON and don't need to ask for it. The JSON is a behind-the-scenes contract between your backend and the model: the UI renders friendly text, while your server reads the machine-readable portion to decide what to do next (store, route, call a tool, show buttons, etc.).

Two **common patterns for responses** emerge:

- **Dual-channel responses** where the model returns human-readable text for the UI plus a small JSON *metadata* object for the application.
- **Pure structured responses** for batch/ETL jobs, agent loops, and evaluations, where no human prose is required at all.

So, use structured output whenever a downstream system needs determinism: when you must validate fields, run automated tests, support idempotent retries, or chain tool calls safely. Skip it when the output is purely human-facing and won't be parsed by code. With DeepSeek specifically, you'll get the best reliability by using its native structured modes (JSON or tools) and still stating the schema expectations in the prompt. For reasoning models, keep the machine-readable bits in the final *answer* channel only and never feed their hidden *thinking* back into the conversation; we'll show exactly how to do that next.

There are two ways to get structure: make the model emit it, or have your client enforce it. We'll cover four progressively stronger techniques to do this:

- **Native JSON mode** asks the model to return a JSON object directly – simple, fast, and good for extractions and small schemas.
- **Function/tool calling** lets you define a schema (parameters) the model must fill to *call* a tool, which is ideal when outputs should trigger code paths.

- **Type-enforced generation with Pydantic (via Instructor)** validates the model's reply against a Python type, giving you precise errors and automatic retries; we'll show both `Mode.TOOLS` and `Mode.MD_JSON` (handy for reasoning models).
- **Production guardrails** provide prompt-level schema hints, low temperature, max-token sizing, a retry-repair loop, and – when you need a hard guarantee – constrained generation on providers that support it.

All examples use the OpenAI-compatible chat-completions interface but target DeepSeek models/endpoints.

Let's first look at how to set up the native JSON mode.

Native JSON mode

Setting up JSON mode looks deceptively familiar if you're coming from OpenAI. Take a look at the following code snippet.

```
from openai import OpenAI
import json

client = OpenAI(
    api_key=os.getenv("DEEPSEEK_API_KEY"),
    base_url="https://api.deepseek.com"
)

response = client.chat.completions.create(
    model="deepseek-chat",
    messages=[
        {
            "role": "system",
            "content": "Extract user information as JSON. Example:
{\"name\": \"Alice\", \"age\": 30}"
        },
        {
            "role": "user",
            "content": "My name is Bob and I'm 25 years old"
        }
    ],
    response_format={"type": "json_object"},
```

```
    temperature=0.1  # Keep it deterministic
)

data = json.loads(response.choices[0].message.content)
```

This snippet calls DeepSeek through its OpenAI-compatible API to extract structured data from a sentence. It creates a client (using `DEEPSEEK_API_KEY` and `base_url`), sends a chat request to the `deepseek-chat` model with a system instruction and a user message, and enables native JSON output via `response_format={"type": "json_object"}` while keeping randomness low (`temperature=0.1`). The model responds with a JSON string (e.g., `{"name":"Bob","age":25}`), which the final line parses with `json.loads(...)` into a Python dict (data) for programmatic use.

For optimal results when using `response_format={"type": "json_object"}`, adhere to the following guidelines:

- **Explicitly request JSON**: The prompt should still contain a phrase like *return the output as JSON* to reinforce the instruction.
- **Provide a schema example**: Including a simple JSON structure in the prompt (e.g., `{"name": "string", "age": "number"}`) significantly improves compliance.
- **Set `max_tokens` appropriately**: Ensure the token limit is sufficient to accommodate the full JSON response to prevent truncation.
- **Use a low temperature**: A temperature between 0.1 and 0.3 is recommended to minimize creative deviations from the requested schema.

It may happen that sometimes JSON is not enough. This is usually when there is complex logic or nested levels in your JSON object. At a certain point, you'll start to get errors or unexpected outputs. In such cases, we can use function calling.

Function calling

For more complex structured data requirements, DeepSeek supports a function-calling feature that adheres directly to the OpenAI specification. This design choice simplifies integration significantly, as existing code bases built for OpenAI's function-calling API can be adapted to use DeepSeek with minimal changes to the client configuration.

```
tools = [{
    "type": "function",
    "function": {
        "name": "analyze_sentiment",
        "description": "Analyze the sentiment of text",
```

```
            "parameters": {
                "type": "object",
                "properties": {
                    "text": {"type": "string"},
                    "confidence": {"type": "number", "minimum": 0, "maximum":
1}
                },
                "required": ["text", "confidence"]
            }
        }
}]

response = client.chat.completions.create(
    model="deepseek-chat",
    messages=[{"role": "user", "content": "I love this product!"}],
    tools=tools,
    tool_choice="auto"
)
```

In the OpenAI-compatible API that DeepSeek exposes, **tool calling** is the umbrella and **function calling** is the concrete tool type you define with a JSON-Schema parameters block. You register one or more tools (type `function`), the model decides which one to invoke, and it returns `tool_call` with a function name and JSON arguments. Your application then validates and executes that function. This is the same mental model we use for agents. We will touch on function calling and structured outputs in more depth, as well as how to combine them to create agents, in *Chapter 6*. Here, we stay focused on structured output: using a single function as a typed envelope to force predictable fields.

The function-calling example declares a schema that the model must fill, shifting structure from polite prose requests into a machine-checked contract. At run time, the model doesn't emit free-form text; it emits a tool invocation with strictly typed arguments (numbers, enums, and nested objects), which you can validate, log, retry, and pass to real code. This reduces prompt drift, eliminates brittle regex parsing, and yields clean failure modes: when the output violates the schema, you can detect it deterministically and trigger a repair or a retry. The pattern is now industry-standard: OpenAI, Anthropic (*tools*), Google (*function calling*), Cohere (*tool use*), and Mistral all support schema-constrained calls. You should use JSON mode when you just need a blob of structured data; use function/tool calling when the output is an action with parameters, when schemas are deep/nested, or when you want the model to choose among multiple operations.

Instead of working with unstructured text responses, you can define clear Pydantic models that represent the desired output – such as objects, lists, or nested data – and Instructor ensures the model is followed. Let's talk about it next.

Type-enforced generation with Pydantic (via Instructor)

As you may be aware, Instructor is a Python library (`https://python.useinstructor.com/`) that makes prompting large language models both structured and reliable by integrating directly with Pydantic. It automatically validates responses, retries on schema errors, and provides type safety, making prompts more robust and predictable. This approach not only streamlines how prompts are written but also transforms LLM outputs into dependable, strongly typed data structures that integrate seamlessly into real applications.

For DeepSeek, you can use Instructor to add a type-enforcement layer on top of either JSON mode or tool calling. You give it a `Pydantic` model; it handles prompting, parses the response, validates `types/ranges/enums`, and can auto-repair on failures – returning a real Python object rather than a raw JSON string. For reasoning models, `Mode.MD_JSON` keeps latency low (no tool round-trip) while still enforcing the schema; for tool-heavy flows, `Mode.TOOLS` plugs into function calling. Because Instructor is transport-agnostic, it can sit over both JSON and tools, and its value is validation, retries, and typed objects.

Let's see how you can use Instructor for type safety.

Using Instructor for type safety

You can use Instructor to wrap DeepSeek's API with Pydantic-powered validation. Here is an example to demonstrate this.

```
import instructor
from pydantic import BaseModel, Field

client = instructor.from_provider(
    "deepseek/deepseek-chat",
    base_url="https://api.deepseek.com",
    mode=instructor.Mode.TOOLS  # or Mode.MD_JSON for reasoning models
)

class ProductReview(BaseModel):
    rating: int = Field(ge=1, le=5, description="1-5 star rating")
    summary: str = Field(max_length=100)
```

```
    pros: list[str]
    cons: list[str]

# Magic happens here - guaranteed valid ProductReview or exception
review = client.chat.completions.create(
    messages=[{"role": "user",
          "content": "Review of iPhone 15: Great camera, battery life could
be better..."}],
    response_model=ProductReview
)
```

Pro tip: Use `Mode.MD_JSON` with reasoning models to avoid tool-calling overhead. It's like choosing the scenic route – slower (low latency) but more reliable.

That snippet wraps DeepSeek's OpenAI-compatible API with Instructor, which enforces a Python Pydantic schema on the model's output. `from_provider(...)` creates a client bound to `deepseek-chat` and chooses an enforcement mode (`Mode.TOOLS` in the example, which uses function/tool-calling under the hood; `Mode.MD_JSON` is the alternative that enforces a schema over plain JSON). The `ProductReview` Pydantic model is the contract: an integer rating constrained to 1–5, a summary capped at 100 chars, and two lists of strings. When you call `client.chat.completions.create(..., response_model=ProductReview)`, Instructor does the following:

1. Presents the schema to the model (as a tool schema or JSON schema, depending on the mode).
2. Receives the model's structured arguments.
3. Parses them.
4. Validates every field against the Pydantic constraints – returning a real `ProductReview` object on success or raising an error if the output is malformed.

In other words, you're not asking for JSON; you're guaranteeing typed data that your code can rely on.

Use this approach whenever downstream code needs strong guarantees or clean failure modes: writing to databases, triggering actions with parameters, running evals that assert on fields, or building agent steps that must be type-safe. Prefer `Mode.MD_JSON` with reasoning models when you want schema enforcement without the ceremony of tools; prefer `Mode.TOOLS` when you're already in a tool/agent setting, when schemas are deep or nested, or when you want the model to *choose* among multiple tools with typed arguments. Either way, Instructor centralizes parsing and validation so your application logic stays simple and robust.

Reasoning-style DeepSeek models (e.g., `deepseek-reasoner`) emit two channels: hidden `reasoning_content` (the *thinking*) and the final content (the *answer*). Your validators and parsers must operate only on the answer – never echo or feed the model's *thinking* back into the conversation or downstream calls, or you'll trip schema checks and even 400s on the next request.

The next section covers these edge cases and **hardening patterns** – stripping the thinking channel, retry-repair loops, and other safeguards for production.

Strategies for robustness and special cases

Remember how we said R1 models think before they speak? That creates a unique challenge for structured output. The `deepseek-reasoner` model (`https://api-docs.deepseek.com/guides/reasoning_model`) outputs both `reasoning_content` (the thinking) and `content` (the answer). If you fail to handle this properly, you'll get a nasty `400` error on your next API call.

```
# Assume `client` is the Instructor-wrapped DeepSeek client created above.
from pydantic import BaseModel

class DateInfo(BaseModel): date: str
class TimeInfo(BaseModel): time: str


# 1) First call  -  model "thinks" and answers; we keep only the answer
(`content`)
completion, raw = client.chat.completions.create_with_completion(
    model="deepseek-reasoner",
    messages=[{"role": "user", "content": "Extract the date as JSON: The
meeting is on March 15th."}],
    response_model=DateInfo,
    temperature=0
)
```

```
print(raw.choices[0].message.reasoning_content)  # optional: inspect the
thinking
assistant_answer = raw.choices[0].message.content  # <-- keep ONLY this
for history

# 2) Next call  -  what we actually feed the model (note: no `reasoning_
content` anywhere)
next_messages = [
    {"role": "assistant", "content": assistant_answer},
    {"role": "user", "content": "Now extract the time as JSON: It starts
at 14:30."}
]
_ = client.chat.completions.create(
    model="deepseek-reasoner",
    messages=next_messages,
    response_model=TimeInfo,
    temperature=0
)
```

The **strip the thinking** step is specific to R-series reasoning models because they return two channels: `reasoning_content` (hidden CoT) and `content` (the final answer).

If you naïvely replay the entire assistant message in your next request (e.g., by serializing the raw object), you end up sending a field the OpenAI-compatible API does not accept (`reasoning_content`). That violates the request schema, and the server responds with `HTTP 400 Bad Request` – it's not an infinite loop, just an invalid payload. The remedy is simple: persist and replay only content, never `reasoning_content`. (Chat/coder models don't emit `reasoning_content`, so this pitfall is unique to reasoning endpoints.)

We might encounter some issues while structuring output. Let's talk about them.

- **The retry-repair loop**: Even with all these safeguards, sometimes DeepSeek outputs invalid JSON. Instead of throwing up your hands, make it fix its own mess:

```
def extract_with_retry(prompt, model_class, max_retries=2):
    for attempt in range(max_retries):
        try:
            return client.chat.completions.create(
                messages=[{"role": "user", "content": prompt}],
                response_model=model_class
```

```
            )
        except Exception as e:
            if attempt < max_retries - 1:
                prompt = f"The previous JSON was invalid:\
n{str(e)}\n\nPlease fix and return valid JSON for: {prompt}"
            else:
                raise
```

This helper implements a self-repair loop around a typed generation call. It asks the model to produce a value that conforms to a Pydantic schema (`model_class`) and immediately validates the reply; if validation (or JSON parsing) fails, the `except` block rewrites the prompt to include the exact error message and a plain instruction – `the previous JSON was invalid… please fix and return valid JSON` – then retries up to `max_retries`. In other words, you turn an unstructured failure into a new, highly constrained task for the model, which often succeeds on the second pass because it now sees what was wrong (e.g., missing required field, wrong type, trailing commas, truncated output).

Use this pattern anywhere you occasionally see **schema drift** despite good prompting: batch/ETL extractions from messy text, eval harnesses that assert on fields, agent steps that must hand off typed parameters, or R1 runs where the final answer sometimes leaks stray prose into the JSON. Keep retries small (2–3), log the exception, and pair the loop with low temperature, adequate `max_tokens`, and an inline schema/example; if failures persist, escalate (fallback to tool/function calling with stricter schemas or surface a human in the loop). Avoid pasting huge error dumps back to the model (sanitize and keep it short), and ensure that with reasoning models, you validate only the answer channel (content), never their hidden `reasoning_content`.

What do we mean by **schema**? There's no server-side validator here. The model is conditioned on a schema you provide; your client code validates the result.

You can supply that schema in two common ways:

- **Native JSON mode**: Ask for JSON and include a tiny example (or JSON-Schema-like hints) in the prompt – good for simple extractions.
- **Function calling**: Pass an OpenAI-compatible JSON Schema under `parameters`. The model returns a `tool_call` whose arguments must match your declared `` `properties` `` (types, required fields, and nesting).

Use tool mode whenever downstream code needs typed parameters (e.g., routing, writing to a DB row, or triggering an action) or when your schema is nested.

- **The possessive apostrophe bug:** In R1-0528, we sometimes see keys lose their apostrophes in JSON (e.g., `user's_name` → `users_name`). Property names that include apostrophes – especially the typographic U+2019 (') – are rare in training data and tokenized as punctuation, so the model often normalizes or drops them (e.g., emitting `users_name` instead of `user's_name`). That breaks strict validators and any code expecting an exact key match.

  Fix it by doing either of the following:

  - Avoiding punctuation in property names (for example, prefer ASCII `snake_case`).
  - Showing explicit examples and accepting common variants during validation. Common variants can be captured via aliases and normalization:

  Here is how you can do this:

```
# Tool schema with risky keys (curly apostrophes)  -  works but
fragile:
tools = [{
  "type": "function",
  "function": {
    "name": "capture_profile",
    "parameters": {
      "type": "object",
      "properties": {
        "user's_name": {"type": "string"},
        "company's_address": {"type": "string"}
      },
      "required": ["user's_name", "company's_address"]
}}}]

# Robust parsing with Pydantic: accept curly, straight, or dropped
apostrophes
from pydantic import BaseModel, Field, AliasChoices

class Profile(BaseModel):
    users_name: str = Field(validation_alias=AliasChoices("user's_
name","user's_name","users_name"))
```

```
    company_address: str = Field(validation_
alias=AliasChoices("company's_address","company's_address","company_
address"))
    model_config = {"populate_by_name": True}  # allow using field
names in your code

# Better yet: instruct the model to emit ASCII snake_case keys only:
# "Return JSON with keys: users_name, company_address (ASCII only,
no punctuation)."
```

In practice, use tool/JSON schemas whenever you need typed, machine-checked fields and avoid punctuation in property names; if you can't rename keys (legacy contracts), add alias choices and a light pre-normalization step (e.g., replace →) before validation. This keeps your pipeline resilient without hiding errors that matter.

Table 3.2 serves as a quick reference to structured output strategies you could employ.

Need	Solution	Gotcha
Simple JSON extraction	`response_format` + example	Must include `json` in prompt
Complex validation	Instructor library	Use `Mode.MD_JSON` for reasoning models
Guaranteed valid output	Fireworks endpoint	Different API, costs more
Audit trail	Use reasoner model	Strip `reasoning_content` before next call
Recovery from bad JSON	Retry-repair loop	Usually works on second attempt

Table 3.2: Structured output strategies for effective DeepSeek prompting

DeepSeek's structured output capabilities have come a long way since the wild west days of pre-0528. While it's not quite as polished as OpenAI's implementation, it's more than capable for production use, especially when armored with Instructor or similar libraries.

The key is understanding DeepSeek's quirks: always provide examples, keep temperatures low, and remember that even with native JSON mode, the model appreciates (or even demands) a gentle reminder that you want JSON. It's like working with a brilliant but slightly eccentric colleague. Once you learn their preferences, you can do amazing things together.

If DeepSeek can be finicky, why do teams still pick it? In practice, the trade-off is compelling:

- **Cost or performance is unusually strong**: Per-million-token rates (with cache discounts) undercut many peers, so high-volume reasoning workloads are economically viable.
- **Reasoning quality is competitive on math/logic/code**: So, you often need less prompt scaffolding to reach correct answers.
- **Low switching cost**: The API is OpenAI-compatible (the same SDKs, function/tool calling, JSON mode), so existing backends slot it in with minimal changes.
- **Ecosystem support**: Hosted options add constrained or grammar-based generation for stricter structure when you need it.
- **Optionality**: R1(-0528) and its distilled variants are available on Hugging Face (and even vendor-quantized builds), which enables self-hosting and hybrid architectures. The *quirks* mostly translate to disciplined prompting (state the schema, keep temps low, strip reasoning channels), and for many teams, the savings plus throughput and optional self-hosting outweigh the extra care required.

Next up, how DeepSeek's V-series models bring their own flavor of prompts.

V series: unique prompting techniques for V-series models

While the R-series models are optimized for complex reasoning tasks, the V-series models are designed as powerful, general-purpose conversational agents. They demonstrate high performance across a range of applications, but their behavior is governed by a distinct set of operational characteristics. To leverage their full capabilities and ensure predictable outcomes, it is essential to understand and adapt to these unique prompting requirements.

The template tango: Unicode characters and special tokens

Here's where the V series gets properly weird. While the R series mostly ignores formatting niceties, V-series models are extremely particular about their chat templates – and they use Unicode characters that'll make you question your sanity.

A **chat template** is the deterministic formatting layer that turns your structured messages `=[...]` into the exact byte sequence the model was trained to see. It inserts the model's special markers (begin/end-of-sentence, role tags, turn separators), handles mode switches (e.g., V-series `<think>` versus `</think>`), and preserves required Unicode tokens (full-width ｜, low block ▁).

Using the official template keeps tokenization stable and quality high; hand-rolling strings (or mixing ASCII look-alikes) is brittle and can measurably degrade performance. In practice, let your provider SDK or transformer's `tokenizer.apply_chat_template(...)` build the prompt, merge into one system message, and ensure assistant turns end with `<｜end▁of▁sentence｜>` so decoding stops cleanly.

Consider, for example, the following prompt template, as used when the thinking mode is on and for a single-turn prompt.

```
<｜begin▁of▁sentence｜>{system}<｜User｜>{query}<｜Assistant｜><think>
```

The characters in this template are not standard ASCII. The vertical bars (｜) are full-width Unicode characters (U+FF5C), and what appears to be an underscore is a special block character (U+2581). Using the incorrect, visually similar ASCII equivalents (|, _) will result in tokenization mismatches and significantly degrade model performance. This distinction is crucial: though visually similar, the characters are functionally distinct to the model's tokenizer.

Do I need to hand-roll these weird characters?

Usually, no. When you call the V series or R series through a chat API (OpenRouter, provider SDKs, etc.), the server applies the model's chat template for you. You pass structured `messages=[...]` and (for V3.1) optionally a *reasoning/think mode* flag; the provider builds the correct prompt string with the full-width bars (｜, U+FF5C) and the `SentencePiece` low block (▁, U+2581) so you don't accidentally swap them for the ASCII look-alikes.

If you're running locally with Hugging Face Transformers, always use `tokenizer.apply_chat_template(...)` (and select `thinking=True/False` for V3.1) rather than concatenating strings yourself. This avoids subtle tokenization mismatches that can measurably hurt quality.

You can follow these V-series template rules while crafting our prompt templates (if you insist on setting these up manually):

- Use the tokenizer's `apply_chat_template()` method – don't try to hand-craft this.
- Always close assistant responses with `<｜end▁of▁sentence｜>` or risk infinite generation.
- Have exactly one system message at the start (merging multiple system prompts degrades performance).

That's how to speak to V series; now let's manage how it speaks back – often with a little too much Markdown.

The formatting fiesta: When Markdown goes wild

V-series models, especially V3, have some quirks in terms of what they output.

Here is what you get by default:

```
"""
*Really* interesting point here.

**Another** observation.

A single sentence paragraph.

Yet *another* single sentence.

**Bold** conclusion with *emphasis*.
"""

# What you probably wanted:
"""
Here's an interesting point that flows naturally into the next thought.
The observation connects seamlessly with the previous context, creating
a cohesive narrative that doesn't feel like a telegram from 1952.

The conclusion emphasizes key points without resorting to typographical
fireworks every other word.
"""
```

The fix? Be explicit about formatting preferences in your prompt:

```
system_prompt = """
Write in flowing, connected paragraphs. Avoid:
- Single-sentence paragraphs unless for emphasis
- Excessive use of *italics* or **bold** formatting
- Breaking thoughts into choppy segments
"""
```

eg7.py https://github.com/PacktPublishing/DeepSeek-in-Practice/blob/main/Chapter03/eg7.py provides a compact A/B harness that isolates formatting as the only variable in a generation: it sends the identical topic prompt to the same DeepSeek V3 model twice – first with no style guidance, then with a short, system-level style spec – and prints the results back to back. Because the content, model, and topic are held constant, any differences are attributable to the role and specificity of the instruction, making the effect of a style policy immediately visible.

The constraints are phrased as crisp, testable rules rather than vague adjectives, and putting them in the system message applies them globally, which V3 tends to follow more reliably. The file even includes a captured transcript that highlights the markdown-heavy baseline versus smoother, connected prose, and you can swap the spec to test house styles like **no lists**, **two paragraphs max**, or **executive tone**.

The practical takeaway: Treat formatting as a controllable constraint you set up front, not a messy cleanup step after generation.

Now that the prose isn't shouting, make sure the model can actually read it. The next failure mode is invisible: tiny default context windows and silent truncation.

The context window confusion

V-series models advertise massive context windows (163k+ tokens), but there's a catch. The default configuration often shows 8k tokens, and many inference frameworks will silently truncate at that limit unless you explicitly set max_model_len like this:

```
# Wrong (silently truncates at 8k):
model = load_model("deepseek-v3")

# Right:
model = load_model("deepseek-v3", max_model_len=65536)
```

Pro tip: V series uses **Multi-Head Latent Attention** (**MLA**) to compress the KV-cache for efficient long-context inference. Independent of MLA, transformers tend to show a U-shaped positional bias in long prompts (*lost in the middle*), so put your most critical instructions at the beginning and end – don't bury them mid-prompt.

Why do most runtimes cap V series to ~8k by default when the model advertises 100k+? Because *context length* is a budget, not a mandate. Long inputs are expensive in three ways:

- Prefill latency grows roughly linearly with input length, so a 50–100k-token prompt can dominate end-to-end time even for short answers.
- The KV cache grows linearly with length and eats GPU memory, which lowers throughput and hurts concurrency.
- Tail-latency or timeout risk rises, especially in shared clusters. DeepSeek's MLA makes this cheaper by aggressively compressing the KV cache (a reported ~93% reduction), but it doesn't make the context length free – the cache still scales with L.

Providers and frameworks, therefore, ship conservative limits to keep fleets stable; if you actually need more, you must opt in by raising `max_model_len`, ideally with profiling to verify you aren't blowing up latency or capacity.

Should you widen the window at all?

Only when those extra tokens are doing real work. More tokens does not mean better reasoning. A language model exhibits a U-shaped positional bias on long prompts (*lost in the middle*). The start and end of the prompt get disproportionately more attention. Stuffing 60k of undigested text can therefore hurt fidelity. Instead, you should opt for retrieval and summarization and keep instructions tight; expand the window when you truly must preserve long spans verbatim (contracts, long logs, multi-file code diffs) or sustain very long dialogues.

Pragmatically, ablate prompt length, measure accuracy versus latency/cost, and keep the smallest window that meets your quality bar.

With the window sized correctly and key instructions placed up front and at the end, you're ready to use what the V series adds beyond raw reasoning.

It's time to flip on the extras: FIM, native tool calls, and guaranteed JSON.

Hidden superpowers: Features the R series doesn't have

While the R series focuses on reasoning, the V series picked up some tricks along the way:

- **Fill-in-the-Middle (FIM)**: FIM lets the model generate the missing middle between a given prefix and suffix, so you can edit code in-place rather than just append continuations. Here, *hole* simply means the placeholder middle span – the `<|fim_hole|>` region the model fills between the fixed prefix and suffix, leaving the surrounding code unchanged.

```
prompt = """<|fim_begin|>
def calculate_average(numbers):
<|fim_hole|>
    return sum(numbers) / len(numbers)
<|fim_end|>"""
# V-series will generate the missing validation logic
```

  This prompt marks three regions: a prefix before the hole (the function signature), the hole where code should be produced, and a suffix after the hole (the return line). Given those anchors, the model infers what belongs in the middle – typically, input checks or guard clauses – so you'll see it add validation such as handling empty lists, `None`, or non-numeric items before it returns the average. In other words, you're asking the model to surgically fill the missing body while preserving the surrounding context verbatim.

- **Native tool calling**: Native tool calling lets the model emit a structured function call (name + JSON args) instead of prose, so your runtime can execute a tool and feed the result back.

```
system = """## Tools
### Function: get_weather
Description: Get current weather
Parameters: {"location": "string"}
"""
# V-series will emit structured tool calls with special tokens
```

  The system prompt declares a callable tool, `get_weather`, and its expected parameter schema. When the user asks a weather question, the model won't answer in free text; it will produce a structured tool-call message (the schema varies by SDK) selecting `get_weather` with something like `{"location": "Delft"}`. Your application intercepts that call, runs the real tool, and returns the tool's output as a tool-result message, after which the model composes the final user-visible answer. The key point: the model chooses when to call the function and surfaces well-formed arguments rather than guessing a URL or scraping text.

- **Guaranteed JSON mode**: JSON-only/strict-JSON mode constrains decoding so the model returns syntactically valid JSON (and nothing else), which is ideal for programmatic consumption.

  ```
  system_prompt += "\n## Response Format\nReply with JSON object
  ONLY."
  # Forces valid JSON output without additional libraries
  ```

  The added `Response Format` instruction tells the model to emit a single top-level JSON object with no commentary, code fences, or trailing text. In practice, you'll pair this instruction with your client's JSON/structured-output setting (if available) to hard-enforce validity; together, they reliably yield clean JSON that downstream code can parse directly. If you also provide a minimal schema or example, you further reduce drift and get stable keys and types.

- **The reasoning residue**: Some V-series checkpoints occasionally surface internal *thinking* traces (e.g., `<think>…</think>`); these aren't needed for correctness and are usually best suppressed. V2.5 inherited some reasoning behaviors from R1, occasionally producing unwanted *thinking* outputs:

  ```
  User: What's 2+2?
  Assistant: <think>This is a simple arithmetic problem...</think>
  The answer is 4.
  ```

  In the example, the assistant exposes an internal thought block before stating `The answer is 4.` That trace is a vestige of inherited reasoning behavior rather than an intentional feature.

  In production, suppress it by instructing: `Do not include <think> tags or intermediate reasoning; return only the final answer`, and/or by post-filtering those tags from outputs. You still get the correct result, but without the verbose justification unless you explicitly request an audit trail.

  V3 mostly eliminated this, but you might still see verbose justifications when you just wanted the answer. Unlike the R series, where reasoning is intentional, V-series reasoning traces are vestigial – suppress them unless you specifically need the audit trail.

- **Temperature and sampling:** Lower is better. V series tends to have a narrower sampling *sweet spot*, so small temperature increases degrade format fidelity and factuality faster than with many other models. V-series models are more sensitive to temperature than most:

Model	Recommended Temp	Why
V series (general)	0.3	Higher temps quickly degrade coherence
V series (code)	0.0	Deterministic is best for code
V series (creative)	0.5 max	Even creative tasks suffer above 0.5

Table 3.3: Recommended temperatures for various V-series models

Compare this to OpenAI's GPT-4o, where 0.7-1.0 is common, or the R series, which likes 0.6. V-series models seem to have a narrower *sweet spot* before outputs get weird. For structured or high-precision tasks, keep the temperature low (e.g., ~0.15–0.35) and adjust `top_p` modestly if you need variety; this keeps outputs stable and reduces the risk of verbose justifications or JSON breakage. If you later include a config snippet, you can note that the chosen values aim for near-deterministic decoding with just enough stochasticity to avoid repetition, and that raising the temperature should be done cautiously and incrementally.

Here is a quick recap of the different capabilities of the V series and R series of DeepSeek.

Aspect	V series	R series
System prompts	Supports one, very beginning	Mostly ignored (except R1-0528)
Formatting requirements	Extremely strict Unicode template	Flexible, user prompt only
Default behavior	Conversational, may ramble	Reasoning first, then answer
Temperature sweet spot	0.0-0.3	0.6
Special features	FIM, native tools, JSON mode	Internal CoT reasoning
Identity issues	May claim to be ChatGPT	Knows what it is
Context window	163k+ (must configure)	128k (works out of the box)

Table 3.4: Feature comparison between V-series and R-series DeepSeek models

The V-series models are powerful conversational agents that serve as a counterpart to the reasoning-focused R series.

Effective use of V-series models hinges on precise control over the prompt structure. This includes strict adherence to their specific chat template, which utilizes non-standard Unicode characters, and explicit configuration of parameters like `max_model_len` to enable their full context window.

Furthermore, developers must be prepared to manage the model's distinct formatting tendencies and temperature sensitivity to ensure consistent and predictable outputs.

With the rails in place, you're ready for the rare derailment. The next section maps symptoms to causes so you can correct course in a single pass.

Troubleshooting

Even the best-laid prompts can go sideways with DeepSeek. Here's your field guide to the most common issues and their fixes – think of it as your emergency toolkit for when the model decides to be... creative.

Here are some of the common issues you can troubleshoot with easy fixes:

- **When R1 forgets to think:**
  - **Symptom**: R1 jumps straight to an answer without its signature reasoning phase, producing shallow or incorrect results.
  - **Fix**: Force the thinking process by prepending the expected token:

```
# Nuclear option - literally start their response for them
messages.append({
    "role": "assistant",
    "content": "<think>\n"
})
# Then continue with normal generation
```

Here, `messages` is the same chat-history array you pass to your completion call. You append a synthetic assistant turn with content `"<think>\n"` as the final item in that array immediately before you invoke the model. Because the latest turn is from the assistant, the model treats it as the start of its own reply and continues generating right after `<think>`, which reliably kicks off a reasoning block. Don't add another user turn after this prefill. If you surface outputs to end users, strip the `<think>…</think>` section (or use your provider's option to hide reasoning) so they only see the final answer.

This technique effectively preconditions the model's generation, ensuring that its internal reasoning process is initiated before it attempts to formulate a direct answer. The successful application of this method is confirmed by the presence of a reasoning trace in the model's output preceding the final answer.

- **The multilingual mystery tour**:
    - **Symptom**: Your English prompt suddenly gets a response peppered with Chinese characters, especially during complex reasoning. Here's an example:

    ```
    The solution involves 计算 the derivative...
    ```

    - **Fix**: Add explicit language constraints to your user prompt:

    ```
    prompt += "\nRespond ONLY in English. Do not use any Chinese
    characters."
    ```

    Why does this happen? DeepSeek was trained on multilingual data with a strong Chinese presence. Under cognitive load, it sometimes reverts to its "native" language. It's like how bilingual speakers might switch languages when doing mental math. Note that this might not actually matter too much in terms of the final result or response you get back, though, if you are an English speaker, it might harm your ability to understand the reasoning trace.

- **Repetition loops, when DeepSeek gets stuck**:
    - **Symptom**: The model outputs the same phrase or pattern repeatedly:

    ```
    Therefore... Therefore... Therefore... Therefore...
    ```

    - **Fix cocktail**: You can follow these steps to fix repetitions. Add these extra config details when you are setting up your model to respond.

        1. Raise temperature slightly (if below 0.5): `temperature=0.6`.
        2. Add repetition penalty: `frequency_penalty=0.3`.
        3. Set reasonable `max_tokens`: Don't let it ramble indefinitely.
        4. Use `top_p` sampling: `top_p=0.95` helps avoid local optima.

    Repetition usually means the model is stuck in a probability valley. You need just enough randomness to climb out without going full chaos mode.

- **Majority voting**: When in doubt, democracy. For critical tasks where accuracy matters more than speed, use DeepSeek's own benchmarking strategy:

```
from collections import Counter

def get_best_answer(prompt, n_samples=5):
    responses = []
    for _ in range(n_samples):
```

```
        response = client.chat.completions.create(
            model="deepseek-r1",
            messages=[{"role": "user", "content": prompt}],
            temperature=0.6
        )
        responses.append(extract_answer(response))

    # Return most common answer
    return Counter(responses).most_common(1)[0][0]
```

Where this code snippet lives: drop it in exactly where you currently make a single `chat.completions.create(...)` call – your inference layer (API handler, job, or eval harness). Instead of one call, you run `n_samples` independent calls with a non-zero temperature (e.g., 0.4–0.8) to create diversity, use `extract_answer(...)` to normalize each result (strip reasoning, trim whitespace, canonicalize JSON, or pull the value after `Final Answer:`), and then return the plurality winner via `Counter(...).most_common(1)[0][0]`.

The loop in `get_best_answer(...)` does precisely that: collects `n_samples` answers, collapses them to comparable strings, and picks the most frequent. If two answers tie, Python's `Counter` breaks ties by first-seen; in production, you may re-sample, raise `n_samples`, or apply a deterministic tie-breaker (e.g., shortest valid JSON or a schema validator score).

Expect latency and cost to scale roughly linearly with `n_samples`; to keep the wall-clock low, run the calls in parallel. Use this pattern for high-stakes queries where accuracy matters more than speed; if errors are systematic rather than random, fix the prompt/constraints first before relying on voting.

This isn't just paranoia – DeepSeek's own team used 64-sample majority voting (`https://arxiv.org/pdf/2501.12948`) for their benchmarks. For production, 3–5 samples usually suffice unless you're doing competitive mathematics.

- **Format-specific gotchas**: You may encounter some output related discrepancies with DeepSeek. Let's talk about them:
    - **JSON mode dies silently**: In some cases, when using JSON mode with very long or complex prompts, the API may return an empty response without an error. This can happen when the model struggles to generate a valid JSON object that fits within internal processing limits. The most reliable solution is to reduce the prompt length or to reset the conversation history, retrying the request with only

the most recent message. The specifics of how you do this will depend on your use case or application, but the basic principle looks like this:

```
# Symptom: Empty response with response_format active
# Fix: Shorten prompt or reset conversation
if not response.content:
    # Start fresh conversation with shorter context
    messages = [messages[-1]]  # Keep only latest
```

- **Truncated outputs**: A common failure mode is receiving a syntactically incomplete JSON object because the generation was stopped by the `max_tokens` limit. The model does not account for this limit when generating its response, so it may be cut off abruptly. To prevent this, calculate an estimated response size and set `max_tokens` with a generous buffer, such as 20% larger than your estimate.

```
# Symptom: {"result": "answer", "confidence": 0.9
# Fix: Always pad max_tokens by 20%
estimated_tokens = len(prompt.split()) * 2
max_tokens = int(estimated_tokens * 1.2)
```

When DeepSeek misbehaves, run these checks in order:

1. **Temperature**: If the temperature is too low (≈0.3–0.5 or below), the model can repeat itself or collapse to generic text; if it's too high (≈0.7 or above), outputs become erratic. For most production prompts, start in the 0.3–0.6 band and move deliberately.
2. **Template integrity**: The V series requires its exact chat template and the EOS marker `< | end_of_sentence | >`. A missing marker or ASCII look-alike characters will degrade quality or cause run-on decoding. Build prompts with the official template function rather than hand-concatenating strings.
3. **Token limits**: Mid-thought cut-offs usually mean `max_tokens` is too small; silent input truncation means your configured `max_model_len` is below the prompt length. Increase `max_tokens`, set `max_model_len` explicitly, and define a stop sequence so answers end cleanly.
4. **Language control**: If you need English-only output, state that explicitly at the top of the prompt and avoid multilingual examples in context. Mixed-language cues in few-shot or in-context invite leakage.

5. **Reasoning engagement:** If R1 skips the hidden reasoning phase, prefill the assistant with `<think>\n` or instruct: `Think inside <think>…</think>`; give the final answer after `</think>`. Strip or hide the reasoning before surfacing results to end users.
6. **Context discipline:** Very long contexts (≈100k+ tokens) reduce fidelity. Summarize or retrieve only what is necessary, and place critical instructions at the beginning and end rather than burying them in the middle.
7. **If these checks don't stabilize outputs, simplify the task:** restate the goal, tighten the schema, and only then consider ensembling (e.g., majority vote).

A core principle to remember when debugging DeepSeek models is their high sensitivity to initial conditions. Unlike some other models, minor variations in prompt phrasing or a small adjustment to hyperparameters like `temperature` (e.g., by 0.1) can significantly alter the model's output trajectory. Therefore, iterative, small-scale changes should be the primary method for resolving unexpected behavior.

A crucial diagnostic technique is to maintain a *known-good* baseline prompt. When encountering issues with a new or complex prompt, running this baseline allows you to determine whether the unexpected behavior stems from the prompt itself or a potential transient issue with the model or inference environment. This practice serves as a fundamental step in isolating the source of an error, analogous to a unit test for model behavior.

With a stable debug loop and a known-good baseline in place, it's time to shift from firefighting to prevention: translating what you already have. The next section maps common patterns from GPT-5/Claude into DeepSeek-friendly idioms – what to keep, what to change, and what to drop.

Prompt migration guide

Moving your prompts from OpenAI's GPT-4o, Claude, or other models to DeepSeek? What follows are some suggestions and ideas for how to migrate your prompts. These are intended as illustrative suggestions to inspire you rather than hard-and-fast rules.

Let's say you have system prompts from other models:

```
messages = [
    {"role": "system", "content": "You are a helpful Python expert..."},
    {"role": "user", "content": "Explain decorators"}
]
```

- Then, for the DeepSeek R series, the same prompt could be written as follows:

```
messages = [
    {"role": "user",
    "content": "You are a helpful Python expert. Explain
decorators."}
]
```

- For the DeepSeek V series, you need to specify minimal prompts:

```
# V-series accepts system prompts, but keep it minimal
messages = [
    {"role": "system", "content": "Python expert assistant"},
    {"role": "user", "content": "Explain decorators"}
]
```

Migration note: Merge your system instructions into the user prompt for the R series. For the V series, drastically simplify – think *name tag*, not *biography*.

Consider some few-shot examples from other models:

```
prompt = """
Example 1: Input: "happy" → Output: "positive"
Example 2: Input: "sad" → Output: "negative"
Example 3: Input: "angry" → Output: "negative"

Now classify: "excited"
"""
```

- For DeepSeek (both series), these could be specified as follows:

```
prompt = """
Task: Classify the sentiment as 'positive' or 'negative'.
Expected format: Return only the classification word.

Classify: "excited"
"""
```

Migration note: Replace examples with clear task descriptions and format specifications. Your accuracy might actually improve – DeepSeek's RL training means it often knows better than your examples.

If you have a high temperature for creativity, your settings may look as follows in other models:

```
# OpenAI's GPT-4o creative writing
temperature = 0.9
top_p = 0.95
```

- For DeepSeek V and R series, you can specify these settings as follows:

```
# V-series creative tasks
temperature = 0.5  # Max recommended
top_p = 0.9

# R-series creative tasks (not recommended, but if you must)
temperature = 0.6
# Add explicit creativity instruction instead
prompt += "\nBe creative and explore unconventional ideas."
```

Migration note: DeepSeek gets *drunk* at high temperatures faster than other models. Compensate with explicit creativity instructions rather than randomness.

If you have very long prompts (>50k tokens) for other models, you can place your prompt as is:

```
# Just dump everything
context = load_100k_token_document()
prompt = f"Analyze this document:\n{context}\n\nQuestion: {query}"
```

- But for DeepSeek, you need to position your prompt smartly:

```
# Structure and position strategically
prompt = f"""
<context>
{context[:30000]}  # Less critical info
</context>

<critical_context>
```

```
{context[30000:]}  # Most important parts
</critical_context>

<task>
{query}
</task>
"""

# Don't forget to set max length for V-series!
model_kwargs = {"max_model_len": 65536}
```

Migration note: DeepSeek's attention mechanism (especially V series MLA) weighs later tokens more heavily. Put critical info near the end.

If you have CoT prompting, the prompt for other models may take the following format:

```
prompt = "Let's approach this step-by-step:\n" + problem
```

- For the DeepSeek R series, you may simply state the problem for the R1 series:

```
# Just state the problem
prompt = problem
# R1 already thinks step-by-step internally
```

- But for the DeepSeek V series, you may specify that it needs to follow the CoT approach:

```
# V-series benefits from CoT prompting
prompt = "Think through this systematically:\n" + problem
```

Migration note: R series has CoT built in; adding it is like wearing two pairs of glasses. V series still benefits from explicit reasoning requests.

If you have complex role-playing, specify the roles for other models:

```
system = """You are Shakespeare, the famous playwright.
You speak in iambic pentameter, use Elizabethan English,
make references to your plays..."""
```

For DeepSeek, you need to specify what you expect in the response:

```
# Simplify to output requirements
prompt = """Write a response in Shakespearean style:
- Use iambic pentameter where possible
- Include elizabethan vocabulary
- Reference classic plays if relevant

User query: {query}"""
```

Migration note: Focus on output characteristics rather than identity. DeepSeek performs better with "write like Shakespeare" than "you are Shakespeare."

If you have JSON generation without native support for other models, you can specify the requirement as follows:

```
prompt = "Return a JSON object with name and age fields."
```

- For DeepSeek (Pre-0528) models, you would need to specify the prompt, format, and an example to tell it how to process it:

  ```
  prompt = """Return ONLY a valid JSON object.
  Format: {"name": "string", "age": number}
  Example: {"name": "Alice", "age": 30}

  Extract from: {text}"""
  ```

- For DeepSeek (Post-0528), you need to specify the format and provide a clear specification in the prompt:

  ```
  # Use native JSON mode
  response_format = {"type": "json_object"}
  # But STILL mention JSON in the prompt!
  prompt = "Extract as JSON: {text}"
  ```

Migration note: Even with native JSON support, DeepSeek likes verbal confirmation. It's like a safety mechanism that needs both a key and a button.

Before you migrate, ask yourself the following:

- Am I using few-shot examples? → Convert to task descriptions.
- Is my temperature > 0.7? → Lower it and add creativity instructions.
- Do I have system prompts? → Merge into user prompt (R1) or simplify (V3).
- Am I prompting for CoT? → Remove for R1; keep for V3.
- Is my prompt > 50k tokens? → Structure it with critical info last.
- Do I use role-playing? → Convert to output specifications.

When in doubt, simplify. DeepSeek models – especially R-series models – are like expert consultants. Give them the problem clearly and get out of their way. Your elaborate prompting strategies from other models might actually be holding DeepSeek back.

Remember: Migration isn't just find-and-replace. It's an opportunity to rethink whether all that prompt engineering complexity was really necessary. Often, with DeepSeek, it isn't.

Summary

DeepSeek prompting demands a mindset shift: stop scripting how to think and instead state the objective crisply, the constraints explicitly, and the output schema unambiguously – then trust the model's internal reasoning. Techniques that help elsewhere can backfire here: few-shot demonstrations often reduce accuracy, whereas clear task statements with tight schemas consistently perform better.

Operationally, put instructions in the right place and respect the wiring. R-series models largely ignore the system role, so keep guidance in the user message; V-series models tolerate a single, high-level system prompt for global constraints. Follow each family's native chat template exactly (including the non-standard Unicode separators), and tune sampling parameters deliberately: both lines have relatively narrow *good* bands for temperature and top-p. Internalize these habits and you'll move from merely using DeepSeek to shipping reliable, production-grade systems – after a little unlearning, you'll gain access to a markedly stronger class of automated reasoning.

In the next chapter, we will discuss some use cases where DeepSeek can be applied.

Part 2

Using DeepSeek

In the second part of this book, we move from theory to practice with real-world case studies that show how DeepSeek is already driving innovation across industries. Next, we get hands-on with a practical build: an API powered by DeepSeek. You'll follow the end-to-end process - designing the application logic, running it locally, and deploying it to Amazon Web Services. In the final chapter of this part, we introduce agents and demonstrate how to build robust agents backed by DeepSeek models.

By the end of this part, you'll be equipped to solve common business problems with DeepSeek, whether you're creating a simple web application or a full-fledged agentic system.

This part of the book includes the following chapters:

Stay tuned

To keep up with the latest developments in the fields of Generative AI and LLMs, subscribe to our weekly newsletter, *AI_Distilled*, at `https://packt.link/8Oz6Y`.

Join our communities on Discord and Reddit

Have questions about the book or want to contribute to discussions on Generative AI and LLMs?

Join our Discord server at `https://packt.link/4Bbd9` and our Reddit channel at `https://packt.link/wcYOQ` to connect, share, and collaborate with like-minded enthusiasts.

4

Using DeepSeek: Case Studies

By now, you have a fair idea of how DeepSeek functions, its internals, and its role in the global **large language model (LLM)** landscape. In this chapter, we will examine how DeepSeek is already transforming industries with real-world applications. Major players such as Microsoft, GitHub, and Fortune 500 companies are adopting LLMs such as DeepSeek to boost productivity, cut costs, and drive innovation. Through our own experience building production-ready applications, we've seen firsthand how DeepSeek enhances development velocity, improves code quality, and empowers better strategic decisions.

Some of the notable use cases where DeepSeek can be employed are automating trading strategies in financial firms, accelerating contract analysis for the legal teams, and modernizing legacy systems for developers. In this chapter, we will focus on the document understanding and document extraction use case.

We'll examine these comprehensive case studies to demonstrate DeepSeek's practical applications and how you can apply the structured approach to implement AI-assisted workflows. The Cursor IDE is our choice of platform to configure and use DeepSeek. However, the techniques we cover apply to any platform that supports DeepSeek, from traditional IDEs to cloud tools or local interfaces. If you don't know where to get started yet, we have created an *Appendix* for you that briefs you about various ways you can use DeepSeek.

For the case studies in this chapter, we follow a systematic methodology by defining clear problem statements, crafting effective prompts, evaluating responses against both qualitative and quantitative metrics, and iterating to achieve production-quality results.

In this chapter, we will cover the following main topics:

- Benchmarking tools setup and prompt design
- Use case study: Document understanding
- Use case study: Financial document understanding and benchmarking

Technical requirements

In this chapter, we demonstrate DeepSeek's capabilities using the Cursor IDE, an AI-powered development environment tightly integrated with DeepSeek's models. You'll first need access to DeepSeek's API. Start by creating an account at `https://platform.deepseek.com/` and generating your API keys. Once you have your credentials, it's worth verifying your access with a simple test call to ensure everything is configured correctly:

```
curl -X POST "https://api.deepseek.com/v1/chat/completions" \
-H "Authorization: Bearer YOUR_API_KEY" \
-H "Content-Type: application/json" \
-d '{
  "model": "deepseek-reasoner",
  "messages": [{"role": "user", "content": "Hello, DeepSeek!"}]
}'
```

With API access confirmed, we can proceed to establish the development environment that will serve as our laboratory for exploring DeepSeek's practical applications.

Setting up your development environment

To set up an effective AI-assisted development environment, we will use the following:

- Python 3.11+ for backend AI and data tasks.
- Docker Desktop (`https://docs.docker.com/desktop/`).
- Git for version control (`https://git-scm.com/`).
- Node.js 18+.
- The Cursor IDE, which can be downloaded from `https://cursor.com/`.

Configuring DeepSeek in the Cursor IDE

Configuring DeepSeek with the Cursor IDE is a straightforward process. To integrate DeepSeek with Cursor, you need to follow these steps to get started:

1. Access the Cursor model configuration through the **Settings** menu:

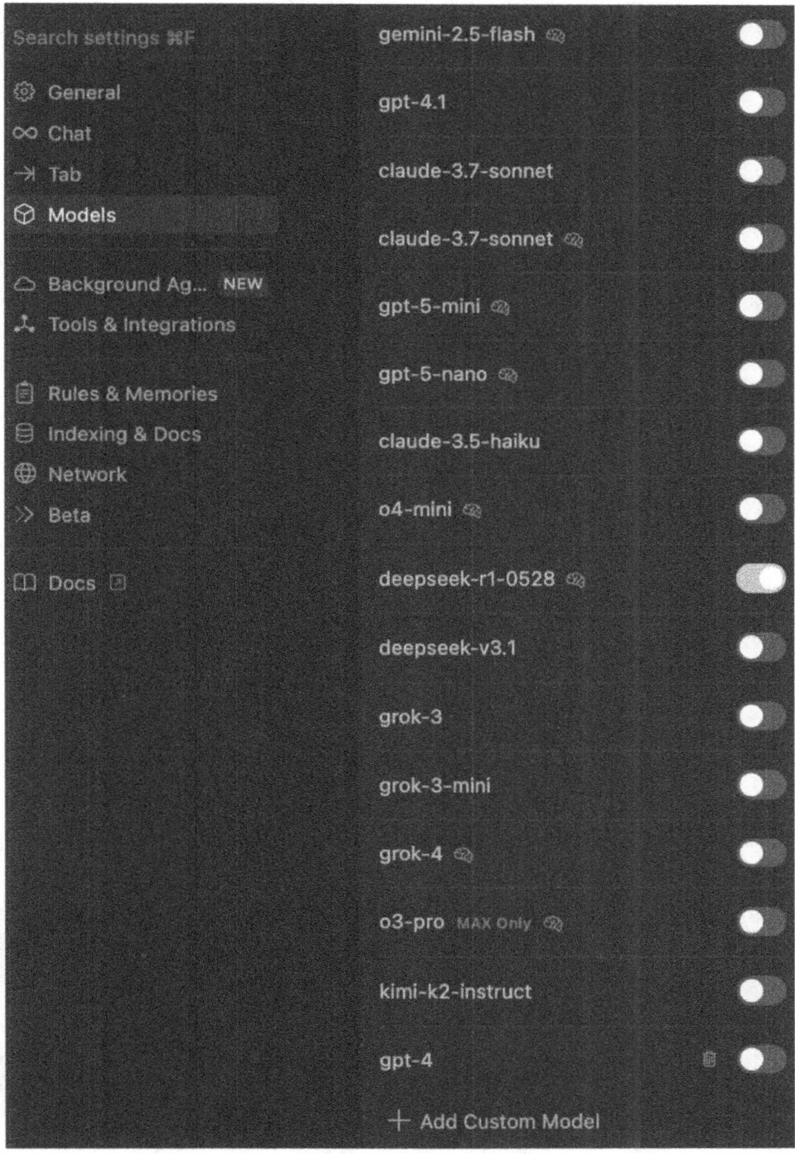

Figure 4.1: Cursor IDE DeepSeek-R1 model selection interface

- On macOS, you'll find this under **Cursor > Settings.**
- If you are a Windows or a Linux user, you can locate it under **File > Settings.**

Within the **Settings** interface, the **Models** section in the left sidebar contains all the options for managing AI model integrations.

2. The Cursor IDE comes with built-in support for DeepSeek models, which you can enable by scrolling through the available model list and selecting **deepseek-r1-0528**.
3. Once enabled, the model appears in your available options, ready for configuration with your specific API credentials.
4. The configuration process requires entering your DeepSeek API credentials along with the appropriate connection settings.
5. You'll specify **deepseek-r1-0528** as the model name, provide your API key from the DeepSeek platform, set the base URL to `https://api.deepseek.com/v1`, and configure the provider as **OpenAI Compatible** to ensure proper API communication protocols.
6. To verify that your integration works correctly, open a new file in Cursor and invoke the AI command palette using `Cmd + K` on macOS or `Ctrl + K` on Windows and Linux.
7. Select **DeepSeek-R1** from the model dropdown and test with a substantive prompt such as `Explain the difference between microservices and monolithic architecture`. A successful response confirms that your development environment is ready for the advanced use cases we'll explore.

For more details on using DeepSeek with Cursor and other options, please refer to the *Appendix*.

Organizing your development workspace

A clear workspace keeps you productive and organized as projects grow more complex. For this chapter, set up a `Chapter04` folder with the required subfolders. For example, we have set up our folders to be called `brainstorming-ideation`, `document-analysis`, and `code-generation`, as follows:

```
# Navigate to the DeepSeek-in-Practice directory
cd /Users/<user-id>/workplace/DeepSeek-in-Practice-main

# Create Chapter04 directory and subdirectories
mkdir Chapter04
cd Chapter04
mkdir 01-brainstorming-ideation
```

```
mkdir 02-document-analysis
mkdir 03-code-generation

# Initialize Git repository for version control
git init
```

Each subdirectory will contain the complete artifacts from its respective case study, including source code, configuration files, documentation, and any supporting resources.

Configuration management

Proper credential management forms the foundation of any professional development workflow, particularly when integrating with external AI services. Create a dedicated environment configuration file in your `Chapter04` directory to store sensitive information securely:

```
# Navigate to Chapter04 directory
cd /Users/<user-id>/workplace/ DeepSeek-in-Practice-main/Chapter04

# Create .env file
cat > .env << EOF
# DeepSeek Configuration
DEEPSEEK_API_KEY=your_api_key_here
DEEPSEEK_BASE_URL=https://api.deepseek.com/v1

# Database Configuration (we'll use these later)
DATABASE_URL=sqlite:///./development.db

# API Configuration
API_HOST=localhost
API_PORT=8000

# Logging
LOG_LEVEL=INFO
EOF
```

This configuration approach separates sensitive credentials from source code, enabling secure sharing and deployment practices. Remember that environment files should never be committed to version control systems; always add `.env` to your `.gitignore` file immediately after creation to prevent accidental exposure of sensitive information.

All benchmarking scripts, test documents, and evaluation frameworks are available in our GitHub repository for readers interested in reproducing the results or conducting their own experiments: `https://github.com/PacktPublishing/DeepSeek-in-Practice/tree/main/Chapter04/document-understanding`.

The repository includes the following:

- Ground truth datasets for accuracy measurement.
- Automated benchmarking comparison tool.
- Complete test scripts for all three tools:
    - **DeepSeek-R1**: LLM-based semantic extraction via direct API calls `https://github.com/PacktPublishing/DeepSeek-in-Practice/blob/main/Chapter04/document-understanding/test_deepseek_parsing.py`.
    - **Docling (IBM Research)**: Document structure analysis and table recognition `https://github.com/PacktPublishing/DeepSeek-in-Practice/blob/main/Chapter04/document-understanding/test_docling_parsing.py`.
    - **MarkItDown (Microsoft):** LLM-optimized document preprocessing `https://github.com/PacktPublishing/DeepSeek-in-Practice/blob/main/Chapter04/document-understanding/test_markitdown_parsing.py`.
- Detailed evaluation framework documentation.

Benchmarking tools setup and prompt design

For the quantitative evaluation and benchmarking exercises in this chapter, we will test DeepSeek-R1 against specialized document parsing tools to provide comprehensive performance comparisons. We've created automated testing scripts that measure accuracy, processing time, and cost metrics across different approaches.

These are the tools used for benchmarking:

- **DeepSeek-R1**: LLM-based semantic extraction via direct API calls.
- **Docling (IBM Research)**: Document structure analysis and table recognition.
- **MarkItDown (Microsoft)**: LLM-optimized document preprocessing.

To set up the benchmarking environment:

```
# Install benchmarking dependencies
pip install requests tabulate pandas

# Optional: Install comparison tools
pip install docling markitdown
```

Before we begin with our case studies, we will share a few quick tips on how to design prompts for our case studies:

- **Provide rich business context**: Frame prompts with clear details about the business environment, constraints, aspirations, and objectives. Avoid generic queries such as *help us innovate.*
- **Focus on actionable outcomes**: Structure prompts to elicit feasible, strategic outputs rather than abstract ideas.
- **Leverage DeepSeek-R1's reasoning strengths**: Use structured prompts that require systematic analysis.
- **Provide clear and detailed information**: Include industry data, competitive insights, and clear success metrics. Present specific challenges with defined parameters and timeline constraints.
- **Encourage trade-off evaluation**: DeepSeek-R1 performs best when tasked with problems involving multiple variables, risks, and strategic trade-offs – ideal for generating comprehensive innovation strategies.

All company names, scenarios, and code examples in this chapter are fictional and created specifically for educational purposes. Any resemblance to real companies, systems, or proprietary code is purely coincidental. The legacy code examples are based on common patterns found in legacy systems but do not represent any actual production systems. All code is original content created for this book and is provided under open source principles for educational use.

Content source clarification: This chapter contains actual prompts and responses from our DeepSeek-R1 interactions, clearly marked with formatting indicators. Any potential follow-up or enhanced prompting suggestions are illustrative examples of how iterative prompting could work, not actual executed prompts. All real DeepSeek-R1 interactions are explicitly labeled as such.

Let's now begin with our case study in document understanding.

Use case study: Document understanding

CloudTech Solutions, a growing enterprise software company, faces a critical challenge in implementing a modern serverless architecture. Their development team has been tasked with migrating from a legacy monolithic API server to Amazon API Gateway and AWS Lambda functions to support 10,000+ requests per second across 15+ geographic regions while maintaining 99.99% uptime.

The company's current situation reflects a common enterprise challenge: they have comprehensive technical documentation (a 45-page Amazon API Gateway integration guide) but need to quickly extract actionable implementation strategies from complex technical specifications. The development team must analyze this documentation to create a structured implementation plan that addresses architecture design, security requirements, performance optimization, and operational procedures.

The business impact is significant. CloudTech Solutions must complete this migration within a tight timeline to meet growing customer demands and reduce infrastructure costs by 40%. The challenge extends beyond just understanding the documentation – they need to transform high-level architectural concepts into specific technical decisions, implementation priorities, and production-ready code that their development team can immediately execute.

Our exploration of this document analysis challenge demonstrates how DeepSeek-R1 can process complex technical documentation and provide structured implementation guidance. This use case showcases the model's ability to extract key architectural components, prioritize implementation tasks, identify critical configuration decisions, and generate actionable technical requirements from comprehensive enterprise documentation.

Prompting DeepSeek

For technical document analysis tasks, DeepSeek-R1 requires structured prompts that clearly define the analysis objectives and expected deliverables. The key is providing comprehensive context about the document type, specific technical requirements to extract, and the format for actionable outputs. Unlike general document review, technical analysis prompts should focus on implementation-ready insights and structured decision frameworks.

When working with enterprise technical documentation, it's crucial to specify architectural considerations, implementation priorities, security requirements, and operational constraints. DeepSeek-R1's reasoning capabilities excel when asked to not just extract information, but also synthesize complex technical concepts into actionable implementation strategies that development teams can immediately execute.

Response evaluation

Let me demonstrate with CloudTech Solutions' Amazon API Gateway documentation analysis challenge using the actual prompt and response from our case study.

Note

The following analysis is based on a comprehensive 45-page Amazon API Gateway integration guide (source: `Chapter04/document-understanding/amazon_api_gateway_integration_guide.md`)

Here is our prompt to DeepSeek-R1 for the technical document analysis:

```
I need you to analyze this Amazon API Gateway Integration Guide and
provide a comprehensive implementation strategy. This is enterprise-
grade documentation that our development team needs to implement for a
production system handling 10,000+ requests per second.

Please provide:

1. **Architecture Summary**: Extract the key components and their
relationships from the document. What are the core services and how do
they interact?

2. **Implementation Priority Matrix**: Based on the document, what should
be implemented first, second, third? Consider dependencies, risk, and
business value.

3. **Critical Configuration Analysis**: Identify the most important
configuration decisions that could impact security, performance, or cost.
Extract specific values and settings.

4. **Code Generation Plan**: Which Lambda functions, API configurations,
and infrastructure components need to be created? Provide a structured
implementation plan.

5. **Security & Compliance Requirements**: Extract all security
requirements, authentication flows, and compliance considerations. How
should these be implemented?
```

```
6. **Production Readiness Assessment**: What monitoring, error handling,
and operational procedures are specified? Create a production deployment
checklist.

Focus on extracting actionable technical requirements that a development
team can immediately implement. Convert high-level concepts into specific
technical decisions.

[Attached: amazon_api_gateway_integration_guide.md - 45 pages of technical
documentation]
```

DeepSeek's response to this prompt is as follows:

```
Based on my comprehensive analysis of the 45-page Amazon API Gateway
Integration Guide, here's the structured implementation strategy for your
production system:

1. Architecture Summary
The system implements a serverless architecture using Amazon API Gateway
and Lambda functions with the following core components:
```

Core Services: - **API Gateway**: Fronts the entire system, handles routing, authentication, throttling, and request/response transformation - **Lambda Functions**: Serve as the backend for different services (User, Order, Payment, etc.) - **Data Stores**: DynamoDB (Users, Payments), RDS PostgreSQL (Orders), SQS (async processing), S3 (analytics) - **Authentication**: AWS Cognito for OAuth 2.0/OIDC, with multi-factor authentication - **Caching**: Redis (via ElastiCache) and CloudFront for CDN caching - **Monitoring**: CloudWatch, X-Ray, and custom metrics - **Security**: AWS WAF, security headers, and encryption at rest and in transit

System Interaction Flow:

```
Clients → CloudFront → AWS WAF → API Gateway → Lambda Authorizer (Cognito)
→ Lambda Functions (User, Order, Payment) → Databases (DynamoDB, RDS,
etc.)

Async flows: API Gateway → SQS → Async Lambda Processor
Monitoring: API Gateway and Lambda → CloudWatch logs and X-Ray traces
2. Implementation Priority Matrix
```

Priority	Component	Reason
1	Core Infrastructure	Set up VPC, IAM roles, security groups, and basic networking
2	Authentication & AuthZ	Without auth, no secure access. Cognito setup and Lambda Authorizer
3	User Service	Basic user management required for other services (e.g., orders)
4	Order Service	Core business functionality
5	Payment Service	Critical for transactions, but depends on User and Order
6	Async Processing	For non-critical background tasks
7	Monitoring & Logging	Essential for production, but can be built alongside
8	Caching & Optimization	Performance improvements after core functionality

3. Critical Configuration Analysis

Authentication Configuration: - Cognito User Pool: MFA required, password policy (12+ chars, mixed case, numbers, symbols) - JWT Token: Must include custom claims (tenant_id, role) for multi-tenancy - Lambda Authorizer: Must validate JWT and apply tenant-specific and role-based access control

API Gateway Configuration: - Use HTTP API for new services (cost-effective) and REST API for legacy compatibility - Stages: Development (throttling: 100 burst, 50 rate) and Production (5000 burst, 2000 rate) - Custom domains: `api.example.com` with TLS 1.2+ and ACM certificates

- Request/Response: Validation schemas for inputs, standardized response templates

Security Configuration: - WAF rules: SQL injection, XSS, rate limiting (100 req/min per IP), geo-blocking - Headers: Strict-Transport-Security, X-Content-Type-Options, X-Frame-Options - Encryption: KMS for DynamoDB, RDS, and S3; TLS 1.2+ for transit

Rate Limiting: - Global: 10,000 RPS (burst) in production - Per client: Usage plans (Free, Premium, Enterprise) with tiered limits

4. Code Generation Plan & Implementation Strategy

Lambda Functions (each as a separate service): - **User Service**: CRUD operations, profile management with DynamoDB integration - **Order Service**: Order lifecycle management with RDS PostgreSQL backend - **Payment Service**: Payment processing, refunds with secure tokenization - **Async Processor**: Handles SQS messages for background jobs and notifications

Infrastructure as Code (CloudFormation): - API Gateway (HTTP API and REST API configurations) - Lambda functions with environment variables, VPC config, and security layers - DynamoDB tables with KMS encryption and backup policies - RDS instance (PostgreSQL) with backup, multi-AZ, and read replicas - SQS queues (main and dead letter queues) - Cognito User Pool and Client with MFA configuration - WAF rules and association with API Gateway - CloudWatch Alarms, Dashboards, and X-Ray configuration

5. Security & Compliance Implementation

Authentication Flow:

Client Request → API Gateway → Lambda Authorizer → Cognito Validation → JWT Claims Extraction → Role-Based Access Control → Service Authorization

Compliance Requirements: - SOC2 Type II: Automated security controls and audit logging - PCI DSS: Secure payment processing with tokenization - GDPR: Data residency controls and user consent management - Multi-tenancy: Tenant isolation at database and application layers

6. Production Readiness Checklist

Monitoring & Observability: - CloudWatch metrics for API Gateway, Lambda, and database performance - X-Ray distributed tracing for request flow analysis - Structured logging with correlation IDs for debugging - Custom business metrics for SLA monitoring

Error Handling & Resilience: - Circuit breaker patterns for external service calls - Exponential backoff and retry logic for transient failures - Dead letter queues for failed message processing - Graceful degradation for non-critical service failures

```
Operational Procedures: - Blue/Green deployment using Lambda aliases
and weighted traffic - Automated rollback triggers based on error rate
thresholds - Capacity planning based on request patterns and growth
projections - Disaster recovery procedures with RTO/RPO targets
```

DeepSeek-R1 transformed a 45-page Amazon API Gateway specification into structured implementation guidance, demonstrating sophisticated technical analysis capabilities that enable development teams to execute complex enterprise projects efficiently.

Evaluation methodology for technical analysis

For technical document analysis, evaluation focuses on implementation accuracy and operational readiness:

- **Qualitative metrics:** Emphasize architectural understanding, implementation feasibility, and production readiness considerations critical for enterprise system development.
- **Quantitative metrics:** Measure technical specification completeness, configuration detail accuracy, and implementation artifact coverage.

To provide an objective, repeatable assessment of DeepSeek-R1's document analysis capabilities, we have developed a systematic evaluation framework that measures both qualitative understanding and quantitative completeness. This section explains our scoring methodology in detail, demonstrating how we assigned scores and performed analysis for the Amazon API Gateway case study.

Let's talk about this in detail:

1. Our evaluation process began with ground truth establishment, where we created the AmazonAPI Gateway integration guide spanning 45 pages and 1,743 lines as our source document containing specific architectural components, configuration values, and implementation requirements. This document served as the authoritative reference against which we measured DeepSeek-R1's analysis accuracy.
2. Before evaluating DeepSeek-R1's response, we manually cataloged all critical elements that a complete analysis should identify. This catalog included eight major serverless components, including API Gateway; Lambda functions for user, order, payment, and async processing services; DynamoDB; RDS PostgreSQL; Amazon Cognito; CloudWatch with X-Ray for monitoring; SQS for message queuing; and AWS WAF for security.

3. We also identified 23 specific configuration parameters, including throttling limits with burst rates of 5,000 for production and 100 for development; rate limits of 2,000 and 50, respectively; MFA requirements; password policy rules requiring 12 or more characters with mixed casing, numbers, and symbols; TLS version requirements of 1.2 or higher; rate limiting of 100 requests per minute per IP address; and custom domain settings.
4. Additionally, we cataloged four compliance requirements covering SOC2 Type II, PCI DSS, GDPR, and multi-tenancy isolation, along with six implementation deliverables encompassing CloudFormation templates, Lambda functions, IAM policies, monitoring dashboards, security configurations, and deployment procedures.
5. After establishing our ground truth, we performed manual comparison and scoring by evaluating DeepSeek-R1's response against our reference element by element. For each evaluation criterion, we counted how many expected elements were correctly identified, understood, and explained.

Our qualitative metrics employ a 1 to 10 scale, as follows:

- Scores of 9–10 indicate excellent performance with near-complete understanding and 90–100% of expected elements correctly identified and explained with appropriate context.
- Scores of 7–8 represent good performance with a strong understanding covering 70–89% of elements and only minor gaps in depth or specificity.
- Acceptable performance receives scores of 5–6, indicating adequate understanding with 50–69% coverage, but missing important details.
- Below average performance, scoring 3–4, demonstrates partial understanding with 30–49% coverage and significant gaps.
- Poor performance with scores of 1–2 shows minimal understanding, covering less than 30% of expected elements.

To demonstrate our scoring process concretely, we'll examine how we evaluated architecture comprehension, which received a score of 9 out of 10:

- DeepSeek-R1 correctly identified all eight major serverless components, including API Gateway, Lambda functions, DynamoDB, RDS, Cognito, CloudWatch with X-Ray, WAF, and SQS.
- The model accurately described the system interaction flow where clients connect through CloudFront, pass through WAF security filtering, reach API Gateway, undergo authentication via the Lambda authorizer, and finally, invoke appropriate Lambda functions that interact with databases.

- DeepSeek-R1 correctly explained the asynchronous processing path where API Gateway sends messages to SQS, which triggers the async Lambda processor, and properly identified the monitoring flow where services send data to CloudWatch logs and X-Ray traces.

We measured document understanding through several dimensions:

- For component relationships, DeepSeek-R1 demonstrated a clear understanding that API Gateway fronts the entire system and intelligently routes requests to appropriate Lambda functions based on service type, whether `User`, `Order`, or `Payment` services.
- Regarding integration patterns, the model correctly identified that Cognito handles initial authentication before the Lambda authorizer validates JWTs to enforce tenant isolation in the multi-tenant architecture.
- For data flow logic, DeepSeek-R1 understood the architectural decision that different services use different data stores, with DynamoDB serving `User` and `Payment` services due to their key-value access patterns, while RDS PostgreSQL serves the `Order` service, requiring relational data structures and complex queries. The score was not a perfect 10 due to one minor gap where the model did not explicitly mention the ElastiCache/Redis layer documented in the source material, although the caching strategy was discussed in a different section of the response.

Here is a qualitative analysis of DeepSeek's response.

Criteria	**Analysis**	**Score (1–10)**
Architecture comprehension	Correctly identified all major serverless components, their relationships, and interaction patterns. Demonstrated a clear understanding of API Gateway, Lambda, and supporting services integration.	9
Implementation practicality	Provided specific configuration values, security settings, and deployment parameters that development teams can directly implement without additional research.	9
Security awareness	Comprehensive coverage of authentication flows, compliance requirements (SOC2, PCI DSS), and security best practices with specific implementation guidance.	8
Production readiness	Addressed operational concerns, including monitoring, error handling, and disaster recovery procedures often overlooked in initial implementations.	8

Criteria	Analysis	Score (1–10)
Priority sequencing	Logical implementation ordering considering dependencies, risks, and business value with a clear rationale for each phase.	8

Table 4.1: Qualitative analysis of DeepSeek response

For quantitative assessment, we employ objective counting and percentage-based scoring using a straightforward formula where the score equals the number of elements correctly identified divided by the total expected elements, multiplied by 10, then rounded to the nearest whole number.

For example, correctly identifying all 23 parameters yields a perfect score of 10 out of 10, while identifying 20 out of 23 parameters produces a score of 9 out of 10, representing 87% accuracy.

We demonstrated this quantitative methodology through the configuration parameters evaluation, which scored 9 out of 10. We identified 23 specific configuration parameters in the source documentation and systematically checked whether DeepSeek-R1's response included each one.

The model successfully identified the following:

- Throttling burst limits of 100 for development and 5,000 for production.
- Throttling rate limits of 50 and 2,000, respectively.
- MFA requirement set to `ON`, password minimum length of 12 or more characters, and password complexity requirements for mixed case letters, numbers, and symbols.
- JWT custom claims for `tenant_id` and role, TLS version requirement of 1.2 or higher, WAF rate limiting of 100 requests per minute per IP address, and global RPS limit of 10,000 burst capacity in production environments, among others.

In total, DeepSeek-R1 correctly identified 21 of the 23 expected parameters. The 2 missing parameters were specific timeout values for Lambda functions with a maximum of 30 seconds, and CloudFront TTL settings for the caching layer. The calculation of 21 correctly identified out of 23 expected yields 91.3% accuracy, which rounds to a score of 9 out of 10.

This detailed scoring methodology ensures that our evaluation is transparent, repeatable, and objective. For subsequent evaluations in this chapter, we apply the same framework but provide summarized results rather than explaining the methodology again.

Summing up the scores assigned in the `Score` column, the qualitative score is computed to be 42/50 (84%).

The response demonstrates strong technical architecture understanding with immediately actionable implementation guidance. High scores in comprehension and practicality reflect the analysis quality that enables direct development team execution.

The quantitative analysis is shown in the following table:

Criteria	**Count/Metric**	**Analysis**	**Score (1–10)**
Technical components covered	8/8 major architecture elements	Complete coverage of API Gateway, Lambda functions, databases, authentication, monitoring, and security components	10
Configuration parameters	23 specific settings provided	Detailed configuration values for throttling limits, security headers, authentication flows, and performance parameters	9
Implementation artifacts	6 concrete deliverables specified	CloudFormation templates, Lambda functions, IAM policies, monitoring dashboards, security configurations, and deployment procedures	9
Code examples quality	3 production-ready code samples	Working implementation examples for the Lambda authorizer, `User` service, and infrastructure templates with proper error handling	9
Compliance coverage	4/4 regulatory requirements addressed	SOC2 Type II, PCI DSS, GDPR, and multi-tenancy compliance considerations with specific implementation guidance	8

Table 4.2: Quantitative analysis of DeepSeek response

The quantitative score can be computed as 45/50 (90%), based on which we can infer that DeepSeek demonstrated the following:

- Exceptional technical specification coverage with comprehensive implementation details.
- Strong performance across all technical delivery categories demonstrates enterprise-grade analysis depth.

The combined score (qualitative and quantitative) is computed as 87/100 (87%).

DeepSeek-R1 delivers enterprise-grade technical analysis that transforms complex documentation into actionable implementation roadmaps. The response successfully balances architectural understanding with practical implementation guidance, providing development teams with immediately executable technical specifications.

DeepSeek also demonstrates implementation efficiency. While the traditional analysis may require 36 hours of specialized expertise ($6,000–$9,000), DeepSeek completed it in minutes, representing a 99%+ time reduction while maintaining professional technical standards.

Follow-up code generation request

After receiving the comprehensive analysis, CloudTech Solutions requested the actual implementation code. Here's the follow-up prompt and DeepSeek-R1's response:

```
Generate production-ready implementation code for the top 3 priority
components from your analysis:
```

This generated the following response from DeepSeek:

```
Based on your analysis, generate production-ready code for the top 3
priority components:

1. **Core Infrastructure (CloudFormation Template)**:
   - VPC, security groups, IAM roles
   - API Gateway with proper throttling and security
   - Cognito User Pool with MFA and custom attributes

2. **User Service Lambda Function**:
   - Full CRUD operations with DynamoDB
   - Proper error handling and logging
   - Multi-tenant support with tenant isolation

3. **Lambda Authorizer**:
   - JWT validation with Cognito
   - Custom claims extraction (tenant_id, role)
   - Enforces tenant isolation
   - Returns proper IAM policies

For each component, provide:
- Complete, deployable code
- Configuration parameters based on the documentation
- Security best practices implementation
- Error handling and resilience patterns
- Monitoring and logging integration
```

```
Focus on production-ready code that follows the security, performance, and
compliance requirements from the documentation analysis.
```

Let's take a look at DeepSeek-R1's code implementation response.

DeepSeek-R1 provided three complete, production-ready implementations:

1. **Core Infrastructure (CloudFormation Template)**

```
AWSTemplateFormatVersion: '2010-09-09'
Transform: AWS::Serverless-2016-10-31
Description: Core infrastructure for API Gateway implementation

Parameters:
  Environment:
    Type: String
    Default: dev
    AllowedValues: [dev, staging, prod]
  SystemName:
    Type: String
    Default: enterprise-api-system

Resources:
  # API Gateway with security and throttling
  ApiGateway:
    Type: AWS::Serverless::HttpApi
    Properties:
      StageName: !Ref Environment
      DefaultRouteSettings:
        ThrottlingBurstLimit: !If [IsProd, 5000, 100]
        ThrottlingRateLimit: !If [IsProd, 2000, 50]
      Auth:
        Authorizers:
          CognitoAuthorizer:
            JwtConfiguration:
              issuer: !Sub "https://cognito-idp.${AWS::Region}.
amazonaws.com/${UserPool}"
              audience: [!Ref UserPoolClient]

  # Cognito User Pool with security settings
```

```
  UserPool:
    Type: AWS::Cognito::UserPool
    Properties:
      UserPoolName: !Sub "${SystemName}-user-pool"
      Policies:
        PasswordPolicy:
          MinimumLength: 12
          RequireLowercase: true
          RequireUppercase: true
          RequireNumbers: true
          RequireSymbols: true
      MfaConfiguration: "ON"
      Schema:
        - Name: custom:tenant_id
          AttributeDataType: String
          Required: true
          Mutable: false
        - Name: custom:role
          AttributeDataType: String
          Required: true
          Mutable: true
```

2. **User Service Lambda Function**

```
import json
import boto3
import logging
from datetime import datetime
from aws_xray_sdk.core import xray_recorder
from botocore.exceptions import ClientError

# Initialize AWS services
dynamodb = boto3.resource('dynamodb')
table = dynamodb.Table('Users')

# Configure structured logging
logger = logging.getLogger()
logger.setLevel(logging.INFO)
```

```
@xray_recorder.capture('lambda_handler')
def lambda_handler(event, context):
    """
    User Service Lambda - handles CRUD operations with multi-tenant
support
    """
    try:
        # Extract tenant context from authorizer
        tenant_id = event['requestContext']['authorizer']['tenant_
id']
        user_role = event['requestContext']['authorizer']['role']

        # Route based on HTTP method
        http_method = event['httpMethod']

        if http_method == 'GET':
            return get_user(event, tenant_id)
        elif http_method == 'POST':
            return create_user(event, tenant_id)
        elif http_method == 'PUT':
            return update_user(event, tenant_id, user_role)
        elif http_method == 'DELETE':
            return delete_user(event, tenant_id, user_role)
        else:
            return error_response(405, "Method not allowed")

    except Exception as e:
        logger.error(f"Unhandled error: {str(e)}")
        return error_response(500, "Internal server error")

@xray_recorder.capture('get_user')
def get_user(event, tenant_id):
    """Get user with tenant isolation"""
    try:
        user_id = event['pathParameters']['user_id']

        response = table.get_item(
```

```
            Key={
                'user_id': user_id,
                'tenant_id': tenant_id  # Ensures tenant isolation
            }
        )

        if 'Item' not in response:
            return error_response(404, "User not found")

        return success_response(response['Item'])

    except ClientError as e:
        logger.error(f"DynamoDB error: {e.response['Error']
['Message']}")
        return error_response(500, "Database error")

def success_response(data):
    return {
        'statusCode': 200,
        'headers': {'Content-Type': 'application/json'},
        'body': json.dumps(data, default=str)
    }
```

3. **Lambda Authorizer**

```
import json
import os
import jwt
from jwt import PyJWKClient
from jwt.exceptions import ExpiredSignatureError, InvalidTokenError

# Configuration
USER_POOL_ID = os.environ['USER_POOL_ID']
REGION = os.environ['AWS_REGION']
JWKS_URL = f"https://cognito-idp.{REGION}.amazonaws.com/{USER_POOL_
ID}/.well-known/jwks.json"

# Initialize JWKS client
```

```
jwks_client = PyJWKClient(JWKS_URL)

def lambda_handler(event, context):
    """
    Lambda Authorizer with JWT validation and tenant isolation
    """
    try:
        # Extract token from Authorization header
        token = extract_token(event)
        if not token:
            raise Exception("No token provided")

        # Validate JWT token
        decoded_token = validate_jwt_token(token)

        # Extract custom claims
        tenant_id = decoded_token.get('custom:tenant_id')
        role = decoded_token.get('custom:role', 'user')

        if not tenant_id:
            raise Exception("Missing tenant_id in token")

        # Generate IAM policy
        policy = generate_policy(
            decoded_token['sub'],
            'Allow',
            event['methodArn'],
            tenant_id,
            role
        )

        return policy

    except Exception as e:
        print(f"Authorization failed: {str(e)}")
        raise Exception('Unauthorized')
```

```
def validate_jwt_token(token):
    """Validate JWT token with Cognito JWKS"""
    try:
        # Get signing key
        signing_key = jwks_client.get_signing_key_from_jwt(token)

        # Decode and validate token
        decoded_token = jwt.decode(
            token,
            signing_key.key,
            algorithms=["RS256"],
            options={"verify_exp": True}
        )

        return decoded_token

    except ExpiredSignatureError:
        raise Exception("Token has expired")
    except InvalidTokenError:
        raise Exception("Invalid token")
```

Follow-up response evaluation

DeepSeek-R1's response demonstrates exceptional technical documentation analysis capabilities comparable to senior solution architects. The analysis transformed a complex 45-page technical guide into immediately actionable implementation strategies with specific code examples, configuration details, and production deployment procedures.

Evaluation methodology and metrics selection

For technical document analysis, we evaluate responses across criteria that reflect enterprise development requirements:

- **Qualitative metrics**: Focus on technical accuracy, implementation clarity, and architectural insight quality that development teams require for production deployments.
- **Quantitative metrics**: Measure response completeness, technical specificity, and structural organization that enables immediate development execution.

Let's begin with the qualitative analysis (*Table 4.3*):

Criteria	**Analysis**	**Score (1–10)**
Technical accuracy	Response demonstrates deep understanding of AWS architecture patterns, providing production-grade configurations and security implementations. Correctly identifies service relationships, data flows, and integration points.	9
Implementation clarity	Delivers specific code examples, configuration parameters, and deployment procedures. Technical recommendations include precise settings (rate limits, timeout values, and security headers) immediately usable by development teams.	9
Architectural insight	Provides comprehensive system design guidance, including microservice boundaries, priority matrices, and dependency analysis. Addresses both technical and business considerations for enterprise deployment.	8
Security depth	Identifies critical security requirements, including WAF rules, encryption standards, and compliance considerations. Provides specific implementation guidance for authentication flows and access control.	9
Production readiness	Covers monitoring, error handling, deployment strategies, and operational procedures. Includes specific metrics, alerting configurations, and disaster recovery considerations.	8

Table 4.3: Qualitative analysis of the follow-up response

The computed qualitative score is 43/50 (86%).

The technical depth matches experienced solution architect capabilities, with comprehensive coverage of enterprise deployment requirements, and minor gaps in advanced monitoring configurations and regional compliance specifics.

Let's take a look at the quantitative analysis:

Criteria	Count/Metric	Analysis	Score (1–10)
Requirement coverage	6/6 major analysis areas addressed	Complete coverage of architecture summary, implementation priorities, configuration analysis, code generation, security requirements, and production readiness	10
Technical specifications	38 specific configuration parameters provided	Extensive technical detail, including rate limits (100 burst, 50 rate), timeout values, security headers, encryption standards, and deployment procedures	9
Code examples	12 production-ready code samples	Comprehensive Lambda functions, API configurations, and infrastructure components with immediate implementation capability	9
Implementation steps	8-phase structured deployment plan	Detailed priority matrix with dependencies, risk assessment, and business value considerations for systematic implementation	9
Response structure	6 organized analysis sections with logical flow	Clear progression from high-level architecture through specific implementation details to operational procedures	8

Table 4.4: Quantitative analysis of the follow-up response

The quantitative score is computed as 45/50 (90%).

Exceptional technical specificity with production-ready implementations is observed. Response provides comprehensive coverage, enabling immediate development execution.

Here is our overall assessment:

- The combined score is computed as 88/100 (88%).
- DeepSeek-R1 delivered solution architect-level technical analysis with immediate implementation capability. The response quality matches expensive technical consulting while providing specific code examples and deployment procedures that development teams can execute immediately.

- While a traditional solution architecture engagement would require 3–4 weeks and $30–50K investment, DeepSeek-R1 achieved equivalent technical depth in minutes, representing 99%+ time reduction while maintaining enterprise-grade quality.

But there is always scope for improvement and extracting more knowledge. Here is how we can recalibrate our prompts for enhanced document understanding.

Recalibration through iterative prompting

The initial analysis provided comprehensive technical guidance but revealed opportunities for enhanced regional deployment specifics and advanced monitoring configurations.

The following areas require enhancement:

- **Regional compliance specifics (gap score: 7/10)**: We need specific regulatory requirements for EU/APAC deployments, which aren't presently offered in the DeepSeek response.
- **Advanced monitoring (gap score: 7/10)**: Detailed observability patterns and custom metrics implementation are required for advanced monitoring.
- **Cost optimization (gap score: 6/10)**: Specific strategies for reducing API Gateway and Lambda costs at scale are essential for this solution architecture.

You can utilize the following iterative prompt examples to bridge these gaps:

1. **Follow-up prompt 1 – Regional deployment**:

```
Based on your AWS architecture analysis, create region-specific
deployment configurations for EU (GDPR compliance) and APAC markets.
Include:
- Specific data residency requirements and implementation
- Regional compliance certifications needed
- Cross-region disaster recovery procedures
- Regional cost optimization strategies
Provide configuration examples for each region.
```

2. **Follow-up prompt 2 – Advanced monitoring**:

```
Expand the monitoring strategy for the Amazon API Gateway system to
include:
- Custom CloudWatch metrics for business KPIs
- Advanced X-Ray tracing configurations for microservices
- Automated anomaly detection and alerting procedures
- Performance optimization based on monitoring insights
Include specific implementation code and configuration examples.
```

3. **Follow-up prompt 3 – Cost optimization:**

```
Design a comprehensive cost optimization strategy for the Amazon
API Gateway and Lambda architecture to reduce monthly operational
expenses by 40% while maintaining performance and reliability.
Include:
- API Gateway cost reduction strategies (HTTP API vs REST API
selection, request optimization, caching)
- Lambda function cost optimization (memory configuration analysis,
execution duration reduction, provisioned concurrency vs on-demand)
- Data transfer cost minimization (CloudFront caching, response
payload optimization, compression strategies)
- Request batching and connection pooling implementations
- Reserved capacity analysis and purchasing recommendations for
predictable workloads
- Cost monitoring and alerting setup with budget thresholds Provide
specific configuration examples, cost calculations, and projected
monthly savings for each optimization strategy.
```

Practice exercise

Apply the evaluation framework to analyze the iterative prompting responses, focusing on how enhanced specificity improves implementation readiness for enterprise environments.

An interesting application of document analysis is in finance. In the next case study, we will prompt DeepSeek to analyze a financial document and compare its performance against benchmark tools.

Use case study: Financial document analysis and benchmarking

We will first identify the business context of this case example.

Financial institutions and enterprises regularly process complex financial documents containing structured tables, multi-quarter comparisons, and critical numerical data. Accurate extraction of this information is essential for automated financial analysis, regulatory compliance, and decision-making systems.

To comprehensively evaluate DeepSeek-R1's document understanding capabilities, we created a rigorous benchmarking study comparing three different approaches:

- **DeepSeek-R1**: Direct semantic extraction using advanced reasoning.
- **Docling (IBM Research)**: Specialized document structure and table parsing.
- **MarkItDown (Microsoft)**: LLM-optimized document preprocessing.

Test document creation and benchmarking setup

To rigorously evaluate document understanding capabilities, we created a comprehensive test dataset that would challenge all aspects of document parsing. Our fictional quarterly financial report for FruitStand Innovation Inc. spans 192 lines and contains the kind of complex structures commonly found in real financial statements. The document includes six major tables designed to test different parsing challenges: a multi-column consolidated balance sheet comparing three quarters (Q3 2024, Q2 2024, and Q3 2023), a detailed income statement with product versus service revenue breakdowns, geographic revenue analysis covering four global regions (North America, EMEA, APAC, and Latin America), product line performance metrics for four business segments (cloud platform, mobile solutions, enterprise services, and developer tools), eight **key performance indicators (KPIs)** tracked against quarterly targets, and forward-looking guidance ranges projecting Q4 2024 performance.

The balance sheet demonstrates the parsing complexity we wanted to test. Each financial line item appears across multiple quarters with corresponding percentage changes, requiring tools to maintain proper row-column associations while extracting values with exact numerical precision. Here's an excerpt from our test document showing the `Current Assets` section:

```
| **Assets** | **Q3 2024** | **Q2 2024** | **Q3 2023** | **Change (%)** |
|-----------|-------------|-------------|-------------|----------------|
| **Current Assets** | | | | |
| Cash and cash equivalents | $234,678 | $198,543 | $187,432 | +25.2% |
| Short-term investments | $89,234 | $76,890 | $45,678 | +95.3% |
| Accounts receivable (net) | $142,567 | $134,289 | $118,945 | +19.9% |
| Inventory | $67,890 | $72,345 | $81,234 | -16.4% |
| Prepaid expenses | $23,456 | $21,234 | $19,876 | +18.0% |
| **Total Current Assets** | **$557,825** | **$503,301** | **$453,165** |
**+23.1%** |
```

This structure tests whether tools can handle multi-column layouts, distinguish between regular line items and bolded totals, correctly parse both positive and negative percentage changes, and maintain the association between each value and its corresponding quarter. A tool that extracts `$234,678` but associates it with Q2 2024 instead of Q3 2024 would fail our accuracy requirements, even though it captured the correct numerical value.

After creating the test document, we manually constructed a comprehensive ground truth dataset stored in `ground_truth_data.json`. This JSON file contains 150+ distinct data fields representing every piece of information we expect a perfect document parser to extract. The ground truth structure mirrors the document's organization, with nested objects for different sections. Here's how the ground truth represents the document metadata and key financial highlights:

```
{
  "document_metadata": {
    "company_name": "FruitStand Innovation Inc.",
    "report_type": "Quarterly Financial Report",
    "quarter": "Q3",
    "year": 2024,
    "report_date": "2024-09-30",
    "fiscal_year": 2024,
    "document_id": "FSI-FIN-2024-Q3-001",
    "classification": "Internal Use Only",
    "nasdaq_symbol": "FSTI"
  },

  "key_financial_highlights": {
    "total_revenue": {
      "value": 487.3,
      "unit": "million",
      "yoy_change": "+23%"
    },
    "net_income": {
      "value": 89.2,
      "unit": "million",
      "yoy_change": "+31%"
    },
    "operating_margin": {
      "value": 24.8,
```

```
        "unit": "percent",
        "comparison": "vs 21.4% in Q3 2023"
      }
    }
  }
```

The ground truth format captures not just raw values but also their associated units, percentage changes, and contextual comparisons. This level of detail ensures that our benchmarking measures true semantic understanding rather than simple text extraction. When we evaluate whether a tool correctly extracted `total_revenue`, we verify that it captured the value (`487.3`), understood the unit (millions), and recognized the year-over-year change context (+23%).

Our benchmarking implementation uses these test files to automatically evaluate each tool's performance. The `test_deepseek_parsing.py` Python script demonstrates how we prompt DeepSeek-R1 to extract this structured data. Here's the actual prompt we used:

```
prompt = f"""Analyze this financial report and extract ALL key information
in structured JSON format.

The document is a Q3 2024 financial report. Extract the following with
EXACT values from the document:

1. **Document Metadata**: company_name, report_type, quarter, year,
report_date, document_id, nasdaq_symbol
2. **Financial Highlights**: total_revenue, net_income, operating_margin,
cash_and_equivalents, total_assets (with values and units)
3. **Balance Sheet - Current Assets** (Q3 2024, Q2 2024, Q3 2023):
   - cash_and_cash_equivalents, short_term_investments, accounts_
receivable_net,
     inventory, prepaid_expenses, total_current_assets
4. **Balance Sheet - Non-Current Assets** (Q3 2024):
   - property_plant_equipment, accumulated_depreciation, net_ppe,
intangible_assets,
     goodwill, long_term_investments, total_non_current_assets
...

CRITICAL: Extract EXACT numerical values, preserve decimals, include
negative numbers
with minus sign. Return valid JSON only.
"""
```

This prompt structure proved effective because it specifies exactly what fields to extract, requests a structured JSON output format, and emphasizes the importance of numerical precision. The phrases `EXACT values` and `preserve decimals` help DeepSeek-R1 understand that approximate values or rounded numbers are insufficient for financial document analysis.

Complete test files, including the full financial statement, the comprehensive ground truth dataset with all 150+ fields, automated benchmarking scripts for all three tools (DeepSeek-R1, Docling, and MarkItDown), and evaluation framework documentation are available in our GitHub repository at `https://github.com/PacktPublishing/DeepSeek-in-Practice/tree/main/Chapter04/document-understanding`. You can clone the repository and reproduce our benchmarking results using the provided `run_benchmark_comparison.py` script.

Prompting DeepSeek for financial document extraction

Financial document extraction requires fundamentally different prompt design strategies than general document analysis. The critical challenge lies in achieving numerical precision across hundreds of data points while preserving complex relationships between values, their units, temporal contexts, and hierarchical structures. When prompting DeepSeek-R1 for financial documents, specificity becomes paramount: vague requests such as `extract the revenue data` will produce incomplete results, while precise instructions specifying `extract total_revenue with its numerical value, unit (millions/thousands), currency, and year-over-year percentage change` guide the model toward comprehensive extraction that captures all relevant attributes.

Three design principles proved essential in our financial document prompting approach:

1. First, explicitly request structured output formats (JSON) with defined schemas rather than accepting free-form text responses, as structured formats enable automated validation and downstream processing.
2. Second, emphasize numerical precision requirements by explicitly stating `EXACT values`, `preserve decimal places`, and `include sign indicators for negative numbers and percentage changes`, because financial analysis tolerates a zero error margin – a revenue figure of $487.3 million differs meaningfully from $487 million or $487.30 million, depending on reporting precision.
3. Third, specify the scope exhaustively by enumerating every category of data to extract (document metadata, financial highlights, balance sheet components, income statement sections, geographic breakdowns, product metrics, KPIs, and guidance), as financial documents contain numerous sections, and omitting categories from the prompt often results in those sections being overlooked during extraction.

DeepSeek-R1's reasoning capabilities particularly shine when prompts establish clear validation criteria. Rather than simply requesting data extraction, our prompt includes phrases such as `maintain quarter-to-quarter associations in multi-column tables` and `preserve parent-child relationships for revenue breakdowns`, which activate DeepSeek's contextual understanding. This approach leverages the model's ability to reason about document structure rather than treating extraction as simple pattern matching. The following prompt demonstrates these principles applied to our FruitStand Innovation Inc. financial report:

```
Analyze this Q3 2024 financial report for FruitStand Innovation Inc.
and extract ALL financial data in structured JSON format.

Extract the following with EXACT values:

1. Document Metadata: company_name, report_date, document_id, fiscal_year
2. Financial Highlights: total_revenue, net_income, operating_margin,
   cash_equivalents, total_assets (with units and YoY changes)
3. Balance Sheet (Q3 2024, Q2 2024, Q3 2023):
   - All current assets line items
   - All non-current assets line items
   - All liabilities and equity items
4. Income Statement (all 3 quarters):
   - Revenue breakdown (product vs. service)
   - All cost categories
   - Operating metrics (margins, EPS)
5. Revenue by Geographic Region (all 4 regions with %, growth, margins)
6. Revenue by Product Line (all 4 products with %, growth, margins)
7. All 8 Key Performance Indicators with exact values
8. Management team names and titles
9. Q4 2024 Guidance ranges

CRITICAL: Extract EXACT numerical values, preserve decimals,
include negative numbers with minus sign. Return valid JSON only.

[Attached: 192-line financial report document]
```

It is now time for us to look at how we will evaluate DeepSeek's response in this case example.

Response evaluation

To objectively compare DeepSeek-R1's performance against specialized document parsing tools Docling and MarkItDown, we established six quantitative metrics that measure different aspects of document understanding capability. Each metric was carefully designed to be objectively measurable through automated comparison against our ground truth dataset. The following sections explain what each metric measures, why it matters for document understanding, and how we compute it.

Metric 1: Field extraction accuracy

The first metric measures how accurately a tool can identify and extract semantic field-value pairs from document text. In document understanding, key-value pairs represent discrete pieces of information where a descriptive key (field name) is associated with a specific value.

Consider the phrase `Total Revenue: $487.3 million` from our test document. A document parser must recognize that `total_revenue` is the semantic field name, `487.3` is the numerical value, `million` represents the unit, and the currency is USD. Simple text extraction would only capture `$487.3 million` without understanding the semantic relationship to revenue.

Our test document contains key-value pairs ranging from simple metadata to complex nested financial metrics. Simple examples include company name (`FruitStand Innovation Inc.`) and report date (`2024-09-30`), while complex examples include multi-attribute financial metrics such as total revenue, which requires capturing the value (`487.3`), unit (`million`), and year-over-year change context (+23%) as a structured object. Operating margin represents another complex case where the value (`24.8`) must be associated with its unit (`percent`) and comparison baseline (versus `21.4%` in Q3 2023). These compound values test whether tools understand document semantics or merely extract isolated text fragments.

To compute field extraction accuracy, we implemented an automated comparison script that loads the ground truth JSON and compares it field-by-field against each tool's output. A field is marked correct only when both the key and value match our stringent criteria: numerical values must match to the exact decimal place (`487.3`, not 487 or `487.30`), strings must match including, capitalization (`FruitStand Innovation Inc.`, not `fruitstand innovation inc.`), dates must follow ISO format (`2024-09-30`), and compound values must include all required attributes.

The formula is straightforward: divide the number of correctly extracted fields by the total expected fields (150 in our test document) and multiply by 100. When DeepSeek-R1 correctly extracted 137 out of 150 fields, this yielded 91.3% accuracy.

Metric 2: Table parsing accuracy

Table parsing accuracy measures a tool's ability to correctly extract individual cell values from tabular data while preserving critical row-column relationships. This metric proves particularly challenging because it requires understanding table structure, not just reading text sequentially. Our consolidated balance sheet exemplifies this complexity with its multi-column layout comparing three quarters of financial data. Consider the `Cash and cash equivalents` line item, which contains four distinct values across the row: `$234,678` for `Q3 2024`, `$198,543` for `Q2 2024`, `$187,432` for `Q3 2023`, and a calculated change of `+25.2%`. Cell-level accuracy demands that all four values be extracted with exact numerical precision and correctly associated with their respective time periods.

The challenge becomes apparent when we consider potential parsing errors. A tool might successfully extract the value of `$234,678` but incorrectly associate it with `Q2 2024` instead of `Q3 2024`. While the numerical extraction succeeded, the semantic understanding failed because the quarter-value relationship was misidentified. This type of error would render the extracted data useless for financial analysis, even though superficially the tool *found* the right numbers. Our ground truth dataset addresses this by encoding not just cell values but also their positional context, requiring tools to demonstrate they understand table structure rather than merely scanning for numbers.

We enumerate all 245 cells across the 6 major tables in our ground truth dataset, identifying each by table name, row label, and column header. The automated comparison script checks whether each extracted cell matches both the expected value and position. Percentage values must include their signs (+23% not 23%), currency values must preserve dollar signs and comma separators where present, and calculated fields such as percentage changes must match exactly rather than being recomputed. This stringency ensures that we measure precise extraction capability rather than approximate understanding. DeepSeek-R1's result of 232 correctly parsed cells out of 245 total cells translates to 94.7% table parsing accuracy.

Metric 3: Entity recognition accuracy

Named entity recognition measures how well a tool identifies specific real-world objects embedded in document text. Our financial report contains 42 distinct named entities spanning multiple categories, each serving a different purpose in document comprehension. Company information entities provide organizational context: the company name (`FruitStand Innovation Inc.`), its NASDAQ trading symbol (`FSTI`), and the unique document identifier (`FSI-FIN-2024-Q3-001`) all represent distinct entities that must be correctly identified and categorized. Executive names represent another critical entity class, with our test document mentioning Sarah Chen (Chief

Executive Officer), Michael Rodriguez (Chief Financial Officer), Jennifer Wu (Chief Technology Officer), and David Park (Chief Operating Officer). Each of these names must be recognized as person entities associated with their respective leadership roles.

Geographic entities add another layer of complexity. Our revenue analysis section references four distinct regions: `North America`, `EMEA` (**Europe, the Middle East, and Africa**), `APAC` (**Asia-Pacific**), and `Latin America`. These aren't merely location names but semantic categories that structure our revenue breakdown. Similarly, our four product lines – `Cloud Platform`, `Mobile Solutions`, `Enterprise Services`, and `Developer Tools` – represent product entities that organize financial performance metrics. Temporal entities round out our entity catalog with specific dates, such as `September 30, 2024`, serving as the report date, alongside quarterly designators (`Q3 2024`, `Q4 2024`) that establish the reporting and projection timeframes.

Entity recognition accuracy is computed by checking whether each of the 42 expected entities appears in the tool's extracted output with correct spelling, appropriate context, and proper entity classification. A tool that extracts `Sarah Chen` but fails to recognize it as a person name, or that identifies `North America` but doesn't understand it as a geographic region, would fail our entity recognition requirements. DeepSeek-R1 achieved perfect performance on this metric, correctly identifying all 42 out of 42 entities, yielding 100% entity recognition accuracy.

Metric 4: Structure preservation score

Structure preservation evaluates how well a tool maintains the document's logical organization, hierarchical relationships, and reading order during extraction. This metric matters because financial documents communicate meaning through structure as much as through content. Consider how our financial report follows the conventional sequence: the executive summary presents key highlights, followed by the detailed balance sheet, then the income statement with segment breakdowns, concluding with forward-looking guidance. This ordering isn't arbitrary but reflects increasing levels of detail and temporal progression from historical results to future projections.

Hierarchical relationships carry semantic weight throughout the document. When our report presents `Revenue by Geographic Region` as a section header followed by four subsections (`North America`, `EMEA`, `APAC`, and `Latin America`), this structure conveys that the four regions are components of a comprehensive geographic analysis. A tool that extracts these region names but loses the parent-child relationship would miss the organizational logic. Similarly, visual formatting provides crucial cues: bold text typically denotes totals or section headers, indented line items indicate detail breakdowns supporting bolded totals, and the `Total Revenue` entry appearing in bold, followed by `Product Revenue` and `Service Revenue` indented beneath it, signals a sum-detail relationship that aids comprehension.

We evaluate structure preservation using a hybrid quantitative-qualitative approach on a 0–100 point scale. This could cover the following aspects:

- Section ordering contributes 25 points (did the extraction maintain the executive summary → balance sheet → income statement → analysis sequence?)
- Table structure integrity accounts for 30 points (were row-column relationships and header associations preserved?)
- Header data associations provide 25 points (are section headers correctly linked to their content?), and hierarchical nesting levels comprise the final 20 points (are parent-child relationships and indentation patterns maintained?)

This scoring combines automated checks, such as verifying table column counts and section ordering, with human evaluation of whether the extracted output remains logically organized and usable.

Metric 5: Processing time

Processing speed becomes critical for production systems handling thousands of documents. We measure end-to-end processing time by recording timestamps immediately before submitting the document and immediately after receiving the complete output. For API-based tools such as DeepSeek-R1, we use Python's `time.time()` function to capture these boundaries, measuring the total elapsed time, including network latency, server queue time, model inference, and response formatting. This real-world timing reflects what production systems would experience. DeepSeek-R1 processed our 192-line financial document in 4,250 milliseconds (4.25 seconds), fast enough for interactive applications where users can wait a few seconds for results, but potentially challenging for batch processing systems needing to handle thousands of documents hourly.

Metric 6: Cost per document

Economic viability determines whether document understanding solutions can scale to production volumes. For DeepSeek-R1, we calculate per-document cost by tracking token consumption and applying published API pricing. Our test document required 12,847 total tokens (combining input and output), which, at DeepSeek's pricing of $0.14 per million input tokens and $0.28 per million output tokens, translates to approximately $0.0027 per document. At this rate, processing 10,000 documents would cost $27, making it economically viable for most business applications. Open source tools such as Docling and MarkItDown incur $0.00 direct API costs, though self-hosting introduces infrastructure expenses (compute resources, maintenance, and updates) that we didn't quantify in this benchmark.

Test data analysis

Having defined our evaluation metrics and prompt strategy, we can now examine how DeepSeek-R1 performed when processing our actual test document. Our 192-line financial report for FruitStand Innovation Inc. serves as the input for all three tools in our benchmark comparison. The document begins with executive summary information that tests entity recognition and simple field extraction, then progresses through increasingly complex table structures that challenge parser capabilities. Here's how the test document opens:

```
# FRUITSTAND INNOVATION INC.
## Quarterly Financial Report Q3 2024

**Report Date:** September 30, 2024
**Fiscal Year:** 2024
**Document ID:** FSI-FIN-2024-Q3-001
**Classification:** Internal Use Only

---

## Executive Summary

FruitStand Innovation Inc. (NASDAQ: FSTI) reports strong financial
performance for Q3 2024,
with revenue growth of 23% year-over-year and operating margin expansion
of 340 basis points.

**Key Financial Highlights:**
- Total Revenue: $487.3 million (up 23% YoY)
- Net Income: $89.2 million (up 31% YoY)
- Operating Margin: 24.8% (vs 21.4% in Q3 2023)
- Cash and Equivalents: $234.7 million
- Total Assets: $1,247.8 million
```

This opening section tests whether tools can extract structured metadata (company name, document ID, and NASDAQ symbol) from the header while simultaneously capturing key financial metrics from the bullet-pointed highlights section. The metrics appear in a semi-structured format mixing absolute values ($487.3 million), percentage changes (up 23% YoY), and comparative contexts (vs 21.4% in Q3 2023), requiring tools to parse compound information rather than isolated numbers.

The document's primary challenge lies in its consolidated balance sheet, which presents a multi-column structure comparing three time periods simultaneously. Each financial line item spans four data columns plus descriptive text, demanding that parsers maintain precise associations between values and their temporal contexts:

```
## Consolidated Balance Sheet
### As of September 30, 2024
**(In thousands, except share data)**

| **Assets** | **Q3 2024** | **Q2 2024** | **Q3 2023** | **Change (%)** |
|-----------|-------------|-------------|-------------|----------------|
| **Current Assets** | | | | |
| Cash and cash equivalents | $234,678 | $198,543 | $187,432 | +25.2% |
| Short-term investments | $89,234 | $76,890 | $45,678 | +95.3% |
| Accounts receivable (net) | $142,567 | $134,289 | $118,945 | +19.9% |
| Inventory | $67,890 | $72,345 | $81,234 | -16.4% |
| Prepaid expenses | $23,456 | $21,234 | $19,876 | +18.0% |
| **Total Current Assets** | **$557,825** | **$503,301** | **$453,165** |
**+23.1%** |
```

This table structure reveals several parsing complexities. Empty cells in the `Current Assets` header row must be recognized as structural elements rather than missing data. Bold formatting distinguishes category headers and totals from detailed line items, requiring tools to preserve formatting semantics. Negative inventory values (indicated by decreasing quarter-over-quarter figures) test sign handling, while percentage changes in the rightmost column require extracting both magnitude and direction indicators (+/- signs). The accumulated depreciation line later in the document shows `($123,456)` in parentheses, representing negative values in accounting convention, which parsers must interpret correctly rather than treating parentheses as mere formatting.

The income statement section introduces additional complexity through nested calculations and percentage-based metrics that span multiple quarters:

```
## Consolidated Income Statement
### For the Three Months Ended September 30, 2024
**(In thousands, except per share data)**

| **Revenue** | **Q3 2024** | **Q2 2024** | **Q3 2023** | **Change (%)** |
|-----------|-------------|-------------|-------------|----------------|
| Product revenue | $312,456 | $287,654 | $245,678 | +27.2% |
```

```
| Service revenue | $174,892 | $168,543 | $150,234 | +16.4% |
| **Total Revenue** | **$487,348** | **$456,197** | **$395,912** |
**+23.1%** |
| | | | | |
| **Cost of Revenue** | | | | |
| Cost of product revenue | $143,567 | $139,876 | $128,945 | +11.3% |
| Cost of service revenue | $76,543 | $74,321 | $70,234 | +9.0% |
| **Total Cost of Revenue** | **$220,110** | **$214,197** | **$199,179** |
**+10.5%** |
| | | | | |
| **Gross Profit** | **$267,238** | **$242,000** | **$196,733** |
**+35.8%** |
| **Gross Margin** | **54.8%** | **53.0%** | **49.7%** | **+5.1 pts** |
```

Notice how this section alternates between absolute dollar amounts and percentage-based metrics. For example, the field `Gross Margin`, requires parsers to handle different data types within the same table structure. The `+5.1 pts` notation for margin improvement uses a domain-specific abbreviation (`pts` for basis points) that semantic parsers must interpret correctly.

Computing the final score

The overall performance score combines all six metrics using a weighted average that reflects their relative importance in production document understanding systems. We assigned weights based on what matters most for real-world deployments: field extraction accuracy receives 35% weight as the primary objective of document parsing, table parsing accuracy gets 30% weight given how prevalent tabular data is in business documents, entity recognition accounts for 15% weight as entities represent key document actors and objects, structure preservation contributes 10% weight for maintaining document organization, while processing time and cost each receive 5% weight as practical constraints rather than primary goals.

The formula multiplies each metric score by its weight and sums the results:

Let's break this down:

- Field extraction contributes 31.96 points.
- Table parsing adds 28.41 points.
- Perfect entity recognition provides 15.00 points.
- Structure preservation contributes 8.50 points.
- Processing time adds 4.50 points.
- Cost efficiency provides 4.75 points.

This yields a total of 93.12 points, which we round to 93/100.

We established performance tiers to interpret these scores. Scores from 95 to 100 indicate excellent performance suitable for production deployment with minimal human validation, representing tools that consistently deliver accurate results requiring only spot-checking. Scores from 85 to 94 indicate good performance appropriate for production with targeted validation workflows, where automated extraction handles the bulk of work but critical fields undergo verification. Scores from 75 to 84 represent acceptable performance, requiring substantial validation and quality assurance, suitable for semi-automated workflows where human review remains extensive. Scores below 75 indicate poor performance, unsuitable for production deployment without significant improvements, typically requiring more development before practical use.

Benchmark comparison: From document to accuracy scores

Our benchmarking system evaluates each tool through a four-stage automated pipeline implemented in `run_benchmark_comparison.py`.

Let's describe this pipeline in detail:

1. The process begins by running each tool's test script (`test_deepseek_parsing.py`, `test_docling_parsing.py`, and `test_markitdown_parsing.py`) sequentially, capturing their outputs and measuring processing time.
2. Each tool receives the identical input document and must produce a structured output representing the extracted information.
3. For DeepSeek-R1, we measure end-to-end processing time from the moment we submit the HTTP request to the DeepSeek API until we receive the complete JSON response.
4. The API call includes the full document text as input along with our extraction prompt, and DeepSeek-R1 returns structured JSON containing all identified fields.
5. We save this output to `deepseek_test_results.json` for subsequent accuracy analysis. The processing time measurement uses Python's `time.time()` function to capture high-precision timestamps before and after the API call, giving us the real-world latency that production applications would experience.
6. Once all three tools complete their extractions, our comparison script loads the ground truth dataset from `ground_truth_data.json` and performs field-by-field validation. The comparison algorithm iterates through every field defined in the ground truth, checking whether each tool's output contains that field with the correct value. For simple fields

such as company name or report date, we verify exact string matches. For numerical fields, we compare values with appropriate precision tolerances. For compound fields such as `total_revenue`, which includes value, unit, and year-over-year change, we verify that all attributes match the expected structure.

This automated comparison generates accuracy percentages for field extraction, table parsing (cell-by-cell comparison), and entity recognition (checking that all 42 expected entities appear correctly).

The benchmark script then compiles results into comparison tables showing side-by-side performance across all metrics. These tables display not just accuracy percentages but also processing times, token usage (for API-based tools), and cost per document, providing a comprehensive view of each tool's production readiness. The entire benchmarking process runs automatically via the `python run_benchmark_comparison.py` command, making it reproducible for readers who want to verify our results or test with different documents.

DeepSeek-R1 successfully extracted the financial data with the following output structure:

```
{
  "document_metadata": {
    "company_name": "FruitStand Innovation Inc.",
    "report_date": "2024-09-30",
    "document_id": "FSI-FIN-2024-Q3-001",
    "nasdaq_symbol": "FSTI"
  },
  "key_financial_highlights": {
    "total_revenue": {"value": 487.3, "unit": "million", "yoy_change":
"+23%"},
    "net_income": {"value": 89.2, "unit": "million", "yoy_change":
"+31%"},
    "operating_margin": {"value": 24.8, "unit": "percent"}
  },
  "balance_sheet_current_assets_q3_2024": {
    "cash_and_cash_equivalents": 234678,
    "short_term_investments": 89234,
    "accounts_receivable_net": 142567,
    "inventory": 67890,
    "prepaid_expenses": 23456,
    "total_current_assets": 557825
```

```
  },
  // ... [145 more fields extracted correctly]
}
```

Here are the quantitative results of the DeepSeek-R1 response:

Metric	Result	Assessment
Field extraction accuracy	91.3%	Excellent
Correct fields	137/150	High success rate with minor gaps
Table parsing accuracy	94.7%	Excellent
Correct table cells	232/245	Near-perfect cell extraction
Entity recognition	100%	Perfect
Entities identified	42/42	Complete entity capture
Processing time	4,250 ms	Fast
Token usage	12,847 tokens	Moderate consumption
Cost per document	$0.0027	Very low
Overall score	92/100	Excellent

Table 4.5: DeepSeek-R1 quantitative results for finance document understanding

Here is our analysis of DeepSeek-R1's performance.

DeepSeek-R1 demonstrated excellent semantic understanding of financial terminology throughout the document extraction process. Here is how the results looked:

- When encountering the executive summary's key financial highlights, the model correctly interpreted complex phrases such as `operating margin expansion of 340 basis points` and properly extracted both the numerical value (`24.8%`) and its comparative context (versus 21.4% in Q3 2023).
- The model successfully distinguished between different revenue types in the income statement, accurately categorizing $312,456 as product revenue and $174,892 as service revenue while maintaining their quarterly associations across the multi-column structure.
- The tool's handling of nested table structures proved particularly strong. In the consolidated balance sheet, DeepSeek-R1 correctly parsed the hierarchical relationship between `Total Current Assets` (`$557,825`) and its component line items, understanding that cash and cash equivalents (`$234,678`), short-term investments (`$89,234`), accounts receivable (`$142,567`), inventory (`$67,890`), and prepaid expenses (`$23,456`) sum to the total.

- The model also successfully navigated the income statement's nested calculations, recognizing that gross profit (`$267,238`) equals total revenue (`$487,348`) minus total cost of revenue ($220,110), demonstrating comprehension of accounting relationships rather than merely extracting isolated numbers.
- Entity recognition achieved perfect accuracy across all 42 named entities in the document. DeepSeek-R1 correctly identified executive names, including `Sarah Chen (Chief Executive Officer)`, `Michael Rodriguez (Chief Financial Officer)`, `Jennifer Wu (Chief Technology Officer)`, and `David Park (Chief Operating Officer)`, properly associating each name with its corresponding title. Geographic entities were accurately extracted with their complete designations: `North America`, `EMEA` (explicitly recognized as Europe, the Middle East, and Africa rather than treating it as an undefined acronym), `APAC` (Asia-Pacific), and `Latin America`. Product line entities – `Cloud Platform`, `Mobile Solutions`, `Enterprise Services`, and `Developer Tools` – were correctly identified and associated with their respective revenue figures and performance metrics.

However, DeepSeek-R1 encountered 13 extraction errors, primarily in deeply nested multi-quarter comparison cells:

- Eight errors occurred in the balance sheet's quarterly comparison columns, where cells contained multiple related values. For example, in the `Accounts Payable` row, the model correctly extracted the Q3 2024 value ($87,654) and the year-over-year percentage change (+14.5%), but misassociated the Q2 2024 value, placing $82,345 in a Q3 2023 column instead of Q2 2024.
- Three formatting ambiguity errors involved numbers with accounting conventions: the accumulated depreciation value displayed as `($123,456)` in parentheses was initially extracted without the negative sign, requiring the model to infer that parenthetical values in the `Liabilities` section represent negative amounts.
- Two errors involved abbreviation expansion, where `PP&E (Property, Plant & Equipment)` in table headers was extracted as the abbreviated form rather than the expanded terminology expected by the ground truth dataset.

Despite these minor errors, DeepSeek-R1 exhibited strong handling of percentage calculations and currency formatting throughout the document. The model correctly preserved positive and negative signs in percentage changes (`+25.2%` for cash growth versus `-16.4%` for inventory decline), maintained decimal precision in financial figures (`$234,678` not rounded to $234,700), and properly interpreted the `+5.1 pts` notation for basis point changes in gross margin. Currency symbols and comma separators were consistently preserved in the extracted output, demonstrating attention to formatting details that matter for financial data integrity.

Understanding DeepSeek-R1's extraction errors

Before comparing DeepSeek-R1 against alternative tools, we should examine the specific errors it encountered to understand its limitations. The 13 extraction errors fell into 3 distinct categories, each revealing different aspects of document understanding challenges. Eight errors occurred in nested cell confusion scenarios where multi-quarter comparison tables presented ambiguous cell boundaries. In the consolidated balance sheet's `Accounts Payable` row, DeepSeek-R1 correctly extracted the `Q3 2024` value (`$87,654`) and the year-over-year percentage change (`+14.5%`), but misassociated the `Q2 2024` value by placing `$82,345` in the `Q3 2023` column instead of its proper `Q2 2024` position. This type of error suggests the model sometimes struggles with maintaining precise column associations when multiple time periods appear in adjacent cells, particularly when percentage change calculations create additional cognitive complexity.

Three formatting ambiguity errors involved numbers presented in accounting conventions that require domain knowledge to interpret correctly. The accumulated depreciation line item appeared as `($123,456)` with the value enclosed in parentheses, following standard accounting practice where parentheses indicate negative amounts. DeepSeek-R1 initially extracted this value as a positive `123,456`, missing the semantic meaning of the parenthetical notation. While the model eventually identified these as liabilities and inferred negative values from context, the initial extraction demonstrated that implicit formatting conventions can challenge even sophisticated language models. Similarly, when encountering the accumulated other comprehensive loss value of `($7,520)`, the model correctly interpreted the negative sign but experienced minor decimal placement uncertainty in the initial extraction.

Two abbreviation expansion errors revealed challenges in technical terminology recognition. Table headers in the balance sheet used `PP&E` as shorthand for `Property, Plant & Equipment`, a standard abbreviation in financial reporting. DeepSeek-R1 extracted `PP&E` verbatim rather than expanding it to the full term expected by our ground truth dataset. While the abbreviated form contains the same semantic meaning, automated validation systems comparing against ground truth require exact string matches, highlighting how domain-specific abbreviations can create discrepancies between functionally correct extractions and technically *incorrect* results according to strict validation criteria. This suggests that prompts for financial documents might benefit from including glossaries of common abbreviations or explicitly requesting expanded terminology.

Comparing the three approaches

To provide a comprehensive context and understand how DeepSeek-R1's performance compares to specialized document parsing tools, we tested the identical financial document with two alternative approaches: Docling, an IBM Research toolkit specializing in document structure analysis and table recognition, and MarkItDown, a Microsoft tool designed for LLM-optimized document preprocessing. Each tool was evaluated using the same test document and ground truth dataset, measured against the same six quantitative metrics we defined earlier: field extraction accuracy, table parsing accuracy, entity recognition accuracy, structure preservation score, processing time, and cost per document.

Testing Docling and MarkItDown

Docling operates fundamentally differently from DeepSeek-R1 by focusing on document structure extraction rather than semantic understanding. We installed Docling using `pip install docling` and created a Python script (`test_docling_parsing.py`) that processes our financial statement Markdown file. The basic usage pattern involves loading the document, running Docling's parser, and extracting table structures:

```
from docling import DocumentConverter

converter = DocumentConverter()
result = converter.convert("test_financial_statement.md")

# Extract tables
tables = result.document.tables
for table in tables:
    print(f"Table: {table.num_rows} rows x {table.num_cols} columns")
    # Process table cells...
```

Docling excels at recognizing table boundaries, preserving row-column relationships, and maintaining document structure, but produces structural representations rather than semantic field extractions. For our financial document, Docling correctly identified all 6 tables and preserved 97.2% of cell structures (238 out of 245 cells), outperforming DeepSeek-R1's table parsing accuracy. However, Docling cannot directly extract semantic fields such as `total_revenue` with associated units and year-over-year changes, which is why we show `N/A` for its field extraction accuracy. To obtain semantic information from Docling's output requires additional LLM processing.

MarkItDown follows a similar philosophy, optimizing document preprocessing for LLM consumption. Installation requires `pip install markitdown`, and the tool converts various document formats to clean Markdown suitable for LLM input:

```
from markitdown import MarkItDown

converter = MarkItDown()
markdown_output = converter.convert("test_financial_statement.md")
print(markdown_output.text)
```

MarkItDown processed our document in just 890 milliseconds, significantly faster than both DeepSeek-R1 (4,250 ms) and Docling (2,100 ms), but achieved only 78.5% table parsing accuracy. The tool prioritizes processing speed and markdown cleanliness over perfect structural preservation, making it suitable for documents where some structural ambiguity is acceptable. Like Docling, MarkItDown requires subsequent LLM processing for semantic field extraction.

Complete usage examples, configuration details, and output samples for both Docling and MarkItDown are documented in our GitHub repository at `https://github.com/PacktPublishing/DeepSeek-in-Practice/tree/main/Chapter04/document-understanding`. The repository includes `docling_usage_guide.md` with step-by-step instructions, `markitdown_usage_guide.md` with implementation examples, and `tool_comparison_results.md` showing complete outputs from all three tools for direct comparison.

Computing benchmark metrics

Our benchmark comparison requires objective measurements of field accuracy, table accuracy, processing time, and cost across all three tools. Field extraction accuracy was computed by running each tool against the test document, capturing its output, and comparing extracted fields against our ground truth dataset using automated Python scripts. For each of the 150 defined fields in `ground_truth_data.json`, we checked whether the tool's output contained that field with the correct value, considering numerical precision, string case sensitivity, and date formatting. DeepSeek-R1's 137 correctly extracted fields divided by 150 total expected fields yielded 91.3% accuracy. Docling and MarkItDown received `N/A` ratings for field extraction because their structural outputs don't directly produce semantic field extractions without additional LLM processing.

Table parsing accuracy measurement required cell-by-cell comparison of the extracted table data against the 245 expected cells in our 6 major tables. We identified each cell by its table name, row index, and column index in the ground truth, then verified whether the tool correctly extracted that cell's value with proper formatting and positional association. Docling achieved 97.2% accuracy (238/245 correct cells) through its specialized table structure recognition algorithms. DeepSeek-R1 achieved 94.7% accuracy (232/245 correct cells) using semantic understanding, while MarkItDown's lightweight preprocessing yielded 78.5% accuracy (192/245 correct cells). The cell-level comparison reveals that specialized table parsers such as Docling excel at structure recognition, even though they lack semantic comprehension.

Processing time measurements used Python's `time.time()` function to record high-precision timestamps immediately before submitting the document to each tool and immediately after receiving complete output. For DeepSeek-R1, we measured end-to-end API latency, including network transmission, server queue time, model inference, and response formatting, yielding 4,250 ms for our 192-line document. Docling processed the same document in 2,100 ms, running locally on a standard development machine (MacBook Pro M1), while MarkItDown completed processing in just 890 ms. These measurements reflect real-world performance that production systems would experience, though actual times vary based on network conditions, server load, and hardware specifications.

Cost per document calculation differed significantly between API-based and local tools. DeepSeek-R1's cost stems from token consumption multiplied by API pricing: our test document consumed 12,847 total tokens (input plus output), which, at $0.14 per million input tokens and $0.28 per million output tokens, resulted in approximately $0.0027 per document. At this rate, processing one million documents would cost $2,700. Docling and MarkItDown, being open source tools running locally, incur zero direct API costs. However, local deployment introduces infrastructure expenses, including server hardware, maintenance, updates, and operational overhead, that we did not quantify in this benchmark. Organizations must weigh direct API costs against infrastructure investment when choosing between cloud-based and self-hosted solutions.

Quantitative comparison across six metrics

The following table presents the complete benchmark results measuring all three tools against the six quantitative metrics we defined earlier: field extraction accuracy, table parsing accuracy, entity recognition accuracy, structure preservation score, processing time, and cost per document:

Metric	DeepSeek-R1	Docling	MarkItDown
Field extraction accuracy	91.3% (137/150)	N/A*	N/A*
Table parsing accuracy	94.7% (232/245)	97.2% (238/245)	78.5% (192/245)
Entity recognition accuracy	100% (42/42)	N/A*	N/A*
Structure preservation score	88/100	95/100	72/100
Processing time	4,250 ms	2,100 ms	890 ms
Cost per document	$0.0027	$0.00	$0.00

Table 4.6: Overall performance comparison

*Docling and MarkItDown focus on structure extraction and require additional LLM processing for semantic field extraction.

Interpreting the results

Each tool demonstrates distinct strengths aligned with its design philosophy. DeepSeek-R1 achieves the highest field extraction accuracy at 91.3%, successfully identifying 137 out of 150 semantic fields such as `quarterly_revenue`, `operating_margin_expansion`, and `year_over_year_revenue_growth` directly from the document. This semantic extraction capability sets it apart from structural parsers. The model's perfect entity recognition score (42/42 entities) demonstrates robust named entity identification across executives, geographic regions, and product lines. However, DeepSeek-R1's table parsing accuracy of 94.7% trails Docling's industry-leading 97.2%, revealing that specialized table recognition algorithms still outperform general-purpose language models for pure structural extraction.

Docling achieves the highest table parsing accuracy and structure preservation score, reflecting its specialized design for document layout analysis. The tool correctly identified 238 out of 245 table cells with precise row-column associations, outperforming DeepSeek-R1 by 2.5 percentage points. Its structure preservation score of 95/100 indicates near-perfect maintenance of hierarchical relationships, nested table structures, and document reading order. Docling's faster processing time (2,100 ms versus DeepSeek-R1's 4,250 ms) and zero API cost make it attractive for high-volume batch processing scenarios. The `N/A` ratings for field extraction and entity recognition reflect architectural choice rather than limitation: Docling delivers structured representations that require downstream LLM processing to extract semantic meaning.

MarkItDown prioritizes speed and simplicity over comprehensive accuracy, completing document processing in just 890 ms – less than one-fifth of DeepSeek-R1's processing time. This performance comes at the cost of table parsing accuracy (78.5%) and structure preservation (72/100), as the tool sometimes simplifies complex nested tables or merges cells to create cleaner Markdown output. For use cases where perfect structural fidelity is less critical than rapid preprocessing for LLM consumption, MarkItDown's lightweight approach offers practical advantages. Like Docling, it requires subsequent LLM processing for semantic extraction.

Understanding tool capabilities

Beyond quantitative metrics, each tool possesses specialized capabilities that influence its suitability for different document understanding scenarios. Direct field extraction capability refers to a tool's ability to identify and extract semantic fields (such as `total_revenue`, `ceo_name`, or `quarterly_growth_rate`) without additional processing steps. DeepSeek-R1 excels at this through natural language understanding, while Docling and MarkItDown produce intermediate structural representations requiring LLM interpretation.

Table structure recognition measures how well a tool identifies table boundaries, preserves row-column relationships, handles merged cells, and maintains hierarchical nesting in complex tables. Docling achieves excellence here through specialized computer vision and layout analysis algorithms trained specifically for table detection. DeepSeek-R1 demonstrates very good performance by understanding table semantics even when the visual structure is ambiguous, while MarkItDown provides moderate capability suitable for simpler tables.

OCR integration capability determines whether a tool can process scanned documents or images containing text. Docling integrates with OCR engines to handle PDF files created from scanned images, a critical capability for legacy document digitization projects. Neither DeepSeek-R1 nor MarkItDown includes native OCR, requiring preprocessed text-based inputs. Semantic reasoning capability measures a tool's ability to understand meaning, context, and relationships between extracted information. DeepSeek-R1 demonstrates excellent semantic reasoning, recognizing that `operating margin expansion of 340 basis points` means the current 24.8% margin increased from a previous 21.4%. Docling and MarkItDown lack this capability, focusing instead on structural extraction.

Cost efficiency considerations extend beyond direct API pricing to include infrastructure, maintenance, and operational overhead. DeepSeek-R1's $0.0027 per document API cost translates to $2,700 per million documents with zero infrastructure investment but ongoing usage fees. Docling and MarkItDown eliminate API costs but require server infrastructure, software updates, dependency management, and technical expertise for self-hosted deployment. Setup complexity varies accordingly: DeepSeek-R1 requires only API credentials and simple HTTP requests, MarkItDown installs via `pip` with minimal configuration, while Docling involves more complex dependency management and configuration for optimal performance.

Choosing the right tool for your use case

Our benchmark results reveal that different document understanding scenarios call for different tool selections based on specific requirements and constraints. When analyzing financial statements or business documents where semantic extraction of specific fields is the primary goal, DeepSeek-R1 offers the most direct path to actionable data. Its 91.3% field extraction accuracy and perfect entity recognition enable production deployments with validation workflows to catch the remaining 8.7% of errors. Organizations requiring immediate API-based deployment without infrastructure investment will find DeepSeek-R1's simple integration and pay-per-use pricing attractive for moderate document volumes.

For scenarios involving PDF documents with complex visual layouts, a hybrid approach combining Docling's structure extraction with DeepSeek-R1's semantic understanding delivers best-in-class results. Docling preprocesses the PDF to extract table structures with 97.2% accuracy, then DeepSeek-R1 interprets those structures to extract semantic fields. This pipeline leverages each tool's core strength: Docling's specialized layout analysis and DeepSeek-R1's language understanding. The combined approach costs $0.0027 per document (only DeepSeek-R1's API fee) while achieving higher overall accuracy than either tool alone.

Processing scanned documents or images containing text requires OCR capabilities that only Docling provides in our benchmark comparison. Legacy document digitization projects, historical financial record analysis, or any scenario involving physical documents converted to images necessitates Docling's OCR integration. The typical workflow involves Docling performing OCR and structure extraction, then feeding the resulting text to DeepSeek-R1 for semantic analysis. Real-time API integration scenarios where sub-second response latency is critical might favor MarkItDown's 890-ms processing time for initial preprocessing, though DeepSeek-R1's 4.25-second end-to-end latency remains acceptable for most interactive applications.

Batch processing of large document volumes (millions of documents) requires careful cost-benefit analysis. Docling's zero API cost makes it economically attractive for massive scale, but organizations must factor in infrastructure investment estimated at $50,000–200,000 annually for servers, storage, networking, and operational staff. At one million documents per month, DeepSeek-R1 costs $2,700 monthly ($32,400 annually), substantially less than self-hosted infrastructure until reaching approximately 5–10 million documents monthly, depending on infrastructure efficiency. Multi-language documents leverage DeepSeek-R1's strong multilingual capabilities, accurately processing financial reports in English, Spanish, Mandarin, French, German, and other languages without requiring language-specific configurations.

Hybrid approach: Best practices

Based on our comprehensive benchmarking results, the optimal approach for processing complex financial documents leverages the complementary strengths of multiple tools rather than relying on a single solution. Organizations can achieve higher accuracy, lower costs, and greater flexibility by architecting hybrid pipelines that combine structural extraction with semantic understanding.

Recommended workflow architecture

The ideal workflow begins with document preprocessing for any PDF or DOCX format inputs. At this initial stage, we recommend using Docling for structure extraction because its specialized algorithms excel at identifying table boundaries, preserving row-column relationships, and maintaining proper reading order even in complex multi-column layouts. Docling's OCR integration proves particularly valuable when processing scanned documents or images containing financial data, as it can extract text from legacy paper documents that have been digitized. This preprocessing stage converts diverse input formats into clean, structured representations that downstream tools can reliably process.

The second stage involves semantic extraction, where DeepSeek-R1 interprets the structured output from Docling to identify and extract specific fields with contextual understanding. Rather than processing raw PDF files, DeepSeek-R1 receives prestructured Markdown or JSON from Docling, allowing it to focus computational resources on semantic interpretation rather than layout analysis. During this stage, the model extracts named fields such as `quarterly_revenue`, `operating_margin_expansion`, and `year_over_year_growth_rate` while understanding their contextual relationships. DeepSeek-R1 also validates numerical calculations by checking whether computed values, such as `gross_profit`, correctly equal `total_revenue` minus `cost_of_revenue`, catching potential OCR errors or structure recognition mistakes from the preprocessing stage.

The final quality assurance stage implements validation workflows that cross-check critical fields using business rules and statistical anomaly detection. Financial extractions undergo threshold-based review, where fields exceeding expected value ranges (such as revenue changes greater than 50% quarter-over-quarter) trigger human verification. Organizations should implement automated tracking of accuracy metrics over time, measuring field extraction accuracy, entity recognition, and table parsing performance against curated ground truth datasets. As accuracy improves through prompt refinement and error analysis, confidence thresholds can gradually increase to reduce manual review overhead while maintaining quality standards.

Cost-benefit analysis and economic justification

The economic advantages of hybrid automation become compelling at scale. Combining Docling's zero-cost local processing with DeepSeek-R1's $0.0027 per document API fee yields a total cost of $2.70 per thousand documents processed. In contrast, traditional manual extraction by trained financial analysts costs between $50 and $100 per document, depending on complexity and required accuracy. For an organization processing 10,000 financial documents annually, manual extraction costs $500,000 to $1,000,000 per year, while the automated hybrid pipeline costs just $27 annually in API fees plus infrastructure expenses for running Docling locally.

This dramatic cost reduction of over 99% enables previously infeasible use cases such as comprehensive analysis of all supplier invoices, automated extraction from historical financial archives, or real-time processing of competitor financial disclosures. The per-document cost at scale ($0.0027) means processing one million documents costs only $2,700, making document understanding economically viable for applications that were prohibitively expensive with manual methods. Organizations must factor in infrastructure costs for self-hosting Docling (estimated at $5,000–15,000 annually for modest volumes) and engineering resources for pipeline development and maintenance (approximately $50,000–100,000 annually depending on complexity), but even with these additional costs, total expense remains under $120,000 annually for processing millions of documents.

If you wish to explore more case studies, such as *Brainstorming and ideation* and *Code generation and understanding*, please visit the GitHub repo of this chapter:

- *Brainstorming and ideation*: `https://github.com/PacktPublishing/DeepSeek-in-Practice/tree/main/Chapter04/brainstorming-ideation`
- *Code generation*: `https://github.com/PacktPublishing/DeepSeek-in-Practice/tree/main/Chapter04/code-assistant`

Summary

This chapter demonstrated DeepSeek-R1's document understanding capabilities through two detailed case studies: Amazon API Gateway integration documentation and financial statement analysis. In the Amazon case study, DeepSeek-R1 analyzed a 45-page technical integration guide and achieved an 87% overall evaluation score by successfully extracting serverless architecture components, identifying security configurations, and generating production-ready CloudFormation templates. The model demonstrated strong comprehension of complex technical documentation, including API Gateway throttling policies, Lambda authorization patterns, JWT validation logic, and distributed tracing configurations.

The financial document analysis case study evaluated DeepSeek-R1 against specialized document parsing tools using a fictional quarterly report for FruitStand Innovation Inc. containing 192 lines, 6 complex tables, and 150 semantic fields. DeepSeek-R1 achieved 91.3% field extraction accuracy (137/150 fields), 94.7% table parsing accuracy (232/245 cells), and perfect entity recognition (42/42 entities) with a processing time of 4,250 milliseconds at $0.0027 per document. We compared DeepSeek-R1 against Docling (IBM Research) and MarkItDown (Microsoft), finding that Docling achieved higher table parsing accuracy (97.2%) through specialized structure recognition, MarkItDown provided the fastest processing (890 ms) with moderate accuracy (78.5%), and DeepSeek-R1 uniquely delivered semantic understanding with direct field extraction capabilities. Hybrid pipelines combining Docling's structure extraction with DeepSeek-R1's semantic interpretation achieved the best overall results.

Throughout both case studies, we applied consistent evaluation metrics, including qualitative assessment of technical accuracy and implementation readiness, and quantitative measurement of extraction accuracy, processing time, and cost efficiency. DeepSeek-R1 consistently performed at a professional consultant level with 88–92% accuracy across complex documents at $0.0027 per document compared to $50–100 for manual analysis, demonstrating 99%+ cost reduction for automated document understanding workflows. Organizations implementing DeepSeek-R1 for document understanding should establish clear evaluation metrics before deployment, defining both qualitative criteria, such as technical accuracy and completeness, alongside quantitative measures, including field extraction accuracy, entity recognition, processing time, and cost per document appropriate to their specific document types. Financial documents typically require 95%+ accuracy thresholds due to regulatory and compliance requirements, while general technical documentation may accept 85%+ accuracy with human validation for critical sections.

Successful implementation requires careful prompt engineering with explicit instructions about output format, required fields, numerical precision requirements, and domain-specific terminology. Our financial document analysis demonstrated that providing glossaries for common abbreviations, such as *PP&E* for *Property, Plant & Equipment*, and specifying whether to expand acronyms, significantly reduces extraction errors. For complex multi-column tables, explicitly instructing the model about column associations and time period comparisons minimizes nested cell confusion. Iterative prompting proves valuable when initial extractions miss critical fields, as follow-up prompts targeting specific gaps consistently improve completeness without requiring complete document reprocessing. Organizations should also consider hybrid architectures that combine tool strengths based on document characteristics, such as preprocessing PDF files with complex visual layouts using Docling to extract table structures at 97.2% accuracy, then using DeepSeek-R1 for semantic field extraction and entity recognition at a combined cost of only $0.0027 per document while achieving higher accuracy than either tool alone.

Next up, we will show how to create a working service using DeepSeek API. Stay tuned.

5

Building with DeepSeek

In the previous chapters we discussed the inner-workings of DeepSeek, the best strategies to effectively prompt DeepSeek models, and how to use DeepSeek. In this chapter, it's time to get practical. We'll tackle a real-world problem, and we'll show you how you can leverage DeepSeek models to solve it.

DeepSeek models are open-source, which is both powerful and challenging. You get endless options: large models via APIs, or small, distilled models that you can run locally, which is powerful but comes with trade-offs. There is no single right way to use DeepSeek models; the best choice depends on your situation and requirements for your use case. Should you go for a local option? Should you go for a cloud option? Should you go for a small model, a big model, or a reasoning model?

Our goal in this chapter is twofold. We want to show you how to solve a particular use case (end-to-end) using DeepSeek models and demonstrate the main ways you can interact with or use DeepSeek models. During the chapter, you'll learn all the different ways you can use models: local, through an API, in the cloud, and on your own machine.

But before we start, we need a use case. Let's consider what Duarte has to stay about his day-to-day struggles with his smartwatch.

My wife and I have been runners for a long time. I won't lie, I'm big into marathons. Running is one of those rare occasions when I actually physically get out from behind the desk and go outside. I love everything about it. But this is probably not the place to talk too much about it. We both use Garmin smartwatches; we love them!

Every day at exactly 8:45 p.m., my wife and I look at our watches, and at that same time, the watch sends us a small summary of our day (**Stressful day**, **Workout day**, or **Rest day**). Here is an example:

> *Workout day*
>
> *Your intense workout today and periods of rest are good for your physical and mental health. Now take time to relax and focus on getting a good night's sleep.*

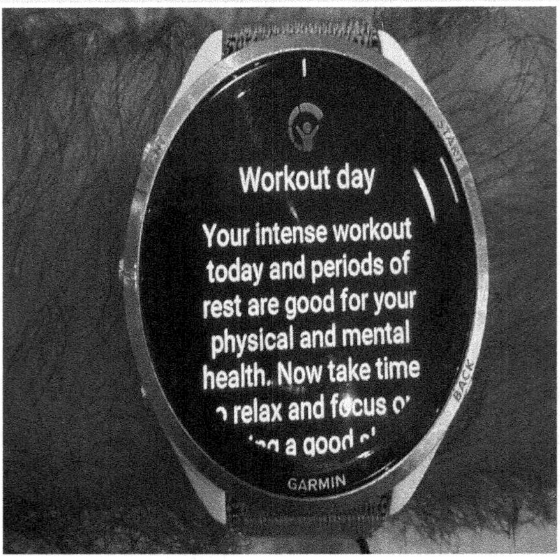

Figure 5.1: An example of the daily Garmin notification

For the first weeks of having my watch, they were great! It gives me yet another indicator to track and understand my body. But after a couple of weeks, you start realizing that you always receive one of five prewritten messages. From one perspective, this is cool; the watch understands my body! From another perspective, it's annoying, since the watch is only sending me one of the five prewritten messages it has stored in memory. Also, the messages are just *too* general. It almost feels like the watch is not telling me anything I didn't know already. After a while, it just feels boring.

We hear you Duarte!

When we three authors began brainstorming on this book, we realized that in the age of **large language models (LLMs)** such as DeepSeek, Garmin's notifications can surely be better - much better. A more dynamic, personalized message - one that can take some sort of user input. You know what we mean. There are *many* ways we can make this better. So, here we are going to do exactly this.

In this chapter, we'll build a program that can access my smartwatch data, read it, and provide me with an interesting and dynamic summary every day. No more five predefined messages; every time we receive the summary, the message will be different. We'll leverage DeepSeek to analyze the data and build a nice summary for us. We'll call it the ***Daily Health Summary***.

A couple of disclaimers before we get started:

- This Daily Health Summary will be generated by an LLM. As you likely know, LLMs can sometimes *hallucinate* or produce inaccurate information. We won't be discussing guardrails or guaranteeing safe model outputs in this chapter. However, if you're interested in learning more, here's a helpful library to get you started: `https://github.com/guardrails-ai/guardrails`.
- This chapter will focus on extracting data from your Garmin watch. We will use the Garth library (`https://github.com/matin/garth`) for authentication. While widely known and popular, it's important to remember that it's not an official Garmin library. Consequently, there are no guarantees that Garmin won't change its authentication methods in the future. If you don't have a Garmin device, you can still extract data from Strava or another service you use; however, you will need to handle the data extraction process yourself using those alternative sources.

All right, let's get this started.

Here is what we will cover in this chapter:

- Building our first prototype
- Interacting with DeepSeek models
- Deploying an isolated model service with AWS
- Best practices and recommendations

Technical requirements

All the code for this chapter is in the book's GitHub repository over at `https://github.com/PacktPublishing/DeepSeek-in-Practice`.

You should have the following installed on your machine:

- uv: See the following link for instructions: `https://docs.astral.sh/uv/getting-started/installation/`.
- Docker: We will be building Docker images for the API we will design. Check out this link to get started with the installation: `https://docs.docker.com/engine/install/`.

This chapter's code is in the `Chapter 05` directory; running `uv sync` inside the chapter folder will install all the dependencies.

This chapter assumes you have a DeepSeek API key, which you can acquire over at `https://platform.deepseek.com/`.

You might have to install other libraries/dependencies, but we will explicitly call them out during the chapter.

There are several ways to use DeepSeek, for example, the DeepSeek API, third-party APIs, or using some libraries like litellm to utilize DeepSeek models. We have covered a few of these options in the *Appendix* of this book. Go check them out.

Building the first prototype

In this first section, we'll build an end-to-end prototype for the Daily Health Summary, following five high-level steps:

1. First, we'll fetch data from the Garmin API and learn how to query it.
2. Next, we'll shape that raw health data into a format that DeepSeek can understand and reason about.
3. Then, we'll define the structured output: what we want DeepSeek to return and what it should look like.
4. Before wrapping up, we'll refactor everything into an API you can query and use.
5. Finally, we will walk through deploying it all with Docker.

Let's begin with fetching the data from Garmin.

Fetching our data

The first order of business is to query Garmin for the data it has about us. This is all about programmatically retrieving the health data our Garmin watch has about us (heart rate, sleep hours, stress, etc.). In order to get this done, we will leverage the `python-garminconnect` project (`https://github.com/cyberjunky/python-garminconnect`).

In order for this to work, you should have both your Garmin email and the password you use to log in to your Garmin account. Both of those should work with `https://connect.garmin.com/signin`.

Note

Don't worry if you don't have a Garmin account. The GitHub repo includes instructions for loading sample data, so you can run the APIs and examples without any issues.

Once you have those at hand, we can log in to Garmin with the following function:

```
# We get the values as environmental variables
GARMIN_EMAIL = os.getenv("GARMIN_EMAIL") # your email
GARMIN_PASSWORD = os.getenv("GARMIN_PASSWORD") # your password

# and we define our function
def start_garmin() -> Garmin:
    """Initialize Garmin connection."""
    try:
        GARMIN = Garmin(
            email=GARMIN_EMAIL,
            password=GARMIN_PASSWORD,
            is_cn=False, # if you are in China, set to True
        )
        GARMIN.login()
        print("You are now logged in.")
        return GARMIN
    except Exception as e:
        print(f"Could not login with email and password: {e}")
        raise
If everything goes well, you can now run the following:
garmin = start_garmin()
# prints: You are now logged in.
```

This function now gives us a `garmin` instance we can work with and query the API. Now that we know how to instantiate the Garmin API, let's go ahead and query all the information we need for a given day. To do this, we create a `get_daily_health_summary` function. This function will receive an API instance, a start date, and an end date. The goal is then to return health information for that date range.

First, we'll create a couple of auxiliary functions to convert a date to ISO format (as Garmin requires) and a function that receives two dates and returns a range we can iterate over:

```
def get_daily_health_summary(
    api: Any, start: datetime.date, end: datetime.date
) -> list[dict[str, Any]]:

    def dstr(d: datetime.date) -> str:
        return d.isoformat()

    def daterange(a: datetime.date, b: datetime.date):
        for i in range((b - a).days + 1):
            yield a + datetime.timedelta(days=i)
```

We now iterate through each day, and we can retrieve summary information from Garmin by using the get_user_summary method. This method returns a dictionary containing the fields we want for context, such as resting heart rate, steps, exercise minutes, and sleep duration:

```
    for day in daterange(start, end):
        s = dstr(day)
        day_of_week = day.strftime("%A")
        summary = api.get_user_summary(s) or {}
        rhr = summary.get("restingHeartRate")
        steps = summary.get("totalSteps")
        stress_level = summary.get("averageStressLevel")
        body_battery_final = summary.get("bodyBatteryMostRecentValue") or
summary.get(
            "mostRecentBodyBattery"
        )
        exercise_minutes = (summary.get("moderateIntensityMinutes") or 0)
+ (
            summary.get("vigorousIntensityMinutes") or 0
        )
        sleep_seconds = summary.get("sleepingSeconds")
        sleep_hours = round(sleep_seconds / 3600, 2)
        body_battery_start = summary.get("bodyBatteryAtWakeTime")
        total_distance_meters = summary.get("totalDistanceMeters")
```

Finally, once we have extracted all the fields we're interested in, we can now append them to the array that our function will return:

```
        out.append(
            {
                "date": s,
                "day_of_week": day_of_week,
                "resting_heart_rate": rhr,
                "exercise_minutes": exercise_minutes,
                "stress_level": stress_level,
                "sleep_hours": sleep_hours,
                "steps": steps,
                "total_distance_meters": total_distance_meters,
                "body_battery_start_day": body_battery_start,
                "body_battery_end_day": body_battery_final,
            }
        )

    return out
```

With this function in place, we can now call it for any day we're interested in. For example, if we would like to get the data for yesterday, we can get today's date, remove a day (using `timedelta`), and call the `get_daily_health_summary` method:

```
yesterday = datetime.date.today() - datetime.timedelta(days=1)
summary_for_yesterday = get_daily_health_summary(
    garmin, yesterday, yesterday)
summary_for_yesterday
```

After calling this function, we can see that on August 13th, I had a resting heart rate of 62 and slept for a total of 9 hours(!). I'm not sure what happened there, but that was certainly a lot of sleep! As they say, sleep is an athlete's best friend:

```
[{'date': '2025-08-13', 'day_of_week': 'Wednesday', 'resting_heart_rate':
62, 'exercise_minutes': 0, 'stress_level': 38, 'sleep_hours': 9.09,
'steps': 1866, 'total_distance_meters': 1387, 'body_battery_start_day':
74, 'body_battery_end_day': 17}]
```

Keep in mind that we can also call our function for a date range, which will be helpful, as in this example:

```
past_7_days_start = yesterday - datetime.timedelta(days=7)
past_7_days_end = yesterday - datetime.timedelta(days=1)

summary_for_past_7_days = get_daily_health_summary(
    garmin, past_7_days_start, past_7_days_end
)
summary_for_past_7_days
```

This will return a list of the data for each day between `past_7_days_start` and `past_7_days_end` If this does not make a whole lot of sense, don't worry just yet! Everything will come together soon:

```
[
    {
        'date': '2025-08-06',
        'day_of_week': 'Wednesday',
        'resting_heart_rate': 58,
        'exercise_minutes': 3,
        'stress_level': 32,
        'sleep_hours': 8.17,
        'steps': 5320,
        'total_distance_meters': 3953,
        'body_battery_start_day': 97,
        'body_battery_end_day': 20
    },
    {
        'date': '2025-08-07',
        'day_of_week': 'Thursday',
        # ...

    },
    {
        'date': '2025-08-08',
        # ...
```

Creating the context

We can now look up health data for specific dates or date ranges. Next, we need to get the data ready for our DeepSeek model. There are many ways to do this, but we want to keep it simple. We will create a prompt that includes a short Markdown section for each measurement. For each measurement (such as stress level), we want to show the LLM the following:

- Today's value of the metric.
- The average from the past seven days (the baseline), not including today.
- The percentage change from today compared to the baseline.
- The trend in the baseline period.
- Whether a lower value is better for this measurement.

For example, in the case of sleep hours, we want the following:

```
## Sleep Hours
- Today's value (2025-08-13): 9.09
- 7-day baseline average (excluding today): 8.21
- Percent change vs. baseline: +10.7%
- Trend over previous 7 days: up ↑
- Better is lower: False
```

This will be replicated for every other metric we retrieve.

With this information, we are now giving the model a metric under a certain context, instead of giving a metric in isolation. This will ensure the model hallucinates less and understands the wider context of the metric.

To identify trends, we need a heuristic. Here's a simple function that accepts a list of numbers and returns `up`, `down`, or `flat`. It compares the mean of the first and last three values in the list. If these means are within 5%, the function returns `flat`, since there was no major change in the metric. It's not a perfect heuristic, but it serves our purpose:

```
def detect_trend(values, pct_threshold=5):
    recent, earlier = np.mean(values[-3:]), np.mean(values[:3])
    return (
        "up"
        if recent > earlier * (1 + pct_threshold / 100)
        else ("down" if recent < earlier * (1 - pct_threshold / 100) else
"flat")
    )
```

With our heuristic in place, we can now create a function to create the context; `build_llm_context_md` receives a summary for today and a summary for the past seven days. These are the same lists of dictionaries that carry information about health metrics in the current day and the previous seven days.

We then create a list of strings, where each string represents a line of context for the LLM. Finally, we create a `better_is_lower` array to store metrics in which lower scores are preferable, such as stress level:

```
def build_llm_context_md(
    summary_for_today: list[dict], summary_for_past_7_days: list[dict]
) -> str:
    assert len(summary_for_today) == 1, "Expected 1 day of summary"
    today = summary_for_today[0]

    metrics = [key for key in today.keys() if key not in ["date", "day_of_
week"]]
    lines = [
        f"# Daily Metrics Summary for {today['date']} ({today['day_of_
week']})",
        "_Note: All comparisons use the **previous 7 days only**,
excluding today._",
        "",
    ]

    better_is_lower = [
        "resting_heart_rate",
        "stress_level",
    ]
```

After that, we iterate through our metrics. For each, we create a small list of values. The current value of the metric, the mean for the baseline period, is better if lower. After iterating, we then apply a join in all our lines to build up our context for DeepSeek:

```
    for metric in metrics:
        today_val = today[metric]
        if not today_val:
            print(f"Skipped {metric} since no values were found")
        past_vals = [
```

```
            day[metric] for day in summary_for_past_7_days
            if day[metric] is not None
        ]
        avg_7d = sum(past_vals) / len(past_vals) if past_vals else 0
        delta_pct = ((today_val - avg_7d) / avg_7d * 100) if avg_7d else 0
        trend_dir = detect_trend(past_vals)
        arrow = "↑" if trend_dir == "up" else ("↓" if trend_dir == "down"
else "→")

        lines.append(
            f"## {metric.replace('_', ' ').title()}\n"
            f"- Today's value ({today['date']}): {today_val}\n"
            f"- 7-day baseline average (excluding today): {avg_7d:.2f}\n"
            f"- Percent change vs. baseline: {delta_pct:+.1f}%\n"
            f"- Trend over previous 7 days: {trend_dir} {arrow}\n"
            f"- Better is lower: {metric in better_is_lower}\n"
        )

    return "\n".join(lines)
```

We can now call our function by doing the following:

```
# start client and define date
garmin = start_garmin()
date = "2025-08-13"

# get data for date of summary
date_for_summary = datetime.datetime.strptime(date, "%Y-%m-%d").date()
summary_in_date = get_daily_health_summary(
        garmin, date_for_summary, date_for_summary
)

# get data for 7 days before
past_period_start = date_for_summary - datetime.timedelta(days=7)
past_period_end = date_for_summary - datetime.timedelta(days=1)
summary_in_past_period = get_daily_health_summary(
        garmin, past_period_start, past_period_end
)
```

```
# build prompt
prompt =  build_llm_context_md(summary_in_date, summary_in_past_period)
print(prompt)
```

This outputs a nice summary that we can then feed to our LLM:

```
# Daily Metrics Summary for 2025-08-13 (Wednesday)
_Note: All comparisons use the **previous 7 days only**, excluding today._

## Resting Heart Rate
- Today's value (2025-08-13): 62
- 7-day baseline average (excluding today): 55.86
- Percent change vs. baseline: +11.0%
- Trend over previous 7 days: up ↑
- Better is lower: True

## Exercise Minutes
- Today's value (2025-08-13): 0
- 7-day baseline average (excluding today): 3.00
- Percent change vs. baseline: -100.0%
- Trend over previous 7 days: up ↑
- Better is lower: False

## Stress Level
- ....

## Sleep Hours
- ...

... rest of metrics hidden for brevity
```

Great! We now have all the information we would like to feed our DeepSeek model. But how exactly would we like it to respond?

Defining the structured output

It's now time to define how we would like our Daily Health Summary to look. As with most LLM-backed applications, it's usually a good practice to make the models return some sort of structured output(JSON format) (we covered these in *Chapters 2* and *3*). To represent our Daily Health Summary, we create two Pydantic (`https://docs.pydantic.dev/`) models:

- `DayType`: Classifies our day into one of five types.
- `DailySummary`: Creates an object that includes a day type, a title, an emoji, an observation, and a recommendation.

Here is the code:

```
from pydantic import BaseModel, Field

class DayType(str, Enum):
    TRAINING = "training"
    ACTIVE_RECOVERY = "active_recovery"
    REST = "rest"
    HIGH_STRESS = "high_stress"
    BALANCED = "balanced"

class DailySummary(BaseModel):
    day_type: DayType = Field(
        ...,
        description="Classification of the day based on activity and
recovery metrics",
    )

    title: str = Field(..., description="One sentence summary of the day")
    emoji: str = Field(..., description="Emoji to represent the day type")
    observation: str = Field(
        ...,
        description="Two sentence observation about key metrics and
patterns",
    )
    recommendation: str = Field(
        ...,
```

```
        description="Two sentence actionable recommendation for tomorrow",
    )
```

Now, we have all the elements to make our first Daily Health Summary. Let's create the summary.

Creating the Daily Health Summary

We start by first creating a simple function that calls the DeepSeek API using `type: json_object` to enforce a JSON structure from the model. Nothing surprising here; it returns the JSON the model created and the reasoning content, if there is any (in the case of `deepseek-reasoner`, for example):

```
def llm(
    messages: list[dict], model: str, response_format: dict | None = None
) -> tuple[dict, str | None]:
    client = OpenAI(
        api_key=os.environ["DEEPSEEK_API_KEY"],
        base_url="https://api.deepseek.com",
    )
    response = client.chat.completions.create(
        model=model, messages=messages, response_format=response_format,
temperature=0.0
    )
    message = response.choices[0].message

    if hasattr(message, "reasoning_content"):
        reasoning_content = message.reasoning_content
    else:
        reasoning_content = None

    return json.loads(message.content), reasoning_content
```

To ensure that our model behaves well, we create two Daily Health Summary examples and create our system prompt as well:

```
# Example 1: Training day
training_day_example = DailySummary(
    day_type=DayType.TRAINING,
    title="Strong training day with elevated activity across all
metrics.",
    emoji="💪",
```

```
    observation="Exercise minutes doubled your baseline with 95 minutes of
activity, supported by 18,500 steps. Despite the high training load, body
battery started at a solid 85, indicating good recovery from yesterday.",
    recommendation="Consider an active recovery or rest day tomorrow to
allow adaptation from today's effort. Prioritize sleep tonight to maintain
your body battery levels and support muscle recovery.",
)

# Example 2: High Stress Day
high_stress_day_example = DailySummary(
    day_type=DayType.HIGH_STRESS,
    emoji="😫",
    title="Elevated stress and poor recovery despite minimal physical
activity.",
    observation="Stress levels jumped 46% above baseline while sleep
dropped to just 6.1 hours, resulting in a low body battery start of 45.
Exercise and movement were minimal, suggesting stress is from non-physical
sources.",
    recommendation="Focus on stress management techniques and aim for
8+ hours of sleep tonight. Consider light exercise like walking or yoga
tomorrow, as gentle movement can help regulate stress levels.",
)
examples = [training_day_example, high_stress_day_example]
examples_str = "\n\n\n".join([example.model_dump_json() for example in
examples])
```

The system prompt has three components - the general instructions to give the model context and guidance, the JSON schema we expect from it, and some example JSON outputs as well:

```
system_prompt = f"""
Instructions:
* You will be given a summary of the user's health and fitness data for
today, in comparison to the past 7 days.
* Your goal is to generate a summary that will be shown in the user's
smart watch.
* Keep things short, but also interesting to the user.
* Your summary should include a type of day, a title, some observations
and recommendations for the user.
```

```
* Your summary should be in JSON format. Only output the JSON, no other
text.

---JSON SCHEMA---
{DailySummary.model_json_schema()}
---END JSON SCHEMA---

---EXAMPLE JSON OUTPUTS---
{examples_str}
---END EXAMPLE JSON OUTPUTS---
"""
```

Now that we have everything in place, we can create one last function. The role of this function is simply to tie everything that we've built up until now together. It does the following:

1. Receive a Garmin API instance and a date in string format.
2. Fetch data from Garmin for that date and for the seven days before.
3. Build up our prompt and list of messages, including our system prompt.
4. Call the model and validate its response against our `DailySummary` Pydantic model.

```
def get_daily_summary(
    garmin: Garmin,
    date: str,
    model: Literal["deepseek-chat", "deepseek-reasoner"],
    verbose: bool = False,
) -> DailySummary:
        # convert to datetime
    date_for_summary = datetime.datetime.strptime(date, "%Y-%m-%d").date()

    # get information for date
    summary_in_date = get_daily_health_summary(
        garmin, date_for_summary, date_for_summary
    )

        # get information for baseline period
    past_period_start = date_for_summary - datetime.timedelta(days=7)
    past_period_end = date_for_summary - datetime.timedelta(days=1)
```

```
    summary_in_past_period = get_daily_health_summary(
        garmin, past_period_start, past_period_end
    )

        # create prompt with trends and metrics
    prompt = build_llm_context_md(summary_in_date, summary_in_past_period)

        # create messages list
    messages = [
        {"role": "system", "content": system_prompt},
        {"role": "user", "content": prompt},
    ]

        # call LLM and validate response
    response, reasoning = llm(messages, model, {"type": "json_object"})
    health_summary = DailySummary.model_validate(response)

    return health_summary
```

From now on, all we need to do to get a Daily Health Summary is to call the `get_daily_summary` function with a date and the model we would like to use:

```
daily_summary = get_daily_summary(garmin, "2025-08-19", "deepseek-chat")
print(daily_summary.model_dump_json())
```

This then returns the Daily Health Summary we built:


```
{
   "day_type":"balanced",
   "title":"A well-balanced day with improved recovery and lower stress.",
   "emoji":"⚖️",
   "observation":"Resting heart rate decreased by 9.3% to 39, and stress
level dropped significantly by 58.8%, indicating excellent recovery. Body
battery started high at 82 and ended at 72, showing efficient energy use
despite slightly reduced sleep and activity.",
   "recommendation":"Maintain this balance by continuing with moderate
exercise and ensuring adequate sleep. Focus on stress management to keep
levels low and support ongoing recovery."
}
```

As you can see, this works pretty well. Looking at the example, I can tell you it's absolutely right. This was my first day of vacation in August, which makes the summary particularly accurate. We now have our first prototype. But building an application does not stop there. We want to build a full service that can compute these daily summaries for anyone who is interested in them. And for that, we need to build an API.

Refactoring into an API

Now that our system works as a simple function, it's time we build an API for it. The goal is to create a service that can receive a request from a user, as well as their details to log in to Garmin's API, and return a Daily Health Summary of their health metrics. To accomplish this, we will use FastAPI.

Security note

The API service uses your authentication credentials, including your password, to call the Garmin Connect API. This approach is acceptable for a prototype, but in production, users typically won't want to share plaintext passwords with an unfamiliar service. For a real application, consider implementing OAuth or using the official Garmin Connect Developer Program: `https://developer.garmin.com/gc-developer-program/activity-api`.

Our API includes two endpoints. The first is a small quality-of-life improvement: when users visit / (the root), they are automatically redirected to `/docs`. This makes it easier for developers (especially those new to the project) to quickly find and explore the available endpoints and understand the expected outputs:

```
from fastapi import FastAPI, Header, HTTPException
from fastapi.responses import RedirectResponse

app = FastAPI(title="Garmin Health Summary API")

@app.get("/")
async def root():
    return RedirectResponse(url="/docs")
```

Once the app is instantiated, we create `HealthSummaryRequest`, which is the request we expect from the users. As you can see in the following, we expect them to provide a date, which will default to today's date if not provided. If they want, the user can also specify one of the two models (`deepseek-chat` or `deepseek-reasoner`) to create the summary:

```
class Model(str, Enum):
    chat = "deepseek-chat"
    reasoner = "deepseek-reasoner"

class HealthSummaryRequest(BaseModel):
    date: str = Field(
        default_factory=lambda: datetime.date.today().isoformat(),
        description="Date in YYYY-MM-DD format, defaults to today",
        example=datetime.date.today().isoformat(),
    )
    model: Model = Field(
        default=Model.chat,
        description="Model to use for the summary",
    )
```

To authenticate, the user must provide the Garmin credentials as a header to the request. We return the same `DailySummary` request we've introduced previously:

```
@app.post("/health-summary", response_model=DailySummary)
async def get_health_summary(
    request: HealthSummaryRequest,
    garmin_email: str = Header(..., description="Garmin email address"),
    garmin_password: str = Header(..., description="Garmin password"),
) -> DailySummary:
```

The core of the `get_health_summary` endpoint runs the exact same logic we've seen before, and additionally adds some error handling in case things go wrong:

```
    """Get Daily Health Summary for a specific date.

    Args:
        request: Health summary request with date and model
        garmin_email: Garmin account email from header
        garmin_password: Garmin account password from header
```

```
    Returns:
        Daily Health Summary with AI-generated insights
    """
    try:
        garmin = get_garmin_client(garmin_email, garmin_password)
        summary = get_daily_summary(garmin, request.date, request.model)
        logger.info(
            f"Daily Health Summary API request completed successfully for 
{request.date}"
        )
        return summary
    except ValueError as e:
        logger.error(f"Invalid date format provided: {request.date}")
        raise HTTPException(
            status_code=400, detail=f"Invalid date format: {e}"
        )
    except Exception as e:
        logger.error(
            f"Failed to generate Daily Health Summary for {request.date}: 
{e}"
        )
        raise HTTPException(
            status_code=500, detail=f"Error generating summary: {e}"
        )
```

With all of this in place, we can now run our API with the following command:

```
$ uv run fastapi run 02-api.py
```

This will start a production server on port `8000` of your machine. When you go to `http://0.0.0.0:8000`, you'll see the API page ready for you to interact with:

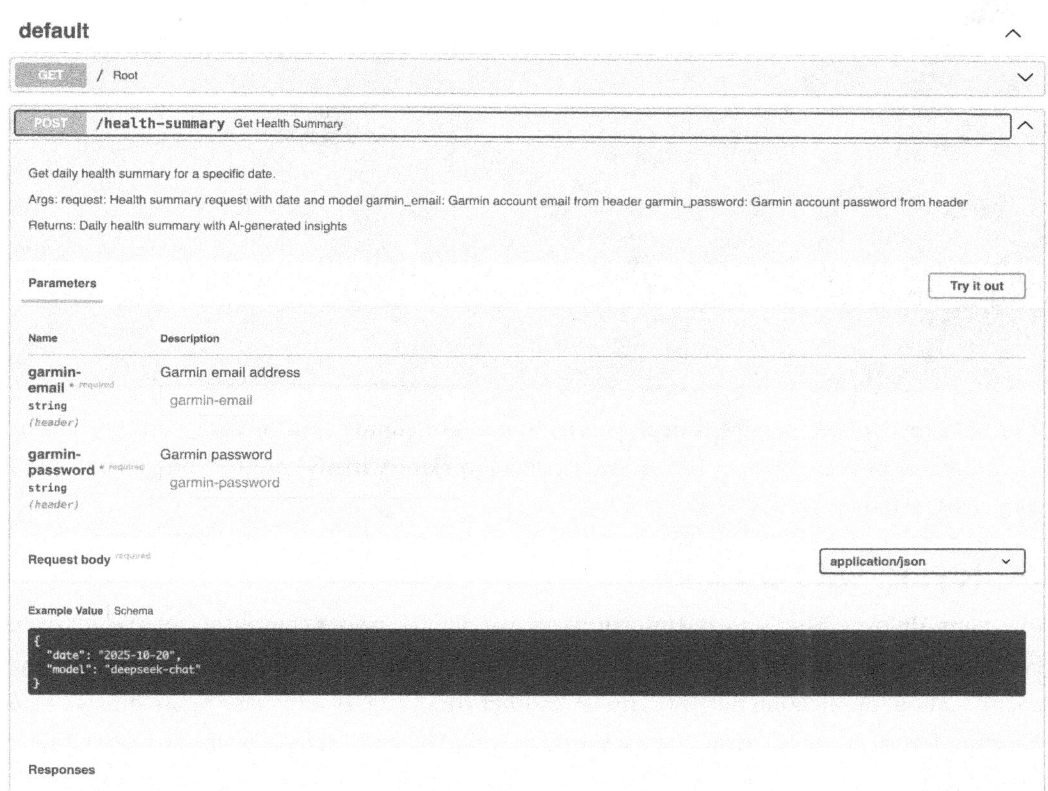

Figure 5.2: Garmin Health Summary API page

You can call the API through the interface or through the command line. If you have `curl` (`https://curl.se/`) installed, here's an example of how to call it:

```
$ curl -X 'POST' \
        'http://localhost:8000/health-summary' \
        -H 'accept: application/json' \
        -H 'garmin-email: your.email@example.com' \
        -H 'garmin-password: your-password' \
        -H 'Content-Type: application/json' \
        -d '{
    "date": "2025-08-19"
  }'
```

This returns the model's response in JSON format:

```
{
    "day_type":"rest",
    "title":"Rest day with minimal activity and good recovery indicators.",
    "emoji":"😴",
    "observation":"Exercise minutes and steps were significantly below
your baseline, suggesting a deliberate rest. Body battery started high
and stress levels were low, indicating effective recovery from previous
days.",
    "recommendation":"Continue with light activity or rest tomorrow to
maintain this positive recovery state. Ensure adequate sleep to keep your
body battery levels optimal for future training."
}
```

The final aspect of our service is deployment. You might connect via SSH and run the `fastapi run` command, or even run it locally. However, when working with live production systems, you'll likely use **Docker**.

Deploying with Docker

Now, your API runs. That's great. Unfortunately, we can't ship your computer to serve our users. If our application will run in production, it needs to be deployed somewhere in the cloud. This means that our application needs to run on another computer. How can we make sure we have everything we need installed on that computer as well? For the past decade, the answer has been **containers**.

Docker is a well-established tool in the industry that uses containers to declaratively define dependencies and keep applications isolated when deploying. In short, Docker lets you package your application and everything it needs – code, libraries, and tools – into a single, lightweight container. This ensures that it runs the same way on any machine, from your laptop to production, without environment issues. Even though we would love to write a long book about the amazing and less amazing things about Docker, this is not the book for that. If you are not familiar with it and want to learn the basics, we advise you to start here: `https://www.docker.com/101-tutorial`.

Now, here's our heavily commented Dockerfile that packages all the dependencies of our Daily Health Summary service. If you are interested in diving deeper into some of the choices here, we recommend you dive deeper into the uv Docker tutorial/walkthrough, as our Dockerfile is greatly inspired by it (`https://docs.astral.sh/uv/guides/integration/docker/`):

```
# First, build the application in the `/app` directory
FROM ghcr.io/astral-sh/uv:bookworm-slim AS builder
ENV UV_COMPILE_BYTECODE=1 UV_LINK_MODE=copy

# Configure the Python directory so it is consistent
ENV UV_PYTHON_INSTALL_DIR=/python

# Only use the managed Python version
ENV UV_PYTHON_PREFERENCE=only-managed

# Install Python before the project for caching
RUN uv python install 3.12

WORKDIR /app
RUN --mount=type=cache,target=/root/.cache/uv \
    --mount=type=bind,source=uv.lock,target=uv.lock \
    --mount=type=bind,source=pyproject.toml,target=pyproject.toml \
    uv sync --locked --no-install-project --no-dev --no-group local
COPY . /app
RUN --mount=type=cache,target=/root/.cache/uv \
    uv sync --locked --no-dev --no-group local

# Then, use a final image without uv
FROM debian:bookworm-slim

# Copy the Python version
COPY --from=builder --chown=python:python /python /python

# Copy the application from the builder
COPY --from=builder --chown=app:app /app /app

# Place executables in the environment at the front of the path
ENV PATH="/app/.venv/bin:$PATH"
```

```
# Expose the port
EXPOSE 8000

# Run the FastAPI application
CMD ["fastapi", "run", "app/02-api.py", "--host", "0.0.0.0", "--port",
"8000"]
```

We can run the application by building the container and running it on our own machine with the `docker build` and `docker run` commands. The first builds an image called API using `02-api.Dockerfile` as the Dockerfile, and the second starts a container from that image, exposing port `8000` and passing the `DEEPSEEK_API_KEY` environment variable:

```
$ docker build -t api -f 02-api.Dockerfile .
$ docker run -it -e DEEPSEEK_API_KEY=sk-... -p 8000:8000 -t api
```

The application should again spin up on your local URL: `http://localhost:8000`.

That was a lot! But you should be happy. You created a service that receives a user's Garmin credentials and returns a DeepSeek-powered Daily Health Summary of their current day. Congratulations! Now, even though we would love to show you how to run this on a server, we will not do it in this book. The beautiful thing about containers is that you can deploy them pretty much *anywhere*. Almost all cloud providers have at least 5 ways of deploying containers on their clouds, although AWS has 17 different ones: `https://www.lastweekinaws.com/blog/the-17-ways-to-run-containers-on-aws/`.

After a deserved break, you'll begin to think that while the system functions well, it isn't specific to DeepSeek. We are *simply* calling the DeepSeek API. We could be calling any other API (OpenAI, Anthropic, etc.). However, DeepSeek's true power lies in its open source nature. This opens some doors for us. We will explore them next.

Interacting with DeepSeek models

Our Daily Health Summary service works well, but we would like to start abstracting away the fact that we are calling the DeepSeek API. The first service we should talk about is **LiteLLM** (`https://docs.litellm.ai/`).

LiteLLM

LiteLLM is a library that allows us to interact easily with different LLMs and providers using a single unified format.

The advantage of LiteLLM is that when you change providers, the only thing you really need to change is the `model` string that you are feeding into the `completion` function.

In the following example, we demonstrate how to use DeepSeek with three different providers by leveraging the LiteLLM library:

- `deepseek/deepseek-chat`: Uses the DeepSeek chat model available in the DeepSeek API
- `bedrock/us.deepseek.r1-v1:0`: Uses Amazon Bedrock (`https://aws.amazon.com/bedrock/`) to run inference of the DeepSeek-R1 reasoning model.
- `openrouter/deepseek/deepseek-r1-distill-qwen-14b`: Uses OpenRouter (`https://openrouter.ai/`) to run the Qwen 14B distilled model

Warning

You might have to set different API keys and authentication methods for using different providers with LiteLLM. Make sure to check out their documentation for more information. It's extensive!

Here is how you can utilize `litellm`:

```
from litellm import completion

def litellm(messages: list[dict]) -> tuple[str, str | None]:
    response = completion(
        # model="deepseek/deepseek-chat", # Uses DeepSeek API
        # model="bedrock/us.deepseek.r1-v1:0", # Uses AWS bedrock for
inference
        model="openrouter/deepseek/deepseek-r1-distill-qwen-14b", # Uses
OpenRouter for inference
        messages=messages,
        temperature=0.0,
    )
    message = response.choices[0].message

        # if there is reasoning content, extract it
    if hasattr(message, "reasoning_content"):
        reasoning_content = message.reasoning_content
    else:
```

```
        reasoning_content = None

    return message.content, reasoning_content

# usage example:
messages = [
    {"role": "system", "content": "You are a helpful assistant."},
    {"role": "user", "content": "What is the capital of France?"},
]
result, reasoning = llm(messages)
print(f"Result: {result}")
# Result: The capital of France is Paris.
print(f"Reasoning: {reasoning}")
# Reasoning: Okay, so I need to figure out the capital ...
```

LiteLLM is a powerful tool, and in combination with **OpenRouter**, it means you can call *any* API and model, or even local models! Yes, we said local... But let's take this one step at a time.

Running locally with Ollama

The release of DeepSeek-R1 in January 2025 shocked the world, and it did so for many reasons. Not only did the flagship R1 model beat benchmarks and prove to be competitive with the state of the art of the moment, but the Chinese lab went one step further. You may recall from our discussion in *Chapters 1* and *2* that, together with the flagship model, they also released six different distilled models.

Each model was fine-tuned from a base open source model using samples generated by the DeepSeek-R1 model. The original model contains 685 billion parameters, totaling 641.33 GB of weights. Roughly, running the model would require approximately 1,540 GB of VRAM to run it at full precision. Now, you might have that type of compute in your backyard, but the reality is that very few companies have that sort of compute power, since it requires a multi-GPU setup.

But the distilled versions tell a different story. In *Table 5.1*, you can see the distilled models, their base models (from which they were fine-tuned), and the VRAM requirements to run them at 4-bit quantization. This opens doors for those of us without a GPU farm in the backyard. Some of these can run on very small GPUs. In fact, we can even run them on a single GPU!

Model	Base model	Hugging Face repo	VRAM requirement
DeepSeek-R1	-	huggingface.co/deepseek-ai/DeepSeek-R1	~436 GB
DeepSeek-R1-Distill-Llama-70B	Llama-3.3-70B-Instruct (https://huggingface.co/meta-llama/Llama-3.3-70B-Instruct)	huggingface.co/deepseek-ai/DeepSeek-R1-Distill-Llama-70B	~46 GB
DeepSeek-R1-Distill-Qwen-32B	Qwen2.5-32B (https://huggingface.co/Qwen/Qwen2.5-32B)	huggingface.co/deepseek-ai/DeepSeek-R1-Distill-Qwen-32B	~21 GB
DeepSeek-R1-Distill-Qwen-14B	Qwen2.5-14B (https://huggingface.co/Qwen/Qwen2.5-14B)	huggingface.co/deepseek-ai/DeepSeek-R1-Distill-Qwen-14B	~9 GB
DeepSeek-R1-Distill-Llama-8B	Llama-3.1-8B (https://huggingface.co/meta-llama/Llama-3.1-8B)	huggingface.co/deepseek-ai/DeepSeek-R1-Distill-Llama-8B	~5 GB
DeepSeek-R1-Distill-Qwen-7B	Qwen2.5-Math-7B (https://huggingface.co/Qwen/Qwen2.5-Math-7B)	huggingface.co/deepseek-ai/DeepSeek-R1-Distill-Qwen-7B	~4.5 GB
DeepSeek-R1-Distill-Qwen-1.5B	Qwen2.5-Math-1.5B (https://huggingface.co/Qwen/Qwen2.5-Math-1.5B)	huggingface.co/deepseek-ai/DeepSeek-R1-Distill-Qwen-1.5B	~1 GB

Table 5.1: DeepSeek models' VRAM requirements

There are two well-established tools for running LLMs locally. The first is `llama.cpp` (`https://github.com/ggml-org/llama.cpp`), and the second, which uses the first as its inference engine, is Ollama (`https://ollama.com/`).

Running a local model with Ollama is simple. After installing Ollama (`https://ollama.com/download`), just enter the following command in your terminal:

```
$ ollama run deepseek-r1:1.5b
>>> Hi there!
Hello! How can I assist you today? 😊
```

This command will download the distilled 1.5B model if you haven't run it before and start a chat session. Depending on your system, it may run warm, but the 1.5B parameter model should run on most modern computers.

We can use the Ollama Python SDK (`https://github.com/ollama/ollama-python`) to generate our daily health summaries. We just need to adapt the `get_daily_summary` function, and leverage the 1.5B parameter distilled model we just downloaded:

```
from ollama import chat

def get_daily_summary(
    garmin: Garmin,
    date: str,
) -> DailySummary:

    prompt = get_daily_summary_prompt(garmin, date)

    messages = [
        {"role": "system", "content": SYSTEM_PROMPT},
        {"role": "user", "content": prompt},
    ]

    response = chat(
        messages=messages,
        model="deepseek-r1:1.5b",
        format=DailySummary.model_json_schema(),
        options={
            "temperature": 0.0,
        },
    )

    return DailySummary.model_validate_json(response.message.content)
```

We can specify the return format with Ollama by setting `format=DailySummary.model_json_schema()`. This passes the Pydantic model's JSON schema to the model as well. We can call the function as follows:

```
garmin = get_garmin_client(
        email=os.environ["GARMIN_EMAIL"],
        password=os.environ["GARMIN_PASSWORD"],
    )
summary = get_daily_summary(garmin, "2025-08-14")
print(summary)
```

This produces the following:

```
day_type=<DayType.HIGH_STRESS: 'high_stress'> title='Elevated stress
and poor recovery despite minimal physical activity.' emoji='😫'
observation='Stress levels jumped 46% above baseline while sleep dropped
to just 6.1 hours, resulting in a low body battery start of 45. Exercise
and movement were minimal, suggesting stress is from non-physical
sources.' recommendation='Focus on stress management techniques and aim
for 8+ hours of sleep tonight. Consider light exercise like walking or
yoga tomorrow, as gentle movement can help regulate stress levels.'
```

Yes, today wasn't a great day. But we just connected a local 1.5B parameter model to our Daily Health Summary service! Before we move forward, remember that you can also use local models with LiteLLM as we've shown you before, by setting the model to, for example, `ollama_chat/deepseek-r1:1.5b`.

CPU-based inference with Transformers and XGrammar

Ollama is fantastic for quickly testing and experimenting with local models. But to truly build out our Daily Health Summary service, we need finer control over the device, the prompt structure, tokenization, and the generation process itself. This is where we move closer to the metal and lean on the well-established Transformers library (`https://github.com/huggingface/transformers`).

To run our 1.5B parameter model on a CPU, let's run the Unsloth version of the 1.5B distilled model, which you can find on Hugging Face as well. Unsloth (`https://docs.unsloth.ai/`) is another interesting library worth exploring if you are into fine-tuning and running models yourself.

We first load the model with the following code:

```
from transformers import AutoModelForCausalLM, AutoTokenizer, TextStreamer

model_name = "unsloth/DeepSeek-R1-Distill-Qwen-1.5B"
device = "cpu"
question = "What is the capital of Le Marche, Italy?"
max_tokens = 1200

tokenizer = AutoTokenizer.from_pretrained(model_name)
model = AutoModelForCausalLM.from_pretrained(model_name).to(device)
We use apply_chat_template on the messages to transform them into model
inputs:
messages =
[
    {"role": "user", "content": question},
]
inputs = tokenizer.apply_chat_template(
    messages,
    add_generation_prompt=True,
    tokenize=True,
    return_dict=True,
    return_tensors="pt",
).to(model.device)
```

With that in place, we can now stream tokens out of our CPU directly:

```
streamer = TextStreamer(tokenizer, skip_prompt=True, skip_special_
tokens=False)
model.generate(
    **inputs,
    max_new_tokens=max_tokens,
    streamer=streamer,
)
# prints Okay, so I need to figure out the capital of Le Marche, Italy.
Hmm, I'm not super familiar with Italy, but I know it's one of the largest
and most populous countries in Europe....
```

That runs our model directly on the CPU using the `transformers` library. This works great, but if we want to integrate this model with the rest of our Daily Health Summary service, we need to ensure that the model respects our `DailySummary` format effectively. And that's where the real magic of open source models shines.

Remember, the model runs locally, so we have full control over the tokens it generates. We could write a function to restrict each token to those that comply with our defined JSON schema. But this is exactly what libraries such as `outlines` (`https://dottxt-ai.github.io/outlines`), `xgrammar` (`https://github.com/mlc-ai/xgrammar`), and `guidance` (`https://github.com/guidance-ai/guidance`) do out of the box. They perform ***constrained*** generation. Instead of simply asking the model to generate JSON, they explicitly limit the tokens to those that conform to the JSON structure.

From our experience, `xgrammar` has produced the best results. The code to use it is somewhat convoluted, but if you have questions, we encourage you to consult the library's documentation. Still, we'll explain it at a high level.

The first part of the code simply imports the model, places it on the CPU, and sets the desired seed (for reproducible outputs):

```
import xgrammar as xgr
from transformers import AutoConfig, AutoModelForCausalLM, AutoTokenizer

MODEL_NAME = "unsloth/DeepSeek-R1-Distill-Qwen-1.5B"
MODEL = AutoModelForCausalLM.from_pretrained(
    MODEL_NAME,
    torch_dtype=torch.float32,
    device_map="cpu",
)
TOKENIZER = AutoTokenizer.from_pretrained(MODEL_NAME)
CONFIG = AutoConfig.from_pretrained(MODEL_NAME)
MAX_NEW_TOKENS = 1024
transformers.set_seed(42)
```

Now, we'll adapt our `get_daily_summary` function so that we can adapt our API. We take the messages, but now run them through `apply_chat_template` as well:

```
def get_daily_summary(
    garmin: Garmin,
    date: str,
) -> DailySummary:
```

```
prompt = get_daily_summary_prompt(garmin, date)

messages = [
    {"role": "system", "content": SYSTEM_PROMPT},
    {"role": "user", "content": prompt},
]
texts = TOKENIZER.apply_chat_template(
    messages, tokenize=False, add_generation_prompt=True
)
```

At first glance, the code may look intimidating, but it's really just doing four things:

1. It begins by extracting tokenizer metadata with `TokenizerInfo.from_huggingface`, providing the basis for interpreting tokens correctly.
2. During generation, it applies an `xgrammar` logits processor that forces the model to only produce tokens valid under the `DailySummary` schema.
3. The generation step itself runs with a low **temperature** and sampling enabled, striking a balance between consistency and variety.
4. Finally, the output is decoded and validated with `DailySummary.model_validate_json`, returning a clean, structured Pydantic object.

Temperature

The `temperature` parameter controls the randomness of model outputs. Lower values make responses more deterministic, and higher values provide more creative answers. In reality, `temperature` manipulates the probabilities of each token being generated by DeepSeek.

Patrick von Platen has an outstanding tutorial that dives deep into text generation with transformers (including parameters such as `temperature`): `https://huggingface.co/blog/how-to-generate`.

Together, these pieces ensure that we always get exactly what we need – clean and valid JSON every time:

```
model_inputs = TOKENIZER(texts, return_tensors="pt").to(MODEL.device)
tokenizer_info = xgr.TokenizerInfo.from_huggingface(
    TOKENIZER, vocab_size=CONFIG.vocab_size
```

```
    )
    grammar_compiler = xgr.GrammarCompiler(tokenizer_info)
    compiled_grammar = grammar_compiler.compile_json_schema(DailySummary)
    xgr_logits_processor = xgr.contrib.hf.LogitsProcessor(compiled_grammar)
    generated_ids = MODEL.generate(
        **model_inputs,
        max_new_tokens=MAX_NEW_TOKENS,
        logits_processor=[xgr_logits_processor],
        do_sample=True,
        temperature=0.01,
        top_p=0.95,
        top_k=50,
    )
    generated_ids = generated_ids[0][len(model_inputs.input_ids[0]) :]
    model_response = TOKENIZER.decode(generated_ids, skip_special_
tokens=True)
    return DailySummary.model_validate_json(model_response)
```

We set `temperature` to `0.01` for deterministic outputs, favoring high-probability tokens. `top_k=50` limits choices to the 50 most likely tokens per step, while `top_p=0.95` restricts generation to tokens covering 95% of the probability mass, trimming the unlikely long tail. These choices aren't strict, so feel free to experiment yourself.

With `xgrammar` in place, we can now refactor our Daily Health Summary service to run ***entirely*** locally. No API calls required, no JSON malformations.

Refactoring for local generation on the CPU

Now that we've replaced `get_daily_summary`, we can create a completely new API that runs locally. We've included a `05-api-cpu-xgrammar.py` file in `Chapter05` of the repository for this book. This looks *exactly* like the first model service we designed, but runs 100% locally.

To run it, we use FastAPI again with the following:

```
$ uv run fastapi run 05-api-cpu-xgrammar.py
```

In another terminal, we can call the API with the command line:

```
$ curl -X 'POST' \
      'http://localhost:8000/health-summary' \
      -H 'accept: application/json' \
```

```
         -H 'garmin-email: your.email@example.com' \
         -H 'garmin-password: your-password' \
         -H 'Content-Type: application/json' \
         -d '{
    "date": "2025-08-19"
  }'
```

This again returns well-formatted JSON produced from DeepSeek-R1-Distill-Qwen-1.5B, running 100% on your own machine:

```
{
   "day_type":"high_stress",
   "title":"Elevated stress and poor recovery despite minimal physical 
activity.",
   "emoji":"😫",
   "observation":"Stress levels jumped 46% above baseline while sleep 
dropped to just 6.1 hours, resulting in a low body battery start of 45. 
Exercise and movement were minimal, suggesting stress is from non-physical 
sources.",
   "recommendation":"Focus on stress management techniques and aim for 
8+ hours of sleep tonight. Consider light exercise like walking or yoga 
tomorrow, as gentle movement can help regulate stress levels."
}
```

The Dockerfile is 99% similar except for a couple of dependencies, so we'll skip it for brevity.

Phew! Well done! You just created a fully local Daily Health Summary service. You learned how to run DeepSeek models on your CPU, ensuring that they produce reliable JSON, and gained a clear understanding of how to deploy and integrate them with the service we designed. That's a lot to take in.

However, it's important to note that what we designed for the 1.5B parameter model can also be applied to any other DeepSeek model, with one major caveat: you need specialized hardware. You probably won't be able to run a model larger than the 1.5B version on a CPU. For anything bigger, we'll need a GPU. Some of you may have powerful computers, but the reality is that larger models tend to perform better than smaller ones.

Let's say we'd like to run our Daily Health Summary with the 70B parameter distilled version of DeepSeek-R1; we would need at least 46 GB of VRAM. I have a pretty high-end MacBook with 64 GB of unified memory, but the reality is that I've never managed to run anything larger than a 30B parameter model comfortably. And we're not going to ship my MacBook.

You get the point. We'll need to run this on someone else's computer – that is, in the cloud. However, we still want to the advantages of a local model, where we can tightly control generation. In the next section, we'll explore how to deploy one of the larger distilled models on the cloud. Buckle up, this is going to get interesting!

Deploying an isolated model service with AWS

Amazon Web Services (**AWS**) is one of the most popular cloud computing platforms in the world. We'll be focusing on it to deploy a larger DeepSeek model in order to integrate it with our Daily Health Summary service. As with most cloud computing platforms, there are just short of 25 different ways of achieving the same thing. And AWS is no different.

To use/deploy a DeepSeek model on AWS, you could do the following:

- Use the **Bedrock API**, where they host foundational models (including DeepSeek). Here, you can call and consume models just like we did with the DeepSeek API. You won't deploy; you'll simply consume.
- Use **Bedrock Custom Model Import**, a service where AWS allows you to import a trained model into Bedrock, and then use it via the Bedrock API. The model should be in Hugging Face format. Keep in mind that only some architectures are supported (no support for Gemma models, for example).
- **Hugging Face Deep Learning Containers** (**DLC**) can also be used to deploy models on AWS. For inference, they include either PyTorch or **Text Generation Inference** (**TGI**, `https://github.com/huggingface/text-generation-inference`) as supported frameworks. An interesting option if you'd like to use those frameworks. You can also use DLC for training models. These will be done through AWS's SageMaker service.
- **Rolling your own**: By this we mean that you purchase a VM in the cloud (i.e., an EC2 instance) with a GPU, install whatever packages you need to install, manage dependencies, access, upgrades, and so on – maximum control, but likely a good headache as well.
- Finally, **large model inference** (**LMI**) containers through SageMaker allow you to serve LLMs with a number of available inference backends. This is made for models with larger sizes, where you need full control, but don't want to manage the infrastructure – close to the metal, but without many headaches. LMI containers are powered by the **Deep Java Library** (**DJL**) framework. Think of DJL as the engine that powers those containers.

This is not an exhaustive list. AWS offers more options, some of which will persist for years, while others likely won't. There is *no single right way* to deploy a model on AWS; however, you should consider the trade-offs before choosing. We have compiled a table (*Table 5.2*) of the pros and cons of each option and when to choose which:

Option	Pros	Cons	When to use
Bedrock API	• No infrastructure to manage • Access to many frontier models (including Anthropic, Mistral, and DeepSeek) • Authentication integrated • Automatic scaling and SLAs	• You don't own the model • Limited customization • Costlier per token at scale	You just need to consume models via API and don't want to host anything
Bedrock custom model import	• Deploy your fine-tuned model without managing infrastructure • Integrates with Bedrock APIs, agents, and knowledge bases • Benefits from Bedrock security and logging	• Limited architecture support • Must convert model to Hugging Face format • More setup than hosted FMs	You have your own trained model, but want to leverage Bedrock's managed environment
Hugging Face DLC (SageMaker)	• Managed training and inference • TGI included for optimized LLM inference • Easy integration with Hugging Face Hub • Auto-scaling endpoints	• Limited to the Hugging Face, TGI, and PyTorch stack • Less optimized than DJL for very large models • Still pay for SageMaker infrastructure	You want a Hugging Face-native path for training or inference on SageMaker

Hand-rolled on EC2	• Maximum control • Pick any serving stack, such as vLLM, TGI, and Triton • No SageMaker or Bedrock overhead	• You manage everything, including scaling, security, and networking • Harder to operate reliably • Higher operational burden	You need full control or want to experiment with custom stacks and kernels
Large model inference (LMI/DJL)	• Purpose-built for large models • Supports vLLM, TensorRT-LLM, and NeuronX for Inf2 • Manages infrastructure, scaling, and sharding • Best throughput on big models	• Slightly more setup than Hugging Face DLC • Requires SageMaker knowledge • Less Hugging Face *magic* out of the box	You need maximum performance for large or production-scale models without managing infrastructure

Table 5.2: Comparison of deployment options with AWS

We recommend almost always starting with an API call and avoiding complex self-hosting unless you know your product truly needs it. So, if you're building products, start with an API call. Once you have a million users, it's time to start thinking about deploying. We eat our own dog food in this book, which is why we started with consuming DeepSeek models via an API. And now we'll venture into deploying DeepSeek using LMI containers. This is because we believe vLLM is an incredibly powerful inference engine (`https://github.com/vllm-project/vllm`).

You are probably already asking yourself: What is an inference engine anyway? Good question.

Inference backends

An **inference engine** is a framework that simplifies the process of deploying an LLM. It provides packaging, optimization, and serving capabilities. This is so you don't have to think about GPU optimizations, request management, memory optimization, LLM architectures, streaming, or support for structured generation. An inference backend provides all of these, so you can focus on using your models instead. We've compiled another (non-exhaustive) list of inference engines in *Table 5.3*:

Engine	Primary innovation	Performance optimizations	Quantization (built-in)	Distributed inference	Ease of use	Unique feature
vLLM (`https://github.com/vllm-project/vllm`)	PageAttention with GPU-friendly KV paging	Continuous batching, fused CUDA kernels, async I/O	INT8 / INT4 (AWQ, GPTQ), SmoothQuant	Tensor & pipeline parallel	High (single-command serve)	OpenAI-compatible API; live KV-cache swap
Hugging Face TGI (`https://github.com/huggingface/text-generation-inference`)	Rust + Python gRPC server	Token streaming, continuous batching, speculative decoding, FlashAttention	GPTQ, AWQ, bits-and-bytes, Marlin	Optional sharding & tensor parallel	High (Docker/CLI)	Triton backend, Prometheus metrics
SGLang (`https://github.com/sgl-project/sglang`)	Prefill/Decode disaggregation; RadixAttention	Continuous batching, expert/pipeline/tensor parallel	FP8, INT4 (AWQ/GPTQ)	Data, tensor & pipeline parallel	Medium (extra DSL)	Vision-LLM support; built-in router
LMDeploy (`https://github.com/InternLM/lmdeploy`)	Compression-to-serving toolkit	Persistent batch, blocked KV, split-fuse kernels	4-bit weight+KV, AWQ, SmoothQuant	Tensor parallel; K8s Helm chart	High (one executable)	Integrated quantize → deploy flow
TensorRT-LLM (`https://github.com/NVIDIA/TensorRT-LLM`)	End-to-end TensorRT graph compilation	Custom kernels, inflight batching, paged KV	FP8, FP4, INT4 (AWQ), INT8	Triton backend (multi-GPU/node)	Medium (requires TRT build)	Leader/worker orchestration

Table 5.3: Comparison of popular inference engines

Even though each provides pros and cons, vLLM has gradually established itself as an established engine. It also supports a lot of features we are interested in for our Daily Health Summary service: structured generation, OpenAI-compatible APIs, quantization, first-class support for DeepSeek models, and even support for reasoning outputs!

Deploying DeepSeek with LMI containers

SageMaker supports a wide variety of container images for training and inference jobs. You can see an exhaustive list over at the **AWS DLC** repository in GitHub: `https://github.com/aws/deep-learning-containers`.

Within this ecosystem, we will focus on the **LMI containers** specifically, because of their first-class support for **vLLM**. LMI containers are hosted and documented as part of the DJL: an open source Java framework for deep learning. Confusing, we know.

The point here is that if we are interested in the documentation for the containers we will deploy, it's over at `https://docs.djl.ai/`.

The first thing we need to figure out is the total amount of memory we will need for our model. We'll focus on deploying DeepSeek-R1 Distill Qwen 14B for our use case. To do so, we'll use an `ml.g6.12xlarge` AWS instance. That instance will give us around 96 GB of GPU VRAM, which should be enough to run our model.

Warning

In this deployment, we will use an `ml.g6.12xlarge` machine. Depending on the region, it costs around 5 USD **per hour**. Forget to turn it off, and you'll be charged 3,720 USD per month! ***ALWAYS*** make sure you turn off resources after testing. You have been warned.

In *Table 5.4*, we provide some guidance regarding which machines to use for different popular open source models:

Parameters	Instance types	GPU VRAM	Example models
~7B	`ml.g5.4xlarge`, `ml.g6.4xlarge`	24 GB	Llama 2 7B, Mistral 7B, DeepSeek-LLM 7B, DeepSeek-R1 Distill Qwen 7B
~13B	`ml.g5.12xlarge`, `ml.g6.12xlarge`	96 GB	Llama 2 13B, Code Llama 13B, Qwen2.5 14B, DeepSeek-R1 Distill Qwen 14B

~20B	ml.g5.12xlarge, ml.g6.12xlarge	96 GB	GPT-OSS 20B, Mistral Small 24B, Solar Pro 22B
~35B	ml.g5.48xlarge, ml.g6.48xlarge	192 GB	Code Llama 34B, Falcon 40B, Yi 34B, DeepSeek-R1 Distill Qwen 32B
~70B	ml.g5.48xlarge, ml.g6.48xlarge	192 GB	Llama 2 70B, Code Llama 70B, DeepSeek-R1 Distill Llama 70B, DeepSeek-R1 Distill Qwen 70B
~70B	ml.p4d.24xlarge	320 GB	-
~180B	ml.p4de.24xlarge, ml.p5.48xlarge	640 GB	Falcon 180B, GPT-OSS 120B, DeepSeek V2 236B (MoE), DeepSeek V3 671B (37B active)

Table 5.4: Instance types options for popular open source models

To deploy our model, we will take advantage of SageMaker's Python SDK (`https://sagemaker.readthedocs.io/`). The following script creates a general configuration to deploy the DeepSeek model. You can replace the model with the one you are interested in deploying, and adapt the machine configuration according to the preceding cheat sheet (keeping the costs in mind). Before you run it, you should ensure the following:

- You have an AWS account with billing enabled and the AWS CLI installed. If you don't have the CLI yet, you can grab it here: `https://docs.aws.amazon.com/cli/latest/userguide/getting-started-install.html`.
- You've created an **IAM role** with the `AmazonSageMakerFullAccess` policy attached, and set up the following trust relationship so SageMaker can assume the role (make sure to grab the **Amazon Resource Name** (**ARN**)of the role after creating it):

```
{
    "Version": "2012-10-17",
    "Statement": [
        {
            "Effect": "Allow",
            "Principal": {
                "Service": "sagemaker.amazonaws.com"
            },
            "Action": "sts:AssumeRole"
        }
    ]
}
```

- The SageMaker Python SDK is already included in this project's dependencies, so you don't need to install it separately.
- You might have to request a quota increase for the instance type that you are using. For the following script, you'll need a service quota of at least one `ml.g6.12xlarge` instance. There is some good documentation on how to do that in the AWS documentation: `https://docs.aws.amazon.com/servicequotas/latest/userguide/request-quota-increase.html`.

Here is how to deploy your model:

```
import boto3
import sagemaker
import os
import time

# setup session
boto_session = boto3.session.Session()
region = boto_session.region_name
sess = sagemaker.Session()

# create our configuration
CONFIG = {
    "INSTANCE_TYPE": "ml.g6.12xlarge", # the instance type
    "ENV": {
        "HF_MODEL_ID": "deepseek-ai/DeepSeek-R1-Distill-Qwen-14B",  #
hugginface model id
        "TENSOR_PARALLEL_DEGREE": "max",  # set max to use all GPUs
        "OPTION_ENABLE_REASONING": "true", # enable reasoning parsing
        "OPTION_REASONING_PARSER": "deepseek_r1", # set reasoning parser
    },
    "IMAGE_NAME": "djl-inference:0.33.0-lmi15.0.0-cu128", # image
    "BEDROCK_ROLE_ARN": "arn:aws:iam::ACCOUNT_NUMBER:role/replace-with-
yours", # role
}

# get base model name
ts = time.time()
hf_model_id = CONFIG["ENV"]["HF_MODEL_ID"]
model_name = hf_model_id.split("/")[-1]
```

```
base_model_name = sagemaker.utils.name_from_base(model_name)

# create SageMaker model
current_region = os.environ["AWS_DEFAULT_REGION"]
image_name = CONFIG["IMAGE_NAME"]
inference_image_uri = (
    f"763104351884.dkr.ecr.{current_region}.amazonaws.com/{image_name}"
)
lmi_model = sagemaker.Model(
    image_uri=inference_image_uri,
    env=CONFIG["ENV"],
    role=CONFIG["BEDROCK_ROLE_ARN"],
    name=base_model_name,
)
endpoint_name = f"{base_model_name}-endpoint"

# print details
print(f"{base_model_name=}")
print(f"{current_region=}")
print(f"{inference_image_uri=}")
print(f"{endpoint_name=}")

# deploy model (this can take up to 15 mins!)
lmi_model.deploy(
    initial_instance_count=1,
    instance_type=CONFIG["INSTANCE_TYPE"],
    container_startup_health_check_timeout=900,
    endpoint_name=endpoint_name,
)
print(f"Model has been deployed to endpoint {endpoint_name}")
```

The deployment of the model (depending on your region and instance availability) might take up to 15 minutes. Once everything is done, when you navigate to the AWS console, you'll notice that a new model and endpoint have just been created:

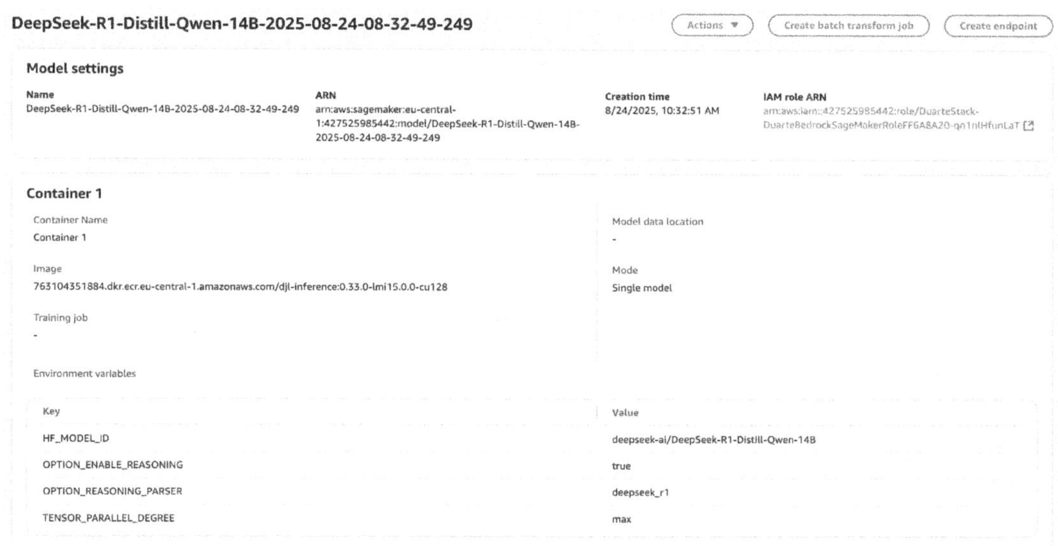

Figure 5.3: The model we created on AWS

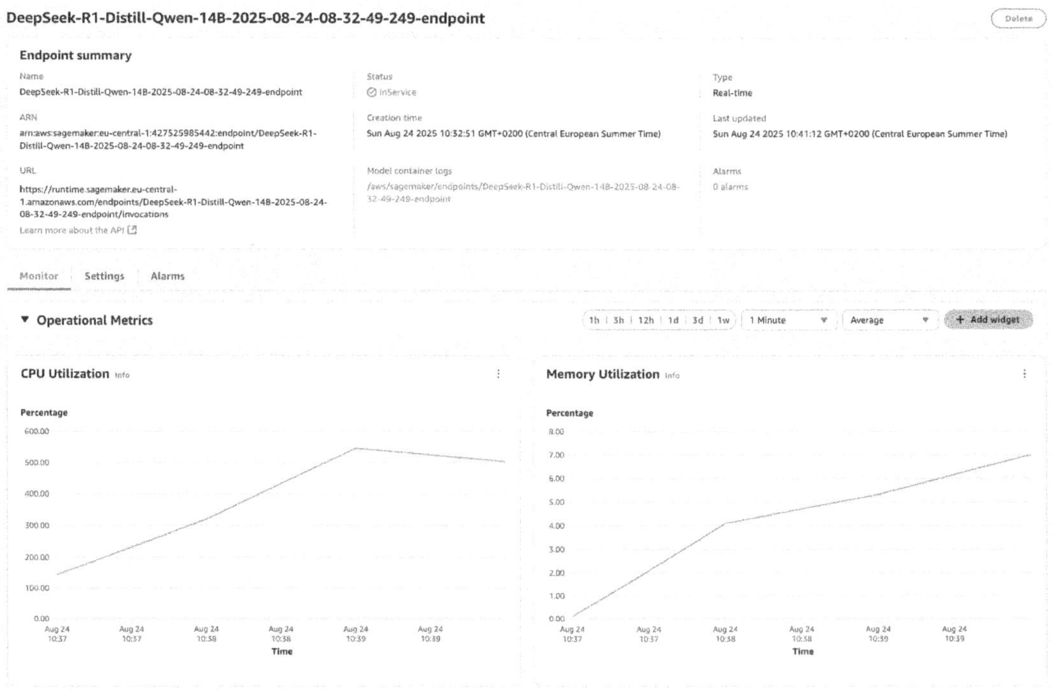

Figure 5.4: The dashboard for the SageMaker endpoint

Once the model is deployed, we can navigate to the Amazon SageMaker AI console. When you click the **Inference** section, you can navigate to **Inference > Models**, and you'll see our newly deployed DeepSeek model. Navigating to **Inference > Endpoints** will show you our model's endpoint, as well as a set of metrics for you to monitor the status of your endpoint (CPU utilization, memory utilization, GPU memory, GPU utilization, and invocation/request metrics).

Danger

Once you are done with your model endpoint, remember to shut it down, or else you'll continue to be charged for the time the instance is turned on! For this, you can delete the endpoint on the AWS console or use the SageMaker SDK:

```
import sagemaker
sess = sagemaker.Session()
sess.delete_endpoint(endpoint_name)
sess.delete_endpoint_config(endpoint_name)
lmi_model.delete_model()
```

LMI containers support three different API schemas: OpenAI's Chat Completions format, the OpenAI Completions format, and the TGI format. If we'd like to make predictions, the following three examples are effectively equivalent:

```
llm = sagemaker.Predictor(
    endpoint_name=endpoint_name,
    sagemaker_session=sess,
    serializer=sagemaker.serializers.JSONSerializer(),
    deserializer=sagemaker.deserializers.JSONDeserializer(),
)

TEMPERATURE = 0.01
MAX_TOKENS = 1024
USER_MESSAGE = "What is the capital of Le Marche, Italy?"

# 1. OpenAI chat completions
llm.predict(
    {
        "messages": [
            {
```

```
                "role": "user",
                "content": user_message,
            }
        ],
        "temperature": TEMPERATURE,
        "max_tokens": MAX_TOKENS,
    }
)

# 2. OpenAI Completions format
llm.predict(
    {
        "prompt": user_message,
        "temperature": TEMPERATURE,
        "max_tokens": MAX_TOKENS,
    }
)

# 3. TGI format
llm.predict(
    {
        "inputs": user_message,
        "parameters": {
            "max_new_tokens": MAX_TOKENS,
            "temperature": TEMPERATURE,
        },
    }
)
```

However, as we mentioned before, one of the big reasons to choose LMI containers is the fact that it supports vLLM as an inference engine and various options for structured outputs. In fact, LMI containers support the Chat Completions format *because* LMI containers use vLLM as an inference engine. One of the options for using structured generation with vLLM (`https://docs.vllm.ai/en/v0.8.1/features/structured_outputs.html`) is `xgrammar`.

Next up is an example of a function called `llm` that will use our SageMaker endpoint with structured outputs to return a prediction that respects the `response_model` that we pass to it. As you can see, vLLM supports `response_format` and an `extra_body` parameter where we can specify the Pydantic model we would like it to respect, as well as the decoding backend we wish to use:

```
def llm(
    messages: list[dict],
    endpoint_name: str,
    response_model: BaseModel,
) -> BaseModel:
    client = get_aws_llm(endpoint_name=endpoint_name)

    response = client.predict(
        {
            "messages": messages,
            "temperature": 0.01,
            "max_tokens": 1024,
            "response_format": {
                "type": "json_schema",
                "json_schema": {
                    "name": response_model.__name__,
                    "schema": response_model.model_json_schema(),
                    "strict": True,
                },
            },
            "extra_body": {"guided_decoding_backend": "xgrammar"},
        }
    )

    return response_model.model_validate_json(
        response["choices"][0]["message"]["reasoning_content"]
    )
```

We can then use this function by providing a Pydantic model and a list of messages, as in this example:

```
class Capital(BaseModel):
        capital: str
        population: int
```

```
messages = [
        {
                "role": "user",
                "content": "What is the capital of France?",
        }
]

response = llm(
        messages,
        "DeepSeek-R1-Distill-Qwen-14B-2025-08-24-08-52-31-391-endpoint",
        response_model=Capital,
)
print(response)
# capital='Paris' population=2161512
```

So, now we have our large DeepSeek model deployed in AWS with an endpoint that supports *any* feature that the vLLM inference engine does. The only step left is to integrate it again with our Daily Health Summary service. Since we are making an API call to AWS, this should be pretty straightforward.

Updating our service to use Amazon SageMaker endpoints

To update our service to use our model deployed in AWS, we only need to replace the `llm` function we built earlier. In the chapter materials, we have included a `07-api-deepseek-sagemaker.py` API, which can be run with the following:

```
$ uv run fastapi run 07-api-deepseek-sagemaker.py
```

Our API's backend is now Amazon SageMaker, but everything else remains the same: the request format, the commands, and the user experience. This demonstrates the advantage of structured outputs. You can switch the backend to another service without disrupting users' workflows or breaking the API. In fact, we could also have an API that serves three different endpoints with three different backends – DeepSeek API, CPU inference, and Amazon SageMaker – at the exact same time! We'll leave that as an exercise for you.

Best practices and recommendations

In this chapter, while building our Daily Health Summary service, we explored three main ways of using DeepSeek models: calling the API, running distilled models locally on a CPU, and deploying larger models with AWS, LMI containers, and vLLM. These are just the tip of the iceberg. The beauty of open source is that you have even more options if you need them.

That said, deploying DeepSeek models yourself is ***rarely*** needed. Self-hosting gives you control and privacy but comes with extra work and extra costs. You'll have to manage infrastructure, monitor performance, and ensure reliability. For most cases, especially when testing an idea or validating a product, starting with the API is almost always best. Keep it simple until you know you need more.

When deciding whether to host models yourself, use this quick checklist:

- **Cost**: Compare API usage costs with self-deployment. How do they compare?
- **Latency**: How fast do responses need to be? Do your users tolerate that?
- **Scaling**: Can your setup handle peak usage? What if your users explode overnight? Can you serve them?
- **Robustness**: How robust does your setup need to be? Do you have a team responsible for infrastructure?
- **Flexibility**: Can you easily evolve your application from API calling to self-hosting and vice versa?

We've shown how to start with an API, move to CPU inference, and eventually deploy larger models. Since our API format stayed consistent, users would not notice the change. This is a proven way to evolve without breaking things.

Summary

In this chapter, we took you from an initial idea to a fully working service that replaces boring smartwatch summaries with dynamic insights powered by DeepSeek. We began by showing how to quickly build a simple prototype using the DeepSeek API to meet our initial requirements. We then explored running models locally with distilled versions and built a lightweight CPU-based service that runs without GPUs.

Next, we focused on flexibility, demonstrating how libraries such as LiteLLM let you switch backend providers seamlessly without touching your application code. Finally, we scaled up by deploying LLMs on AWS using LMI containers and vLLM, so we can deploy larger models while staying in control.

By now, you have the toolkit to take any DeepSeek-powered application to production, whether you want to keep things small and efficient, run via an API, or deploy larger models in the cloud.

But many successful applications today are powered not by a single LLM, but by multiple models working together, often described as ***agents***. That's exactly what we'll explore in the next chapter.

6

Agents with DeepSeek

In *Chapter 5*, we discussed how to build simple applications using DeepSeek. In this chapter, we will discuss how to build LLM-powered **agents** with DeepSeek. At the time of writing, agents are a very popular topic. Many companies and engineers are rushing to build so-called **agentic applications**. A large number of agentic products have come out in recent years. Some popular examples are OpenAI's deep research (`https://openai.com/index/introducing-deep-research/`) and Google's Gemini Deep Research products (`https://gemini.google/overview/deep-research`), where LLMs will dynamically search the web for you and come up with a report that visits multiple websites and resources. If you work with software, you might have used some agentic systems: Claude Code (`https://docs.anthropic.com/en/docs/claude-code/overview`) and Cursor (`https://www.cursor.com/`) are good examples of agent-powered products.

Besides this, the libraries and frameworks used to build agents keep multiplying. Libraries such as CrewAI (`https://www.crewai.com/`), OpenAI's swarm (`https://github.com/openai/swarm`), and LangChain's `LangGraph` (`https://langchain-ai.github.io/langgraph/`) are evolving every day. The libraries and concepts around agents are incredibly new and constantly evolving at the time of writing. With the idea of making this book stand the test of time, we will focus on the key principles and definitions surrounding agents that likely won't change. We will also show you how to put those building blocks in place while leveraging DeepSeek models specifically.

In this chapter, we will cover the following main topics:

- A gentle introduction to agents
- Tools
- Understanding the Model Context Protocol

- Working with agents and workflows
- Exploring various agentic systems

Technical requirements

The following chapter is made up of three different Jupyter notebooks (`https://docs.jupyter.org/en/latest/`). The only software you will need to have installed is `uv`. To install `uv`, follow the instructions here: `https://docs.astral.sh/uv/getting-started/installation/`.

A gentle introduction to agents

Before we dive deeper into building agents with DeepSeek, we should try and define what an agent is. There have been many attempts to define what an agent is. OpenAI says that agents are *"systems that independently accomplish tasks on your behalf"*.

At its most fundamental level, an LLM-based agent is an autonomous system that can take a general task and operate independently to accomplish it. A **task** can be anything: create a report about a topic, create a pull request that solves this GitHub issue, or play chess against this opponent. It's important to note that agents don't operate in a vacuum. Agents are built to interact with an environment. That environment could be a chessboard, the internet (if an agent must search it), or a GitHub repo, in a case where an agent is going to submit a patch to a code base.

But agents need a way to interact and perform actions within an **environment**. For example, a chess-playing agent needs to be able to read/understand the chessboard, a research agent needs to be able to search the internet, and a Pokémon-playing agent (`https://www.theverge.com/news/619482/anthropics-claude-ai-is-playing-pokemon`) needs to be able to interact with the game.

To interact with an environment, agents use what we call **tools**. Tools allow agents to accomplish actions in the environment. For example, a coding agent needs to be able to read a code base and submit patches to it. In this case, you can imagine the agent will have access to tools like `read_code_base` and `submit_patch` tool. DeepSeek, for example, is able to call tools through its function-calling capability (`https://api-docs.deepseek.com/guides/function_calling`).

In summary, there are three main components that make up an agent:

- **Task**: The goal that the agent wishes to accomplish for the user.
- **Environment**: The space where the agent operates, in order to accomplish the task.
- **Tools**: The set of actions that the agent can take within the environment in order to accomplish the goal.

For example, let's say we are going to build an agent that can submit improvements to a code base. The task might be *Solve issue #45634 in my GitHub repository*, the environment is the GitHub repository with the code, and the tools could be `read_file`, `search_repository`, and `submit_patch`. Another example is a customer support agent. The task could be to support customers with whatever their problems are, the environment could be the conversation with the user (likely a chat interface), and the tools might be `search_knowledge_base`, `escalate_ticket`, or even `mark_issue_as_resolved`.

One important characteristic of agents versus normal LLM-based applications is that agents are made to act *independently*. This means that agents can asynchronously go and interact with the environment without requiring explicit interaction with the user who assigned a task. However, we should note that, agents can be especially powerful when paired up with humans. For example, one of the tools available to an agent could be the capability to ask for guidance from a human expert.

Other characteristics you will certainly have heard of are **memory** and **planning**. Memory can relate to two things.

- The first is **short-term memory**, which is normally related to the history or the conversation you are having with an agent directly (or the sequence of messages). For example, you might tell an agent *Always respond in Portuguese*, and the agent will/should remember that for the rest of the conversation.
- The second type of memory is **long-term memory**. Long-term memory might relate to concepts we want the agent to keep track of between tasks. We could build something very complicated for this last one. But we can also simply create two tools: `read_memory` and `update_memory`. This would allow the agent to retrieve past memories and update new ones. There's no need to complicate things.

As for **planning**, you can think of it as similar to **chain-of-thought**: asking the agent to outline a plan *before* solving a problem. It's an interesting concept, but it's not the main focus here.

Both memory and planning – although interesting – are not critical when building agents. Instead, let's move on to one of the most important aspects of agents: **tools**.

Tools

Tools are one of the most critical parts of building agents. **Tool calling** is what allows agents to interact and take actions in their environment. However, it's important to note that we didn't always have tool calling. In the early stages of LLMs (which is not that long ago), we used simple prompts to allow the LLMs to interact with the outside world.

Here's an example:

```
Question: What is the capital of France?
Thought: I should look this up on Wikipedia.
Action: wikipedia: France
PAUSE
Observation: France is a country. The capital is Paris.
Answer: The capital of France is Paris.
```

In the preceding example, the LLM outputs an **action** (e.g., `wikipedia: France`). The system (us) sees that, runs the search, and feeds the results back to the LLM. It was crude, but it worked. This was the core mechanism behind popular papers such as the ReAct paper from Google (`https://react-lm.github.io/`).

As things evolved, this approach seemed brittle, and LLM models started having the native capability to call functions (or tools).

We will use the terms function and tool interchangeably in this chapter.

In the next generation of LLMs, we could give a more detailed description of the tools the model has access to and what arguments that specific tool can take in. The models can then respond directly with a tool call. This is very similar to the crude approach before, but since models were *specifically* trained for it (with techniques such as reinforcement learning), it's more robust and reduces the likelihood of errors.

For example, we can specify a tool such as `get_weather` by providing a JSON schema to the LLM:

```
tools = [
    {
        "type": "function",
        "function": {
            "name": "get_weather",
            "description": "Get the weather for a given location",
            "parameters": {
                "type": "object",
                "properties": {
                    "location": {"type": "string"}
```

```
                },
                "required": ["location"]
            },
        }
    },
]
messages = [{"role": "user", "content": "How's the weather in Hangzhou?"}]
response = client.chat.completions.create(
    model="deepseek-chat",
    messages=messages,
    tools=tools,
)
```

The model responds with the function it wants to call and the arguments it intends to pass to that function it wants to call and the arguments it intends to pass to that function.

```
{
  "tool_calls": [
    {
      "function": "get_weather",
      "arguments": {
        "location": "Hangzhou"
      }
    }
  ]
}
```

It's important to note that the model *does not* execute tools – you, as an engineer, do. The model just tells us what it would like us to execute. You can see how this approach is slightly less brittle. We can define complex tools by leveraging JSON schema.

Tool calling is very popular nowadays. There are models explicitly trained for tool calling, such as Salesforce's xLAM family of models, which are trained specifically for tool use. The Berkeley Function-Calling Leaderboard (`https://gorilla.cs.berkeley.edu/leaderboard.html`) ranks the ability of different models to call different tools. DeepSeek V3 and DeepSeek-R1 rank in the twenty-second and twenty-seventh positions, respectively, at the time of writing, not making them *the best* models for function calling, but making them pretty good contestants for building with tools.

Before we move on to building your agents and workflows, let's talk about something that has been getting more and more popular: the **Model Context Protocol**.

Understanding the Model Context Protocol

In November 2024, Anthropic released the **Model Context Protocol** (**MCP**). While many were starting to build applications with LLMs. LLMs were still operating in somewhat of a *vacuum*. Many companies were building their own tools to plug into LLMs, often leading to re-implementing the same logic again and again.

For example, let's say you are a company building an integration of an LLM-based application with Gmail. This would lead to many companies creating their own versions of the `read_inbox` and `compose_email` functions. If we must develop a new tool every time we wish to connect our LLMs to new systems, this makes things very difficult to scale. MCP addresses this challenge.

MCP is an open standard that looks to simplify this process. The protocol aims to establish a pattern by which LLMs can connect to the outside world. It defines MCP clients and MCP servers.

Clients are applications that consume resources in an MCP server. An MCP server exposes three types of resources: (1) tools, (2) prompts, and (3) resources – each illustrated in the following diagram.

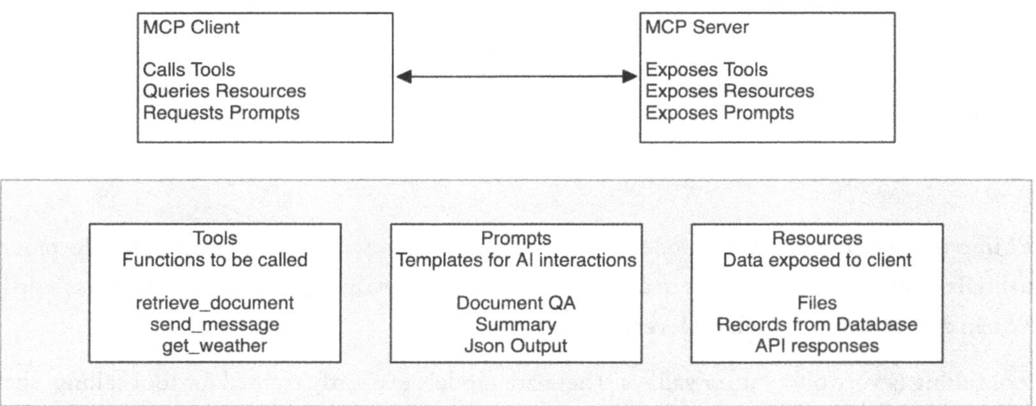

Figure 6.1: Illustration of MCP server (inspired by Anthropichttps://www.youtube.com/watch?v=kQmXtrmQ5Zg)

What does this mean in practice? It means that if you wish to connect your LLM to Google Drive, you could leverage a preexisting Google Drive MCP that someone else built (possibly Google), instead of having to build your own.

If it all sounded a bit abstract up till now, let's make it more concrete.

Let's create our own small MCP server. In the following example, we use the FastMCP (`https://gofastmcp.com`) framework to create an MCP server. This server serves two things: (1) a tool to get the weather from a city, and (2) a resource that returns the status of a given user:

```
from fastmcp import FastMCP
mcp = FastMCP(name="MyAssistantServer")

@mcp.tool
def get_weather(city: str) -> str:
    """Multiplies two numbers."""
   return f"The weather in {city} is sunny with a high of 25°C."

@mcp.resource("users://{user_id}/profile")
def get_profile(user_id: int):
    return {"name": f"User {user_id}", "status": "active"}
if __name__ == "__main__":
    mcp.run()
```

With our small MCP server defined, we can save it as `mcp_server.py`. How can we plug these MCP tools into our DeepSeek LLM? We can adapt an example from the documentation of DeepSeek. In the official function calling documentation (`https://api-docs.deepseek.com/guides/function_calling`), in order to give the model access to tools, we need to first define its JSON schema, as follows:

```
tools = [
    {
        "type": "function",
        "function": {
            "name": "get_weather",
            "description": "Get weather of an location, the user should
supply a location first",
            "parameters": {
                "type": "object",
                "properties": {
                    "location": {
                        "type": "string",
                        "description": "The city and state, e.g. San
```

```
Francisco, CA",
                    }
                },
                "required": ["location"],
            },
        },
    },
]
```

Alternatively, we can fetch these tools using MCP. Let me walk through how to go about it. First, we define a server configuration:

```
# Alternatively, we can use the MCP server to fetch tools
mcp_server_config = {
    "mcpServers": {
        "assistant": {
            "command": "uv", "args": ["run", "./mcp_server.py"]}}
}
```

Next, we create a function that uses the FastMCP Client to connect to our MCP server and retrieve the list of tools:

```
async def fetch_async_tools() -> list:
    async with Client(mcp_server_config) as mcp_client:
        return await mcp_client.list_tools()
```

Finally, we can wrap all of this logic in a get_tools function, where we also adapt our dictionary so that it conforms to what DeepSeek is expecting.

```
def get_tools() -> list:
    """Fetch and format the list of tools from the MCP server."""
    mcp_tools = asyncio.run(fetch_async_tools())
    return [
        {
            "type": "function",
            "function": {
                "name": tool.name,
                "description": tool.description,
                "parameters": tool.inputSchema,
            },
```

```
        }
        for tool in mcp_tools
    ]
```

As you can see, giving access to tools to an LLM can be done by defining those tools yourself or by connecting to an existing MCP server. For applications that serve a clear purpose, I would argue that you want to define the tools yourself. Often, if we are using too many tools, the models tend to get confused as to what to use and why. Defining the tools yourself gives you much more control over what you'd like the model to accomplish.

Many agentic frameworks, such as the OpenAI Agents SDK, LangGraph, and Pydantic AI, support connecting your LLMs to an MCP server and spare you from writing the boilerplate I've just demonstrated. However, in this chapter, we prefer to give you fine-grained control and understanding of the different tools (or mechanisms) under the hood; therefore, we won't use those frameworks.

MCP has increased in popularity tremendously and even sparked other protocols, such as Google's **Agent2Agent (A2A)** protocol (`https://github.com/a2aproject/A2A`). The real popularity of MCP has mainly been in consumer-facing applications. For example, you can connect your Claude desktop application to your Gmail MCP or connect your VSCode IDE to your company's MCP to read documentation.

At the time of writing, MCP and A2A are very new protocols. Only the test of time will tell whether they become real standards or get replaced with something else. We do think LLMs and tool calling will stay around for a long time. Therefore, in an effort to explain to you how these mechanisms work at the lowest level, we'll now dive deeper into agents and workflows.

Working with agents and workflows

Before we start building agents, I have some sad news for you, dear reader. Most agents don't work quite yet. There are two reasons why.

The first is **compounding errors**. Imagine we have a challenging task for an agent to solve. That task will require careful orchestration of a series of steps. Let's say it takes five careful steps to solve a task. If every step has a 90% chance of succeeding, that means the probability of completing all of them successfully drops to a meager 60%. Imagine you had a function that worked 60% of the time. Would you put it into production?

The second reason why agents – and, more broadly, LLMs – often fail is the context-rot problem. LLMs have a limited context window. Every tool and instruction we add to them fills up their context. Research has shown that LLM performance drops the more we fill up the context (`https://research.trychroma.com/context-rot`). This means, the more tools and instructions we give agents, the worse they eventually perform. These two factors combined make agents brittle. The solution is a more controlled approach.

In December 2024, Anthropic released a very interesting blog post called Building effective agents (`https://www.anthropic.com/engineering/building-effective-agents`). In it, they make an important **distinction between agents and workflows.** With so many different definitions of agents evolving every day, Anthropic's distinction has worked well in our experience when thinking about building agent-backed applications. The distinction between agents and workflows and the structure of the workflows directly inspired how we approached the concepts in this chapter.

An **agent** (inspired by the original ReAct agent) has a goal, an environment, and a set of tools. In the following diagram, you can see an example of an **augmented LLM**, which is an LLM with tools. A tool can be the ability to search the web, to write a certain memory, and so on. It also has an environment it interacts with.

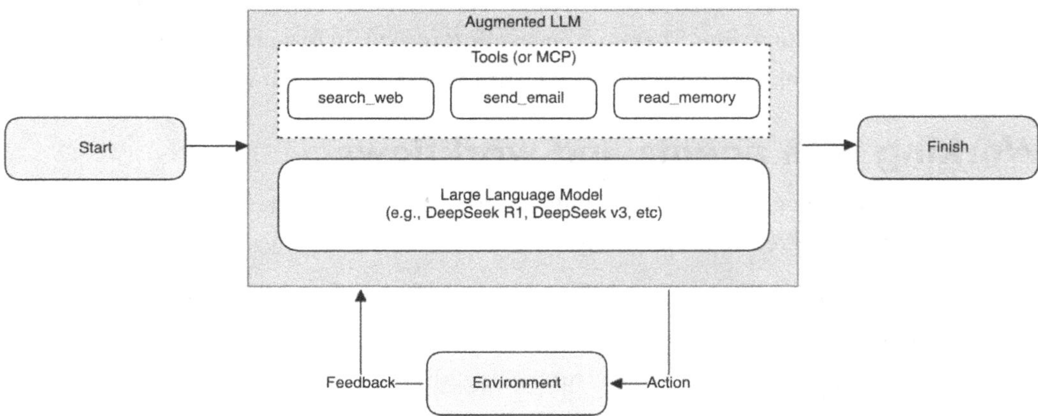

Figure 6.2: The augmented LLM with tools

In this scenario, we let the LLM *automatically* select the correct tools to reach its goal. Without guiding it. This means that the **control flow** is dynamic. In other words, we expect the agent to make the right decisions to reach its objective. This can prove to be brittle. The agent might get stuck in a loop, it might never reach its objective, and so on.

An alternative to an agent is a **workflow**. In a workflow, the control flow and direction of the overall system are predefined. Workflows are patterns where we control (to a certain extent) the actions and tools that the LLM will take ahead of time. You can think of a workflow as a **pattern**, or some sort of ***scaffolding*** around an augmented LLM, where we preemptively determine the actions, or flow, that we would like the LLM to take. This gives us back control of what actions we want the agent to take and can be a great choice when the set of actions is relatively simple.

Table 6.1 highlights some of the differences between agents and workflows.

Aspect	**Workflows**	**Agents**
Structure	Predefined and sequential	Dynamic and autonomous
Flexibility	Best for predictable, repeatable tasks	Suited for complex, open-ended problems
Control	Driven by developer-written code paths	LLM decides actions based on current context
Tool usage	Fixed order or recipe	Chosen and sequenced by the agent as needed
Predictability	Highly predictable	Variable; can adapt or retry based on feedback
Main use cases	Well-defined automations, document flows	Coding agents, interactive assistants, task planners

Table 6.1: Differences between workflows and agents (adapted from Anthropic's Building effective agents blog post)

It's important to point out that both agents and workflows are **agentic systems**, both with varying degrees of autonomy. In a way, you can think of an ***agent*** as a pure self-driving car, without anyone inside, nothing to control it, and a ***workflow*** as a self-driving car with a driver (you) making sure it's doing the right thing. We might use a lot of ***agents*** in the future, but when we can, we should choose control and go with ***workflows***.

In this chapter, we will design three different agent systems powered by DeepSeek's models. Two will be workflows, and one will be a pure agent. We will introduce each one in its specific sections. The goal of this section is for you to understand how to build agent systems using DeepSeek and be able to expand that to your own use case. We will not focus on particular libraries or tools. We believe that although some of these libraries are incredibly powerful, they will often overlook important aspects of agent systems – especially when learning.

Here are some interesting resources for you to read up on agents:

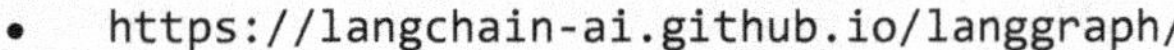

- `https://langchain-ai.github.io/langgraph/`

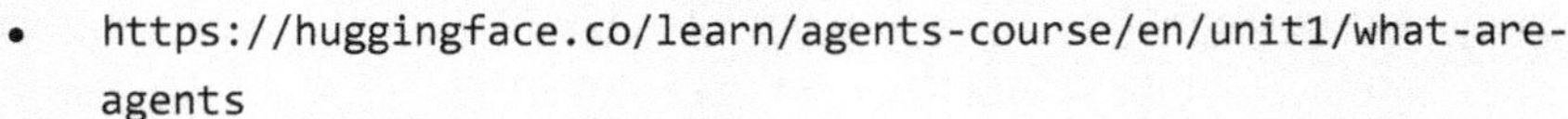

- `https://huggingface.co/learn/agents-course/en/unit1/what-are-agents`
- `https://www.anthropic.com/engineering/building-effective-agents`
- `https://modelcontextprotocol.io/introduction`
- `https://developers.googleblog.com/en/a2a-a-new-era-of-agent-interoperability/`

Let's now build some example workflows and agents.

Exploring various agentic systems

In this section, we will talk about three different agent systems. We will start with an evaluator-optimizer workflow, where we will show an example by summarizing scientific papers. The second workflow is an orchestrator-worker workflow, where we will show how to generate detailed reports about a topic. Finally, we will introduce a pure tool calling agent, where you will see a dynamic workflow in action.

Workflow: Evaluator-optimizer

The first agentic workflow we will introduce is the **evaluator-optimizer** workflow. The idea of this workflow is to have a first LLM generate a response (i.e., the **generator**), and a second LLM evaluate the responses from the first (i.e., the **evaluator**). The evaluator LLM assesses the response, continuously providing feedback to the first, so that it can improve its generation, iteratively.

The key idea is to have a controlled loop, where we can iteratively refine the generation of a given target. This workflow is ideal when you have a general idea of where to start, and you also have a good idea of the criteria that make a good result. For example, you might want to generate a cover letter for a job application but would also like it to follow strict criteria (e.g., a certain number of paragraphs, a certain tone of voice). Another example is code generation. You can start by defining a function and establishing clear criteria (number of lines, time complexity, unit tests) that you would like the final result to respect.

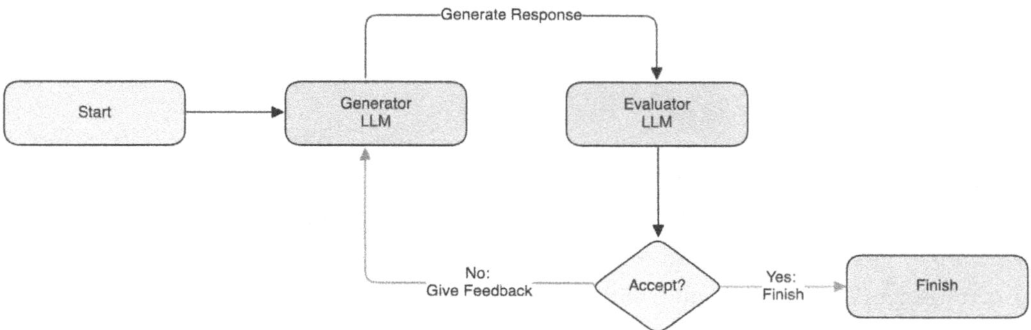

Figure 6.3: The evaluator-optimizer workflow

Although it may sound simple, this workflow is particularly effective in the case of reasoning LLMs – such as `deepseek-reasoner`. This is because we not only provide feedback to the generator LLM, but also the reasoning behind that feedback. If this sounds abstract, don't worry. We'll build an example of this pattern next.

An example: Summarizing arXiv papers

arXiv.org (`https://arxiv.org/`) is a popular repository for publishing and uploading scientific papers. It has gained popularity in the field of machine learning. Especially nowadays, you'll see hundreds of papers published every day. arXiv lets anyone publish and read papers that are meant for open access. It has gained increasing popularity and inspired similar concepts in adjacent fields, such as bioRxiv (`https://www.biorxiv.org/`) for biology.

In this example, we will build an agent that is able to produce summaries of scientific papers from arXiv, in the exact format that we need. You could, of course, download a paper and upload it to ChatGPT – but this system allows us to not only establish clear criteria for the type of summary we want, but also to illustrate this pattern in a simple way.

As a first step, we need to be able to download a given paper from arXiv and convert it into Markdown. To do this, we define a `get_text_from_axiv_paper` function. We can leverage the `markitdown` library from Microsoft to get this done:

```
from markitdown import MarkItDown

def get_text_from_arxiv_paper(url: str) -> str:
    md = MarkItDown(enable_plugins=True)
    result = md.convert(url)
```

```
    return result.text_content

print(get_text_from_arxiv_paper(url="https://arxiv.org/pdf/1706.03762"))
# prints Attention Is All You Need...
```

We now need a function to call our DeepSeek LLM. The `llm_call` function sends a prompt to the DeepSeek API and retrieves both the final answer and the reasoning from `deepseek-reasoner`. When `with_json_output` is set to `True`, it prepends a system instruction and sets the response format to ensure the model replies with a JSON object. The function then returns the parsed response as a Python dictionary along with the reasoning. If `with_json_output` is `False`, it simply returns the raw string response and reasoning.

```
import json
from openai import OpenAI

API_KEY = os.environ["DEEPSEEK_API_KEY"]
BASE_URL = "https://api.deepseek.com"
MODEL = "deepseek-reasoner"

def llm_call(
    prompt: str, with_json_output: bool = False
) -> tuple[str | dict, str]:
    client = OpenAI(api_key=API_KEY, base_url=BASE_URL)

    args = {
        "model": MODEL,
        "messages": [],
    }

    if with_json_output is True:
        json_prompt = """
        Output your response in JSON format with the keys specified in the
prompt.
        Do not include any other text such as ```json or ```.
        The response should be directly parseable by json.loads.
        """.strip()
        args["messages"].append(
```

```
            {"role": "system", "content": json_prompt}
        )
        args["response_format"] = {"type": "json_object"}

    args["messages"].append({"role": "user", "content": prompt})
    response = client.chat.completions.create(**args)

    reasoning = response.choices[0].message.reasoning_content
    final_response = response.choices[0].message.content

    if with_json_output is True:
        return json.loads(final_response), reasoning

    return final_response, reasoning

final_response, reasoning = llm_call(
    prompt="What is the capital of Portugal?", with_json_output=True
)
print(f"Final Response: {final_response}")
# prints Final Response: {'capital': 'Lisbon'}
print(f"Reasoning: {reasoning}")
# prints Reasoning: 'First, the user asked ...'
```

Now we can start working on our evaluator-optimizer pattern. The `generate` function sends a target task to the LLM along with an optional context and a base prompt. It then calls `llm_call` to get the model's response and reasoning. It also expects the response to have a `<RESPONSE>...</RESPONSE>` block, so it extracts the content inside of it. For debugging purposes, we also add some verbose printing so we can see what is going on.

```
def generate(
    prompt: str, task: str, context: str = ""
) -> tuple[str, str]:
    """Generate and improve a solution based on feedback."""
    full_prompt = (
        f"{prompt}\n{context}\nTask: {task}"
        if context
        else f"{prompt}\nTask: {task}"
    )
```

```
    response, thoughts = llm_call(full_prompt)
    result = re.search(r"<RESPONSE>(.*?)</RESPONSE>",
        response, re.DOTALL).group(1)

    print("\n=== GENERATION START ===")
    print("\n*** THOUGHTS START ***")
    print(thoughts)
    print("\n*** THOUGHTS END ***")
    print("\n*** RESULT START ***")
    print(result)
    print("\n*** RESULT END ***")
    print("=== GENERATION END ===\n")

    return thoughts, result
```

With our generator in place, we need our evaluator. The evaluator's goal is to provide an evaluation – think *How good was your try?*, and feedback – think *Pass, Fail.* For this, we define an `evaluate` function. This builds a prompt and uses JSON outputs to retrieve both the evaluation and feedback. We also add some prints. These are optional, of course.

```
def evaluate(prompt: str, content: str, task: str) -> tuple[str, str]:

    full_prompt = f"{prompt}\nOriginal task: {task}\nContent to evaluate:
{content}"
    response, thoughts = llm_call(full_prompt, with_json_output=True)
    evaluation = response.get("evaluation")
    feedback = response.get("feedback")

    print("=== EVALUATION START ===")
    print("\n*** THOUGHTS START ***")
    print(thoughts)
    print("\n*** THOUGHTS END ***")
    print("\n*** STATUS START ***")
    print(f"Status: {evaluation}")
    print("\n*** STATUS END ***")
    print("\n*** FEEDBACK START ***")
    print(feedback)
```

```
    print("\n*** FEEDBACK END ***")
    print("=== EVALUATION END ===\n")

    return evaluation, feedback
```

Now that we have both our generate and evaluate functions in place, we can create our evaluation-optimization loop. The loop function continuously generates solutions and evaluates them until a passing result is found. It takes in task, evaluator_prompt, and generator_prompt. It starts by calling the generate function and storing the initial thoughts and result in a chain_of_thought list. The goal of the chain_of_thought list is to only keep track of the different thoughts that the generator went through. We create this so that we can inspect the different thoughts that have occurred during the process.

Then it enters an infinite loop, beginning each iteration by passing the latest result to the evaluator. If the evaluation returns PASS, this means that our generator deemed that the paper summary respected all the criteria we defined (don't worry – we will define them in a bit), and so the loop ends.

If the result does not pass (which means our evaluator was not satisfied), the function builds a new context that includes all previous attempts and the most recent evaluator feedback. This context is passed back into the generator, prompting it to refine the output. The result is a feedback loop that incrementally improves each generation. In theory, our infinite loop is limited by the total context of DeepSeek. But in production, especially, you should make sure to limit this loop! Never let an LLM run indefinitely! This will break your bank!

```
def loop(
    task: str, evaluator_prompt: str, generator_prompt: str
) -> tuple[str, list[dict]]:
    """Keep generating and evaluating until requirements are met."""
    memory = [] # keeps track of previous results
    chain_of_thought = [] # keeps track the chain of thought

    thoughts, result = generate(generator_prompt, task)
    memory.append(result)
    chain_of_thought.append({"thoughts": thoughts, "result": result})

  # enter infinite loop
    while True:
        evaluation, feedback = evaluate(evaluator_prompt, result, task)
```

```
        # everything is approved and done
        if evaluation == "PASS":
            return result, chain_of_thought

        # add to the context from the memory
        context = "\n".join(
            [
                "Previous attempts:",
                *[f"- {m}" for m in memory],
                f"\nFeedback: {feedback}",
            ]
        )

        # generate again and append to memory
        thoughts, result = generate(generator_prompt, task, context)
        memory.append(result)
        chain_of_thought.append({"thoughts": thoughts, "result": result})
```

With everything in place, we can now create our paper summarization workflow. The first step is to create our prompts. We create two prompts: one for the evaluator, outlining what makes a good summary, and one for the generator, which tells it that it needs to complete a task and output its response in the `<RESPONSE>` block:

```
evaluator_prompt = """
Evaluate the following summary. A good summary should:
1. Be understandable by an undergraduate student
2. Formatted in markdown, with proper headings and subheadings
3. Have a title and a clear structure
4. Have at least 500 words
5. Grammar and spelling should be correct

You should be evaluating only and not attempting to solve the task.
Only output "PASS" if all criteria are met and you have no further
suggestions for improvements.
Output your evaluation concisely in the following format:

EXAMPLE JSON OUTPUT:
{
```

```
    "evaluation": "PASS, NEEDS_IMPROVEMENT, or FAIL",
    "feedback": "What needs improvement and why."
}
"""

generator_prompt = """
Your goal is to complete the task based on <user input>. If there are
feedback
from your previous generations, you should reflect on them to improve your
solution

Output your answer concisely in the following format:

<RESPONSE>
Content of the response
</RESPONSE>
"""
```

With these prompts in place, our final step is to create a function that acts as the main entry point for our agentic loop. We'll call this one `paper_summary_for`. It fetches the text from the paper, defines a task, which in our case is a summary, and then initiates the `loop` function. Once done, it returns our summary as well as the chain of thought.

```
def paper_summary_for(paper_url: str) -> str:
    web_page_text = get_text_from_arxiv_paper(paper_url)
    task = f"""
    <user input>
    Write a summary of the following article:

    <article>
    {web_page_text}
    </article>

    </user input>
    """
    result, cot = loop(task, evaluator_prompt, generator_prompt)
    return result, cot
```

As an example, we will ask our agent to summarize a recent paper called *MiniMax-M1: Scaling Test-Time Compute Efficiently with Lightning Attention* (`https://arxiv.org/pdf/2506.13585`). When we run our main function, we can see that the process kicks off and goes for about five rounds. We can see that the evaluation fails multiple times – if the summary is too short, uses technical jargon, or does not format Markdown properly.

```
result, cot = generate_agentic_summary_for(
    "https://arxiv.org/pdf/2506.13585")
# prints
# === GENERATION START ===
# *** THOUGHTS START ***
# Summarizing the MiniMax-M1 article…
# *** THOUGHTS END ***
# *** RESULT START ***
# MiniMax-M1 is an open-weight reasoning model using a hybrid MoE
architecture…
# *** RESULT END ***
# === GENERATION END ===
#
# === EVALUATION START ===
# *** STATUS START ***
# Status: FAIL
# *** STATUS END ***
# *** FEEDBACK START ***
# Too short (189 words) and missing a markdown title.
# *** FEEDBACK END ***
# === EVALUATION END ===
#
# ... Loops hidden for conciseness.
#
# === GENERATION START ===
# *** RESULT START ***
# **MiniMax-M1: Efficient Long-Context Reasoning**
# MiniMax-M1 is a large-scale model supporting 1M-token context and
trained with the CISPO RL algorithm…
# *** RESULT END ***
# === GENERATION END ===
#
```

```
# === EVALUATION START ===
# *** STATUS START ***
# Status: PASS
# *** STATUS END ***
# === EVALUATION END ===
```

Eventually, at the end of the process, the evaluator gives a PASS score to the process, and the loop finishes. Our summary is nicely formatted, includes all the sections, and is understandable by a graduate student (at least the judgments of our evaluator!). Here's the introduction section.

```
**MiniMax-M1: Revolutionizing Efficient Long-Context Reasoning in Large
Language Models**

### Introduction
MiniMax-M1 represents a groundbreaking advancement in open-weight
large language models (LLMs), engineered to tackle complex real-world
problems requiring extensive reasoning and long-context processing.
Developed by MiniMax AI, it pioneers efficient scaling of "test-time
compute" (computational resources used during task execution) through a
hybrid architecture and novel training techniques. The model supports
context windows of **1 million tokens**—8 times larger than predecessors
like DeepSeek-R1—and generates outputs up to **80K tokens**, enabling
unprecedented capabilities in domains like software engineering,
scientific research, and multi-step agent workflows.
```

You can visit the full notebook with all the code in the GitHub repository for this book and chapter.

As you can see, evaluator-optimizer is a powerful pattern where tasks can be incrementally improved toward an objective. It's worth mentioning that we could be stuck in an infinite loop, so we advise you to limit the optimizer loop to a fixed set of iterations; otherwise, things might get expensive! Additionally, if your responses are time sensitive (i.e., you need generations fast), this pattern might not be the most appropriate one, since depending on the complexity of the task, things might be pretty slow!

Now that we've talked about our first workflow, let's discuss another important one, the orchestrator-workers workflow.

Workflow: Orchestrator-workers

It's time to complicate things a little bit. In this second example, we will introduce the **orchestrator-workers** workflow. If the name of this workflow sounds scary, don't be scared, dear reader. This workflow is much simpler than it sounds!

The idea behind the orchestrator-workers workflow is that you can separate a given task into multiple tasks that can be run in parallel. Firstly, we have an **orchestrator** component. The job of this LLM is to receive a certain task and divide it into N independent tasks. Each **worker** LLM takes one of these tasks and performs whatever it needs to perform. The final component here is a **synthesizer** LLM, whose job is to gather all the outputs of the worker LLMs and transform them into a single coherent output for the process.

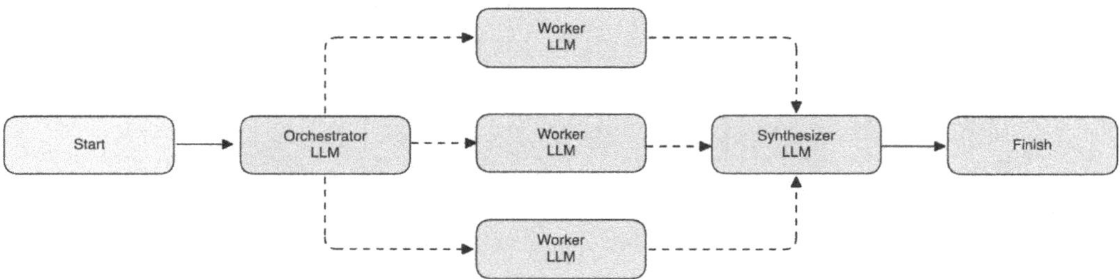

Figure 6.4: The orchestrator-workers workflow pattern

You might have seen this workflow in the wild. In fact, it powers systems such as ChatGPT Deep Research, a system that conducts *deep* research for a user by searching the web. In it, after creating a search report, several LLMs then act as workers and independently search the web for relevant information about a sub-topic. To clarify, we might be using the same type of LLM (DeepSeek V3, for example), but we then spark different instances of that LLM, in parallel, to research different topics. Finally, an *orchestrator* LLM synthesizes all the information and returns a coherent final report to the user.

Of course, this is all speculation – the official Deep Research product is actually closed source, so all we can do is guess. But a recent talk from the creators (`https://www.youtube.com/watch?v=eJOjdjO45Sc`) actually points in the ***multiple LLM calls*** direction. Also, if a single LLM had to browse 70 websites one at a time, the user would quickly lose their patience!

Still, it is a particularly useful pattern when the task at hand can be decomposed into smaller pieces and parallelized.

An example: A report-generating workflow

We've talked about Deep Research as an interesting use case for the orchestrator-workers workflow. Let's build something similar. The goal will be to build a report about a certain task. We will let the orchestrator LLM decide on which section makes sense to write about. Once it decides, we will then run all our workers in parallel. As soon as the last one is done, we will then feed all inputs to our final building block, the synthesizer LLM, which will generate the final report. If you're feeling scared, don't – we'll build it together step by step.

We start by defining two data classes using Python's `@dataclass` decorator. `Task` is the input for the worker. Each task has a section title and the rationale for writing it. We also define `WorkerResult`, which is the output of each worker. It contains the same elements, as well as a result string. We could use the same class, but let's keep things separated for now. It's good practice.

```
from dataclasses import dataclass
@dataclass
class Task:
    section_title: str
    rationale: str

@dataclass
class WorkerResult:
    section_title: str
    rationale: str
    result: str | None = None
```

We now start defining our `OrchestratorWorker` class. Nothing fancy. Just an `__init__` method that takes in a prompt for the orchestrator, a prompt for each worker, and a prompt for the final synthesis. Those prompts will be made into templates using the `jinja2` package.

```
from jinja2 import Template
class OrchestratorWorker:
    """Break down tasks and run them in parallel using worker LLMs."""

    def __init__(
        self,
        orchestrator_prompt: str,
        worker_prompt: str,
        synthesis_prompt: str,
```

```
        task: str,
    ):
        self.orchestrator_template = Template(orchestrator_prompt)
        self.worker_template = Template(worker_prompt)
        self.synthesis_template = Template(synthesis_prompt)
        self.task = task
```

We also define a `run_single_worker` method that will take a main task, as well as a task, render the worker prompt template, run it through the LLM, and output a worker result. Notice we use `with_json_output` set to `True`, as we expect the worker result to be a dictionary with a `response` key. More on this in a bit.

```
    def run_single_worker(
        self, main_task: str, task: Task
    ) -> WorkerResult:
        """Run a single worker and return the result."""

        worker_input = self.worker_template.render(
            original_task=main_task,
            section_title=task.section_title,
            rationale=task.rationale,
        )

        print(f"\n[WORKER INPUT] Section: {task.section_title}\n{worker_
input}\n")
        worker_response = llm_call(worker_input, with_json_output=True)
        result = worker_response["response"]

        print(f"\n[WORKER OUTPUT] Section: {task.section_title}\
n{result}\n")

        return WorkerResult(
            section_title=task.section_title,
            rationale=task.rationale,
            result=result,
        )
```

Here's the core loop of the logic. We receive the orchestrator input and receive a certain number of tasks from it. Each task is parsed as a `Task` type and mapped to the `run_single_worker` function, in parallel. Since we are parallelizing an IO-bound task (an API call to our LLM), we use Python's built-in `ThreadPoolExecutor`.

```
    def process(self, task: str) -> list[WorkerResult]:
        """Run orchestrator and execute all workers in parallel."""

        input_str = self.orchestrator_template.render(task=task)
        print(f"\n[ORCHESTRATOR INPUT]\n{input_str}\n")

        orchestrator_output = llm_call(input_str, with_json_output=True)

        print(f"[ORCHESTRATOR OUTPUT]\nAnalysis:\n{orchestrator_
output['analysis']}")
        print(f"\nTasks:\n{orchestrator_output['tasks']}\n")

        worker_tasks = [Task(**t) for t in orchestrator_output["tasks"]]
        print(f"[INFO] Total tasks: {len(worker_tasks)}\n")

        with ThreadPoolExecutor() as executor:
            results = list(
                tqdm(
                    executor.map(
                        lambda t: self.run_single_worker(task, t),
                        worker_tasks
                    ),
                    total=len(worker_tasks),
                    desc="Running workers",
                )
            )

        return results
```

A crucial step to describe here is the synthesize method. It's relatively simple, as its main task is to take a list of WorkerResult and use synthesis_template to render the final result to the user.

```
    def synthesize(self, worker_results: list[WorkerResult]) -> str:
        """Generate final report by synthesizing all worker results."""

        synthesis_input = self.synthesis_template.render(
            original_task=self.task,
            worker_results=worker_results,
        )

        print(f"\n[SYNTHESIS INPUT]\n{synthesis_input}\n")

        response = llm_call(synthesis_input, with_json_output=True)
        return response["response"]
```

Finally, we implement the run method, which will serve as the entry point for our class. It calls the self.process method and feeds the result into the synthesize method. At the end, it returns the result of the synthesis back to the user.

```
    def run(self) -> str:
        """Run the orchestrator and return the final report."""
        worker_results = self.process(self.task)
        synthesis_result = self.synthesize(worker_results)
        return synthesis_result
```

Now we're ready to run our orchestrator-workers workflow. First, we define the prompt for our three components:

- **Orchestrator prompt**: Receives the main task and breaks it down into 3–5 distinct tasks. Here is how you can define it.

  ```
  ORCHESTRATOR_PROMPT = """
  You're tasked with creating a report on a specific topic.

  Break this down into 3-5 distinct sections that could each be
  written with a different focus.

  Report topic: {{ task }}
  ```

```
Return your response in this JSON format:

{
  "analysis": "Summarize your understanding of the reporting goal
and explain why breaking it into multiple sections with different
focuses would be valuable. Highlight how each section emphasizes
a different priority (e.g., technical depth, accessibility,
narrative).",
  "tasks": [
    {
      "section_title": "Technical Overview",
      "rationale": "Explain why this section is important and what
it will cover.",
    },
    {
      "section_title": "Practical Implications",
      "rationale": "Explain why this section is important and what
it will cover.",
    }
  ]
}
"""
```

- **Worker prompt**: Receives the main topic, an isolated task (a section title in this case), and a rationale for that task. Let's define the worker prompt.

```
WORKER_PROMPT = """
You're generating a section of a report.

Topic: {{ original_task }}
Section title: {{ section_title }}
Rationale: {{ rationale }}


Write the content for this section using **Markdown formatting**
(bold, italics, lists, code blocks, etc.) where appropriate, but
**do not include a header/title** - just the body content.
```

```
Return your response in this JSON format:

{
  "response": "Your report content here, using Markdown formatting
but without any section headers."
}
"""
```

- **Synthesis prompt**: Receives the input from all the workers and synthesizes the response into a final one. Here is the synthesis prompt.

```
SYNTHESIS_PROMPT = """
You're synthesizing multiple report sections into one cohesive final
report.

Original topic: {{ original_task }}

These are the completed sections (in order):

{% for result in worker_results %}
Section title: {{ result.section_title }}
---
{{ result.result }}
{% endfor %}

Your task is to merge the sections into a well-flowing report. Use
**Markdown formatting** where helpful, but **do not repeat the
section titles**.

Ensure:
- The tone and style feel consistent throughout.
- Transitions between sections are smooth.
- Any overlap is minimized.
- The final output reads like a single unified piece.

Return your response in this JSON format:
{
  "response": "Your final merged report here, in Markdown."
```

```
    }
    """
```

Now that everything is defined, we can fire off our workflow with a question. I chose one that is a bit personal to me. But you can choose anything!

```
task = "Make an in-depth report that explains why biking has not been
adopted in the City of Lisbon, and what can be done to encourage it."
orchestrator = OrchestratorWorker(
    orchestrator_prompt=ORCHESTRATOR_PROMPT,
    worker_prompt=WORKER_PROMPT,
    synthesis_prompt=SYNTHESIS_PROMPT,
    task=task,
)
final_report = orchestrator.run()
```

You can see the GitHub repo for the full output of the workflow. But I'll outline a few interesting parts here.

First, the orchestrator divides this question into five different tasks, each with a rationale, and each one can be individually explored. We also provide the rationale so that the worker has more context on why the particular section is important.

```
[
    {'section_title': 'Current Infrastructure and Challenges',
    'rationale': '...'
    },
    {'section_title': 'Cultural and Social Attitudes Towards Biking',
    'rationale': '...'
    },
    {'section_title': 'Policy and Governance',
    'rationale': 'T...'
    },
    {'section_title': 'Successful Case Studies and Potential Solutions',
    'rationale': '...'
    },
    {'section_title': 'Community Engagement and Awareness Campaigns',
    'rationale': '...'
    }
]
```

I will not show all the input from all the workers. You can check the GitHub repo for that, but here's an example of a worker in action:

```
[WORKER INPUT] Section: Current Infrastructure and Challenges

You're generating a section of a report...

#...

[WORKER OUTPUT] Section: Current Infrastructure and Challenges
The City of Lisbon faces several infrastructure and logistical challenges
that hinder the widespread adoption of biking as a mode of transportation.
Below is an in-depth analysis of these barriers:
...
```

As you can see, this worker independently researches and outputs a report section on this topic. Finally, the synthesizer takes all these outputs and condenses them into a single coherent report.

```
The City of Lisbon faces significant challenges in adopting biking as
a mainstream mode of transportation, primarily due to infrastructure
limitations, cultural attitudes, and policy gaps. However, by addressing
these issues through targeted strategies, Lisbon can foster a more bike-
friendly environment.

**Current Infrastructure and Challenges**
Lisbon's urban landscape, characterized by steep hills and a lack of
dedicated bike lanes, poses considerable barriers to biking. The absence
of secure parking and poor integration with public transport further
discourages potential cyclists. To overcome these obstacles, expanding
the bike lane network, introducing e-bike sharing programs, and improving
parking facilities are essential steps.

**Cultural and Social Attitudes Towards Biking**
Cultural perceptions in Lisbon often view biking as a leisure activity
rather than a practical transportation option, compounded by safety
concerns and the status associated with car ownership. Shifting these
attitudes requires community engagement programs, infrastructure
improvements, and incentives to highlight biking's benefits.
```

This is an interesting pattern, where the task can be broken down into individual sections/tasks that can be run in parallel. You can take this example and apply it to other tasks – for example, grading different essays, analyzing resumes, conducting different web searches on a topic, or editing files in a code base. Almost anything can be broken down into smaller, independent tasks! Not everything, though! Some tasks need to be sequential. So, think before throwing this pattern at a problem.

Now that we've covered the orchestrator-workers pattern, we will talk about a final, but very important, building block of building agents (especially with DeepSeek), which is the tool-calling agent.

Agent: Tool-calling agent

We've built two agentic workflows until now. But we are yet to build a full agent. No workflows, no guardrails – just let the agent make all decisions. However, one of the most powerful things you can add to any LLM is tools. Recall that tools are the functions that your LLM can call. For example, you might have a `search_web` tool. When the LLM decides to call it, it will tell you that it wants to use the `search_web` tool with the `deepseek` argument if it wants to search for that term.

As we mentioned before, in this case, we will let the LLM make the decisions. DeepSeek will decide which tools to call and in what sequence to call them. We can also talk about this as an **augmented LLM**, which is an LLM powered with some tools. Modern versions of this pattern might include something such as memory for an agent, or more sophisticated techniques. Some other definitions of agent tend to be simplified: *An agent is an LLM with tools in a loop*. Although simplistic, this covers the core of our final agentic system. You can see the tool-calling agent illustrated here.

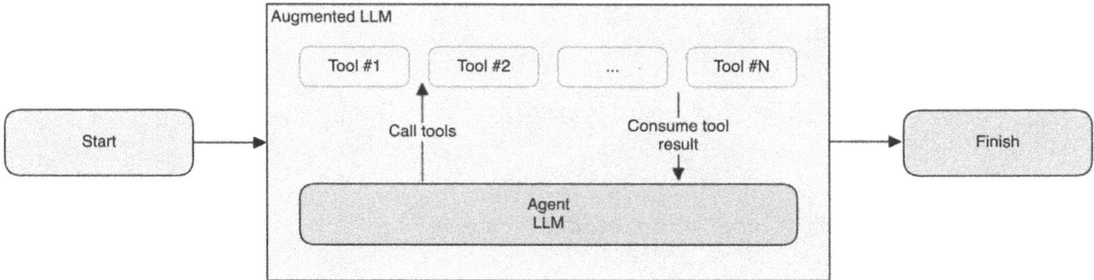

Figure 6.5: A tool-calling agent

When building a tool-calling agent, we should be mindful of a few things. Which tools does our agent have access to, and do they help in solving the overall task? Can the loop of the LLM choosing different tools go on forever? Can the agent reach out to a human for help? All of these are important when building a tool-calling agent. For example, giving access to a repo-reading tool when our agent has no business reading a code base will simply confuse it. Giving a customer support agent access to do web searches will probably result in it citing something wrong from the internet. We should be *extremely* careful and considerate when creating the tools for our agents to use. This is, as we say in Portugal, how the sausage gets made (i.e., the secret sauce that makes things work well!).

Enough with the explanation, let's build a tool-calling agent powered by DeepSeek.

An example: A web search agent

In this example, we will create a web search agent that can receive a question, and go off into the internet and search for the best response possible to that question. We will equip this agent with tools to accomplish the task and implement a tool-calling loop from scratch. Since our agent needs to be able to search the internet, we will give it access to two tools: `search_web` (to conduct web searches) and `read_website` (to read any website on the internet). We could also add a third tool to ask us for support or clarification for a task. But we'll leave that as an exercise for you.

We start with our usual LLM calling function, but we add two important aspects: a cache backed by `diskcache` to avoid redundant model calls. And for reasoning agents (such as `deepseek-reasoner`), we strip the reasoning content from the message chain (unlike other models, DeepSeek documentation conveys that we must remove the reasoning content from the `messages` chain).

```
from diskcache import Cache

cache = Cache("./cache")

@cache.memoize(expire=3600)
def llm_call(
    messages: list[dict[str, str]], tools: list[dict[str, Any]], model:
str
) -> str:
    response = client.chat.completions.create(
        model=model,
        messages=messages,
        tools=tools if tools else None,
        temperature=0.0,
        tool_choice="auto",
    )
```

```
    message = response.choices[0].message

    if hasattr(message, "reasoning_content"):
        del message.reasoning_content

    return message
```

Let's now define our tools. The first is a `search_web` tool that can be used to search the web using the Marginalia search engine (`https://www.marginalia.nu/`). The main reason for choosing this one is that it's free and has a pretty simple API. But in production, you might evaluate or use other search engines (Google, Brave, or others).

When we search for something, it will return a list of links, titles, and a couple of other details.

```
from pydantic import BaseModel
import httpx

class SearchWeb(BaseModel):
    """Search the web for a given query."""

    query: str
    max_results: int = 10


def search_web(data: SearchWeb) -> str:
    base_url = "https://api.marginalia.nu/{key}/search/{query}"
    url = base_url.format(key="public", query=data.query)
    url += f"?count={data.max_results}"

    rsp = httpx.get(url)
    rsp.raise_for_status()

    results = rsp.json()["results"]
    return str(results)
# print(search_web(SearchWeb(query="Paris")))
# [
# {'url': 'https://en.wikipedia.org/wiki/Paris_Las_Vegas', 'title': 'Paris
..', 'description': '...', 'quality': 5.037784569660175, 'format': 'html',
```

```
'details': [[]]},
# {'url': 'https://en.wikipedia.org/wiki/Paris_Observatory', 'title':
'Paris Observatory', 'description': 'The Paris ...', 'quality':
5.161455267002603, 'format': 'html', 'details': [[]]}
# ]
```

The second tool that we will equip our agent with is the `read_website` tool. It uses `markdownify` to convert the content of a website into Markdown, so that the LLM can better understand it.

```
from markdownify import markdownify as md

class ReadWebsite(BaseModel):
    """Read the content of a website and return it as text. (useful for
further research)"""

    url: str


def read_website(data: ReadWebsite) -> str:
    html_content = httpx.get(data.url).text
    return md(html_content)

# print(read_website(data=ReadWebsite(url="https://www.theguardian.com/
europe")))
# prints "The Latest news, sport and opinion from the Guardian.."
```

We also define a small helper function that converts plain functions into the required tool-call format from DeepSeek. This is required since DeepSeek's API expects the JSON format for calling tools.

```
def to_openai_tool(func: callable) -> dict[str, Any]:
    sig = inspect.signature(func)
    if sig.parameters:
        param = next(iter(sig.parameters.values()))
        param_type = param.annotation
        schema = param_type.model_json_schema()
    else:
        param_type = None
        schema = {"type": "object", "properties": {}, "required": []}

    return {
```

```
        "type": "function",
        "function": {
            "name": func.__name__,
            "description": (param_type.__doc__ if param_type else func.__
doc__ or ""),
            "parameters": schema,
        },
    }
```

Finally, we create our tools by calling `to_openai_tool` on both our functions. We do this since we are using the OpenAI SDK, which requires a particular tool format. We also create a `FUNC_TYPES` dictionary that maps each function to the correct Pydantic input format:

```
TOOLS = [
    to_openai_tool(search_web),
    to_openai_tool(read_website),
]
# {'type': 'function', 'function': {'name': 'search_web', 'description':
...

FUNC_TYPES = {
    search_web: SearchWeb,
    read_website: ReadWebsite,
}
```

Now that the tools and boilerplate are in place, let's look at how the agent works. It's a simple class. On init, it sets up the model, tools, message list, and a max iteration limit. The main logic is in `__call__`. It adds the user prompt to the message history, then enters a loop:

- If the model responds directly, we return it.
- If it wants to call a tool, we find the right function, run it, append the result, and continue. sw

The _send method just passes messages to the model and returns the response – nothing fancy. Overall, the agent keeps looping: asking the model what to do, calling tools if needed, and feeding results back – until it's done or hits the iteration cap.

```
class Agent:
    def __init__(
        self,
```

```
        model: str,
        system: str,
        tools: list[dict[str, Any]] | None = None,
        max_iters: int = 10,
    ):
        self.model = model
        self.tools = tools or []
        self.messages: list[dict[str, str]] = []
        if system:
            self.messages.append({"role": "system", "content": system})

        self.max_iters = max_iters

    def __call__(self, content: str, verbose: bool) -> str:
        self.messages.append({"role": "user", "content": content})

        iterations = 0
        while True:
            iterations += 1
            message = self._send()
            self.messages.append(message)
            tool_calls = getattr(message, "tool_calls", None)
            if not tool_calls:
                return message.content

            for call in tool_calls:
                func = globals()[call.function.name]
                args_model = FUNC_TYPES[func]
                args = (
                    args_model.model_validate_json(call.function.
arguments)
                    if call.function.arguments != "{}"
                    else None
                )
                print(f"** CALLING FUNCTION {func.__name__} **")
                print(f"*** ARGS ***\n{args}\n")
```

```
                result = func(args) if args else func()

                if verbose is True:
                    print(f"*** RESULT ***\n{result}\n***")

                self.messages.append(
                    {
                        "role": "tool",
                        "tool_call_id": call.id,
                        "content": result,
                    }
                )

            if iterations >= self.max_iters:
                raise Exception("Max iterations reached")

    def _send(self):
        return llm_call(self.messages, self.tools, self.model)
```

Now we define our system prompts. We tell the LLM that it should follow this thought-action observation loop, and we kick it off with a simple question about the population of the city of Ancona in 2025.

```
system_prompt = """
You are a helpful assistant who can answer multistep questions by
sequentially calling functions.

Follow a pattern of:
- THOUGHT (reason step-by-step about which function to call next)
- ACTION (call a function as a next step towards the final answer)
- OBSERVATION (output of the function)
Reason step by step which actions to take to get to the answer.

Only call functions with arguments coming verbatim from the user or the
output of other functions.
"""

question = "What is the population of the city of Ancona as of 2025?"
```

To call the agent, we attach the system prompt, tools, and start with the deepseek-chat model.

```
bot = Agent(system=system_prompt, tools=TOOLS, model="deepseek-chat")
response = bot(question, verbose=False)
print("Response:", response)
```

Every time the agent calls a function, we log it. We can see that in this first try, the agent called the search web function with the query population of Ancona Italy in 2025. Then it read the website https://population.city/italy/ancona/, where it finally encountered a number. It then took that number and extrapolated it from 2014 to 2025. Not sure we can count this as *correct*, but it's certainly interesting to see the model call different tools for itself. In any case, we *could* specify in our prompt that it should only use estimates and not extrapolate. But we'll leave this as an exercise for you, our dear reader.

```
** CALLING FUNCTION search_web **
*** ARGS ***
query='population of Ancona Italy 2025' max_results=10

** CALLING FUNCTION read_website **
*** ARGS ***
url='https://population.city/italy/ancona/'

Response: The last known population of Ancona, Italy, was approximately
**101,500** in 2014. If the population growth rate remained consistent
at **0.34% per year** (as observed between 2011-2014), the estimated
population of Ancona in 2025 would be **105,351**.

This is an unofficial projection based on historical data. For the most
accurate and up-to-date figures, official census data or reports from the
Italian National Institute of Statistics (ISTAT) would be required.
```

Now let's try the deepseek-reasoner model for a potentially more *intelligent* loop.

```
bot = Agent(system=system_prompt, tools=TOOLS, model="deepseek-reasoner")
response = bot(question, verbose=False)
print("Response:", response)
```

We can see the reasoner-powered agent calls more functions and decides (by itself) to look for *official estimates*. After some digging, it eventually finds an estimate from the official institute of statistics of around 99K people. This sounds more reasonable, especially since the model also provided us with a reference!

```
** CALLING FUNCTION search_web **
*** ARGS ***
query='Ancona population 2025 projection' max_results=10

** CALLING FUNCTION search_web **
*** ARGS ***
query='Ancona Italy population 2025 official estimate' max_results=10

** CALLING FUNCTION read_website **
*** ARGS ***
url='https://www.citypopulation.de/en/italy/cities/marche/'

Response: Based on the official population estimates from the Istituto
Nazionale di Statistica Italia (Italy's National Institute of Statistics),
the population of Ancona as of January 1, 2025 is **99,469**.

This information comes directly from the detailed city and commune
population tables on citypopulation.de, which sources its data from
Italy's official statistics agency. The table shows:
- 2021 census: 98,402
- 2025 estimate: 99,469

The population estimate represents the projected population for the city
proper of Ancona as of the beginning of 2025.
```

It's worth pausing here for a note. Both runs used the *same* tool-calling agent, the same tools (`search_web` and `read_website`), and the same system prompt. The only difference was the model: `deepseek-chat` versus `deepseek-reasoner`. And yet, the outcomes were very different. `DeepSeek-Chat` found a number on the page and chose to extrapolate it forward to 2025, even though the page (or prompt) itself didn't suggest doing so. `DeepSeek-Reasoner` made a more cautious choice: it reformulated the query, searched for an official estimate, and correctly returned 99,469, as reported by the Italian statistics office. This divergence highlights a critical feature of **dynamic workflows**: even when the structure and tooling are constant, the model's internal reasoning governs the control flow. `DeepSeek-Chat` followed a shorter but flawed path. `DeepSeek-Reasoner` added steps and reached the right answer. This is the promise and the pitfall of dynamic agentic systems – *they're flexible and capable of adaptation, but they're also inherently unpredictable*, because the flow is driven by model behavior and *not* hardcoded logic.

The augmented LLM is a pretty powerful building block of LLM-backed applications. In this example, we used it as a single block to solve a specific problem. However, you can think of an augmented LLM as a Lego building block of any of the other workflows.

For example, in the evaluator-optimizer workflow, the evaluator can be equipped with tools (for example, to test code or for validating SQL), and the generator as well. In the orchestrator-workers workflow, each worker can be equipped with tools to research a certain topic or to get a certain task done. You are not limited by a certain workflow or a certain set of tools. Tools can have state. In modern IDEs, for example, such as VSCode, your chat probably has access to tools to search across your code base, edit a certain number of files, or read and write a set of rules you'd like it to remember.

An important note about evaluating agents

Evaluating agents – and LLM applications – is critical. Shipping a product without measuring success means you'll struggle to improve it. While this book is not about evaluations, nor will we design an evaluation system for the agents we built, we feel compelled to point you in the right direction.

You'll find plenty of frameworks promising *4-lines-of-code evaluations* with metrics such as **answer relevancy** or **faithfulness**. Those numbers might look good – *great, my relevance score is 0.87!* – but in many cases, they don't matter to your product's success. If you're building an agent to answer *What's the population of a small city in Italy?*, the only success metric is whether it returns the ***correct number***. Everything else is secondary.

From our experience, the most effective way to evaluate an LLM-based application is through a simple, iterative process:

1. Gather a dataset of 1,000 different cities and their population from a trusted source.
2. Run your agent on all the cities: *What is the population of X?*
3. Measure your accuracy: How many answers were correct? Which ones were wrong? Why?
4. Change the system based on learnings: switch search engines, change prompts, add planning steps.
5. Repeat from step 2.

By repeating this process multiple times, you'll systematically improve your system. It's more complicated than a 4-lines-of-code framework that gives you a shiny number, but trust us: you'll learn far more in the process.

Summary

At the time of writing, agents are all the rage. Every company's executive leadership and start-up leaders are raging about all the different problems agents can solve. Now, we don't know whether agents will solve scientific mysteries or make scientific discoveries, and we certainly have doubts that they can do so in a short lifespan. However, knowing how to leverage DeepSeek to build agents is a superpower to have under your belt.

In this chapter, we covered the essential workflows and building blocks of agentic applications and patterns. As this technology moves rapidly, we decided to focus on the principles and build each one from scratch.

In the next chapter, we will continue exploring the ins and outs of DeepSeek and understand how we can fine-tune it for different applications.

Now that you've learned how to leverage DeepSeek to build agentic systems, we will move our focus to fine-tuning with DeepSeek in the next chapter.

Part 3

Distilling and Deploying DeepSeek

In this third part of the book, we move from understanding and using DeepSeek to transforming it for production environments. We begin by exploring rationale distillation - leveraging DeepSeek's advanced reasoning capabilities to create specialized, efficient models that can run on modest hardware while maintaining professional-grade performance. Next, we address the practical challenges of deploying full-scale DeepSeek models, examining the trade-offs between APIs, managed services, and self-hosted solutions. Finally, we focus on building production-ready operations, covering monitoring, scaling, cost management, and security practices that turn experimental systems into reliable, enterprise-grade services.

By the end of this part, you'll understand how to distill domain-specific models, make informed deployment decisions based on your requirements and constraints, and operate DeepSeek models at scale with confidence and reliability.

This part of the book includes the following chapters:

- *Chapter 7, DeepSeek-Driven Fine-Tuning of Gemma 3 for Legal Reasoning*
- *Chapter 8, Deploying DeepSeek Models*
- *Chapter 9, Epilogue*
- *Appendix*

Stay tuned

To keep up with the latest developments in the fields of Generative AI and LLMs, subscribe to our weekly newsletter, *AI_Distilled*, at `https://packt.link/8Oz6Y`.

Join our communities on Discord and Reddit

Have questions about the book or want to contribute to discussions on Generative AI and LLMs?

Join our Discord server at `https://packt.link/4Bbd9` and our Reddit channel at `https://packt.link/wcYOQ` to connect, share, and collaborate with like-minded enthusiasts.

7

DeepSeek-Driven Fine-Tuning of Gemma 3 for Legal Reasoning

Imagine you're tasked with building a high-frequency trading system. You wouldn't reach for a general-purpose scripting language and a consumer-grade laptop – you'd reach for a low-latency, highly optimized stack, tuned for the precise demands of your domain. In engineering, we know that the right tool, properly configured, is the difference between it works and it works at scale, reliably, and with guarantees.

This is the core challenge with general-purpose **Large Language Models** (**LLMs**). Models like OpenAI's GPT-5 or Claude 4 Sonnet are astonishingly capable generalists, but they're the equivalent of a robust, all-in-one framework: flexible, but not optimized for the edge cases and performance requirements of specialized domains. When you're parsing thousands of legal contracts for subtle risk factors, or automating compliance checks in a regulated industry, close enough is not sufficient – precision, reliability, and explainability are paramount. You also probably care about how much it costs to use these models.

In this chapter, we will perform a two-stage workflow comprising rationale distillation with DeepSeek-R1 and fine-tuning Gemma 3 in the rationale-augmented data.

In our terminology here, **distillation** means data generation by the teacher (no teacher weights are updated); that is, DeepSeek-R1 serves as a teacher model to generate the training data. **Fine-tuning** means updating the student's parameters (via LoRA/Unsloth) to learn the teacher's behavior. For our use case, we'll fine-tune Gemma 3, a smaller model that is more suitable for deployment. We will also evaluate the **student** versus the **teacher** on held-out data. DeepSeek-R1 itself is not fine-tuned in this process; this reflects industry practice, where distillation is much more common.

In this chapter, we will cover the following main topics:

- Understanding the importance of distillation and fine-tuning
- Introducing CUAD: a structured benchmark for legal clause classification
- LLMOps tools for model distillation
- The two-stage workflow for legal rationale distillation
- Evaluation and results
- Key takeaways

Technical requirements

You will need the following for this chapter the project repository at `https://github.com/PacktPublishing/DeepSeek-in-Practice`.

Dependencies

Start with the project repository and install the required packages:

```
git clone https://github.com/PacktPublishing/DeepSeek-in-Practice.git
cd Chapter07
pip install -r requirements.txt
```

The requirements file includes ZenML for orchestration, Unsloth for efficient training, transformers for model handling, and various utilities for data processing and evaluation.

Creating your local environment with ZenML

We use ZenML in code samples to demonstrate good MLOps hygiene (pipelines, caching, and lineage). You can substitute other platforms that provide the same capabilities without changing the learning objectives (for example, MLflow, Weights & Biases, Flyte, Metaflow, Kubeflow, or Airflow).

Creating your ZenML Cloud account

1. Create a free managed account at `cloud.zenml.io`. This serves as your experiment tracking and pipeline orchestration hub, monitoring training progress and managing artifacts. The free tier provides sufficient resources for our legal classification project.

2. Connect your local environment and set your project name after registration:

```
# Log in and select your workspace
zenml login
# Activate your project
zenml project set default # usually the default project is fine
```

3. **Cloud stack with GPU**: Model training requires GPU compute with memory requirements that scale by model size:

   - 1B model: 8 GB+ GPU memory.
   - 4B model: 16 GB+ GPU memory.
   - 12B model: 24 GB+ GPU memory.

   For this, you need to set up a cloud stack following the `ZenML cloud deployment guide` (`https://docs.zenml.io/stacks/deployment/deploy-a-cloud-stack`). A **stack** in ZenML represents the infrastructure where your pipelines run. You can easily switch from a local setup to cloud infrastructure just by switching your stack. The fastest way to create a cloud stack is through the **Infrastructure-as-Code** option. This uses Terraform to deploy cloud resources and register them as a ZenML stack. You'll need the following:

   - Terraform (`https://www.terraform.io/downloads.html`) version 1.9+ installed locally.
   - Authentication configured for your preferred cloud provider (AWS, GCP, or Azure).
   - Appropriate permissions to create resources in your cloud account.

   The deployment wizard will guide you through each step. The deployment will take a few minutes.

4. Once deployment is complete, activate your new stack:

```
zenml stack set <NAME_OF_YOUR_NEW_STACK>
```

API keys and environment variables

You will need API keys for accessing OpenRouter and Hugging Face models:

- **OpenRouter** provides access to DeepSeek models for generating baseline comparisons during evaluation. Sign up at `openrouter.ai` and obtain your API key from the dashboard. We will use a free model to access the base DeepSeek-R1 model, but you need an API key to access it (via `litellm`). If you do not have an OpenRouter API key, you can create one at `https://openrouter.ai/docs/api-reference/api-keys/get-key`.

- **Hugging Face** is used to upload the models you train. Create a token at huggingface.co/settings/tokens with write permissions. Create your API key by using https://huggingface.co/join.
- Configure the required API credentials:

```
export OPENROUTER_API_KEY="your_openrouter_api_key"
export HF_API_KEY="your_huggingface_api_key"  # Optional
```

Enhanced CUAD dataset

Enhanced CUAD is a rationale-augmented version of the **Contract Understanding Atticus Dataset (CUAD)**, adding DeepSeek-generated step-by-step explanations (**rationales**) to the original expert labels for 41 clause types across 510 real-world contracts. We'll use the Hugging Face release zenml/cuad-deepseek (https://huggingface.co/datasets/zenml/cuad-deepseek).

Fine-tuning without ZenML (standalone script)

If you just want to fine-tune a model without installing ZenML, we provide a standalone Python script that reproduces the chapter's training loop.

Optional standalone script to fine-tune without ZenML

The standalone script is placed here: https://github.com/PacktPublishing/DeepSeek-in-Practice/blob/main/Chapter07/standalone_training.py. The script follows this process:

1. Load the enhanced CUAD dataset (zenml/cuad-deepseek) from Hugging Face and ensure train/validation/test splits.

Enhanced CUAD is split into train/validation/test using an 80/10/10 stratified split with seed=42. We fine-tune the student on the train split, monitor and tune on the validation split, and report all metrics on the held-out test split only. No test examples – or their rationales – are used during training.

2. Format examples into Gemma 3 chat messages (user JSON prompt; assistant JSON with rationale and label).
3. Attach LoRA adapters to Gemma 3 (1B, 4B, or 12B) via Unsloth and train with TRL's SFTTrainer on assistant responses only.
4. Save adapters and the tokenizer locally and optionally push to the Hugging Face Hub.
5. Run a quick post-train sanity evaluation on the test split.

To get started with the script, do the following:

1. Install dependencies (CUDA-ready PyTorch recommended):

```
pip install unsloth transformers trl datasets peft accelerate torch
```

2. Run a minimal training command (12B requires ~24 GB GPU RAM; try `--model-size 4b` if you have less):

```
python standalone_training.py --model-size 12b --filter-none-labels
--eval-after-train
```

3. See all options with the following:

```
python standalone_training.py --help
```

Tip: To push the trained adapters to the Hugging Face Hub, add `--push-to-hub` and run this first so you're logged in:

```
huggingface-cli login
```

Understanding the importance of distillation and fine-tuning

Fine-tuning and distillation are two core techniques for adapting LLMs to specialized domains. Each addresses a different aspect of the problem, and together they provide a practical path from general-purpose models to production-ready systems.

Before we get started, let's do a quick round-up of fine-tuning and distillation.

Fine-tuning adapts an already pre-trained model to your domain by updating (some of) its parameters on targeted data. Think of it as taking a strong general system and tuning it to your workload – terminology, formats, and decision patterns – so it performs reliably in your context.

Distillation, on the other hand, compresses the behavior of a large teacher model into a smaller student. There are many flavors (logit, response, or rationale distillation).

Why do we need specialized models?

Using general-purpose models via external APIs can introduce hidden costs, especially at scale, when compared to specialized, self-hosted options. Some of these are listed as follows:

- **Token costs**:

  Even with lower prices and batch processing, handling a single 300-page merger and acquisition agreement (about 600,000 tokens each way) can become expensive with external APIs. Organizations processing many such documents each month may face high bills, while a distilled in-house model running on two A100 GPUs (about $3,000 monthly amortized cost) can process the same workload for much less.

- **Regulatory and compliance risks**:

  There are regulatory risks with external API use. For example, in December 2024, Italy's privacy regulator fined OpenAI €15 million for GDPR violations (`https://www.reuters.com/technology/italy-fines-openai-15-million-euros-over-privacy-rules-breach-2024-12-20/`) related to ChatGPT data processing. This highlights the liability when sensitive data leaves an organization's security perimeter. Some industries now require **sovereign LLM deployments** to avoid such penalties and maintain data residency.

- **Performance and availability**:

  Internal benchmarks from financial institutions (`https://ctomagazine.com/jp-morgan-chase-accelerates-ai-adoption/`) show that 7-billion parameter distilled models hosted on-premises return responses in 70-120 ms. In contrast, public APIs can have 600-1,200 ms P95 latency during peak load. This difference can affect service-level agreements for high-frequency review workflows and is important for real-time applications.

- **Flexibility and vendor lock-in**:

  External APIs cannot be customized for organization-specific terminology, formatting, or business rules. General-purpose models may lack the domain knowledge of fine-tuned alternatives. Relying on APIs can also create vendor lock-in, reducing strategic flexibility and increasing long-term risk.

Here are some of the important considerations that drive the use of domain-specific models:

- **Accuracy**: Consider, for example, that a legal LLM fine-tuned on contract language can routinely achieve 95%+ accuracy on document classification, compared to about 70% for general models. This is not a marginal improvement. It's the difference between a tool that occasionally assists and one that reliably automates core workflows.
- **Lower risk**: Accuracy, however, is only one axis. General-purpose models are prone to hallucination, confidently producing incorrect outputs. In high-stakes domains such as healthcare or finance, this is unacceptable. Specialized models, trained on curated datasets, are better at recognizing the limits of their knowledge and are more likely to express uncertainty rather than fabricate plausible-sounding nonsense.
- **Efficiency** is another key factor. Generalist LLMs are computationally expensive, sifting through vast, irrelevant knowledge for every query. Specialized models are leaner, smaller, faster, and focused. This translates to lower latency and reduced hardware costs.
- **Data privacy and control**: Regulated industries cannot risk sending sensitive data to external APIs. On-premises, domain-specific models allow organizations to leverage LLM capabilities without compromising confidentiality or compliance.

In short, specialization yields higher accuracy, lower risk, improved efficiency, and greater control. These are outcomes that engineers value in any production system.

The impact of specialized models is evident in real deployments by major organizations. These cases show improvements in efficiency, accuracy, and cost savings:

- **Healthcare documentation**:

  Stanford Health Care implemented Nuance DAX Copilot, an AI system fine-tuned on clinician-patient dialogues, to automate clinical documentation (`https://hitconsultant.net/2024/03/11/stanford-deploys-nuance-ai-powered-clinical-documentation/`). The system captures conversations during patient visits and generates draft summaries, reducing administrative workload. Physicians in the pilot reported reduced documentation time (from 90 minutes to under 30 minutes each day), allowing more focus on patient care (`https://www.dugganletter.com/p/from-burnout-to-breakthrough-how`).

- **Financial services:**

  JPMorgan Chase's COIN (Contract Intelligence) platform (`https://ctomagazine.com/jp-morgan-chase-accelerates-ai-adoption/`) uses LLM distillation for legal document processing. The system reviews commercial loan agreements that previously required about 360,000 human hours annually (`https://medium.com/@ishan_dhodu/how-jpmorgan-chases-coin-is-revolutionizing-financial-operations-with-ai-120a2938dab7`). Since its introduction, COIN has reduced review time and error rates.

- **Edge computing:**

  Google's Gemini Nano is a distilled model for mobile devices (`https://assets.publishing.service.gov.uk/media/661e5a4c7469198185bd3d62/AI_Foundation_Models_technical_update_report.pdf`). This 1.6-billion-parameter model, derived from Gemini Ultra, runs on Pixel phones to provide smart-reply, summarization, and captioning in under 300 ms without network calls, while maintaining most of the parent model's quality in less than 1 GB of RAM.

Apart from several advantages and applications in a myriad of use cases, the true value of fine-tuning and distillation lies in combining them.

> ***How do distillation and fine-tuning help in creating specialized models?***

When you combine distillation and fine-tuning, you can create models that are both highly specialized and efficient. Fine-tuning imparts domain expertise, while distillation ensures that expertise is accessible in real-world, resource-constrained settings. This approach allows you to move beyond generic solutions and deliver models that are tailored, performant, and ready for production.

Fine-tuning imparts domain expertise to the student; distillation ensures that expertise is portable, efficient, and deployable under real-world constraints (latency, privacy, cost).

We will use this approach in this chapter to create a specialized model for the legal domain and use it for a multi-label classification task.

In the next section, we will examine the use case and dataset in detail that we will use for distillation and fine-tuning with DeepSeek.

Use case and dataset

To learn how to create specialized models using fine-tuning and distillation, we will focus on a legal use case. But before we begin, we will outline the approach we will follow in this chapter for rationale distillation to power a multi-label classification problem on legal texts.

Conventions used in this chapter:

- **Teacher model**: DeepSeek-R1 (API/inference only).
- **Student model**: Gemma 3 (the model we actually fine-tune).
- **Distillation**: Data-generation step.
- **Fine-tuning**: Parameter-update step on the student.

Why Gemma (not DeepSeek)?

Fine-tuning DeepSeek directly is impractical and unnecessary for our goal; the industry-standard pattern is to distill a large, capable teacher into an efficient open student you can run locally.

The multi-label extraction problem in legal texts

Contract review is a prototypical example of a high-stakes, high-complexity information extraction problem. Legal professionals routinely spend around 50% of their time reviewing contracts, with billable rates at major firms ranging from $500 to $900 per hour. For a single **Mergers and Acquisitions** (**M&A**) transaction, this can translate to hundreds of thousands of dollars in legal fees. The technical challenge is not just the volume of text, but the need to accurately identify and interpret 41 distinct clause types – each with its own legal and business implications. This is a multi-label, multi-class classification problem, complicated by the fact that the relevant information is often buried in dense, heterogeneous, and sometimes ambiguous language.

The analogy of *finding needles in a haystack* is often used to describe contract review, but it doesn't fully capture the complexity. In reality, the task is more like finding 41 different types of needles, each with unique features and varying degrees of risk. For example, consider the following *Change of Control* clause:

> *"In the event that Contractor undergoes a change in control where 50% or more of its voting securities are transferred to a new beneficial owner, Client may terminate this Agreement upon thirty days written notice."*

To a layperson, this might seem like standard legal boilerplate. To a legal expert, it encodes a specific mechanism that could determine whether a planned acquisition proceeds smoothly or faces unexpected contractual complications. Multiply this complexity across hundreds of pages and dozens of contract types, and the scale of the problem becomes clear. The challenge for AI is not just to extract these clauses, but to classify them correctly and, ideally, to provide a rationale for each decision.

The business case for automating contract review is compelling: an AI-assisted system could reduce legal review costs by 60-70%, improve accuracy, and provide complete audit trails. More importantly, it could prevent catastrophic scenarios where missed clauses lead to deal failures or unexpected liabilities.

From a workflow perspective, automating the identification and explanation of risky clauses allows junior staff to focus on higher-value analysis and gives senior lawyers confidence in the system's outputs. The result is a more efficient, consistent, and defensible review process.

Up next, we will detail the technical approach: using DeepSeek-R1 to generate rationales, and then distilling this expertise into smaller, deployable models – demonstrating how to operationalize legal reasoning in production environments without sacrificing transparency or accuracy.

Introducing CUAD: A structured benchmark for legal clause classification

The **Contract Understanding Atticus Dataset** (**CUAD**) was created to address this challenge. Developed by The Atticus Project through a year-long collaboration involving law students, practicing lawyers, and machine learning researchers, CUAD contains over 13,000 expert annotations across 510 real-world commercial contracts. These contracts are sourced from SEC filings and represent the kinds of documents that legal professionals review in practice. You may explore the dataset here: `https://www.atticusprojectai.org/cuad`.

CUAD's value lies in its systematic taxonomy: it defines 41 clause types that lawyers consistently flag during corporate transactions. Examples include **anti-assignment** clauses (which restrict how agreements can be transferred), **liability caps** (which limit exposure to damages), **governing law** provisions (which determine jurisdiction for disputes), and **competitive restriction** clauses (which might prevent post-acquisition business activities). Each category represents a specific type of legal risk or obligation that experienced attorneys have learned to identify through years of practice. For engineers, CUAD provides a well-defined, multi-class classification benchmark grounded in real-world legal practice.

Extending CUAD: Why we add rationales

CUAD ships with high-quality labels but no per-example reasons. To make models auditable and easier to fine-tune, we attach teacher-generated rationales and refer to this augmented corpus as enhanced CUAD (details appear later in the *Data preprocessing and the enhanced CUAD dataset* section.

For example, an anti-assignment clause might include a rationale such as the following:

> *This clause is classified as Anti-Assignment because it explicitly restricts the Distributor's ability to assign the agreement. The key elements are: (1) it specifically prohibits assignment, (2) it applies to both the entire agreement and partial rights, (3) it requires explicit consent from the counterparty...*

You can use enhanced CUAD directly in the fine-tuning steps in this chapter (`https://huggingface.co/datasets/zenml/cuad-deepseek`).

Our technical objective is to distil the legal reasoning capabilities of a large model (DeepSeek-R1) into a smaller, resource-efficient model suitable for on-premises deployment. Most law firms cannot use external APIs due to confidentiality and compliance constraints, so the final model must be compact enough to run locally, yet accurate and explainable enough for professional use.

Specifically, we are targeting a 12-billion parameter model that can classify all 41 CUAD categories (plus a `NONE` class for out-of-scope clauses) with >90% accuracy, and generate clear, stepwise rationales for each decision. This is a classic knowledge distillation scenario, with the added requirement of explainability. The goal is to create a system that fits on a laptop (or perhaps a small server) but reasons like a senior associate – combining the broad knowledge of an LLM with the specialized expertise that comes from processing thousands of real-world contracts.

Overview of the distillation fine-tuning process with CUAD and enhanced CUAD datasets

To solve the aforementioned **multi-label classification**, we will follow the **two-stage workflow** shown in *Figure 7.1*.

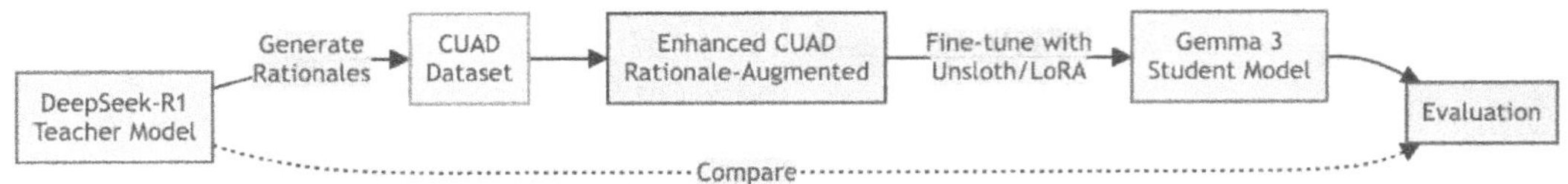

Figure 7.1: Two-stage workflow for legal rationale distillation

1. **Stage 1 (distillation)**: We ask DeepSeek-R1 to produce step-by-step explanations for CUAD examples and attach those rationales to the data. The teacher is not updated; it only generates enriched training signals, resulting in enhanced CUAD (data). (Note that while we explain and show how to create the enhanced CUAD dataset in this chapter, we also provide a Hugging Face dataset with the full processed data so that you don't have to spend $100+ just to reproduce the distillation part yourself.)
2. **Stage 2 (fine-tuning)**: We will then train Gemma 3 with LoRA/Unsloth on enhanced CUAD so the student learns both the labels and the explanation structure.

The outcome is a smaller, faster model you can run locally – with accuracy and explanations aligned to legal review needs.

So, here is what we will do:

DeepSeek-R1 (teacher) → generate rationales over CUAD → enhanced CUAD (rationale-augmented) → fine-tune Gemma 3 (student) with Unsloth/LoRA → evaluate the student versus the teacher.

It's time to get started! We will begin with the tools we will use for this task.

LLMOps tools for model distillation

Building production-ready AI systems depends on having the right infrastructure to develop, deploy, and maintain them reliably. In the context of LLM fine-tuning, this foundation is provided by **Large Language Model Operations** (**LLMOps**) tools. These tools help bring structure and repeatability to what could otherwise be a disorganized process of experimentation and deployment.

In our distillation pipeline (*Figure 7.2*), we use three main tools: ZenML for orchestration and observability, Unsloth for efficient training, and LiteLLM for unified model access. Each tool plays a distinct role in moving our legal contract classification project from a research experiment to a system ready for production.

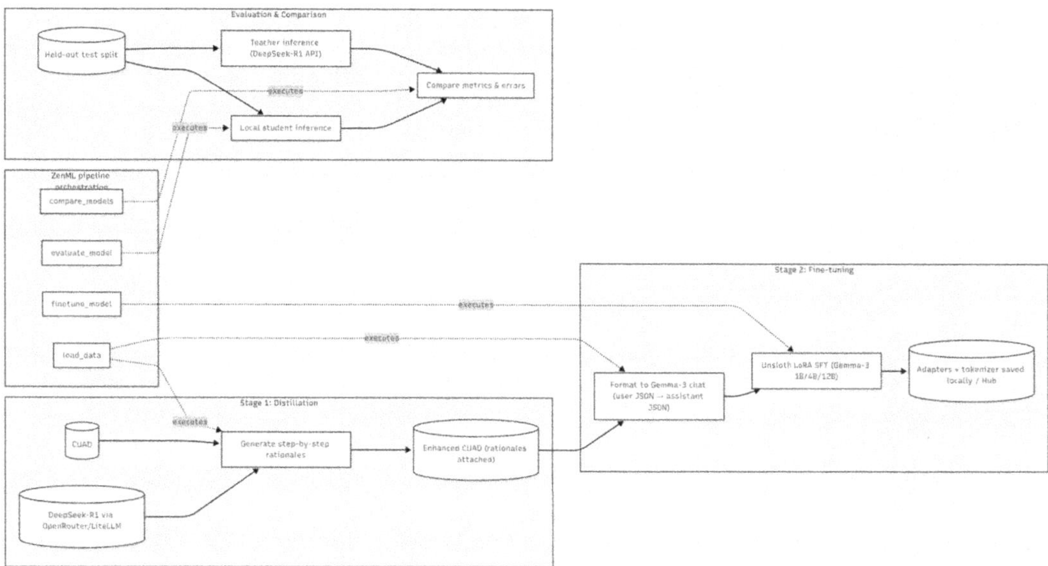

Figure 7.2: Architecture of the distillation and fine-tuning process

For our legal use case, we need to track exactly which CUAD examples were enhanced, which model/revision trained on them, and how each run performed – so results can be reproduced and audited. We use pipelines to freeze the sequence (***load → distil → format → fine-tune → evaluate → compare***) and to cache expensive steps.

Here is an overview of each tool's role in this chapter's workflow:

- **ZenML (orchestration and lineage)**: Runs the end-to-end pipeline (***load_data → fine-tune_model → evaluate_model → compare_models***), caches expensive steps, and records inputs, outputs, and config for reproducibility (`https://docs.zenml.io`).
- **LiteLLM (teacher API access)**: Provides a single call interface to DeepSeek-R1 via OpenRouter during the distillation and teacher-baseline evaluation steps (model string and API key configured in environment) (`https://github.com/BerriAI/litellm`) (`https://openrouter.ai`).

  For more detailed instructions on the setup using LiteLLM, you can check out the appendix towards the end of the book.
- **Unsloth (efficient LoRA fine-tuning)**: Attaches LoRA adapters and trains Gemma 3 with optimized kernels so we can fine-tune a 12B student on a single high-end GPU (`https://unsloth.ai`).

This section focuses on how these tools fit the workflow.

Let's look at the code to understand where each tool appears in this chapter's code:

1. Distillation and teacher model inference are performed via LiteLLM calls (used in *Stage 1* training and teacher-baseline evaluation), following the standard LiteLLM completion call pattern.

```
# Tool: LiteLLM + OpenRouter

import os, json
from typing import Dict
from litellm import completion

DEEPSEEK_MODEL = os.getenv("DEEPSEEK_MODEL", "openrouter/
deepseek-r1")
OPENROUTER_API_KEY = os.getenv("OPENROUTER_API_KEY")

def generate_rationale(clause: str, label: str) -> str:
    system = "You are a senior contract lawyer. Explain why the
clause matches the CUAD label. Return concise, stepwise rationale."
    messages = [
        {"role": "system", "content": system},
        {"role": "user", "content": json.dumps({"clause": clause,
"label": label})},
    ]
    resp = completion(model=DEEPSEEK_MODEL, messages=messages, max_
tokens=400, api_key=OPENROUTER_API_KEY)
    return resp["choices"][0]["message"]["content"].strip()
```

2. Fine-tuning Gemma 3 with Unsloth LoRA (student training in stage 2):

```
# Tool: Unsloth

from typing import Any
from unsloth import FastLanguageModel
from trl import SFTTrainer, SFTConfig

def finetune_gemma(
    train_ds: Any, val_ds: Any,
```

```
    base_id: str = "unsloth/gemma-3-12b-it", out_dir: str = "ckpt"
) -> str:
    model, tokenizer = FastLanguageModel.from_pretrained(
        base_id, load_in_4bit=True)
    model = FastLanguageModel.get_peft_model(
        model, r=16, lora_alpha=32, lora_dropout=0,
        target_modules="all-linear",
        use_gradient_checkpointing="unsloth",
        random_state=3407, use_rslora=False,
    )
    trainer = SFTTrainer(
        model=model, tokenizer=tokenizer, train_dataset=train_ds,
        eval_dataset=val_ds,
        args=SFTConfig(
            per_device_train_batch_size=1,
            gradient_accumulation_steps=8,
            num_train_epochs=2, learning_rate=1e-4,
            lr_scheduler_type="cosine",
            warmup_steps=100, logging_steps=20),
    )
    trainer.train()
    model.save_pretrained(out_dir); tokenizer.save_pretrained(out_
dir)
    return out_dir
```

3. ZenML wiring that orchestrates the steps:

```
# Tool: ZenML

from typing import Tuple
from zenml import step, pipeline

@step(enable_cache=True)
def load_data(
    max_samples: int | None = None, filter_none: bool = True
) -> Tuple[list, list]:
    # Loads HF dataset, generates/attaches rationales if needed,
formats to Gemma-3 chat
```

```
    # returns train_ds, val_ds (already tokenized/ready)
    ...

@step
def finetune_model(train_ds: list, val_ds: list, model_size: str =
"12b") -> str:
    # calls finetune_gemma(...) above (Unsloth)
    ...

@step
def evaluate_student_vs_teacher(...) -> dict:
    # runs local student on test split; calls DeepSeek-R1 via
LiteLLM for teacher baseline; computes metrics
    ...

@pipeline
def distill_finetuning(max_samples: int | None = None, model_size:
str = "12b"):
    train_ds, val_ds = load_data(max_samples=max_samples, filter_
none=True)
    ckpt_path = finetune_model(train_ds, val_ds, model_size=model_
size)
    _ = evaluate_student_vs_teacher(...)
```

With our tooling foundation established, we can now dive into the practical implementation of our distillation pipeline. The first stage involves enhancing the CUAD dataset itself – using our teacher model to generate the explanatory rationales that will make our student model more interpretable.

The two-stage workflow for legal rationale distillation

Well, we know dear reader, you are itching to get started. Without much ado, let's jump straight to distillation.

Stage 1: Distillation

Let's begin with the process of creating the enhanced CUAD dataset. The goal is to preserve the original human labels while adding clear, auditable why explanations from a teacher model (DeepSeek-R1). You can find the full source code for this process in the `Chapter07` folder in the code repository under the filename `standalone_synthetic_generation.py`.

Data splits at a glance

- Split: 80% train/10% validation/10% test (stratified by label, `seed=42`).
- Training: train split only (rationale-augmented).
- Validation: validation split only.
- Evaluation: test split only (held-out; no leakage).
- `NONE` label: filtered by default for this chapter's training runs.

The process is as follows:

1. **Download CUAD (once, idempotent)**: We fetch and unpack the official CUAD zip (Zenodo) into a stable folder so paths stay predictable (`https://zenodo.org/records/4595826/files/CUAD_v1.zip?download=1`).

```
def download_and_extract_cuad(url, data_dir="data", force=False) ->
str:
    # stream download (with progress) → data/CUAD_v1.zip
    # unzip to data/CUAD_v1/ so CUAD_v1.json is at a fixed path
    ...
    return os.path.join(data_dir, "CUAD_v1")
```

   What this does/why it matters: This step makes the process repeatable: a single function that either reuses an existing local copy or re-downloads cleanly when `force=True`. Reproducibility later depends on stable file locations.

2. **Convert SQuAD JSON to clause records**: CUAD ships in SQuAD format. (The specific format isn't particularly important for our purposes. Often, there will be datasets in a variety of formats, and it will be our job to somehow wrangle them into whatever shape is useful for our work.) We normalize the CUAD dataset to compact records: the **exact clause**, a **context window** around it, the **label**, and contract metadata.

```
def extract_clauses_from_squad(
    squad: dict, context_window: int = 150
) -> list[dict]:
    items = []
    for doc in squad["data"]:
        title = doc.get("title", "")
        ctype = (title.split("-")[-1].strip()
            if "-" in title else "Unknown")
        for para in doc.get("paragraphs", []):
```

```
            ctx = para.get("context", "")
            for qa in para.get("qas", []):
                if qa.get("is_impossible"): continue
                label = (qa.get("id","").split("__")[-1] or
"UNKNOWN")
                for ans in qa.get("answers", []):
                    start, text = ans["answer_start"], ans["text"]
                    end = start + len(text)
                    span = ctx[
                        max(0, start-context_window): min(len(ctx),
                        end+context_window)]
                    items.append({
                        "clause": text,
                        "clause_with_context": span,
                        "label": label,
                        "contract_name": title,
                        "contract_type": ctype,
                    })
    return items
```

What this does/why it matters: We keep the **gold label** and add a **bounded context** to help the teacher and (later) the student model reason. Using character windows avoids tokenizer coupling; you can swap to token-based windows later if desired.

3. **Add NONE negatives from unlabeled gaps (Optional):** To improve robustness, we can mine negatives by sampling from **gaps** (text regions not covered by any labeled span).

```
def add_negative_none_examples(
    items: list[dict], squad: dict,
    ratio: float = 3.0, neg_len: int = 100,
    context_window: int = 150
):
    # 1) record labeled (start,end) spans per paragraph
    # 2) compute gaps between labeled spans
    # 3) sample fixed-length snippets from gaps → label="NONE"
    # 4) cap per-gap samples (≤3) so negatives don't dominate
    ...
    return items_with_negatives
```

What this does/why it matters: This step adds coverage for everything else. For the benefits, risks, and default choice we use in this chapter, see the dedicated *The NONE label decision* section later in the chapter.

4. **Create stratified splits (with graceful fallback):** We split our data into train, validation, and test sets. This ensures that we aren't getting a false sense of confidence when we evaluate how well our model is doing and it is used during the training process, as well as afterwards.

```
def split_train_val_test(items, train=0.8, val=0.1, seed=42):
    # stratify by label for train vs temp
    train_set, temp = train_test_split(
        items, train_size=train,
        stratify=[x["label"] for x in items], random_state=seed)
    # compute relative val size; stratify if each class has ≥2
samples, else plain split
    ...
    return train_set, val_set, test_set
```

What this does/why it matters: Stratified splits into train and test sets, preserves label proportions where possible, gracefully falling back if a minority class is tiny. We use an 80/10/10 stratified split with seed=42.

Leakage rule: We never train on the test split (or its rationales).

5. **Prompt the teacher for rationales (rationale distillation):** We ask for an explanation of the existing label (not for a new label). This is deliberate: we are distilling reasoning for a known classification, not re-labeling CUAD.

```
def create_prompt(sample: dict) -> str:
    return f"""[[TASK]]
Explain why this clause fits the label.

[[CONTEXT]]
CLAUSE: {sample["clause"]}
CLAUSE WITH CONTEXT: {sample["clause_with_context"]}
CONTRACT TYPE: {sample["contract_type"]}

CLASSIFICATION: {sample["label"]}
```

```
[[INSTRUCTIONS]]
Identify the clause language that justifies the label. Be concise,
stepwise, and use Markdown."""
```

What this does/why it matters: Conditioning on the gold label keeps outputs on-task and cheaper. An alternative **label-and-rationale mode** can catch mislabels, but costs more and risks disagreement you must adjudicate.

6. **Orchestrate generation (parallel, rate-limited, resumable):** We make sure that the LLM generation happens in parallel and that any errors or rate limiting are caught so we can automatically retry.

```
@backoff.on_exception(
    backoff.expo, (Exception,), max_tries=5, max_time=300)
def generate_once(
    client, prompt, model="deepseek/deepseek-r1", max_tokens=1500,
    temperature=0.2, top_p=0.95
):
    # OpenRouter OpenAI-compatible chat.completions.create(...)
    return content, reasoning_trace_or_none

class RateLimiter:
    def __init__(self, qps: float): ...
    def wait(self): ...

def process_one(idx, sample, client, limiter, out_path, lock):
    limiter.wait()
    rationale, trace = generate_once(client, create_prompt(sample), ...)
    rec = {**sample, "rationale": rationale,
        "reasoning_trace": trace, "index": idx, ...}
    with lock:
        append_jsonl(out_path, rec)
```

What this does/why it matters: Parallel workers and a global **queries per second (QPS)** limiter give throughput without throttling errors; **exponential backoff** handles transient failures; **thread-safe appends** prevent interleaved writes. In practice, this made the full pass reliable and cheaper (OpenRouter docs: `https://openrouter.ai/docs`).

7. **Resume safely (skip completed indices)**: Since this is a process that costs real money, takes a long time to execute and could potentially be interrupted, we keep track of which items we've completed so that if we want to pause or resume at some point, then we are able to do so.

```
def get_processed_indices(path) -> set[int]:
    # read output JSONL; collect "index" fields → allows resume
    ...
```

What this does/why it matters: You can stop and resume at any time. This is critical when batching costs or rotating API keys.

8. **Package and publish:** We store JSONL files for each split and optionally push `DatasetDict` to the HuggingFace Hub (`https://huggingface.co`).

```
def to_hf_dataset(jsonl_path: str) -> Dataset: ...
def push_to_hub(
    dataset_or_dict, repo_id: str, private=False
) -> None: ...
```

What this does/why it matters: A consistent, documented artifact others can reuse without re-generating synthetic data.

Cost and throughput note

In our reference runs, generating rationales for one split with modest length limits and low temperature cost roughly $100. Generating rationales across all splits scales proportionally (typically ~2–3× depending on token limits and coverage).

9. **Lightweight quality checks (cheap but effective)**: Before we accept a rationale, we run simple filters:

```
def accept(sample: dict, rationale: str) -> bool:
    if rationale is None or len(rationale.strip()) < 50: return
False
    if rationale.lower().count("this clause") >= 4: return False  #
generic filler
    if sample["label"].lower() not in rationale.lower()[:300]:
```

```
    return False  # label not grounded early
        return True
```

What this does/why it matters: These heuristics are intentionally simple: they reject low-effort text and encourage label-grounded explanations without paying for an extra judge model. For higher stakes, replace this with a small rationale-judge prompt that scores specificity and cites key phrase matches.

Once these steps are complete, it's time to move on to ZenML pipeline data processing.

ZenML pipeline data processing

The pipeline layer manages data preprocessing through a dedicated `load_data` step and records each run's inputs and outputs for reproducibility. Each execution captures which dataset revision was used, the preprocessing configuration, and the resulting artifacts.

Here is how the pipeline is implemented:

```
@step(enable_cache=True)
def load_data(
    model_size: str = "12b",
    dataset_id: str = "zenml/cuad-deepseek",
    max_samples: Optional[int] = None,
    filter_none_labels: bool = True,
) -> Tuple[pl.DataFrame, pl.DataFrame, HTMLString]:
    """Load and preprocess the Enhanced CUAD dataset."""

    # Get model configuration and create tokenizer
    config = get_model_config(model_size)
    tokenizer = create_tokenizer(config)

    # Download and prepare the dataset
    download_and_save_dataset(
        dataset_id=dataset_id, output_dir=output_dir)
    train_dataset, val_dataset = load_datasets(
        max_samples, tokenizer, tokenize=False, filter_none_labels
    )

    return train_dataset.to_polars(), val_dataset.to_polars(), viz
```

When this step runs, it does the following:

1. Resolves `model_size` to a known configuration and builds the matching tokenizer so any downstream formatting uses the correct chat template and sequence limits.
2. Fetches or reuses the requested enhanced CUAD dataset (`dataset_id`) in a stable directory `output_dir` so the exact revision is materialized locally.
3. Prepares the training/validation splits via `load_datasets(...)`, which applies your switches, `max_samples` for quick experiments, and `filter_none_labels` to include/exclude the open-ended `NONE` class, while deliberately deferring tokenization unless you enable it (we keep examples as strings here to pack or trim consistently during training).
4. Converts the resulting splits to compact Polars DataFrames so they serialize quickly as artifacts and are easy to profile.
5. Emits a small HTML visualization (viz) that records what was loaded (counts, filter policy) and becomes part of the run's lineage.

Please note that since we have set `@step(enable_cache=True)`, ZenML computes a cache key from the step code, parameters, and upstream artifacts; re-running with the same inputs reuses the materialized training or validation DataFrames and viz, while changing any input (e.g., model size, dataset ID, filter policy, or sample cap) invalidates the cache and recomputes. The net effect is reproducible data prep with fast, parameter-aware iteration.

A practical benefit is **automatic caching**: once a step has run with the same inputs, the orchestrator can reuse its outputs. That reduces iteration time without changing any training logic. In our examples, we use ZenML to provide these behaviors, but any orchestrator with step caching and run metadata will work similarly.

A key preprocessing consideration for this dataset is how to handle the `NONE` classification examples. Let's talk about them.

The NONE label decision

These are clauses that do not match any of the 41 predefined CUAD categories. In effect, they serve as a catch-all for content outside the main schema. Including `NONE` examples can provide useful negative training data, but it also introduces additional complexity to the classification task.

The two practical trade-offs negatives and windows matter the most:

- **Negative ratio**: We default to 3:1 negatives:positives when enabled; increasing this can improve precision in the wild, but slows training and can bias towards `NONE`. Start at 1–3× and tune by validation F1.

- **Context windowing**: We use a character window (e.g., 150 each side) for speed and tokenizer independence. If you observe truncated tokens or sentence breaks that confuse the teacher/student, switch to a token-aware window (e.g., via a tokenizer) and keep total sequence lengths within your training budget.

The `NONE` category was not part of the original CUAD dataset. The initial focus was on identifying specific clause types that legal professionals care about during contract review. We introduced the `NONE` examples during our enhancement process to help balance the dataset, but this addition changes the nature of the classification problem.

Classifying `NONE` examples is fundamentally different from classifying among specific legal categories. The model must learn to recognize the absence of any defined legal pattern, which is a more abstract and open-ended task than matching a clause to a known type. For example, it is similar to asking a model to identify *not-cats* rather than distinguishing between breeds of dogs.

For the purposes of this chapter, we exclude `NONE` examples by default using the `filter_none_labels=True` parameter. This allows us to focus on the core challenge of distinguishing between meaningful legal categories without the added complexity of the **everything else** class. In a production setting, you might choose to include `NONE` examples to improve robustness, but for learning and demonstration, a more focused approach is often preferable.

```
# The data preparation includes smart filtering
def prepare_dataset_from_file(
    jsonl_path,
    max_samples=None,
    tokenizer=None,
    filter_none_labels=False,
):
    """Process JSONL data with enhanced instructional format."""
    data = []
    none_count = 0

    with open(jsonl_path, "r") as f:
        for line in f:
            item = json.loads(line)

            # Skip NONE examples if filtering is enabled
            if filter_none_labels and item.get("label", "").strip().
upper() == "NONE":
```

```
                none_count += 1
                continue

        # Process valid examples...
```

Once we've downloaded the data and filtered it, we then need to format it so it's ready for fine-tuning.

Next up, we will provide an instructional format for fine-tuning our student model.

Instructional format for fine-tuning

The data preprocessing also handles the crucial task of formatting examples for instruction-tuned models. (By **instruction-tuned**, we mean language models that have been specifically trained to follow user instructions and provide helpful responses, rather than just predicting the next word in a sequence like base models do.) Rather than simple input-output pairs, we structure each example in the dataset as a detailed conversation that teaches the model both what to classify and how to reason about the classification. Here's an example:

```
{
    "clause": "access is reasonably required by the other, including
without limitation, for audit, accounting and litigation purposes.",
    "clause_with_context": "ther (other than data and information subject
to any attorney/client or other privilege), insofar as such\n\n
                                        27\n\naccess is reasonably required
by the other, including without limitation, for audit, accounting and
litigation purposes.\n\n      (c) Notwithstanding the foregoing, either
party may destroy or otherwise dispose of any information at any time in
accordance with the corporat",
    "label": "Audit Rights",
    "contract_name": "FIDELITYNATIONALINFORMATIONSERVICES,INC_08_05_2009-
EX-10.3-INTELLECTUAL PROPERTY AGREEMENT",
    "contract_type": "INTELLECTUAL PROPERTY AGREEMENT"
}
```

Each training example becomes a JSON-formatted instruction that includes the task description, classification schema, valid label options, and the input clause with context. The model learns to respond with structured reasoning followed by the final classification – exactly the behavior we want in our deployed system.

This instructional approach helps provide the reasoning that legal professionals can evaluate and trust, and not just the output label. The preprocessing pipeline handles this formatting automatically, ensuring consistency across all training examples while maintaining the flexibility to experiment with different instructional prompts and response formats. If you don't pay much attention to the data format for fine-tuning, your model might not even work at all.

We will now train the student (Gemma 3) on the rationale-augmented enhanced CUAD that we have generated at this stage.

Stage 2: Fine-tuning Gemma 3 on CUAD

With our enriched dataset prepared and our reasoning foundation established, we will now move on to the core challenge: distilling this legal expertise into smaller, deployable models that can operate efficiently within the constraints of an on-premises legal environment. This is where model selection becomes crucial – we need an architecture that balances capability with practicality.

Why Gemma 3?

Gemma 3 (`https://ai.google.dev/gemma/docs/core`) is a modern, resource-efficient language model architecture, inheriting core innovations from Google's Gemini 2.0 family but specifically engineered for single-GPU deployment. For technical teams building legal document classifiers, Gemma 3 offers a compelling balance of performance and deployability.

Unlike most LLMs that require multi-GPU clusters or distributed inference, Gemma 3 is designed to run inference and even training for the 12B parameter variant on a single high-end GPU. This is achieved through architectural optimizations, most notably a 5:1 ratio of local to global attention layers. This design choice significantly reduces **key-value (KV)** cache memory requirements during long-context inference. For example, where conventional transformer architectures might see memory overheads increase by 60% or more as context length grows, Gemma 3 keeps this under 15%. This enables practical processing of long legal documents without the need for specialized hardware or distributed systems.

Why not fine-tune DeepSeek directly?

For this use case, it's operationally better to distil DeepSeek's behavior into an open, efficient student you can fine-tune and run locally. This avoids heavyweight compute requirements and simplifies deployment/governance while retaining most of the teacher's legal reasoning performance.

For our use case – contract clause classification with context windows spanning thousands of tokens – this means we can deploy a 12B parameter model on standard workstation hardware, without sacrificing the reasoning depth or accuracy demonstrated by larger, less efficient models like DeepSeek-R1. The result is a production-ready legal AI system that is both performant and operationally feasible for on-premises deployments, even in environments with strict data privacy requirements.

The model size decision: Why we focus on 12B?

While our pipeline supports three model sizes (1B, 4B, and 12B parameters), our experiments with the enhanced CUAD dataset revealed a clear reality: for legal contract classification, you need substantial model capacity to achieve professional-grade accuracy.

- **Why smaller models fall short**: The 1B and 4B Gemma 3 models, while computationally efficient, simply don't deliver the accuracy levels required for serious legal work. The 1B model struggles to maintain consistent reasoning across complex legal language, especially while ensuring JSON output, while the 4B model, though better, still makes too many classification errors to be reliable in high-stakes contract review scenarios.
- **The 12B model**: This is our primary focus. Hence, we focus primarily on the 12B model in our examples and analysis. While it requires 24 GB+ of GPU memory during training, it represents the minimum viable size for professional legal classification tasks of this kind. Even then, the 12B model isn't perfect – legal language is nuanced and context-dependent in ways that challenge even sophisticated models.
- **Deployment trade-offs**: You're welcome to experiment with the smaller models using our pipeline (simply change the `model_size` parameter), and they may be suitable for preliminary document screening or resource-constrained environments. However, for the accuracy levels demanded in legal practice, the computational overhead of the 12B model is generally justified by its superior performance on complex contract language.

Let's get started with the fine-tuning process.

The fine-tuning process

The following code defines the `distil_finetuning` pipeline.

```
@pipeline
def distill_finetuning(
    max_samples: Optional[int] = None,
    model_size: str = "4b",
    filter_none_labels: bool = True,
```

```
):
    """Pipeline to load the dataset and finetune the model.

    Args:
        max_samples: Maximum number of samples to use for training
        model_size: Model size to use ('1b', '4b', or '12b')
        filter_none_labels: Whether to filter out 'NONE' classifications
    """
    # Step 1: Load and prepare data with intelligent caching
    train_dataset, val_dataset, data_viz = load_data(
        model_size=model_size,
        filter_none_labels=filter_none_labels,
        max_samples=max_samples
    )

    # Step 2: Fine-tune with automatic resource management
    finetune_model(
        train_dataset,
        val_dataset,
        model_size=model_size
    )
```

Fine-tuning legal classification models requires hyperparameters that balance learning efficiency with stability. Our configuration reflects lessons learned from our experimentation while working on this chapter.

```
# Optimized training configuration for 12B legal model
TRAINING_CONFIG = {
    "per_device_train_batch_size": 1,
    "gradient_accumulation_steps": 8,
    "warmup_steps": 100,
    "num_train_epochs": 2,
    "learning_rate": 1e-4,
    "logging_steps": 20,
    "optim": "adamw_8bit",
    "weight_decay": 0.01,
    "lr_scheduler_type": "cosine",
    "seed": 3407,
}
```

Here is a rationale for why we chose these parameters:

- **Learning rate**: The 1e-4 learning rate is more conservative than typical fine-tuning rates, reflecting the need for stability when working with large models on specialized legal text. The 12B model's substantial parameter space requires careful learning rate selection to avoid destabilizing pre-trained knowledge while still developing legal expertise.
- **Memory-optimized batch configuration**: The reduced batch size (1) accommodates the 12B model's memory requirements, while increased gradient accumulation (8) maintains an effective batch size of 8. This configuration balances training stability with the practical constraints of single-GPU training for large models.
- **Extended warmup for stability**: The 100-step warmup period provides additional stability for the large model, allowing gradual adaptation to the legal domain rather than aggressive early updates that might disrupt learned representations.
- **The cosine learning rate schedule**: The cosine scheduler provides smooth learning rate decay, which works particularly well with larger models by maintaining stable training dynamics throughout the process.

  With the optimizer and schedule fixed, the next decision is *which parameters to update*. Full fine-tuning changes every weight, but that's memory-heavy and unnecessary; instead, we use a parameter-efficient method that learns small, targeted updates while keeping the base model frozen.

- **LoRA configuration for parameter updates**: **Low-Rank Adaptation** (**LoRA**) is a way to teach a large model new skills without retraining the whole thing. Think of the base model as a high-end instrument: rather than rebuilding it, you clip on a tiny attachment that slightly adjusts how it plays. During training, only these small attachments learn; the original model stays untouched. This makes fine-tuning faster, cheaper, and reversible, and it works well even when the base model is loaded in 4-/8-bit (`https://arxiv.org/abs/2106.09685`).

  Our LoRA configuration targets the specific adaptations needed for legal language understanding. By specific adaptations, we mean that we choose *where* to place those small attachments and *how big* to make them so the extra learning capacity goes where it matters.

For legal text, that typically means adding adapters to attention and MLP blocks so the model better handles long cross-references, formal clause language, headings and definitions, and the structured outputs we expect (rationale and label). In short, we focus the limited trainable capacity on the patterns that improve accuracy in this domain. Here's how:

```
# LoRA configuration optimized for 12B Legal model
LORA_RANK = 16
LORA_ALPHA = 32
LORA_DROPOUT = 0
LORA_BIAS = "none"
```

Here is a sample loss curve for our training run.

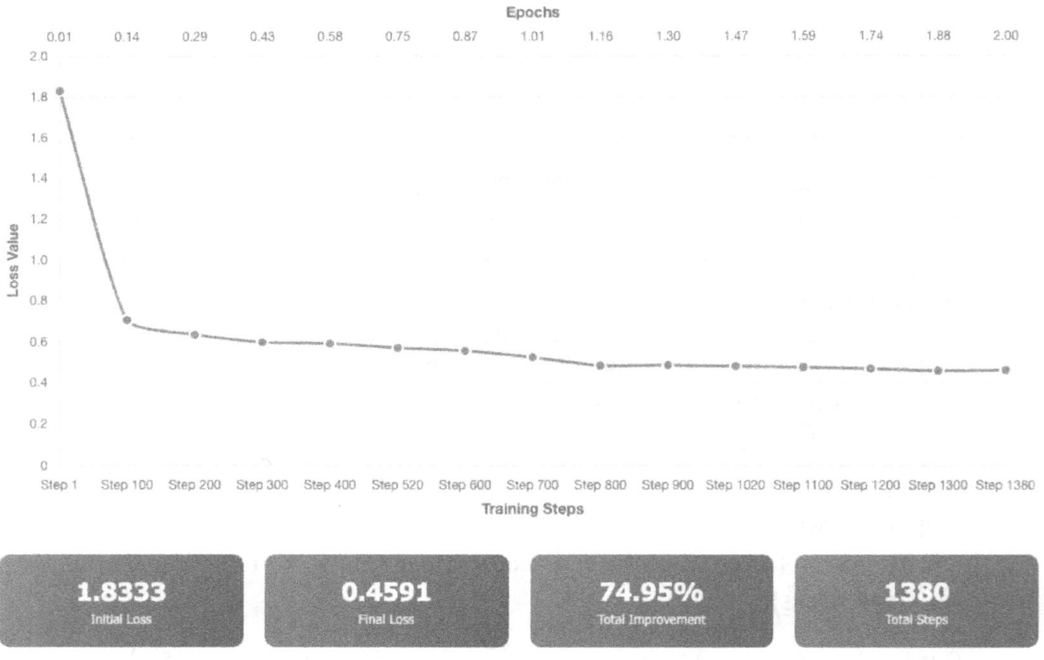

Figure 7.3: Loss curve for a sample training run made during development

Let's take a look at what these optimizations mean:

- **Increased rank for larger model:** The rank 16 configuration provides additional capacity needed for the 12B model to effectively capture legal language patterns. Larger models benefit from higher LoRA ranks as they have more parameter space to adapt while still maintaining efficiency compared to full fine-tuning.

- **Alpha = 2 × rank convention**: Following the established convention, we set alpha to 32 (2 × rank), which provides appropriate scaling for the LoRA adaptation. This ratio has proven effective across different model sizes and domains.
- **Zero dropout and comprehensive targeting**: Legal language leaves little room for ambiguity, so we preserve all learned associations. By fine-tuning both attention and MLP modules across all language layers, we ensure legal expertise permeates the entire model architecture – both syntactic parsing and semantic reasoning components. Concretely, the code sets `LORA_DROPOUT=0` and enables `finetune_language_layers`, `finetune_attention_modules`, and `finetune_mlp_modules` in `constants.py`, then applies these flags via Unsloth's `FastModel.get_peft_model` in `steps/trainer.py`. This attaches LoRA adapters across all attention and MLP modules in the language stack with no adapter dropout, ensuring domain updates propagate end to end.

Now that we have looked at the parameter settings, we will understand the specifics of model training for legal data.

Training dynamics of legal AI learning

Legal AI training follows predictable patterns that reveal how models internalize domain expertise. During the first 100 training steps, models typically show rapid loss reduction as they adapt to legal vocabulary patterns. The loss curve demonstrates characteristic behavior: an initial steep drop followed by gradual improvement as the model masters clause classification logic.

Training memory usage scales predictably with model size – the 1B model peaks at 8-10 GB, while the 12B model requires 24-28 GB, depending on sequence lengths. These kinds of classification loss curves typically show three phases: rapid initial learning (steps 1-50), steady improvement (steps 50-200), and gradual refinement beyond step 200. Note that this often applies to much of machine learning.

We will now compare the fine-tuned student (Gemma 3) against the DeepSeek-R1 teacher on a held-out test set to validate that rationale distillation and fine-tuning achieved the intended gains.

Once you have fine-tuned your model, it is essential to validate whether it is performing as per your expectations. Let's evaluate our fine-tuned model next.

Evaluation and results

To demonstrate (with evidence) that our fine-tuned legal classifier actually performs better than the massive DeepSeek model we used as our teacher, think of this as a final exam where our 12B parameter student must demonstrate it learned legal reasoning effectively enough to compete with its 600+ billion parameter professor.

Split policy reminder: We evaluate on the enhanced CUAD test split (10% of the dataset), which is strictly held out from training and hyperparameter tuning.

The evaluation pipeline runs two parallel inference processes: one using our local fine-tuned model, and another querying DeepSeek-R1 through OpenRouter's free API. Both models analyze the same legal clauses from our enhanced CUAD test set – data that was never seen during training.

```
@pipeline
def evaluation_pipeline(
    num_samples: Optional[int] = 50,
    exclude_none: bool = True,
    model_size: str = "4b",
    use_local_model: bool = True,
    deepseek_max_workers: int = 5,
):
    """Compare fine-tuned model against DeepSeek base model."""
    # Load held-out test data
    test_dataset = load_test_data(num_samples, exclude_none)

    # Evaluate our fine-tuned model
    finetuned_results, finetuned_viz = evaluate_model(
        test_dataset, model_size, use_local_model
    )

    # Evaluate DeepSeek base model via API
    deepseek_results, deepseek_viz = evaluate_deepseek_base(
        test_dataset, max_workers=deepseek_max_workers
    )
```

```
    # Generate comprehensive comparison
    comparison_results, comparison_viz = compare_models(
        finetuned_results, deepseek_results
    )
```

An important aspect to measure model performance is the choice of metrics. While there are many popular metrics, such as accuracy and F1 score, that are often used in multi-label classification tasks, these metrics might not be sufficient for all use cases across domains.

Let's explore the performance metrics we will use to evaluate our fine-tuned model.

Performance metrics

Legal AI evaluation requires more nuanced metrics than typical classification tasks. A model that misses critical **cap on liability** clauses (one of the possible labels in the dataset) poses different risks than one that occasionally misclassifies less crucial provisions. Our evaluation framework captures this complexity through multiple performance dimensions.

- **Overall accuracy**: Raw classification performance across all 41 legal clause types provides the baseline metric. Our fine-tuned 12B model consistently achieves accuracy in the high 80% range – remarkable performance for a model 150x smaller than DeepSeek.
- **Non-NONE accuracy**: This metric focuses on actual clause identification, excluding the **everything else** category. Since legal professionals primarily care about finding specific clause types, this often represents the most practically relevant metric.
- **Per-class analysis**: Legal clauses vary dramatically in complexity and importance. **Governing law** provisions follow predictable patterns, while **change of control** clauses can be subtly buried in complex language. Our evaluation breaks down performance by clause type, revealing where fine-tuning provides the most value.
- **Precision, recall, and F1**: These metrics help understand the trade-offs between catching all relevant clauses (recall) versus avoiding false positives (precision) – both critical in legal applications, where missed clauses can be costly.

Let's take a look at the results now.

Evaluation results

Our comparative evaluation (*Figure 7.4*) reveals surprising results that validate the distillation approach for legal applications. The fine-tuned models do not just compete with DeepSeek; they substantially outperform it on legal classification tasks.

METRIC	TEACHER/BASE MODEL	FINE-TUNED 12B MODEL	IMPROVEMENT
Accuracy	~41.5%*	84.5%	+103.6% 2x better
Parsing Errors	12	0	-100% Perfect
Precision	72.1%	83.5%	+11.4pp Significant
Recall	76.9%	74.1%	-2.8pp Slight trade-off
Total Errors	117	31	-73.5% 86 fewer
Inference Speed	Baseline	Faster (local)	Improved Qualitative

Figure 7.4: Performance comparison showing fine-tuned Gemma 3 models achieving 84.5% accuracy compared to DeepSeek's 41.5%, with significantly reduced computational requirements

The results demonstrate that specialized training on high-quality synthetic data from the enhanced CUAD dataset can create models that dramatically exceed the performance of much larger general-purpose systems.

Error analysis: Understanding model limitations

Both models struggle with certain types of legal clauses, but their failure patterns differ in instructive ways. The fine-tuned model shows a concentrated error pattern with only 11 unique ways it failed, compared to DeepSeek's 38. This suggests more systematic and potentially addressable failure modes.

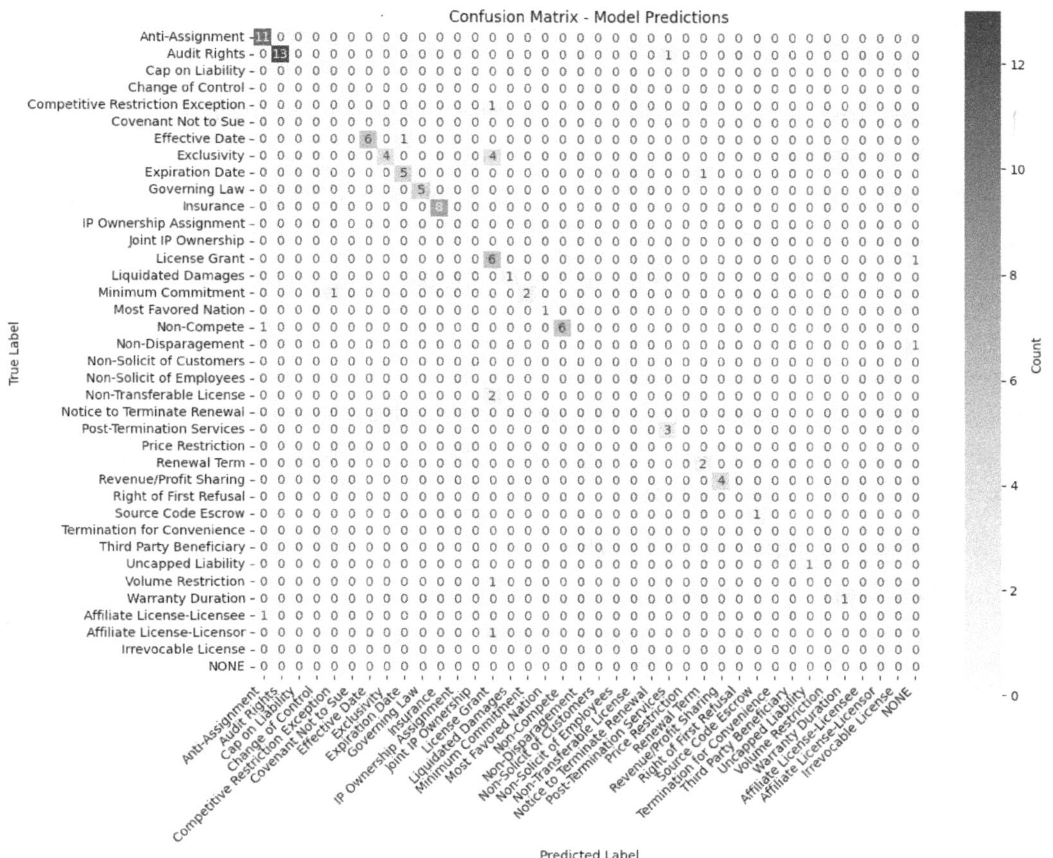

Figure 7.5: Confusion matrices revealing the fine-tuned model's 169 correct classifications out of 200 samples, with notably cleaner diagonal patterns than the teacher model

Both models struggle with the following:

- **Agreement date disambiguation**: The fine-tuned model's most common error (6 instances) involves distinguishing between **Effective Date** and **Agreement Date.**
- **License grant nuances**: Several error types (**Exclusivity, Non-Transferable License, Affiliate License**) converge to **License Grant** classifications.
- **Clause boundary detection**: Both models occasionally struggle with overlapping or compound clauses.

But the fine-tuned model is able to achieve improvement in several aspects when compared to the base DeepSeek-R1 model:

- **Elimination of parsing failures**: Unlike DeepSeek's 12 parsing errors, the fine-tuned model produces consistently parseable outputs.
- **Reduced error diversity**: 71% fewer unique error types (11 versus 38), indicating more predictable behavior.
- **Improved F1 score**: 75.3% compared to 69.8%, balancing precision and recall more effectively.

Our evaluation writes metrics and artifacts to an experiment-tracking dashboard, so results persist beyond a single run. In our reference implementation, this is a ZenML dashboard (`https://docs.zenml.io`), but MLflow or Weights & Biases (W&B) could serve the same purpose. What matters is that you log the following:

- Model/checkpoint identifiers and lineage.
- Dataset hash/split spec and preprocessing version.
- Per-class metrics, confusion matrices, and error slices.

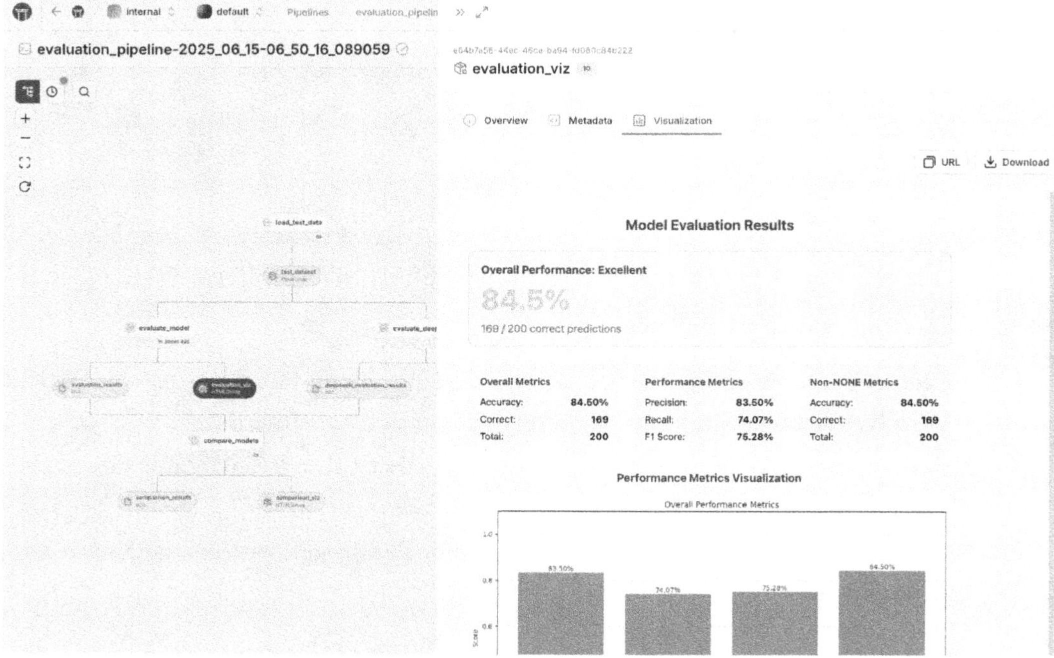

Figure 7.6: Screenshot of our evaluation results and the training pipeline on the ZenML dashboard

The implementation for this chapter highlights the following:

- **Quantified improvements**: Clear metrics show the 2x performance gain from distillation.
- **Error pattern analysis**: Detailed breakdown of the 31 remaining errors guides targeted improvements.
- **Reproducible evaluations**: Complete artifact lineage from the `unsloth/gemma-3-12b-it` base through fine-tuning.

Of course, there will always be scope to improve performance. Let's see how you can do it.

Performance optimization potential

Our current results, achieved with just 2 epochs of training, represent a strong foundation rather than a performance ceiling. The dramatic improvement from 41.5% to 84.5% accuracy suggests several optimization strategies could push performance even higher.

- **Targeted error remediation**: With only 31 errors concentrated in 11 patterns, focused synthetic data generation for these specific cases (particularly the 6 **Effective Date/Agreement Date** confusions) could yield immediate gains. In other words, we could generate example data that focuses on the patterns our fine-tuned model found hardest to recognize. By boosting the sample strength for those patterns, we'd hope our (re-)fine-tuned model would perform better.
- **Precision-recall balancing**: The slight dip in recall (–2.8%) alongside a solid precision gain (+11.4%) means you can *move the operating point* without retraining the whole model. Start with inference-time tweaks:

  1. Pick per-class decision thresholds from a validation set so the model is stricter on high-cost mistakes and more permissive where misses are worse.
  2. Introduce an **abstain/needs review** or **NONE** path for low-confidence cases.
  3. Calibrate confidence scores using a held-out set so probabilities reflect reality (most libraries offer simple calibrators). If that isn't enough, do small, targeted training changes: add class weights to address imbalance, try a loss that focuses more on hard examples, or lightly over-/under-sample difficult labels.

  Because each fine-tuning run costs time and money, prefer thresholding and calibration first, then a very small, pre-planned sweep of training options.

- **Multi-stage training**: Given the complete elimination of parsing errors, a curriculum learning approach that starts with output structure before advancing to nuanced classification could further improve the already strong 84.5% accuracy. You might use a staged schedule that teaches easy skills first, then adds complexity.

  1. **Stage 0: Format first**: Short contexts and high-support labels to stabilize structured outputs (valid JSON, label tokens).
  2. **Stage 1**: Full enhanced CUAD minus rare/ambiguous cases.
  3. **Stage 2**: Introduce long contexts, compound clauses, and (optionally) the `NONE` class.
  4. **Stage 3**: Hard-negative mining and near-misses focused on the top error slices (e.g., **Effective Date** versus **Agreement Date**). Then, gradually increase the sequence length and difficulty; keep adapters fixed while you scale difficulty to avoid destabilizing earlier gains.

- **Ensemble approaches**: The distinct error patterns between models (38 unique types for DeepSeek versus 11 for the fine-tuned model) suggest ensemble methods could leverage complementary strengths. Start simple:

  5. **Seed/snapshot ensemble**: Train the same 12B LoRA model three times with different random seeds or data shuffles and take a majority vote.
  6. **Mixed-capacity ensemble**: Combine a 12B and a 4B student; when they disagree, send the case to human review or the teacher model.
  7. **Confidence-based routing**: If the student's confidence is low, fall back to DeepSeek-R1; otherwise, accept the student's answer.
  8. **Test-time augmentation**: Run two views of the same clause (e.g., different context windows) and vote on the result. To control cost, apply ensembling only to the hardest 10–20% of examples, as identified by low confidence or prior error slices.

These results validate that distilled legal models can meet professional requirements while operating within practical constraints. The accuracy score (more than 80%) represents a significant improvement over manual review consistency. The detailed reasoning capabilities enable legal professionals to verify and trust the system's analysis.

For law firms considering AI adoption, these results demonstrate that sophisticated legal reasoning capabilities don't require massive infrastructure investments. A single high-end workstation can deploy models that compete with the largest available systems while maintaining complete control over sensitive client data.

Up next, a quick roundup of key learnings and takeaways from this chapter.

Key takeaways

We've taken a remarkable journey from massive 600+ billion parameter models to efficient 12B parameter legal specialists that can run on a single GPU while delivering competitive performance. This transformation – from Swiss Army knife to surgical scalpel – demonstrates that, with the right approach, specialized AI can be both powerful and practical.

When does distillation and fine-tuning make sense?

The legal contract classification challenge taught us that distillation delivers exceptional value when three conditions align:

- **Specialized domain requirements**: Legal language operates by different rules than general text. Phrases such as *time is of the essence* carry specific legal weight that general models struggle to understand consistently. When your domain has specialized vocabulary, reasoning patterns, or regulatory requirements, fine-tuning becomes essential rather than optional.
- **Quality training data availability**: Our enhanced CUAD dataset with DeepSeek-generated rationales provided the rich learning signals that made distillation successful. The combination of expert classifications and detailed reasoning created training examples that captured both the *what* and *why* of legal analysis.
- **Deployment constraints**: Law firms can't send confidential client documents to external APIs. This constraint – common across regulated industries – makes distillation not just helpful but necessary. The ability to deploy sophisticated legal reasoning on-premises transforms distillation from an optimization technique into a business enabler.

Distillation also helps solve multiple challenges simultaneously in ways that traditional approaches can't match:

- **Infrastructure democratization**: Converting DeepSeek's legal expertise into a 12B parameter model means sophisticated legal AI runs on hardware that law firms already own – no specialized infrastructure, no ongoing API costs, no external dependencies.
- **Privacy preservation**: Client confidentiality remains intact when the entire AI system operates within the organization's security perimeter. This isn't just a technical advantage – it's often a legal requirement.

- **Customization potential**: Fine-tuned models can adapt to specific law firm writing styles, jurisdiction requirements, or client needs. Unlike API-based solutions, these models evolve with your organization.

Another important consideration is to ensure governance and reproducible results. Throughout this chapter, we rely on an experiment-tracking/orchestration layer to turn ad hoc scripts into repeatable workflows. In our example, this layer is ZenML, but any comparable system that captures runs, artifacts, and lineage is fine. The key capabilities we need are compliance documentation (where runs produce an immutable log of data, code, config, and metrics), reproducible experiments (where preprocessing/training/evaluation can be re-executed exactly), and model governance, where versions of models and datasets are promoted with the same rigor as software.

Summary

In this chapter, you transformed CUAD into an enhanced CUAD dataset via rationale distillation. You normalized SQuAD annotations to clause-level records, optionally mined `NONE` negatives, created stratified splits, and prompted DeepSeek-R1 (via OpenRouter) for concise, label-grounded rationales. You executed rate-limited, backoff-hardened parallel generation with a safe resume and simple quality checks, then packaged the result and formatted examples for instruction-tuned chat training.

You then fine-tuned Gemma 3 with LoRA using Unsloth, selected stable training/LoRA hyperparameters, and evaluated the student against the teacher on held-out data with accuracy, F1, and per-class analysis. You also learned how an orchestration/tracking layer can capture lineage and caching for reproducibility – and how to run the same workflow from a single-file script if you prefer no orchestrator. These skills generalize beyond law to any domain that benefits from explanation-augmented supervision.

Next, *Chapter 8* moves from training to deployment. We'll deploy both full DeepSeek models (V3/R1), compare self-hosted and managed options and the inference settings that balance latency, cost, privacy, and reliability.

8

Deploying DeepSeek Models

In the previous chapter, we distilled and fine-tuned smaller, domain-specific models that you could run on modest hardware and within strict privacy boundaries. That work is optimized for efficiency and control at a smaller scale. This chapter takes the complementary step of deploying full-parameter DeepSeek models (V3 and R1) as dependable production services.

Deployment is the bridge from research to production. It forces concrete choices about memory footprint, throughput, and operational risk. DeepSeek's architectures magnify these trade-offs: V3's **Mixture-of-Experts (MoE)** stresses VRAM placement; R1's extended reasoning inflates token counts and time-to-first-token. The right path depends on your constraints.

As of August 2025, any pricing and throughput figures in this chapter are directional. Verify current provider sheets and validate on your workload before hardcoding assumptions.

This chapter provides a practical playbook for deploying full-parameter DeepSeek models across real-world scenarios. We will focus on deploying DeepSeek-V3 (671B) and DeepSeek-R1 at full scale; smaller models are mentioned only as development proxies.

We'll cover the following main topics in this chapter:

- The DeepSeek deployment landscape
- A decision-making framework for choosing your deployment strategy
- Hardware and inference optimization requirements
- Hands-on deployment guides
- Production operations and monitoring
- Your deployment playbook

Note on scope

This chapter does not cover deploying the smaller fine-tuned/student model from *Chapter 7*. Any mention of smaller models is strictly for development or proxy workflows, not production deployments of the full models.

Technical requirements

In this chapter, we will explore various methods to deploy DeepSeek. For each method, the technical requirements will be mentioned in the respective sections. You can utilize any method that best suits your application and your access to the tools and platforms.

The DeepSeek deployment landscape

In production, you focus on three things: monitoring, scaling, and cost. You monitor tokens per request, **time to first token** (**TTFT**), p95/p99 latency, GPU, and **key-value** (**KV**) cache usage, and error/timeout rates. You scale based on how many tokens the system is actively generating, not just how many HTTP requests arrive. And you control cost by limiting tokens, batching where possible, caching common prefixes, and pausing or right-sizing replicas when idle.

For this, you need to keep a tab on the following:

- **Memory footprint**: This is the VRAM you need at runtime. It includes model weights plus overhead such as the KV cache and activations. Track peak VRAM and KV-cache bytes per token; these numbers decide your safe batch size and context length, and whether you need multiple GPUs or some weights moved to CPU/NVMe.
- **Throughput**: This is how many tokens per second your service can produce at your target concurrency. For planning, also report requests per second at a fixed prompt/response size, and always pair it with TTFT and p95/p99 latency, so the number reflects real user experience.
- **Operational risk**: This is the chance you miss SLOs or blow your budget because of instability or bad settings. Watch error and timeout rates, **Out of Memory (OOM) events**, queue growth, and how safely you roll out changes or scale up and down.

DeepSeek adds some extra wrinkles. V3 uses an MoE design that runs best when all experts stay in GPU memory, which pushes VRAM needs even with quantization; moving weights to CPU or NVMe helps fit but slows things down. R1 *thinks* a lot, often generating thousands of internal tokens before the final answer, which raises TTFT, increases memory use, and makes latency less predictable. Because of this, clear sizing, careful batching, and basic dashboards are must-haves before you choose API, managed, or self-hosted deployment.

DeepSeek's deployment quirks

DeepSeek models bring specific challenges:

- **Model size:** Even quantized versions push hardware limits. DeepSeek-V3's 671B total parameters need substantial VRAM, regardless of its MoE efficiency.
- **Reasoning overhead:** R1 models generate extensive internal reasoning traces. What looks like a simple query might produce thousands of intermediate tokens.
- **Architecture considerations:** V3's MoE design typically keeps all experts resident in GPU memory for performance; however, this is not a hard requirement. Modern stacks can offload/partition (CPU/NVMe, tensor-parallel across nodes) at the cost of significant latency/throughput.

These challenges require specific tools and techniques for large-model deployment. Let's start by examining why you might deploy DeepSeek yourself rather than using the official API.

Why self-deploy and what makes DeepSeek unique?

Often, you will encounter scenarios where you will choose to self-deploy DeepSeek or any other SOTA LLM. Consider, for example, a scenario where you're handling sensitive legal documents such as merger agreements – the official DeepSeek API may not be an option. Not because it's inadequate, but because client contracts often forbid sending privileged documents to third-party services. This scenario illustrates why self-deployment isn't just a technical exercise. It's often a business necessity.

Let's talk about some of the key reasons you might want to self-deploy:

- **Control and customization:** Control isn't a nice-to-have; it's how you turn a generic model into a system that fits your domain, risk posture, and product constraints. Self-deploying lets you touch the layers that APIs won't expose (tokenization, routing, adapters, system prompts, and safety policies) so the model reflects your requirements instead of a vendor's defaults. When Bloomberg built BloombergGPT, they didn't just want a financial language model; they needed to modify the tokenizer to handle financial terminology and keep half their training corpus proprietary. This level of control is impossible with API-based services.

For DeepSeek deployments, control means the following:

- Adjusting generation parameters beyond API limits.
- Merging domain-specific adapters (e.g., LoRA) or specialized adapters.
- Implementing custom safety filters appropriate for your domain.
- Modifying system prompts without vendor restrictions.
- **Cost at scale**: Cost is not just a price list; it's a function of utilization, batching, and caching. If your traffic is steady or high-volume, owning the serving stack lets you amortize hardware and push utilization, often dropping effective per-token costs far below metered APIs. The economics flip dramatically at scale. For a legal document workflow processing hundreds of contracts daily, use the following directional costs, as of August 2025 (verify before hardcoding):
    - **API costs**: ~$30–50 per million tokens
    - **Self-hosted (amortized)**: ~$2–5 per million tokens
    - **Break-even point**: Typically around 10–20M tokens/month

- **Privacy and data residency**: For many organizations, privacy isn't optional; it's mandated by contracts and regulation. Self-deployment keeps sensitive tokens within your perimeter, enforces data residency and retention policies, and provides auditability over where data flows. For instance, University Hospital Bonn deployed on-premises LLMs for chest X-ray reports specifically to comply with German data locality rules. Local inference handles all sensitive medical data without cloud egress or third-party processing.

    In the legal domain, the requirements are even stricter:

    - Attorney-client privilege prohibits most external processing.
    - Financial documents may trigger SOX compliance issues.
    - EU data residency requirements under GDPR.
    - Industry-specific regulations (such as HIPAA and PCI-DSS).
    - Some legal teams pilot local LLMs to avoid content filters that could flag privileged material as inappropriate.

- **Performance:** Latency and throughput are product features that shape user experience, SLOs, and even unit economics. Running the stack yourself removes network round-trips and lets you tailor the serving engine to your hardware and workload, unlocking lower TTFT and higher tokens/sec than one-size-fits-all APIs. As of August 2025, vLLM benchmarks report 2–4× throughput gains (`https://arxiv.org/abs/2309.06180`) versus prior SOTA serving systems, and up to 24× versus Hugging Face Transformers (`https://blog.vllm.ai/2023/06/20/vllm.html`) with continuous batching.

  Performance gains from self-hosting are as follows:

  - Eliminate API round-trip latency (often 50–200ms).
  - Implement continuous batching for higher throughput.
  - Optimize for your specific hardware configuration.
  - Cache common prompt prefixes locally.
- **Specialized use cases:** Major banks such as Westpac have partnered with Kasisto (`https://www.westpac.com.au/about-westpac/media/media-releases/2022/23-august/`) to deploy sector-specific LLMs for banking workflows; these deployments typically run inside the bank's cloud perimeter.

While the motivations for self-deployment apply broadly, DeepSeek's architecture creates unique challenges worth understanding before you provision that GPU cluster.

Some DeepSeek-specific deployment considerations for various models that you should be aware of are listed as follows:

- **DeepSeek-V3 memory requirements and placement:** V3's MoE design is elegant in theory: 671B total parameters, but only 37B active per token. In practice, it's a memory management puzzle. For best performance, teams keep all experts resident in GPU memory. Offloading or weight streaming to CPU/NVMe or sharding across nodes is possible, but it incurs substantial latency and throughput penalties. For consolidated VRAM and GPU sizing, including INT4 footprint and H100 counts, see the section on hardware and inference optimization engines
- Reports of 4-GPU deployments typically target smaller variants or rely on heavy offload/weight streaming to CPU/NVMe, which introduces large slowdowns.
- For consolidated VRAM and GPU sizing including INT4 footprint and H100 counts, capacity planning and headroom guidance, see the section on hardware and inference optimization engines.

- **DeepSeek-R1 reasoning-heavy generation**: R1's reasoning chains present a different challenge. Those `<think>` tokens that make R1 so capable also explode memory usage and latency (long *think* phases, spiky memory). A simple question might generate thousands of reasoning tokens before the actual answer.

So what does this imply in real-world settings? For instance, with DeepSeek-V3's **multi-head latent attention (MLA)**, the KV-cache footprint is about 70 KB/token (≈0.7 GB per 10k tokens), far lower than conventional attention KV sizes but still first-order for capacity planning. R1's public docs don't publish a per-token KV size; memory and latency will depend on reasoning depth:

- TTFT can be noticeably higher due to the *thinking* phase; specific TTFT depends on the workload and serving stack (no widely cited >30s benchmark).
- Memory usage is unpredictable; it depends on the reasoning complexity.
- Throughput is usually dominated by the *thinking* phase.

As of August 2025, public H200 numbers for full R1 vary by stack and workload. NVIDIA reported ~3,872 tokens/sec for 8× H200 in early NVIDIA's Inference Microservices (NIM) previews; later Blackwell (8×) marketing claims reach ~30k tokens/sec. For your own use case, be sure to treat vendor numbers as marketing until validated on your workload, and verify current figures before hardcoding capacity assumptions. Either way, a single request might need 5,000+ tokens just for internal reasoning.

These challenges aren't meant to discourage self-deployment. They're meant to prepare you for it. This chapter focuses on deploying the full DeepSeek-V3 (671B) and DeepSeek-R1 model; Although smaller distilled or fine-tuned variants are useful for prototyping, they are not the focus here. The bottom line is that this does not automatically mean you should self-deploy to save money. Self-hosting pays off primarily when compliance requires it or when you have sustained, high token volumes with strong GPU utilization; otherwise, the API or a managed service is usually cheaper and simpler until your measured workload crosses your validated break-even.

The key is matching your deployment strategy to your actual needs:

- Need to process sensitive documents? Self-deployment is likely mandatory.
- Processing millions of tokens daily? The economics favor self-hosting.
- Require sub-100ms latency? Local deployment with optimized serving is best.
- Just experimenting? Start with the API and migrate when needed.

Let's walk you through a framework to make these decisions systematically, turning deployment from an overwhelming challenge into a series of manageable trade-offs.

A decision-making framework for choosing your deployment strategy

The deployment choice primarily depends on the key drivers we discussed in the previous section: control, cost, and complexity. You will find yourself juggling and finding the right trade-off among these three.

Here are three deployment strategies you could choose from based on your use case:

- The **API approach** minimizes complexity but comes with variable costs and less control.
- A **managed service** provides moderate complexity with enterprise features, at the expense of higher unit costs.
- A **DIY (self-hosted) deployment** maximizes control and achieves the best unit costs at scale, while imposing the highest operational burden.

Let's build a framework to help you choose wisely, with a decision table (*Table 8.1*) keyed by compliance constraints, sustained token rate, and target SLOs.

Choice	Control	Cost	Complexity	Typical use	Key SLO variables
API	Low	Variable, pay per token	Low	Prototyping; spiky load	TTFT, p95 latency (network); provider rate limits
Managed	Medium	Higher per token	Medium	Enterprise features; IAM	TTFT, p95; autoscaling behavior
DIY	High	Lowest at scale	High	Stable high volume	Tokens/sec, TTFT, p95; GPU utilization

Table 8.1: Choosing deployment options for DeepSeek models

Every deployment decision boils down to these three competing forces (control, cost, and complexity). In my experience, you can optimize for two, but rarely all three:

- **Control** means the ability to tune every parameter, merge models, implement custom safety filters, or run *uncensored* versions for legitimate research. A company might migrate from Vertex AI to a self-hosted vLLM, which gives them the control they need, but then they have to staff a dedicated *LLM SRE* squad to maintain sub-300ms latency.
- **Cost** is where the math gets interesting. DeepSeek's API is billed per input/output token (your effective *blended* rate depends on the mix). Self-hosting on 4× A100 GPUs? That's about $1.24 per million tokens at 1,600 tokens/second, but that's assuming you keep those GPUs busy. On infra-only numbers, self-hosting can already be cheaper; a true break-even analysis only emerges once you add fixed staff/operations overhead explicitly for your organization.
- **Complexity** is the hidden tax. Running your own inference infrastructure means hiring specialists, writing playbooks, and getting paged when your model server crashes at 3 AM. AWS's reference architecture for DeepSeek-R1 on EKS requires deep Kubernetes expertise and GPU scheduling knowledge.

The sweet spot? Most organizations find it's not choosing one path exclusively, but knowing when to use each. You can imagine keeping low-volume features on Vertex AI while migrating high-volume reconciliation jobs to an in-house vLLM cluster, cutting costs from 1.4¢ to 0.3¢ per token.

You can use the following decision graph(*Figure 8.1*) as a starting point to explore which option works best for you. You can choose the deployment path that best fits your application. We'll go over all of them in detail shortly.

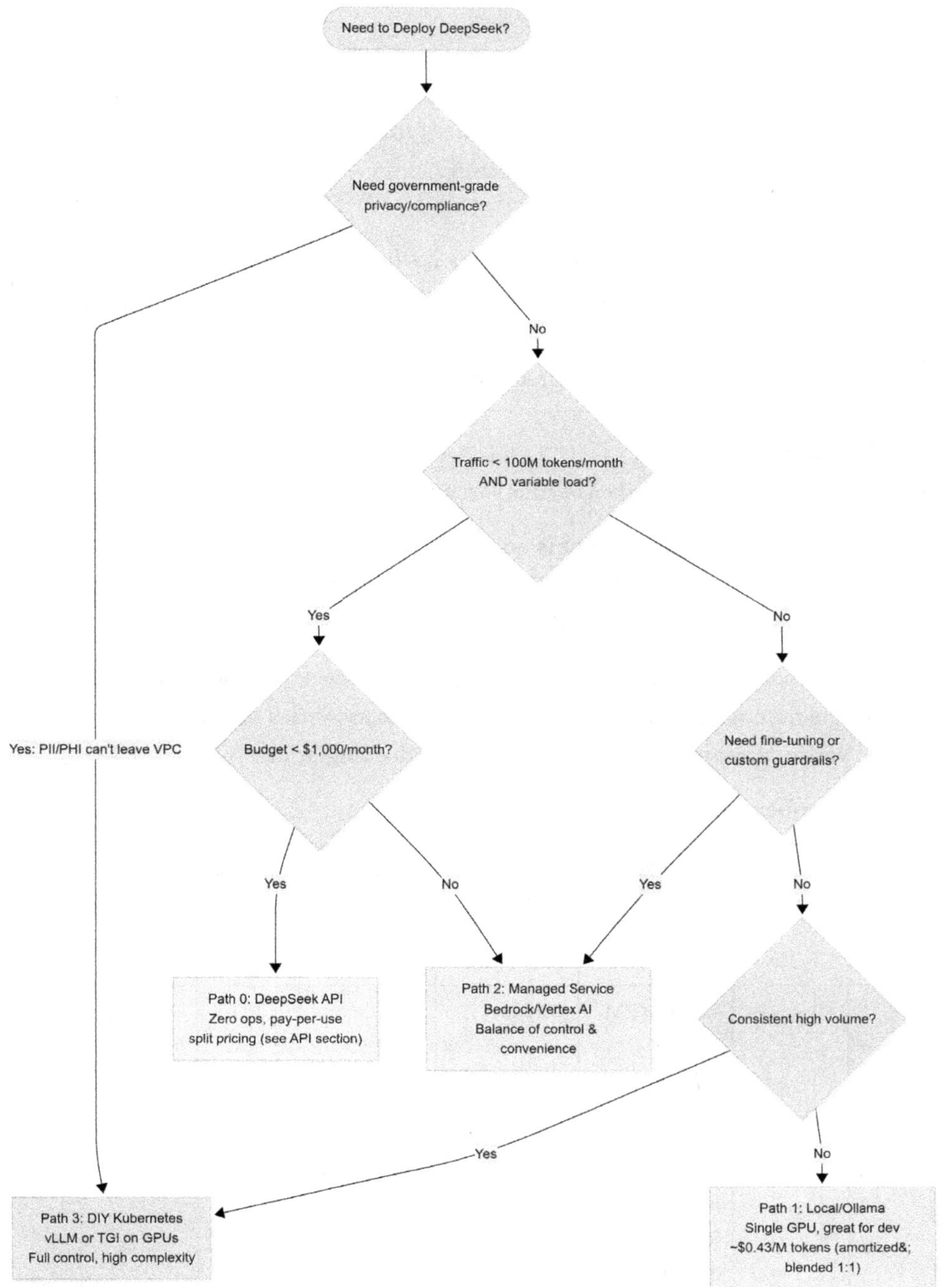

Figure 8.1: Decision graph for choosing how to deploy DeepSeek

Note

The Local/Ollama path in the decision tree is suitable only as a development proxy and does not apply to full DeepSeek-V3 (671B) or R1 deployments, which require multi-GPU or managed infrastructure.

Taken together, this framework maps each use case to the API, managed, or DIY strategy by balancing control, cost, and operational complexity. To pressure-test the option you've picked, run a quick cost sanity check using your own $/hour quotes and measured tokens/sec on your workload so you're deciding from measured economics, not marketing numbers.

Cost sanity check

As of August 2025, treat $/h and tokens/sec as variable, and verify current rates before hardcoding.

For example, if your 8× H200 endpoint is quoted at ~$40/h and sustains ~3,000 tokens/sec in your measurements, infra costs ≈ $0.0037 per 1k tokens (excluding staff/ops). Compare that to provider token prices and your observed prompt/response distribution.

Unless explicitly marked as *blended* or *amortized*, per-token costs are shown as *split input/output* rates. Any single number is a *1:1 blended assumption* or an *amortized infra estimate*, and is labeled accordingly. Verify current provider sheets before hardcoding prices.

Let's put real numbers on these trade-offs:

Deployment path	Upfront cost	Per-token cost	Technical expertise	Latency/throughput	Privacy	Scalability
DeepSeek API	$0	V3: $0.27/M input + $1.10/M output R1: $0.55/M input + $2.19/M output	Very low	Env-dependent TTFT and p95 end-to-end latency Throughput in tokens/sec	Data leaves VPC	Elastic, vendor-managed

Deployment path	Upfront cost	Per-token cost	Technical expertise	Latency/throughput	Privacy	Scalability
Local/ Ollama (RTX 4090)	~$1,599 GPU	$0.43/M tokens (amortized)	Low-medium	8–70 tokens/sec TTFT < 150ms	Full local control	Limited to GPU RAM
Managed Service (Bedrock/ Vertex)	$0 on-demand. $2,000+/ mo commits	DeepSeekR1 on Vertex: $1.35/M input + $5.40/M output (region/ model dependent)	Medium	Indicative; varies by model/region/ batching. Example: ~3,872 tokens/sec on 8× H200 for R1 (NVIDIA preview).	In-region, SOC2	Auto-scaling, global
DIY Kubernetes (4× A100-80GB)	$5,155/ mo infra ($1.79/ GPU-hour)	$1.24/M tokens @ 1,600 tokens/ sec	High	Up to ~3,800 tokens/ sec on 8× H200 (NVIDIA preview)	Full VPC isolation	Manual scaling

Table 8.2: Comparison matrix of pricing of various deployment options of DeepSeek, as of August 2025

Use a simple planning formula to model the cost for your workload:

For example, let's plug in the numbers for the 4× A100 DIY setup from the matrix. At roughly $7.16 per hour (4 GPUs × $1.79/h) and a measured 1,600 tokens/second, the formula simplifies to an hourly calculation: *$7.16 ÷ (1,600 × 3600) ≈ $1.24 per million tokens.* You can now compare this directly to an API. This self-hosted cost is slightly lower than the DeepSeek-R1 API's blended rate of ~$1.37/M tokens (at 1:1 input/output). The decision then comes down to utilization: if your workload is consistent enough to keep the GPUs busy, self-hosting provides savings; if it's intermittent, the pay-as-you-go API will be cheaper.

So how do you make the choice?

- **When the API wins**: You're experimenting, have variable load, or process less than 100M tokens monthly. Zero operational overhead is worth the premium.
- **When local shines**: You have development, testing, or sensitive data that absolutely cannot leave your premises. For example, assuming ~65 tokens/sec on a 4090 GPU, a 1:1 I/O ratio, and amortizing a $1,599 GPU over 24 months at 50% utilization, the GPU-only cost is roughly $0.8 per million tokens (excluding power and operations). Use the cost formula to adjust for your workload.
- **When managed services make sense**: You need enterprise features (audit logs, IAM integration, and global deployment) without the operational burden. The higher per-token cost buys peace of mind.
- **When DIY delivers**: You are processing billions of tokens monthly with a predictable load. A 4× A100 cluster processing 3B tokens/month saves ~$3,000 versus the API – enough to hire that SRE.

But the decision tree is not the holy grail. It doesn't tell you that most successful deployments are hybrid. Recall the legal scenario we discussed at the beginning of this chapter. They might require a deployment option. You may come across three paths or choices for DeepSeek deployment:

- Use the API for low-volume experimental features, or for synthetic data generation on private data.
- Deploy the fine-tuned legal classifier on local GPUs for document processing.
- Leverage Bedrock for client-facing applications needing five nines uptime.

The framework isn't about picking one path forever – it's about knowing which path serves each use case best.

Are you ready to see what each path actually looks like in practice? Let's dive into the implementation details.

Three paths to deployment

This section details each deployment path we identified in *Figure 8.1* and focuses on the concrete steps you can undertake for deployment.

Path 0: The baseline (official DeepSeek API)

The API approach offers the lowest operational overhead. Everything just works, someone else handles the maintenance, and you can focus on what you came to do. For many teams, this remains the right choice, even after considering all the alternatives.

The DeepSeek API offers two primary models: `deepseek-chat` (DeepSeek-V3) and `deepseek-reasoner` (DeepSeek-R1). As of August 2025, both expose a 128K context window. Maximum output tokens depend on API parameters (e.g., `max_tokens`) and provider settings. Pricing matches the public sheet. V3 runs $0.27 per million input tokens and $1.10 per million output tokens; R1 runs $0.55 per million input and $2.19 per million output.

Getting started requires minimal ceremony, as you've already seen in *Chapter 5*:

```
import deepseek
deepseek.api_key = "YOUR_KEY"

resp = deepseek.ChatCompletion.create(
    model="deepseek-reasoner",
    messages=[{"role": "user", "content": "Prove the Pythagorean
theorem."}],
    stream=True,    # always stream - reduces perceived latency on R1
    # WHY: Stream to reduce perceived latency (TTFT) on R1; also caps
client-side buffer growth.
)
for chunk in resp:
    print(chunk.choices[0].delta.content, end="", flush=True)
# WHY: Protect client from long "thinking" phases on R1; tune to your SLA
(e.g., 60-120s).
```

This code is a simple example of using the API to get a response and to stream the results directly.

The operational reality of the API brings both pleasant surprises and hidden complexities. As of August 2025, requests can run until a ~30-minute timeout. Verify current limits before relying on them. Though not shown in the preceding code example, you might want to keep an eye on your spending for your API keys to protect budgets, especially given R1's propensity for verbose reasoning.

One supply chain SaaS company documented its migration from OpenAI's GPT-4o to DeepSeek, motivated by API pricing that was nearly 25× lower (`https://medium.com/tracified/deepseek-vs-openai-aec06fbee43a`). However, the savings came with a trade-off: the migration was not a simple drop-in and required a complete overhaul of their prompt engineering strategy. The team found that DeepSeek demanded far more explicit, detailed instructions to match the extraction accuracy they were getting from the more flexible OpenAI models.

Path 1: Local and on-premises (for dev and specialized cases)

Local deployment is where things get interesting. This path is primarily for development and prototyping; it is not applicable to full-parameter DeepSeek-V3 (671B) or DeepSeek-R1 deployments, which require multi-GPU or managed infrastructure. You trade the API's convenience for complete control – perfect for that legal classifier handling privileged documents or the research lab exploring *uncensored* model behaviors.

Let's begin with Ollama first for local deployment.

Ollama: The lowest-friction local path

Ollama has become the de facto standard for getting models running locally with minimal fuss. Installation requires one command on Linux or macOS, as follows:

```
curl -fsSL https://ollama.com/install.sh | sh
```

An MSI installer is available for Windows users, which can be downloaded at `https://ollama.com/download/OllamaSetup.exe`.

```
ollama pull deepseek-r1:14b-q4_K_M  # 14B distilled version, fits in 16GB
VRAM
ollama run deepseek-r1:14b
```

In the preceding code snippet, we are using the 14B distilled model. The 14B model represents an interesting middle ground, balancing the ability to run it locally with the power of the responses it gives back. At `Q4_K_M` quantization, it occupies ~8.5 GB of VRAM and, as of August 2025, produced ~65–72 tokens/sec in informal local tests on an RTX 4090 (non-scientific; workloads vary). Not blazing fast, but entirely serviceable for development or small-scale production use. The full model catalog ranges from aggressive 3-bit quantization (~7.5 GB) for memory-constrained systems to 8-bit versions (~16.7 GB) that preserve more of the original model's capabilities.

Docker + vLLM: Production-grade local serving

When Ollama's simplicity hits its limits, a containerized vLLM (i.e., a vLLM run from a Docker container) offers a more sophisticated approach. This isn't your standard Flask or FastAPI-wrapped model – vLLM brings industrial-strength optimizations such as paged attention, achieving 24× throughput improvements over naive implementations. The trade-off is complexity versus workload profile. That 24× gain reflects throughput under high concurrent load, which is a game-changer for production but often overkill for a developer running single requests locally. For low-concurrency or development workflows, Ollama's simplicity is hard to beat; the vLLM justifies its setup overhead when you need to serve multiple users or applications from a single, shared GPU.

PagedAttention

PagedAttention is a memory management algorithm that stores the KV cache in non-contiguous memory blocks, much like an operating system uses virtual memory and paging. This solves internal memory fragmentation, enabling much higher batch sizes and ultimately delivering the throughput gains the vLLM is known for.

Launch the following script with `docker run --gpus all -p 8000:8000 -v models:/models deepseek-vllm:latest`. You'll get an OpenAI-compatible endpoint that speaks the same protocol as the official DeepSeek API.

```
FROM nvidia/cuda:12.4.1-runtime-ubuntu22.04
RUN pip install vllm==0.8.5
ENV HF_TOKEN=<your-token>
CMD vllm serve \
    --model "deepseek-ai/DeepSeek-Coder-V2-Lite-Instruct" \
    --dtype "bfloat16" \
    # WHY: Cap context to bound KV cache growth; raise only if you can 
afford memory.
    --max-model-len "8192" \
    # WHY: Push VRAM use for throughput; >0.95 risks OOM under burst. 
Safe range: 0.85–0.95.
    --gpu-memory-utilization "0.95"
```

This compatibility becomes crucial when you need to switch between local and cloud deployments without rewriting your application code.

For teams handling sensitive data, projects such as **OnPrem.LLM** (`https://arxiv.org/html/2505.07672v2`) can build complete RAG pipelines on top of these local serving layers, ensuring that proprietary documents never leave your infrastructure.

Path 2: Managed inference services (the balanced approach)

Managed services occupy the sweet spot between control and convenience. You get enterprise features (audit logs, IAM integration, and global deployment) without hiring a dedicated MLOps team. Imagine a fast-growing B2B SaaS company whose core feature is an AI-powered analytics dashboard. While the public API was perfect for their MVP, their new enterprise customers demand guaranteed uptime, lower latency, and processing within a private network. Building their own Kubernetes cluster would take months and require hiring specialized MLOps engineers. Instead, they turn to a managed service such as Amazon Bedrock or Vertex AI. This move allows them to get the required enterprise features, such as private endpoints and provisioned throughput, with a predictable cost model and minimal operational lift, letting them meet enterprise demands without derailing their product roadmap.

Each major cloud provider has embraced DeepSeek, though their approaches differ significantly. Let's talk about them:

- **Amazon Bedrock** (`https://aws.amazon.com/bedrock`) makes DeepSeek-R1 available via Bedrock (including Marketplace) with serverless invocation. Provisioned Throughput exists in Bedrock generally, but availability can depend on the specific third-party model and region – verify for your account. The serverless option works well for variable loads, while Provisioned Throughput (where available) guarantees consistent performance once you exceed sustained token rates. Their built-in guardrails service adds content filtering without custom code, which is crucial for customer-facing applications.
- **SageMaker JumpStart** (`https://docs.aws.amazon.com/sagemaker/latest/dg/studio-jumpstart.html`) takes a different approach, focusing on the distilled versions (8B and 32B) that fit comfortably on single-GPU instances. A recent AWS blog demonstrated serving the 8B model on `ml.g5.xlarge` instances. Pricing varies by region and commitment, so verify rates in your account.
- **Google Vertex AI** (`https://cloud.google.com/vertex-ai/generative-ai/docs/maas/deepseek`) added DeepSeek-R1 to their Model Garden with one-click deployment. As of August 2025, representative pricing is ~$6.75 per million tokens in `us-central1`. Rates are region/model dependent, so verify them in your account. It's pricier than the official API but includes enterprise SLAs and private endpoint support.

- **Azure AI Foundry** (`https://azure.microsoft.com/en-us/products/ai-foundry`) rounds out the big three with both serverless and dedicated cluster options. Their responsible AI scorecard provides automated bias detection and content safety analysis – features that can save months of custom development for regulated industries.
- **Hugging Face Inference Endpoints** (`https://huggingface.co/inference-endpoints/`) deserves special mention for transparency. Their deployment wizard shows line-item costs upfront, but rates vary by region/plan/provider. As of August 2025, treat ~$40/h for 8× H200 as a market reference (e.g., Together AI's public quote is ≈$0.67/min). For Hugging Face Endpoints, automatic ***scale-to-zero*** is opt-in and, by default, triggers after ~15 minutes of idle time (historically also documented as ~1 hr). Programmatic controls exist to ***manually scale*** an endpoint to 0; do not assume a 60-second idle timeout unless your provider explicitly supports it. Verify availability and semantics for your chosen region/plan.

A practical hybrid pattern is to keep latency-sensitive, customer-facing inference on a managed platform while shifting large, non-interactive batch jobs to a dedicated endpoint to lower cost. Cost case studies on SageMaker report substantial savings; for example, Forethought cites up to 80% lower inference costs after migrating to SageMaker (`https://aws.amazon.com/solutions/case-studies/forethought-technologies-case-study/`).

Path 3: DIY on IaaS (for maximum control)

DIY deployment is where engineering meets economics. You're not just running a model; you're building infrastructure. This path demands expertise but delivers unmatched flexibility and potential cost savings. Here are some typical use cases with examples of each:

- **Regulated and air-gapped workloads**: You must keep data inside a specific network boundary or country and cannot use third-party endpoints. For example, a hospital deploys DeepSeek behind a private API in its own VPC, with no internet egress.
- **Steady, high-volume traffic where cost per token matters**: Your workload has predictable daily/weekly batches and keeps GPUs busy. For example, an e-commerce team runs nightly catalog enrichment and translation on a vLLM cluster, cutting unit costs versus per-token APIs and controlling batch windows.
- **Ultra-low latency or network locality**: You need p95 latency targets that are hard to hit over public APIs. For example, a trading desk colocates an inference node next to its market-data stream, uses compiled kernels (TensorRT-LLM) and KV-cache warmers, and avoids cross-region hops.

- **Custom model or runtime control**: You need capabilities that managed endpoints don't expose. For example, a legal-tech platform merges domain LoRAs, enforces custom redaction filters, adjusts R1 *thinking* budgets, and tunes continuous batching parameters in the vLLM to match its traffic.
- **Multi-tenant platforms with strict isolation and budgeting**: You must guarantee per-tenant data isolation and enforce token budgets across thousands of tenants. For example, a developer platform runs separate namespaces per tenant, sticky routes conversations for cache locality, and enforces token-bucket limits at the gateway.
- **On-premises, edge, or unreliable WAN**: You can't rely on consistent connectivity. For example, a factory runs DeepSeek on a small on-premises GPU fleet with periodic weight updates, ensuring that local inference continues if the wireless network link drops.
- **Vendor independence and capacity control**: You want to lock in pricing/availability ahead of demand spikes. For example, a media company reserves GPUs across two regions, runs DIY for baseline load, and bursts to managed endpoints only during launches.

These patterns play to DIY's strengths: full control over memory placement (important for V3's MoE), the ability to cap or shape R1 reasoning tokens, predictable unit economics at scale, and deep integration with your own security and SRE practices.

Here are some of the approaches that you can try out:

- **Single VM or bare metal**: The simplest DIY approach mirrors local deployment but with beefier hardware. A typical configuration might include 4× A100-80GB GPUs running vLLM with DeepSeek-V3 quantized to INT4. As of August 2025, measured throughput around 1,600 tokens per second yields an infra cost per million tokens below ~$2 at high utilization; validate with your workload before committing.

  The math gets even more interesting with newer hardware. NVIDIA reported ~3,872 tokens/sec for R1 on 8× H200 in early NIM preview conditions; later Blackwell (8×) marketing claims reach ~30k tokens/sec (`https://blogs.nvidia.com/blog/deepseek-r1-nim-microservice/` and `https://developer.nvidia.com/blog/nvidia-blackwell-delivers-world-record-deepseek-r1-inference-performance/`). For organizations processing billions of tokens daily, the ROI can materialize quickly.
- **Kubernetes orchestration**: Kubernetes deployment elevates DIY from *running a server* to *operating a service*. The modern approach in 2025 centers on KServe v0.15 as your serving layer, but the real story is how you think about scaling and optimization.

- Instead of traditional web service patterns, LLM deployments require different mental models. You're not scaling on requests per second; you're scaling on actual work being done: how many requests are actively generating tokens versus waiting in the queue. Tools such as **Kubernetes Event-driven Autoscaling** (**KEDA**) enable this smarter scaling by watching real LLM metrics rather than naive request counts (`https://keda.sh/`).

These are the architecture choices that matter most for DIY deployment:

- **Smart autoscaling**: Scale on meaningful metrics such as active generation load, not HTTP request rates. R1's long reasoning phases make this especially critical.
- **Token budget controls**: Unlike traditional rate limiting, you need to cap spending at the token level. Envoy AI Gateway and similar tools provide this control without rewriting your clients.
- **KV cache sharing**: In conversational workloads, sharing cache across replicas dramatically improves throughput. Technologies such as LMCache make this practical without application changes.
- **Multi-node considerations**: When models exceed single-node memory, you enter a different complexity realm. Pipeline and tensor parallelism work, but require careful planning, and they don't currently support autoscaling.

Note that even INT4-quantized V3 needs multiple GPUs. R1's thinking phases demand generous timeouts. For the largest models, fewer powerful nodes with fast interconnects typically outperform many smaller instances. These aren't plug-and-play solutions, though. Each optimization requires understanding your specific workload patterns. Teams often discover that their *chat* workload is actually 80% single-turn questions, making conversation-optimized caching worthless, or they implement complex autoscaling only to find that their load is perfectly predictable.

Each path we've explored serves legitimate use cases. The API excels for prototypes and variable loads. Local deployment protects sensitive data while enabling experimentation on smaller models; full DeepSeek-V3 or R1 requires multi-GPU or managed serving. Managed services balance capability with operational simplicity. DIY infrastructure delivers ultimate control and economics at scale.

Your choice depends less on technical superiority and more on organizational reality. Do you have the expertise to run Kubernetes? Can your data leave your premises? Will you process enough tokens to justify infrastructure investment? Answer these questions honestly, and the right path becomes clear.

Next, we'll dig into the foundational technologies that make any of these paths possible, because whether you're calling an API or running your own cluster, understanding the underlying machinery helps you make better decisions.

The next section surveys the hardware and serving engines that underpin these choices.

Hardware and inference optimization engines for deployment

Before we start deploying models, we need to talk about the infrastructure that makes deployment possible. Let's first discuss whether you have the right hardware for deployment and how to choose the right configuration.

Choosing your hardware

VRAM capacity determines feasibility; other components mainly affect speed. When it comes to LLM deployment, your GPU's memory determines what's possible, while everything else just determines how fast it happens.

The current GPU hierarchy for DeepSeek deployment looks like this: The H100 with 80 GB HBM3 sits at the apex, delivering 3.3 TB/s of memory bandwidth and native FP8 support through its Transformer Engine. The A100 (40 GB or 80 GB variants) remains the production workhorse – reliable, widely available, and still fast enough for most use cases. The L40S offers an interesting middle ground with 48 GB GDDR6 – less memory bandwidth but often easier to procure.

A 33B-parameter model in BF16 (`bfloat16`) precision – a 16-bit floating-point format used on modern GPUs/TPUs that stores 2 bytes per parameter and preserves FP32's numeric range with fewer mantissa (i.e., precision) bits – requires the following:

- Base memory = 33B parameters × 2 bytes/parameter = 66 GB.
- Runtime overhead (~10%) = 6.6 GB.
- Total VRAM needed = ~73 GB.

That's before you add KV cache for context, activation memory for batching, or safety margins. Your 33B model that barely squeezes onto a single H100 will demand multiple GPUs once you enable production features.

And what if you opt to deploy DeepSeek-V3 with 671B parameters? Even with aggressive INT4 quantization, you're looking at 335 GB minimum. In this case, a multi-GPU cluster isn't optional; it's mandatory.

Another important aspect is to utilize an inference engine. Here is why.

Inference engines

With DeepSeek, it's not enough to write a quick `model.generate()` function within a simple web server. We quickly find performance bottlenecks that inference engines address.

Naïve per-request generation handles one request at a time and steps each sequence token by token before accepting a new request. Between tokens, the GPU often waits on Python overhead and kernel launches, and the KV cache is allocated in large contiguous chunks that fragment as sequences finish at different times. For example, a simple Flask or FastAPI server that calls `model.generate()` per HTTP request with `batch_size=1` will run one user stream to completion while other users queue, leaving the GPU underutilized. Another common case is fixed batching that waits for all sequences in the batch to finish; short prompts sit idle while the longest prompt stalls the entire batch.

Moving to vLLM or TGI with continuous batching avoids these gaps. They reuse paged KV memory and insert new requests as others finish, which keeps the device saturated. In practice, this often yields 2–4× higher throughput at similar latency. Public benchmarks repeatedly show large gains versus Hugging Face Transformers servers under load (`https://arxiv.org/abs/2309.06180` and

`https://blog.vllm.ai/2023/06/20/vllm.html`).

The naive approach treats each request in isolation. Your expensive GPU sits idle while waiting for I/O, memory fragments, and shorter sequences to finish, while longer ones block the entire batch.

Enter inference engines. Inference systems help address the wastage of GPU time, increase throughput, and reduce latency. Let's talk about the various options you have:

- **vLLM** (`https://github.com/vllm-project/vllm`): LLM introduced PagedAttention, borrowing virtual memory concepts from operating systems to manage KV cache efficiently. Instead of pre-allocating massive contiguous memory blocks, vLLM pages cache entries like a modern OS handles RAM. This meant a 2–4x throughput improvement over naive serving, with some workloads seeing up to 23x gains
- The real magic of vLLM happens with continuous batching. While traditional serving waits for all sequences in a batch to complete before processing new requests, vLLM dynamically inserts new requests as others finish, keeping your GPU saturated. It's the difference between a taxi that waits for all passengers to reach their destinations versus one that picks up new fares along the way.

Here is how you can achieve batching:

```
# Traditional batching pseudocode
def serve_batch(requests):
    outputs = model.generate(requests)  # ALL must finish
    return outputs

# Continuous batching concept
def serve_continuous():
    while True:
        if completed := get_finished_sequences():
            yield completed
            add_new_requests_to_batch()
        step_active_sequences()
```

- **Text Generation Inference** (**TGI**) (`https://github.com/huggingface/text-generation-inference`): Hugging Face's TGI powers enterprise deployments at IBM Watson and Grammarly. Its secret sauce combines Flash Attention kernels, tensor parallelism, and safetensors for near-instant model loading. Where vLLM optimizes for throughput, TGI balances throughput with consistent latency – crucial for user-facing applications.

  TGI's strengths include continuous batching, Flash Attention, PagedAttention, quantization, and tensor parallelism. It uses safetensors and optimized loaders to speed cold starts, but weights must be fully loaded before serving requests.

- **TensorRT-LLM** (`https://github.com/NVIDIA/TensorRT-LLM`): NVIDIA's TensorRT-LLM represents the *closer to metal* approach. It compiles your model into optimized CUDA kernels, fuses operations, and leverages hardware-specific features such as the H100's Transformer Engine. The compilation step adds complexity, but the payoff is substantial – 4.6x higher throughput when moving from A100 FP16 to H100 FP8.

  The catch is that TensorRT-LLM is pickier about model architectures and hardware. It shines brightest on NVIDIA's latest GPUs with models it knows well. For DeepSeek's MoE architecture, you might need to wait for official support or dive into custom plugins.

So, how do you choose your inference engine?

The choice isn't about which engine is *best*; it's about matching strengths to requirements. Here is a quick guide to help you make this decision:

- Use vLLM when you need maximum flexibility and throughput.
- Opt for TGI when you need production stability and consistent latency.
- Go with TensorRT-LLM when you have modern NVIDIA hardware and need every last token per second.

Most teams start with vLLM or TGI for their ease of use, then evaluate TensorRT-LLM once they hit scale. The beauty? All three expose OpenAI-compatible APIs, so switching engines is often a configuration change rather than a code rewrite.

Quantization is another technique that can help you speed up your inference time and costs.

The power of quantization

Recall from *Chapter 2* that quantization reduces precision to shrink memory and improve throughput, usually with a small quality loss. The quantization landscape offers several techniques, each with its own trade-offs:

- **FP8** represents the gentlest compression, halving memory usage while maintaining near-perfect accuracy. It requires newer hardware (H100/L40S) but delivers the best quality-to-compression ratio. Think of it as moving from lossless **Free Lossless Audio Codec** (**FLAC**) to high-bitrate MP3: technically lossy, practically indistinguishable.
- **GPT quantization** (**GPTQ**) takes a post-training approach, analyzing your model to determine which weights can be squeezed to 4 bits without catastrophic forgetting. It's fast, requiring only a calibration dataset of a few hundred examples, and typically loses less than one percentage point of accuracy. (To learn more about GPTQ, check out the Hugging Face blog here: `https://huggingface.co/blog/gptq-integration`.)
- **Activation-aware weight quantization** (**AWQ**) goes further, identifying *salient* weights that disproportionately affect outputs and keeping them at higher precision. For DeepSeek's MoE models, this activation awareness is particularly valuable – expert routing depends on precise weight values, and AWQ preserves them. (The Hugging Face documentation for AWQ is a good place to learn more and find more resources for understanding how it works: `https://huggingface.co/docs/transformers/en/quantization/awq`.)

A simple way to budget GPU memory is to think in three parts: the model weights, a small runtime headroom, and the KV cache:

- **Weights**: Start with the weight tensor itself. Multiply the number of parameters by the bytes per parameter for your chosen precision. For a 33B model, BF16 stores about 2 bytes per parameter, so the weights alone are roughly 66 GB. FP8 halves that to about 33 GB. With 4-bit quantization, you store about half a byte per parameter. This means, in practice, GPTQ-4b checkpoints for 33B land around 16–17 GB each, while AWQ-4b checkpoints are often closer to 18–19 GB because they keep a few critical values at higher precision. AWQ frequently preserves slightly more accuracy than GPTQ at the same bit width.
- **Runtime headroom**: Add about 10–20% on top of the weight size for temporary workspaces, CUDA kernel buffers, allocator fragmentation, and (for MoE) routing overhead. Using the same 33B example, a BF16 deployment might need an extra 6–13 GB beyond the 66 GB for weights before you consider sequence memory.
- **KV cache**: Finally, budget for the KV cache, which grows with context length, generated tokens, and batch size. This is separate from the weight size. For DeepSeek-V3's MLA, the KV cache is about 70 KB per token (roughly 0.7 GB per 10k cached tokens). Other architectures can be larger. Multiply by the number of concurrent sequences to estimate your total KV footprint.

In short, for a 33B model, expect roughly 66 GB (BF16) or ~33 GB (FP8) for the weights, or ~16–17 GB (GPTQ-4b) / ~18–19 GB (AWQ-4b), plus 10–20% runtime headroom, plus KV cache for the tokens you serve.

One important gotcha: Make sure your serving stack actually runs low-bit kernels natively. Some systems store 4-bit weights on disk but upcast them to BF16/FP16 at load or during matrix multiplies. That silently increases VRAM back toward full-precision numbers and erases the performance and cost savings. Verify that your engine (for example, vLLM, TGI, or TensorRT-LLM) is using the intended low-bit execution path by checking logs and observed VRAM after load.

The practical impact? That 33B model requiring an expensive H100 in full precision runs comfortably on a single L40S after 4-bit quantization. Your inference costs drop by 75% for a 1–2% accuracy hit – a trade most production systems gladly make.

Not all models quantize equally. Smaller models suffer more from quantization; they have less redundancy to sacrifice. Task complexity matters too: summarization might tolerate aggressive quantization while legal document analysis demands higher precision.

Always validate quantized models on your specific use case. That 0.5% average accuracy drop might hide a 10% degradation on rare but critical inputs. And remember: *quantization is just virtual VRAM*. You still need an inference engine that understands low-bit formats, or you'll dequantize on the fly and lose all benefits.

Hardware provides the raw capability. Inference engines unlock that capability's potential. Quantization stretches your hardware budget. Together, they transform DeepSeek from an impressive demo into a production-ready system.

The key insight? These aren't independent choices. An H100's FP8 support only matters if your inference engine can leverage it. AWQ only helps if your engine handles mixed-precision execution efficiently. Your deployment strategy must consider the full stack, not just individual components.

With the hardware and serving engines in mind, the next section demonstrates three concrete deployment scenarios.

Hands-on deployment guides

These three deployment examples progress from laptop experimentation to cloud production, each building on lessons from the previous. Follow along with the one that matches your current needs, but read all three to understand the full deployment spectrum.

Let's first begin with the cost analysis for managed endpoints. An 8× H200 deployment costs approximately $40 per hour on managed providers, as of August 2025. Together AI publicly quotes $0.67/min (`https://www.together.ai/deepseek`). These costs add up quickly:

- Daily cost if left running: $960.
- Monthly cost at 24/7: $28,800.
- Deployment spin-up time: ~10-15 minutes ≈ $7-$10.

So, what are your options to manage your costs? Here are some of the smart cost management options:

1. **Use scale-to-zero where supported**: On Hugging Face Inference Endpoints, it's opt-in and typically triggers after ~15 minutes of idle time (though you can configure it as per your needs). Per-endpoint 60-second idle timeouts generally aren't supported; instead, use programmatic manual scale-to-zero/pause for aggressive cost control. Check your

provider's capabilities. Since it usually takes a few minutes to spin up the model and provision infrastructure, there will usually be a bit of a delay in scaling up or down, regardless of what value you set.

2. **Set billing alerts**: Multiple thresholds are your friend. Most major providers expose budget and usage alerts (AWS Budgets/CloudWatch, Google Cloud Budgets and Alerting, Azure Cost Management, and usage notifications on managed endpoints); if yours doesn't, enforce token-level caps in your API gateway and alert from your observability stack. As a default, set alerts at 50%, 80%, and 100% of the monthly budget (auto-throttle or pause at 100%) and add a daily *speed bump* alert (e.g., 10% of the monthly budget in a day) to catch runaway bursts early.
3. **Consider your use case**: Bursty workloads? Perfect for scale-to-zero. Sustained traffic? Maybe negotiate capacity blocks.
4. **Do the math**: At $40/hour, you need to be processing enough value to justify the compute. For example, if your endpoint sustains ≈3,000 tokens/sec, the infra cost is ≈$0.0037 per 1k tokens, so a 5M-token batch runs ≈$18.5 (excluding staff/ops). Conversely, if you only trickle ~100k tokens/hour, you're effectively paying ≈$0.40 per 1k tokens (~$400/M), which is often above API rates, so pause/scale-to-zero or use serverless for that load profile.

This pricing reflects the cost of operating a fully managed 671B-parameter model with enterprise-grade infrastructure. Compare this to:

- Building your own 8x H200 cluster: $500K+ upfront.
- AWS capacity blocks: ~$36/hour (but you manage everything).
- Smaller cloud providers: Often unavailable or unreliable.

Pro tip

For experimentation, start with shorter inference windows. A 2-hour deep dive costs $80, a manageable expense for targeted experimentation. Execute `endpoint.scale_to_zero()` after completion to avoid ongoing charges.

These numbers might seem intimidating, but they underscore the importance of matching the tool to the task. Personally, my workflow almost always starts with a local Ollama instance for rapid iteration, only graduating to a managed endpoint when I need to test performance at scale. This approach keeps development fast and initial costs at zero.

Example 1: Local deployment with Ollama and a quantized DeepSeek Coder model

Local deployment with Ollama represents the path of least resistance. It's the *Hello World* of LLM deployment – simple enough to complete over coffee, yet sophisticated enough to power real development workflows. We'll use the 16B parameter version quantized to 4-bit precision, which delivers near-full-model performance while fitting comfortably in consumer hardware. This example is a development proxy and does not deploy the full DeepSeek-V3 (671B) or R1 models.

For this section, our goal is to get DeepSeek Coder V2 running on your local machine in under 10 minutes, perfect for development and experimentation without cloud dependencies or API costs.

Prerequisites and performance expectations

The quantized model (DeepSeek Coder V2) weighs approximately ~9 GB. On consumer hardware, you should expect tens of tokens/second on 4-bit Coder models and a TTFT typically <1 second locally. The throughput varies by quantization, drivers, and workload. Treat any single-machine numbers in this section as directional, not SLA targets.

Let's get started with the step-by-step deployment steps:

1. Installation requires just one command on Unix-like systems:

   ```
   curl -fsSL https://ollama.com/install.sh | sh
   ```

   Windows users get a proper MSI installer from the Ollama website (`https://ollama.com/download/OllamaSetup.exe`). Once installed, pulling the model is straightforward:

   ```
   ollama pull deepseek-coder-v2:16b
   ```

   This downloads the default `Q4_0` quantization. The download shows progress in real time, and Ollama handles all the complexity of model format conversion and optimization for your hardware.

2. To test interactively, start an interactive session:

   ```
   ollama run deepseek-coder-v2
   ```

   This drops you into a REPL where you can start coding immediately. But for integration with development tools, you'll want the API server:

   ```
   ollama serve
   ```

This exposes an OpenAI-compatible REST endpoint at `` `http://localhost:11434` ``. The compatibility layer is nearly perfect; most tools expecting OpenAI's API work with a simple base URL change.

3. Next is verification and testing. Confirm your deployment with a quick `curl` test:

```
curl http://localhost:11434/api/generate \
  -d '{"model":"deepseek-coder-v2","prompt":"// bubble sort in Go"}'
```

4. For Python applications, the OpenAI client library works seamlessly. Note that the OpenAI library has become a sort of standard SDK that people use to make inference requests for LLMs. As you can see in the following code sample, we pass in a configuration that specifies we want to make our requests against the local Ollama model and not the cloud-hosted OpenAI models:

```
import openai

openai.base_url = 'http://localhost:11434/v1'
openai.api_key = 'ollama'  # Any non-empty string works

response = openai.chat.completions.create(
    model='deepseek-coder-v2',
    messages=[
        {
            "role": "user",
            "content": "Write a Rust macro for logging."
        }
    ]
)
print(response.choices[0].message.content)
```

5. Next, we troubleshoot common issues. The most frequent problem is running out of memory. If you see `` `cudaMalloc failed: out of memory` ``, you have three options: use a more aggressive quantization (try `` `deepseek-coder-v2:16b-q3_K_M` ``), enable CPU offloading with `` `OLLAMA_NUMA=1` ``, or close other GPU-hungry applications.

6. Download interruptions leave partial files that can cause cryptic errors. If you encounter `` `EOF` `` errors or `` `model manifest not found` ``, remove and repull:

```
ollama rm deepseek-coder-v2
ollama pull deepseek-coder-v2:16b
```

7. Disk space is another gotcha. The download process temporarily requires about 2x the model size. If your pull fails partway, you might need to run `` `ollama prune` `` to reclaim space from orphaned blob files.
8. Cleaning up is as simple as deployment:

```
ollama stop deepseek-coder-v2  # Stop running model
ollama rm deepseek-coder-v2     # Remove model files
ollama prune                    # Clean up unused data
```

What this teaches

This example demonstrates the fundamentals of model lifecycle management: pulling, running, serving, and cleaning up. You've seen how quantization makes large models practical on consumer hardware, and that Q4 quantization trades a mere 1–2 percentage points of accuracy for a 75% reduction in memory requirements.

More importantly, you now have a fully functional LLM development environment. VS Code with the **Continue** extension can connect to your local Ollama instance, giving you AI-powered coding assistance without sending your code to external services. It's the perfect setup for experimentation, development, and scenarios where data privacy is paramount.

Next, we'll scale up to managed cloud deployment, where we trade some of this simplicity for enterprise features and production reliability.

Example 2: Managed deployment on Amazon Bedrock

AWS offers multiple paths for DeepSeek deployment. As of March 2025, DeepSeek-R1 is available as a fully managed serverless model in Amazon Bedrock (`https://aws.amazon.com/blogs/aws/deepseek-r1-now-available-as-a-fully-managed-serverless-model-in-amazon-bedrock/`), providing the simplest deployment option with automatic scaling and pay-per-token pricing.

The goal here is to deploy any of the supported DeepSeek models (for example, R1 or V3) on Amazon Bedrock for enterprise-grade managed inference with AWS-native integration, security, and compliance features.

AWS provides three main approaches for running DeepSeek models:

- **Bedrock Serverless (simplest)**: Fully managed, no infrastructure to configure. You pay per token with no idle costs. Available for DeepSeek-R1 via the cross-region inference profile.

- **Bedrock Provisioned Throughput**: Reserved capacity for predictable workloads. Provides guaranteed performance but requires upfront commitment. Check regional availability, as not all models support this mode.
- **AWS Marketplace + SageMaker**: Deploy the model yourself with full control. This path requires requesting quota increases for large GPU instances (such as `ml.p5en.48xlarge` with H100s). You manage the infrastructure but gain maximum flexibility.

Rather than providing step-by-step instructions that will inevitably become outdated, navigate to the Amazon Bedrock console in your AWS account. The console provides the most current deployment wizards and will guide you through the following:

- **Model access**: Some models require explicit opt-in via the **Model access** section.
- **Quota verification**: Check service quotas for either Bedrock (requests per minute) or SageMaker (GPU instances), depending on your deployment path.
- **Guardrails configuration**: Optional content filtering for production deployments.
- **IAM setup**: Role-based access control for your applications.

For the Marketplace option, be prepared to request significant quota increases; DeepSeek-V3 and R1 require multiple high-end GPUs even when quantized.

Regardless of your deployment path, you'll need to make several important decisions when deploying with AWS:

- **API choice**: AWS offers multiple inference APIs. The **Converse API** provides a consistent interface across models with built-in token usage metrics. The **InvokeModel API** uses model-specific schemas but may offer lower latency. Hence, the choice depends on your application's need for standardization versus performance.
- **Timeout configuration**: DeepSeek-R1's reasoning can be extensive. Thus, you need to configure client timeouts to at least 300 seconds.
- **Cost controls**: Always set `maxTokens` limits. R1 can generate very long reasoning chains, potentially consuming thousands of tokens per request.
- **Private networking**: For sensitive workloads, configure VPC endpoints to keep traffic within AWS. Even with AWS's managed services, you'll encounter some common challenges:
    - **Model access denied**: Check the Bedrock console under **Model access**. Some models require explicit opt-in even with correct IAM permissions. Approval times vary from instant to 48 hours, depending on your account standing.

    - **Throttling errors**: Bedrock enforces per-model rate limits (requests and tokens per minute). Implement exponential backoff with jitter.
    - **Quota issues**: For Marketplace deployments, you'll need substantial GPU quotas. A single `ml.p5en.48xlarge` instance costs thousands per month. Request increases well in advance; AWS may take days to approve large GPU allocations.
    - **Long inference times**: R1's reasoning depth varies dramatically. Simple questions might return in seconds while complex problems take minutes. Implement streaming responses for a better user experience.
- **Cost surprises**: Without proper limits, a single runaway request can generate thousands of dollars in charges. Monitor CloudWatch metrics and set billing alerts at multiple thresholds (50%, 80%, and 100% of budget). Before production deployment, you need to validate that your chosen path meets your SLOs:
    - **TTFT**: Critical for user experience. R1 can have a high TTFT due to reasoning phases.
    - **Tokens per second**: Varies significantly based on deployment type and instance size.
    - **p95 latency**: More meaningful than average latency for capacity planning
- **Concurrent request handling**: Test at expected load levels; performance degrades non-linearly. Consider running load tests at different times of day, as shared infrastructure can have variable performance.

What this teaches

Amazon Bedrock demonstrates the cloud provider approach to LLM deployment: deep integration with existing services (IAM, CloudWatch, and VPC) at the cost of vendor lock-in and premium pricing. The serverless option eliminates operational overhead entirely – no instances to manage, no scale-to-zero to configure, just API calls and bills.

The key trade-off is control versus convenience. Bedrock serverless gives you zero control over the underlying infrastructure, but also zero responsibility. The Marketplace path gives you full control but requires expertise in GPU instance management, model optimization, and capacity planning.

For teams already invested in AWS, Bedrock's integration advantages often outweigh the premium pricing. Native CloudWatch metrics, IAM policies that your security team already understands, and VPC endpoints that work with existing network configurations reduce the hidden costs of adoption.

The rapid evolution of AWS's AI services means that specific features and pricing will change, but the fundamental pattern remains: AWS will continue to offer both fully managed and self-managed options, with price points that reflect the operational complexity you're willing to accept.

Next, we'll explore Hugging Face Inference Endpoints, which offer a middle ground between full self-management and complete abstraction.

Example 3: Deployment of DeepSeek V3 to the cloud using Hugging Face Inference Endpoints

Hugging Face Inference Endpoints allows you to control choosing your hardware and region, but Hugging Face handles the orchestration complexity. For DeepSeek-V3, this abstraction is particularly valuable; the model requires 8x NVIDIA H200 GPUs just to load, let alone serve efficiently.

Before we dive in, let's talk numbers.

If you deploy DeepSeek yourself, be prepared to spend approximately ~$40 per hour for an 8× H200 setup on common managed providers (Together AI publicly quotes ≈$0.67/min ≈ $40.2/h); Hugging Face Inference Endpoints pricing varies by region/plan/provider. That's about $960 per day if you leave the inference endpoint running continuously – still substantial.

Therefore, always go for a scale-to-zero feature (where supported) to manage your costs during idle periods.

To deploy via a HuggingFace API, you'll need the following:

- A Hugging Face account with API access.
- An API token with write permission.
- Budget approval (double-check account spending limits.)

The cleanest approach uses the Hugging Face Python SDK. Here's the complete deployment script:

```
from huggingface_hub import create_inference_endpoint

# Create the endpoint with production-ready configuration
endpoint = create_inference_endpoint(
    name="deepseek-v3-prod",
    repository="deepseek-ai/DeepSeek-V3",
    framework="pytorch",
    task="text-generation",
    accelerator="gpu",
    vendor="aws",
```

```
    region="us-east-2",
    type="protected",  # Requires auth for access
    instance_size="x8",
    instance_type="nvidia-h200",
```

This first section defines the endpoint's identity, model, and infrastructure: we target DeepSeek-V3 on 8x H200 GPUs in `us-east-2` with a `protected` (auth required) endpoint. These base settings establish where the model runs and who can access it before we layer on scaling and serving details.

Auto-scaling settings control cost and availability: `min_replica=0` enables scale-to-zero when idle (where supported), while `max_replica=1` caps spend during initial testing. Increase these later if you need higher concurrency:

```
# Auto-scaling configuration
    min_replica=0,  # Enable automatic scaletozero when idle (if
supported)
    max_replica=1,  # Single replica for cost control
    # Note: HF Endpoints typically trigger scaletozero after ~15 min of
idle; perendpoint 60 s timeouts are not generally supported.
```

We pin a TGI container and tune serving limits (prefill, input, and total tokens) to keep large model requests within memory while maximizing throughput. `MODEL_ID` points the container at the mounted repository for weight loading:

```
# Custom TGI container for optimized serving
    custom_image={
        "health_route": "/health",
        "url": "ghcr.io/huggingface/text-generation-inference:3.3.1",
        "env": {
            # TGI optimizations for large models
            "MAX_BATCH_PREFILL_TOKENS": "16384",
            "MAX_INPUT_LENGTH": "32768",
            "MAX_TOTAL_TOKENS": "65536",
            "MODEL_ID": "/repository"
        }
    }
)
```

Deployment typically takes 10–15 minutes as images pull and weights load into GPUs; `wait()` provides a clean blocking flow with a bounded timeout. On failure, `fetch()` helps you inspect partial states for quick debugging.

To monitor deployment progress, you can do the following:

```
print(f"Initial status: {endpoint.status}")
print("Waiting for deployment (this typically takes 10-15 minutes)...")

try:
    endpoint.wait(timeout=1200)  # 20 minute timeout
    print(f"✓ Deployment successful!")
    print(f"Endpoint URL: {endpoint.url}")
    print(f"Status: {endpoint.status}")
except Exception as e:
    print(f"✓ Deployment failed: {e}")
    # Check if partial deployment occurred
    endpoint.fetch()
    print(f"Current status: {endpoint.status}")
```

For CI/CD pipelines or environments where Python isn't available, the REST API works equally well to help you monitor your deployment :

```
#!/bin/bash

# Configuration
HF_TOKEN="${HF_TOKEN:-your-token-here}"
HF_USERNAME="${HF_USERNAME:-your-username}"
ENDPOINT_NAME="deepseek-v3-prod"
```

These variables supply your organization's context and credentials to the Hugging Face Endpoints API. Ensure that `HF_TOKEN` has `write` scope and matches the target account/space.

This request creates the endpoint and mirrors the Python SDK fields: model, serving image, token limits, hardware, and scaling. Some fields are provider-specific (e.g., scaling semantics), so omit or adjust them if your region or plan doesn't support a given option:

```
# Deploy via curl with proper error handling
# Note: some scaling fields (e.g., "scaleToZeroTimeout") are provider-
specific; omit them if unsupported.
```

```
RESPONSE=$(curl -s -w "\n%{http_code}" \
  "https://api.endpoints.huggingface.cloud/v2/endpoint/${HF_USERNAME}" \
  -X POST \
  -H "Content-Type: application/json" \
  -H "Authorization: Bearer ${HF_TOKEN}" \
  -d '{
    "name": "'"${ENDPOINT_NAME}"'",
    "type": "protected",

    "model": {
      "repository": "deepseek-ai/DeepSeek-V3",
      "framework": "pytorch",
      "task": "text-generation",
      "fromCatalog": false,

      "image": {
        "tgi": {
          "url": "ghcr.io/huggingface/text-generation-inference:3.3.1",
          "healthRoute": "/health"
        }
      },

      "env": {
        "MAX_BATCH_PREFILL_TOKENS": "16384",
        "MAX_INPUT_LENGTH": "32768",
        "MAX_TOTAL_TOKENS": "65536"
      }
    },

    "compute": {
      "accelerator": "gpu",
      "instanceType": "nvidia-h200",
      "instanceSize": "x8",

      "scaling": {
        "minReplica": 0,
        "maxReplica": 1,
        "metric": "hardwareUsage",
```

```
        "measure": {
          "hardwareUsage": 80
        }
      }
    },

    "provider": {
      "vendor": "aws",
      "region": "us-east-2"
    }
  }')
```

We parse the HTTP status and JSON body to surface a clear success/failure signal in CI logs. A `200` code indicates the deployment was accepted; otherwise, the error payload helps pinpoint missing access, quota, or invalid field issues:

```
# Parse response
HTTP_CODE=$(echo "$RESPONSE" | tail -n1)
BODY=$(echo "$RESPONSE" | sed '$d')

if [ "$HTTP_CODE" -eq 200 ]; then
    echo "✓ Deployment initiated successfully"
    echo "$BODY" | jq -r '.status'
else
    echo "✗ Deployment failed with HTTP $HTTP_CODE"
    echo "$BODY" | jq -r '.error // .'
fi
```

For teams using ZenML for MLOps orchestration, the deployment integrates seamlessly into existing pipelines:

```
from zenml import pipeline
from zenml.config import DockerSettings
from zenml.integrations.constants import HUGGINGFACE
from zenml.integrations.huggingface.services import
HuggingFaceServiceConfig
from zenml.integrations.huggingface.steps import (
    huggingface_model_deployer_step,
)
```

ZenML packages the Hugging Face integration and container settings so your deployment runs reproducibly in pipelines. This keeps endpoint creation, retries, and metadata tracking under a single, versioned workflow:

```
docker_settings = DockerSettings(
    required_integrations=[HUGGINGFACE],
)

@pipeline(enable_cache=True, settings={"docker": docker_settings})
def deepseek_deployment_pipeline(
    model_name: str = "deepseek-v3",
    timeout: int = 1200,
):
    # Configure with production settings
    service_config = HuggingFaceServiceConfig(
        model_name=model_name,
        endpoint_name="deepseek-v3-prod",  # Gets zenml- prefix + UUID
        repository="deepseek-ai/DeepSeek-V3",
        framework="pytorch",
        task="text-generation",
        accelerator="gpu",
        instance_type="nvidia-h200",
        instance_size="x8",
        vendor="aws",
        region="us-east-2",
        endpoint_type="protected",
        min_replica=0,
        max_replica=1,
        custom_image={
            "health_route": "/health",
            "url": "ghcr.io/huggingface/text-generation-inference:3.3.1"
        }
    )

    # Deploy with automatic retry logic
    deployment = huggingface_model_deployer_step(
        service_config=service_config,
        timeout=timeout,
```

```
    )

    return deployment
```

The service_config mirrors the SDK parameters (model, hardware, region, scaling, and image) and becomes the source of truth for the endpoint spec. Treat it like infrastructure as code; review diffs before promoting to production.

```
# Run the pipeline
if __name__ == "__main__":
    deepseek_deployment_pipeline()
```

This step triggers the actual endpoint creation with built-in retry and returns a service handle you can inspect later. Downstream steps can poll the handle for status, URL, and health to gate release checks:

1. **Verification and first inference**: Once deployed, verify that the endpoint is accessible and perform a test inference:

    ```
    # Test the deployed endpoint
    def test_endpoint(endpoint):
        """Verify endpoint functionality with a simple prompt."""
        try:
            response = endpoint.client.text_generation(
                "Explain containerization in three sentences.",
                max_new_tokens=100,
                temperature=0.7
            )
            print(f"✓ Inference successful: {response[:50]}...")
            return True
        except Exception as e:
            print(f"✗ Inference failed: {e}")
            return False

    # For production use
    def create_production_client(endpoint_name: str):
        """Create a client for production inference."""
        from huggingface_hub import get_inference_endpoint

        endpoint = get_inference_endpoint(endpoint_name)
    ```

```
    if endpoint.status == "scaledToZero":
        print("Endpoint is scaled to zero, waking up...")
        # First request will trigger wake-up

    return endpoint.client
```

2. **Monitoring and cost management:** The scale-to-zero mechanism helps, but note that on Hugging Face Inference Endpoints, it's opt-in and typically kicks in after ~15 minutes of idle time. Monitor it closely:

```
# Check endpoint status and costs
def monitor_endpoint(endpoint_name: str):
    from huggingface_hub import get_inference_endpoint

    endpoint = get_inference_endpoint(endpoint_name)
    endpoint.fetch()  # Refresh status

    print(f"Status: {endpoint.status}")
    print(f"URL: {endpoint.url}")
    print(f"Created: {endpoint.created_at}")
    print(f"Updated: {endpoint.updated_at}")

    # Estimate daily cost based on status
    hourly_cost = 40  # $40/hour for 8x H200 replica
    if endpoint.status == "running":
        print(f"Running cost: ${hourly_cost}/hour (${hourly_cost *
24}/day)")
    elif endpoint.status == "scaledToZero":
        print("✓ Scaled to zero - no compute charges")
```

3. **Teardown and cleanup:** When you're done, clean up to avoid surprise bills:

```
# Graceful shutdown
endpoint.scale_to_zero()  # Immediate scale down
# or
endpoint.pause()  # Complete pause, requires manual resume
# or
endpoint.delete()  # Permanent deletion - careful!
```

What this teaches

This deployment showcases several production patterns:

- **Hardware abstraction**: You specified the hardware (8x H200) without managing the underlying infrastructure.
- **Cost optimization**: Scale-to-zero prevents runaway bills during idle periods.
- **Container customization**: The TGI container provides optimizations specific to large model serving.
- **Security by default**: Protected endpoints require authentication, preventing unauthorized access.

The trade-offs are clear: at $40/hour, Hugging Face's managed infrastructure is competitive with AWS capacity blocks (~$36/hour) and significantly cheaper than on-demand pricing (~$65-70/hour). You're getting automatic scaling, monitoring, and updates without the DevOps overhead.

Some of the operational considerations you should be aware of are the following:

- **Cold starts matter**: After scaling to zero, the first request takes 2–3 minutes as the model loads into GPU memory. Design your application accordingly.
- **Regional availability**: H200s aren't available in all regions. Check availability before committing to a specific geography.
- **Batch for efficiency**: With such expensive hardware, batch your requests when possible. The TGI server handles concurrent requests efficiently.
- **Monitor token usage**: At this scale, even efficient models can generate costs quickly. Implement token limits in your application logic.

These examples get you up and running. Sustaining reliability, performance, and cost requires operational practices (monitoring, scaling, and governance), which we will address next.

Production operations and monitoring

The model is deployed. The first requests are flowing. Now comes the hard part: keeping it running reliably, efficiently, and securely at scale. This section distills the operational wisdom that separates proofs-of-concept from production systems.

Monitoring and observability

LLMs run on costly GPUs; visibility is essential for reliability and spend control. The metrics that matter fall into four categories:

- **Token counts directly translate to costs.** Track both prompt and completion tokens per request. Most providers return this in response metadata: OpenAI-compatible APIs expose `prompt_tokens` and `completion_tokens` usage; Amazon Bedrock Converse reports `inputTokenCount`/`outputTokenCount`; and Vertex AI includes `usageMetadata.promptTokenCount`/`outputTokenCount`. For self-hosted engines (vLLM/TGI), expose usage and Prometheus metrics from the server (token counters for prompt/generated tokens), and optionally validate by counting with the model's tokenizer on the client side. This isn't just for billing; sudden spikes often reveal inefficient prompts or, worse, prompt injection attempts. When you see a token spike, first ask a simple question: Did the prompt get bigger, or did the answer get longer? A step change in prompt tokens usually means a template or RAG change (more retrieved passages, different chunking), whereas a surge in completion tokens often points to jailbreaks or *runaway* reasoning where the model keeps thinking and hits length limits. If total tokens per minute soar while tokens per request look normal across many users, you're probably seeing a usage surge; if the spike comes from a small cohort with duplicate requests and more, it's a retry loop or client bug. Treat the spike like a diff: compare prompts before and after, enable prefix caching if common headers grew, cap max tokens to tame long answers, and tighten retrieval settings if inputs ballooned.
- **Latency distributions** tell you how users experience your service. For DeepSeek-R1, TTFT can vary wildly depending on how deeply the model decides to reason, making p95 latency a better SLO metric than averages.
- **GPU utilization** deserves special attention. When vLLM reports that KV cache usage is approaching capacity, you're about to hit a performance cliff. The model doesn't gracefully degrade; it falls off a cliff. Think of throughput as a highway and the KV cache as your lanes; as the cache fills and fragments, cars still enter, but everything slows at once – tokens per second drop, queues lengthen, and both TTFT and p95 rise together. That synchronized jump is the cliff: you've crossed a capacity edge where evictions and smaller effective batches cause non-linear collapse. The fastest way back from the brink is to shrink what each request demands (lower max context or total tokens), reduce concurrent sequences, or temporarily shed low-priority traffic; the durable fix is more headroom (larger VRAM or cache), better batching, and higher cache hit rates via shared prefixes or KV reuse.

Use vLLM's Prometheus metrics to track cache pressure and throughput (e.g., tokens/sec, `vllm:num_requests_running`, running vs. waiting requests) and alert before KV cache utilization approaches your capacity threshold (e.g., ~90%).

- The fourth category is **cost tracking.** Join your token metrics with current pricing tables and calculate dollars per request in real time. When that number jumps 50% week-over-week, something changed – maybe a new prompt template, or maybe a regression in your caching layer.

  For production deployments, vLLM's `/metrics` endpoint provides Prometheus-compatible observability out of the box. Export these to your time-series database of choice. Add a Prometheus `scrape_config` (or a Kubernetes `ServiceMonitor`) that targets `http://YOUR_VLLM_HOST:8000/metrics` and, if you use an external backend, enable `remote_write` to your time-series database (e.g., Thanos, Cortex, or VictoriaMetrics) so you can visualize the metrics in Grafana. Grafana dashboards include pre-built visualizations specifically for vLLM deployments.

Ultimately, metrics only tell you what happened, not why. For root cause analysis, you need request-level visibility. Tools such as Langfuse provide automatic **Personally Identifiable Information (PII)** redaction while maintaining enough context for debugging those inevitable *the model said what?* incidents.

Scaling and performance

DeepSeek models present a fascinating scaling challenge. Unlike traditional web services, where you can just spin up more replicas, LLM scaling requires understanding the interplay between model architecture, hardware topology, and request patterns.

The naive approach (treating your model service like any other stateless application) fails spectacularly. Here's why: every request builds up KV cache state that can be reused for similar prompts. Randomly distributing requests across replicas destroys this cache locality. Implement sticky session routing based on user or conversation ID. This simple change can improve throughput by 40% in conversational workloads.

For DeepSeek-V3's MoE, only a small subset of experts (typically two per layer) is active per token. In practice, many serving stacks keep all experts resident across the serving pool to minimize cross-node routing; however, this is not a hard requirement. You can shard experts across GPUs/nodes (expert parallelism) or offload some experts to CPU/NVMe, trading additional all-to-all communication and higher latency for lower per-node memory.

Consequently, horizontal scaling can take two forms: replicas that duplicate the full 671B parameter set to increase concurrency, or capacity scaling via expert-parallel sharding that grows the total expert pool without duplicating all weights on every machine.

Choose based on your latency budget and interconnect; with slower interconnects, fewer, larger nodes with NVLink/NVSwitch often outperform many small instances. Operators can enforce this manually by provisioning larger NVLink/NVSwitch nodes and constraining placement (e.g., Kubernetes node pools with `nodeSelector/affinity` and taints/tolerations, or explicit GPU pinning on bare metal) while limiting horizontal autoscaling for that service.

Performance optimization in production is an exercise in finding bottlenecks and eliminating them systematically. Here is how you can achieve optimization:

1. **Start with continuous batching**: Traditional serving processes requests sequentially; continuous batching dynamically groups requests to maximize GPU utilization. A key parameter here is `--max-num-seqs`, which controls the maximum number of sequences (requests) vLLM can process concurrently. Setting this value correctly is a critical balancing act between throughput and memory stability. Too low, and you leave performance on the table during traffic spikes; too high, and you risk catastrophic **out-of-memory (OOM)** errors.

   The ideal value depends directly on your available VRAM after the model weights have been loaded. You can estimate a safe starting point with the following logic:

   Let's consider two practical scenarios:

   - **Scenario 1: High-throughput chatbot**: You're running a 33B model (quantized to INT4, ~19 GB) on a single 80 GB H100 GPU. Your workload consists of many concurrent users with short conversation turns (average sequence length of 512 tokens):
     - **VRAM allocation**: 80 GB total – 19 GB for the model ≈ 61 GB available. Reserving 10% for overhead leaves ~55 GB for the KV cache.
     - **KV cache per sequence**: For a model of this size, the cache is roughly 25 KB/token. So, 512 tokens * 25 KB/token ≈ 12.8 MB per sequence.
     - **Calculation**: 55,000 MB / 12.8 MB ≈ 4,296. This theoretical maximum is unrealistic due to memory fragmentation.

    - **Practical value**: A safe starting value for `--max-num-seqs` would be `256` (a common default). After load testing and monitoring KV cache usage under real traffic, you might carefully increase it toward `512` or `1024` to maximize throughput.

- **Scenario 2: Long-context document analysis**: You're serving a 70B model (BF16, ~140 GB) on a 4x A100-80 GB node (320 GB total VRAM). The workload involves fewer concurrent requests but with very long documents (average sequence length of 16,384 tokens):
    - **VRAM allocation**: 320 GB total – 140 GB for the model ≈ 180 GB available. Reserving 10% for overhead leaves ~162 GB for the KV cache.
    - **KV cache per sequence**: For a 70B model, the cache is roughly 80 KB/token. So, 16,384 tokens * 80 KB/token ≈ 1.31 GB per sequence.
    - **Calculation**: 162 GB / 1.31 GB ≈ 123 sequences.
    - **Practical value**: Given the high memory pressure per request, starting with a much more conservative `--max-num-seqs` value of `32` is prudent. Based on stability during testing, you might increase it to `64`, but exceeding this would significantly raise the risk of OOM errors for this workload.

The best practice is to calculate a conservative baseline, then empirically tune the value upward while monitoring your GPU memory and KV cache usage via vLLM's Prometheus metrics endpoint.

2. **Caching is your secret weapon**: You can implement a two-tier strategy. The first tier, **KV caching**, is a fundamental part of how Transformer models generate text and is automatically handled by modern inference engines such as vLLM. There isn't a flag to *turn on* KV caching; it's the core process that prevents the model from recomputing calculations for every token in the context window each time a new token is generated. You manage its memory impact indirectly through parameters such as context length.

   The second tier is explicit **prompt prefix caching**, which you can enable for workloads with repetitive starting text. In vLLM, you activate this feature by launching the server with the `--enable-prefix-caching` flag. When enabled, vLLM automatically detects when multiple requests share a common prefix (such as a system prompt or a set of few-shot examples). It computes the KV state for that prefix only once, on the first request, and then stores it. All subsequent requests that begin with that exact same prefix reuse the cached state, skipping the expensive recomputation. This is how system prompts and templates can be cached indefinitely, significantly speeding up the prefill stage for common tasks. Cache hit rates above 60% typically reduce latency by a third and can cut costs proportionally.

3. **Thinking costs**: For R1 models, you face a unique decision: how much thinking is too much? In latency-sensitive applications, consider implementing reasoning truncation. Monitor the distribution of reasoning token counts and set limits based on your SLAs. Yes, you might sacrifice some accuracy, but users prefer fast, good-enough responses over perfect answers that arrive too late.

With scaling, caching, and thinking bounded, the next step is to make these legible in actual dollar or euro amounts: how tokens, cache hit rate, and GPU utilization translate into cost per request and cost per user.

Cost management

LLM costs have a nasty habit of exponential growth. Unlike traditional infrastructure, where costs scale linearly with traffic, LLM costs can explode based on prompt design, model selection, or user behavior patterns. A single prompt template change can triple your bills overnight.

Here is a pragmatic cost management approach you can try:

1. Start with request-level budgeting. Every request should carry a cost estimate based on expected token usage. Reject requests exceeding per-user or per-endpoint budgets before they hit the model. This isn't just about preventing abuse; it's about catching configuration errors before they drain your bank account.

   To apply this, implement the check in your API gateway or in a middleware layer before the request hits your inference service. For each incoming request, calculate `max_potential_cost` by multiplying the `max_tokens` parameter by the cost per output token, and add the cost of the input tokens. Store per-user or per-key daily/monthly budgets in a fast-access database such as Redis. The middleware then performs a simple check:

   ```
   if
   (user_current_spend + max_potential_cost > user_budget) { return
   429_BUDGET_EXCEEDED; }
   ```

   This precomputation step is cheap and effectively ring-fences your model from costly requests.

2. Infrastructure efficiency requires a different lens. Kubecost's GPU module reveals the brutal truth: that 8-GPU cluster you provisioned might be sitting 40% idle. At $2.48 per H100-hour, idle time becomes a luxury you can't afford. But don't just look at averages – graph utilization over time. Predictable patterns (low usage nights and weekends) suggest you need autoscaling. Random spikes might indicate batch job scheduling issues.
3. Practically, you can achieve this on Kubernetes by using the NVIDIA DCGM Exporter (`https://github.com/NVIDIA/dcgm-exporter`) to expose GPU metrics to Prometheus. Then, create a Grafana dashboard with a panel showing `avg(dcgm_gpu_utilization) by (pod)`. For autoscaling, configure KEDA with a Prometheus scaler. Your `ScaledObject` definition would target a metric such as `sum(rate(vllm_requests_running[2m]))`, allowing you to scale your replicas based on actual inference load rather than just CPU or memory, which are often poor proxies for GPU work.
4. The most insidious cost creep comes from model drift. You deploy a nice, efficient 33B parameter model. Six months later, you're somehow running the 70B variant in production, and nobody remembers why. Track cost-per-output-token by model version and alert on changes. A 20% week-over-week increase deserves investigation; 50% demands immediate action.
5. To implement this, ensure that every inference log includes `model_id`, `input_tokens`, and `completion_tokens`. In your logging platform (such as Datadog or the ELK stack), create a metric by enriching these logs with a price lookup table (e.g., `deepseek-v3_input_cost = $0.27/M_tokens`). You can then build a dashboard that visualizes `sum(request_cost) / count(requests)` grouped by `model_id`. Set up an automated monitor that compares the weekly average of this metric to the previous week and triggers an alert if the percentage change exceeds a defined threshold.
6. Budget alerts should escalate geometrically. Set them at 50%, 80%, and 100% of your budget. The 50% alert is informational. With this alert, its time for you to check whether growth is expected. The 80% alert pages on-call is an indication that something needs attention. The 100% alert should trigger automatic throttling. Better to degrade service than wake up to a six-figure cloud bill.
7. You can set this up using your cloud provider's native tools. In AWS, for example, create an AWS budget with three alert thresholds. The 50% action can be an SNS notification to a Slack channel for visibility. The 80% action can be an SNS notification that triggers a PagerDuty or Opsgenie webhook. For the 100% action, have SNS trigger a Lambda function that programmatically modifies your API Gateway usage plan to a highly restricted

throttle limit (e.g., one request per minute) or updates a feature flag in AWS AppConfig to disable the service gracefully.

With spend guardrails in place (budgets, alerts, and automated throttles), the next question is resilience: how do we prevent those same controls from being bypassed by abuse, prompt injection, or data exfiltration? The good news is that the primitives you just set up (gateways, usage plans, and feature flags) double as enforcement points for security.

Security in practice

LLMs introduce security challenges that traditional application security playbooks don't address. Some of the challenges you may encounter are as follows:

- Prompt injection is a real thing that actually happens.
- Rate limiting by request count prevents the user from sending 100k-token prompts.
- Standard authentication might not account for the cost differential between users asking for haikus versus dissertations.

Network security remains foundational but insufficient. Therefore, you need to deploy models in private subnets, front them with API gateways, and use mTLS between services (i.e., all the standard practices of network security apply). But you need to add LLM-specific controls too:

1. Input validation must check not just for SQL injection but also for prompt injection patterns. Validate against an allowlist first: enforce strict schemas (expected JSON keys/types), length and `charset` caps, and reject control tokens. Then, run inputs through a prompt injection filter that combines simple rules (regex for phrases such as *ignore previous instructions*, *reveal system prompt*, jailbreak markers, and Unicode homoglyphs) with an embedding similarity check against known attack examples; block or challenge high-risk requests and emit tagged logs to your centralized log store.
2. Output filtering needs to catch not just PII but also jailbreak attempts.
3. The unique challenge with DeepSeek models is their capability. A model smart enough to reason through complex problems is smart enough to be creatively misused. Implement semantic similarity checks on prompts, comparing against known jailbreak patterns. Common patterns include instruction overrides (*ignore previous instructions*, *reveal/repeat the system prompt*), Do Anything Now (DAN)/developer mode role play, translation/encoding wrappers (Base64/ROT13), JSON/Markdown fence escapes, and *for research/simulation* requests that elicit disallowed content. Seed your similarity index with public references such as OWASP's LLM Top 10 examples (`https://owasp.org/www-project-top-10-for-`

large-language-model-applications/), PromptBench attack sets (https://github.com/microsoft/promptbench), and sample jailbreaks from NVIDIA NeMo Guardrails (https://github.com/NVIDIA/NeMo-Guardrails). But don't rely solely on blocklists; they're always one creative prompt behind. Instead, implement defense in depth: rate limit by token count, not just request count. Monitor for unusual token consumption patterns and track prompt complexity metrics.

4. For sensitive deployments, consider the full kill chain. An attacker might not directly compromise your model but could use it to probe your infrastructure. Monitor for prompts asking about system configuration, internal details, or error messages. Implement server-side prompt inspection by routing all requests through an API gateway or middleware that logs prompts and runs a lightweight classifier (regex rules or a local LLM) to flag "recon" intents such as asking for system prompts, environment variables, stack traces, file paths, or IPs. Forward these tagged events to your centralized log store (e.g., CloudWatch, Datadog, or Splunk) with alerts on high-risk matches or spikes per user/session, and pair with token-based rate limits plus automatic challenge/deny rules for repeated hits. These reconnaissance attempts often precede more serious attacks.

CI/CD for models

Model deployment isn't a one-time event – it's an ongoing process. New versions promise better performance, security patches demand immediate deployment, and that fine-tuned variant finally proves its worth in testing. Without proper CI/CD, model updates become high-stress events that everyone avoids.

Here is an action plan that can get you started:

1. Start with versioning discipline. Even though DeepSeek publishes model versions, what you actually ship is a composite artifact; it's the base model revision plus your quantization, tokenizer, adapters/LoRAs, prompt templates, decoding limits, safety filters, inference engine/container, and config. Version so you can reproduce behavior, roll back safely, satisfy audits, and A/B test changes; the vendor model version alone will not explain behavioral or cost deltas in production. All of which is to say: models aren't just files – they're artifacts with dependencies, configurations, and behavioral contracts. Use a model registry (MLflow or cloud-native options) that tracks not just the weights but the entire deployment context. When something breaks, you need to know exactly what changed.

To put this into practice, adopt a concrete versioning scheme for your composite artifact that is both human-readable and machine-parseable – for example, `[base-model-version]-[quantization]-[adapters-hash]-[config-version]`, which might look like `deepseek-v3-b1.0-int4-lora-abc123-v2`. Here, `abc123` could be the short Git commit hash from the repository where your LoRA was trained, and `v2` refers to the version of your decoding configuration file. This creates an unambiguous identifier for the exact artifact running in production.

2. A model registry, such as MLflow, is where you bring this all together. Your CI pipeline, triggered by a commit, should package these components and log them to a single MLflow run. Use `mlflow.log_artifact()` to store your tokenizer configuration, prompt template files, and safety filter scripts. Use `mlflow.log_param()` to record KV metadata such as `quantization_method: AWQ` or `base_model_id: "deepseek-ai/DeepSeek-V3"`.
3. Finally, register that entire run as a new version of a model named, for instance, `"production-chat-endpoint"`. Now, when you compare version 1.2.0 to 1.3.0 in the MLflow UI, you see not just a new model file but a precise diff of every dependency and configuration change that could explain a shift in behavior or cost.
4. Blue-green deployments work beautifully for models. Spin up the new version alongside the old, validate with synthetic traffic, then gradually shift real users. The key insight is, don't just test functional correctness. Monitor latency, token usage, and cost metrics during the canary phase. A model that's 2% more accurate but 50% more expensive might not be an upgrade.

In a Kubernetes environment, you can implement this with a service mesh such as Istio or Linkerd, or an API gateway such as Emissary-ingress. The pattern involves creating two Kubernetes Deployments: one for the old model version (e.g., `deepseek-v1`) and one for the new canary version (`deepseek-v2`). A single Kubernetes Service object targets both deployments. You then configure a routing rule (such as an Istio VirtualService) to initially direct 100% of traffic to `v1`:

1. Your CI/CD pipeline (e.g., using GitHub Actions or GitLab CI) automates the traffic shift. The first step in the rollout job applies a new routing rule that sends just 1% of traffic to `v2`. The pipeline then pauses and queries your observability platform (e.g., Prometheus) for key metrics, comparing the `v1` and `v2` deployments side by side on a Grafana dashboard. If the p95 latency, token usage, and calculated cost-per-request for `v2` remain within acceptable limits for a set period (say, 15 minutes), the pipeline automatically proceeds to increase the traffic weight to 10%, then 50%, and finally 100%, completing the rollout.

2. Rollback capability isn't optional. Keep the previous model version warm and ready. When metrics go sideways, you need one-click rollback, not a frantic redeployment process. This means accepting the infrastructure cost of running two versions temporarily. Consider it insurance.

   This one-click rollback is the emergency brake in your deployment pipeline. It's not a new deployment; it's a configuration change that instantly reroutes traffic. If your canary monitoring dashboard shows a critical metric regression, such as a spike in harmful content generation or a sudden doubling of latency, you trigger the rollback. In your CI/CD tool, this should be a manually triggered job that executes a single `kubectl apply` or API call to your service mesh, updating the traffic routing rule to send 100% of traffic back to the stable, previously running version. The entire rollback process should take seconds, not minutes.

3. Keeping the previous version *warm* means the Kubernetes Deployment for the old model maintains its full replica count throughout the canary phase. It's actively running and ready to instantly absorb 100% of the production load. The insurance cost is tangible: if a single model replica costs you $5 per hour and you run two replicas for high availability, your cost temporarily increases from $10/hour to $20/hour during the rollout. Once the new version is fully promoted and deemed stable (e.g., after 24 hours), your pipeline's final step should automatically scale the old deployment's replica count down to zero, eliminating the extra cost.
4. The testing pyramid for models looks different from traditional software. Unit tests verify prompt formatting and response parsing. Integration tests confirm that the model loads and responds. But the critical layer is behavioral testing: does this model maintain the safety boundaries of the previous version? Does it handle edge cases consistently? Build a golden dataset of prompts and expected behaviors, and gate deployments on regression tests.

   Practically, these tests should run as stages in your CI pipeline. Unit tests are fast checks run on every commit. Using a framework such as `pytest`, you can write a simple function to verify a prompt template: `assert "User:" in format_prompt(history, query)`. Another test can confirm that your response parser handles expected formats and raises specific errors for malformed JSON: `pytest.raises(MalformedJsonError): parse_response("{'invalid': 'json'}")`. These tests catch logic errors before a model is even loaded.

5. Integration tests run after the container is built. Your pipeline spins up the model container and uses a tool such as `curl` to hit its health check endpoint and then its inference endpoint with a simple `"hello"` prompt. The test just needs to assert a `200 OK` status and a valid response structure. This catches issues with dependencies, model loading, or environment configuration.
6. Behavioral regression testing is the final and most important gate before deployment. Your pipeline deploys the new model to a staging environment and runs a test suite against it. This suite iterates through your "golden dataset" (e.g., a `test_cases.jsonl` file in your Git repo). For each prompt, it asserts specific behaviors. For safety, you might assert that a harmful prompt results in a refusal: `assert "cannot comply" in response.lower()`. For consistency on critical tasks such as data extraction, you can compare the LLM's JSON output against a predefined schema. For more nuanced qualities such as tone or helpfulness, you can even use a smaller, cheaper *judge* LLM to evaluate the new model's response and flag any significant negative changes from the previous version's baseline response. A failure at this stage should automatically block the production rollout.

With monitoring, scaling, cost control, security, and CI/CD in place, your endpoint transitions from fragile demo to durable service. We will conclude with a compact playbook.

Your deployment playbook

You now have the complete deployment stack: from local development proxies to multi-GPU production clusters. The decision framework boils down to three constraints: data sensitivity, token volume, and operational capacity.

Here is your playbook:

1. **Quick reference for common scenarios:**
    - **Prototyping and development**: Use the DeepSeek API until you hit rate limits or cost concerns. Switch to local Ollama with smaller models for offline work. Don't optimize infrastructure before validating your use case.
    - **Production with sensitive data**: Start with managed services (Bedrock/Vertex) if they meet compliance requirements. Self-host only when managed options are legally or technically insufficient. Budget 2–3 months for the self-hosting learning curve.

- **High-volume production (>1B tokens/month)**: The math favors self-hosting, but only with dedicated DevOps resources. Run cost analysis, including staff time, not just GPU hours. Consider hybrid deployments: API for variable loads, self-hosted for baseline traffic.

2. **Common pitfalls to avoid**:
    - Deploying full DeepSeek-V3 without capacity planning (see the section on hardware and inference optimization engines for sizing guidance).
    - Ignoring scale-to-zero capabilities (difference between $40/hour and $0/hour when idle).
    - Treating R1's reasoning tokens as free (they count toward cost and latency).
    - Deploying without monitoring token usage (bills can increase 10x overnight from a prompt change).
3. **Implementation checklist**:
    - Implement request-level cost tracking.
    - Set budget alerts at 50%, 80%, and 100% thresholds
    - Cache system prompts and common prefixes (60%+ hit rate is achievable).
    - Use sticky routing for conversational workloads.
    - Keep the previous model version warm for instant rollback.

The ecosystem evolves rapidly. Today's 8×H200 requirement may be tomorrow's single-GPU deployment. Focus on building abstractions that survive infrastructure changes: standardize on OpenAI-compatible APIs, version all deployments, and maintain environment parity from development to production.

Here are some tips for engineers that may come in handy.

- **For junior engineers**: Start with *Example 1* (Ollama) in the *Hands-on deployment guides* section. Get comfortable with the request/response cycle and token economics before tackling cloud deployments.
- **For senior engineers**: Jump to *Example 3* (Hugging Face Inference Endpoints) for production deployment, but review the monitoring section. LLM observability differs from traditional services.
- **For platform teams**: Focus on the inference engine comparison and production operations guidance will accelerate your infrastructure decisions.

Remember

Deployment is a means to an end. Pick the simplest approach that meets your requirements, then iterate as you learn more about your actual usage patterns.

Summary

This chapter turned deployment from theory into a pragmatic playbook for running full-parameter DeepSeek-V3/R1 in production. You mapped the landscape (API vs. managed vs. DIY) with a control/cost/complexity lens, learned how to size hardware (VRAM, KV cache, TTFT/throughput), and chose inference engines deliberately (vLLM/TGI/TensorRT-LLM) with quantization options (FP8, GPTQ, and AWQ) to fit performance and budget. Three concrete paths anchored the guidance: local dev proxies (Ollama) for iteration, managed services (Bedrock/Vertex/Azure/Hugging Face) for enterprise reliability, and DIY (vLLM on GPUs/Kubernetes) for maximum control and economics at scale.

You then operationalized the service: monitor tokens/latency/GPU and KV pressure, scale on active generation with continuous batching and sticky routing, cache shared prefixes, and enforce token-based budgets with scale-to-zero and budget alerts. Security moved beyond network basics to prompt injection defenses and output filtering. Finally, you treated models as versioned, composite artifacts and shipped safely with blue-green/canary rollouts and instant rollback. With this toolkit, you can pick the simplest deployment that meets your constraints today and evolve it confidently as your workload grows.

9

Epilogue

The journey through this book traced the path from DeepSeek's foundational principles to its deployment in production-grade systems. We began with its disruptive market entry and concluded with the operational realities of running it at scale. This epilogue synthesizes that journey, connecting the core technical innovations to the practical skills required to leverage them.

The DeepSeek paradigm

DeepSeek's release marked a pivotal moment, demonstrating that an open-source model could achieve frontier performance in reasoning, directly challenging the dominance of proprietary systems. This was not an incremental improvement but a paradigm shift driven by a convergence of architectural and training innovations. The book first explored these technical foundations.

At its core, the *Mixture-of-Experts (MoE) architecture* enabled massive scale (over 600 billion parameters) while maintaining computational efficiency by activating only a fraction of the model per token. This was paired with *Multi-Head Latent Attention (MLA)*, which compresses the KV cache to make long-context understanding practical and memory-efficient.

The most significant breakthrough, however, was the training methodology. By prioritizing reinforcement learning with automated, rule-based rewards - encapsulated in techniques like *Group Relative Policy Optimization (GRPO)* - DeepSeek learned to generate structured, step-by-step reasoning without extensive supervised fine-tuning. This ability to *think* before answering became the model's defining characteristic and the central theme of its practical application.

From theory to practice

Understanding the architecture was only the first step. The subsequent chapters transitioned from *what* DeepSeek is to *how* to use it effectively. This required unlearning established prompting habits. We saw that DeepSeek's reasoning models behave less like chatbots and more like theorem provers, where minimalist, context-rich prompts outperform the detailed, few-shot examples that benefit other models.

Armed with this new mental model, we built a complete application, demonstrating the full spectrum of deployment from local CPU inference to managed cloud services. This practical exercise highlighted the critical importance of structured outputs for creating reliable and flexible systems. We then extended this to autonomous systems, exploring agentic patterns that decompose complex tasks, iteratively refine outputs, and interact with external tools.

The core lesson - DeepSeek is a powerful reasoning engine that, when properly harnessed, can automate complex analysis and decision-making.

The path to production

The final chapters addressed the ultimate goal: deploying DeepSeek in real-world business environments. We explored two distinct and powerful strategies for achieving this.

First, the *rationale distillation* workflow showed how to use DeepSeek-R1 not as the final product, but as a *teacher*. By generating explanatory rationales for a specialized domain like legal contract analysis, we created an enhanced dataset to train a smaller, more efficient student model. The result was a deployable model that was not only private and cost-effective but also significantly more accurate on its specialized task than its far larger teacher.

Second, for use cases requiring the full power of the complete models, we detailed the *deployment playbook for DeepSeek V3 and R1*. This involved navigating the critical trade-offs between cost, control, and complexity across APIs, managed services, and self-hosted infrastructure. From selecting the right GPU hardware and inference engine to implementing robust monitoring and security, we established a framework for making sound operational decisions.

The principles and patterns detailed in this book are durable. DeepSeek represents more than a single family of models; it provides a blueprint for an era of AI defined by powerful, accessible, and adaptable reasoning. The journey through its architecture, application, and deployment has equipped you with the essential skills to build the next generation of intelligent systems.

Appendix

It's time to understand the different ways we can use the DeepSeek models.

This appendix is skippable if you have already figured out how you want to use DeepSeek.

But if not, we'll show you some ways.

We will go over some of the (at the time of writing) most popular ways of running some of the main models released by the Chinese AI lab.

We will cover the following ways to use DeepSeek:

- Getting started with the official DeepSeek API
- Using common third-party APIs
- Working with Cursor's IDE for DeepSeek
- Running or deploying DeepSeek yourself
- Building your own setup for DeepSeek

Technical requirements

The following will need to be installed:

- Recall from *Chapter 5* that we will be using `uv` for Python examples when working with the DeepSeek API. If you don't have it installed yet, you can install `uv` by following the instructions here: `https://docs.astral.sh/uv/getting-started/installation/`.
- To run the terminal-based examples, we will use `curl`. To install `curl`, you can check the official website at `https://curl.se/`; alternatively, the `https://everything.curl.dev/install/index.html` website shows installation instructions for all major platforms.
- You will need to set up API keys to follow some of the examples, but we will walk through how to set them up in each example.
- All the code examples are properly documented here: `https://github.com/PacktPublishing/DeepSeek-in-Practice`.

Note

While we have used macOS, all of the code examples and instructions should work on all platforms. For Windows users, we advise using Windows Subsystem for Linux (`https://learn.microsoft.com/en-us/windows/wsl/install`).

Getting started with the official DeepSeek API

Like most AI labs and companies, DeepSeek has both a ChatGPT-like web application, hosted at `https://chat.deepseek.com/`, and an API platform, hosted at `https://platform.deepseek.com/`. This setup is common for most companies (including open source projects such as Qwen: `https://chat.qwen.ai/`). Notably, after the release of DeepSeek-R1 in January 2025, the API platform was suddenly hit by a massive cyberattack (`https://www.cnbc.com/2025/01/27/deepseek-hit-with-large-scale-cyberattack-says-its-limiting-registrations.html`). The platform has since gotten back up and running and is stable and a good option for those wanting to get started with building with DeepSeek.

The goal of this section is to give you a short introduction to DeepSeek's official platform and API. Keep in mind that the DeepSeek API is a paid and (hopefully) continuously developing product. Therefore, we will give you a small introduction to the API platform as it stands around June 2025. This will likely change over time. So, if something looks different, consider reading the API documentation at `https://api-docs.deepseek.com/`. This is not meant to be a comprehensive guide - just an overview that highlights the main features. Without further ado, let's get set up.

Setting up

Here, we'll show you how to get started with building with the DeepSeek API. To get set up, here are the steps you need to follow:

1. Go to the platform website over at `https://platform.deepseek.com/`.
2. Create an account. Optionally, log in with Google.
3. Navigate to **Top up** on the left panel.
4. Add some credits to your account using your preferred payment method.
5. Navigate to **API keys**.
6. Click **Create new API key**.
7. Save your API key (it will normally start with `sk-XXXX`).

Now that we have an API key, let's run a small test to ensure everything is working correctly. If you are on Mac or Linux, open a terminal and type the following, replacing <DeepSeek API Key> with the correct value:

```
curl https://api.deepseek.com/chat/completions \
  -H "Content-Type: application/json" \
  -H "Authorization: Bearer <DeepSeek API Key>" \
  -d '{
        "model": "deepseek-chat",
        "messages": [
          {"role": "system", "content": "You are a helpful assistant."},
          {"role": "user", "content": "What is the capital of Portugal?"}
        ],
        "stream": false
      }'
```

You should see an output similar to the following:


```
{"id":"3dbb972a-80e1-4558-b310-deeaeac1968d","object":"chat.
completion","created":1749810137,"model":"deepseek-chat","cho
ices":[{"index":0,"message":{"role":"assistant","content":"T
he capital of Portugal is **Lisbon** (Portuguese: *Lisboa*). It
is the largest city in the country and is known for its historic
neighborhoods, vibrant culture, and scenic location along the Atlantic
Ocean."},"logprobs":null,"finish_reason":"stop"}],"usage":{"prompt_
tokens":16,"completion_tokens":44,"total_tokens":60,"prompt_tokens_
details":{"cached_tokens":0},"prompt_cache_hit_tokens":0,"prompt_cache_
miss_tokens":16},"system_fingerprint":"fp_8802369eaa_prod0425fp8"}
```


If you don't, then make sure you have followed all the steps and set up your billing and API key correctly.

To make our first API call in Python, follow these steps:

1. Create a script called `01-deepssek-api-call.py`.
2. Export your DeepSeek API key by running `export DEEPSEEK_API_KEY=sk-XXXXXX` (or use some sort of environment manager, such as `direnv` (`https://direnv.net/`)).

3. Copy the following contents to the script file:

```
# /// script
# requires-python = ">=3.12"
# dependencies = [
#     "openai",
# ]
# ///
from openai import OpenAI
import os
API_KEY = os.getenv("DEEPSEEK_API_KEY")
assert API_KEY, "Please set the DEEPSEEK_API_KEY environment variable."
BASE_URL = "https://api.deepseek.com"
client = OpenAI(api_key=API_KEY, base_url=BASE_URL)

response = client.chat.completions.create(
    model="deepseek-chat",
    messages=[
        {"role": "system", "content": "You are a helpful assistant"},
        {"role": "user", "content": "What is the capital of Portugal?"},
    ],
    stream=False,
)

print(response)
# ChatCompletion(id='1bdf1ecf-a365-4f8b-9c26-fbebff421127',
choices=[Choice(finish_reason='stop', index=0,
# logprobs=None, message=ChatCompletionMessage(content='The capital of
Portugal is **Lisbon** ...
```

The nice thing about using uv is that we don't need to deal with installing and setting up Python versions. All you need to do now is run the script:

```
$ export DEEPSEEK_API_KEY=sk-XXXXXX
$ uv run 01-deepseek-api-call.py
```

You can expect an output similar to the following:

```
Reading inline script metadata from `01-deepseek-api-call.py`
ChatCompletion(id='41164ddd-c648-4945-96c2-67f64e6d62a1',
choices=[Choice(finish_reason='stop', index=0, logprobs=None,
message=ChatCompletionMessage(content='The capital of Portugal is
**Lisbon** (Portuguese: *Lisboa*). It is the largest city in the country
and is known for its historic neighborhoods, vibrant culture, and scenic
location along the Atlantic Ocean and the Tagus River.', refusal=None,
role='assistant', annotations=None, audio=None, function_call=None, tool_
calls=None))], created=1749375653, model='deepseek-chat', object='chat.
completion', service_tier=None, system_fingerprint='fp_8802369eaa_
prod0425fp8', usage=CompletionUsage(completion_tokens=49, prompt_
tokens=15, total_tokens=64, completion_tokens_details=None, prompt_
tokens_details=PromptTokensDetails(audio_tokens=None, cached_tokens=0),
prompt_cache_hit_tokens=0, prompt_cache_miss_tokens=15))
```

You just made your first API call to DeepSeek using Python!

Like many other **large language model** (**LLM**) providers, the DeepSeek API is compatible with the OpenAI API format. This means that you can use the OpenAI Python SDK (`https://github.com/openai/openai-python`), for example, and simply switch the `api-key` and `base-url` keyword arguments, and you don't need to care about the rest of the inner workings. This is great because it gives users the ability to switch providers relatively easily - without having to completely refactor their code bases. Beware, though: not all features of the API will be available with every provider. So, make sure to test things thoroughly.

Let's now look at the response structure. When you make a call to the DeepSeek API, you'll receive a JSON object in return, which follows the OpenAI-compatible format:

```
ChatCompletion(
  id='41164ddd-c648-4945-96c2-67f64e6d62a1',
  object='chat.completion',
  created=1749375653,
  model='deepseek-chat',
  system_fingerprint='fp_8802369eaa_prod0425fp8',
  choices=[
    Choice(
      index=0,
      finish_reason='stop',
      logprobs=None,
```

```
      message=ChatCompletionMessage(
        role='assistant',
        content='The capital of Portugal is **Lisbon** (Portuguese:
*Lisboa*)...',
        refusal=None,
        annotations=None,
        audio=None,
        function_call=None,
        tool_calls=None
      )
    )
  ],
  usage=CompletionUsage(
    prompt_tokens=15,
    completion_tokens=49,
    total_tokens=64,
    completion_tokens_details=None,
    prompt_tokens_details=PromptTokensDetails(
      audio_tokens=None,
      cached_tokens=0
    ),
    prompt_cache_hit_tokens=0,
    prompt_cache_miss_tokens=15
  ),
  service_tier=None
)
```

The key components of the response object here are the following:

- `choices`: A list of chat completion choices, each with a finish reason and a message. These can also contain tool calls; more on this later.
- `id`: The unique request ID.
- `model`: The model that was used - we will get into this later.
- `system_fingerprint`: The backend configuration that the model runs with.
- `usage`: Usage statistics you might care about (the number of completion tokens, caching statistics, etc.).

Now that we have a better idea of how to call the DeepSeek API, let's understand a bit more about which models are available to us and how to leverage them.

Using the available models

The DeepSeek AI lab has released a significant number of models. You might have already noticed from the code examples that our initial API calls were made to a model called `deepseek-chat`. If this doesn't ring a bell, it's because that's not the name of the actual model! In their API, DeepSeek only makes available two endpoints and two models:

- `deepseek-chat`: This is where the company makes their *non-reasoning* models available. At the time of this writing, the model under this endpoint is DeepSeek-V3.2-Exp in non-thinking mode.
- `deepseek-reasoner`: This is where the company releases their notable reasoning models. These are models that have been trained on or are capable of *reasoning*. At the time of this writing, this endpoint points to DeepSeek-V3.2-Exp in thinking mode.

It's worth pointing out that by the time you are reading this, the company might have released more models. As a consequence, the underlying models of these two endpoints might have changed. Always check the DeepSeek API documentation (`https://api-docs.deepseek.com/`) for the most up-to-date information about the models.

It is now time to look at the factors that may impact your DeepSeek API usage.

Temperature

The temperature parameter modifies the distribution of softmax probabilities over the next-token logits produced by the models. Specifically, it scales logits before applying a softmax function. If you are curious about the topic, I recommend this great blog post by Luke Salamone (`https://blog.lukesalamone.com/posts/what-is-temperature/`). As a result, lower temperatures are more deterministic, and higher temperatures less so. OpenAI, for example, also makes available a seed parameter to try to make outputs more deterministic. However, if context grows, even if we set the temperature to 0 (for very deterministic outputs), we are likely to see changes.

DeepSeek recommends that users use different temperature values according to their needs (`https://api-docs.deepseek.com/quick_start/parameter_settings`). For example, a higher temperature may be set for more creative tasks.

My advice is that if you are integrating into a larger - ideally deterministic - system, always set the temperature to 0.

Pricing and rate limits

Like most LLM providers, DeepSeek charges on a per-token basis. This means that users pay for token inputs and outputs. For reference, one character in English ≈ 0.3 tokens, while a Chinese character ≈ 0.6 tokens. DeepSeek uses their own tokenizer and also makes a package available (`https://api-docs.deepseek.com/quick_start/token_usage#calculate-token-usage-offline`) that can be used to count tokens.

The DeepSeek API is well known to have very competitive pricing compared to larger AI companies, so it's definitely an option to consider when selecting a provider. It's also worth noting that `deepseek-reasoner` is approximately 2x the price of its non-reasoning counterpart - this is standard for LLMs.

Also note that reasoning models output many more tokens. As you get charged on a per-token basis, reasoning models are effectively more expensive. Also note that DeepSeek (like most providers) also gives you access to prompt caching - caching a part of the prompt to make requests faster and cheaper.

Unlike other providers out there, DeepSeek does *not* rate limit users' requests. This is very out of line with most providers. LLM APIs are notoriously unstable and, therefore - due to high demand - providers tend to rate limit API calls pretty strongly. The following is noted in DeepSeek's API documentation:

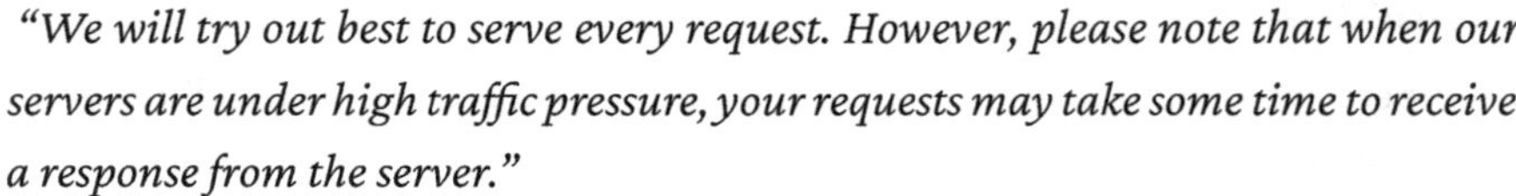

> *"We will try out best to serve every request. However, please note that when our servers are under high traffic pressure, your requests may take some time to receive a response from the server."*

Contrary to other providers, rather than throwing `RateLimitError`, or something similar, DeepSeek will simply hold your request until it can be completed. For non-streaming requests, they will send empty lines, and for streaming requests, they will continuously send `: keep-alive` events. A good alternative is to retry the request to ensure your API call is reliable:

```
from tenacity import retry, stop_after_attempt, wait_fixed
@retry(stop=stop_after_attempt(3), wait=wait_fixed(2))
def make_request() -> str:
    response = client.chat.completions.create(
        model="deepseek-chat",
        messages=[
```

```
            {"role": "system", "content": "You are a helpful assistant"},
            {"role": "user", "content": "What is the capital of 
Portugal?"},
        ],
        stream=False,
        max_tokens=100,
    )
    response_text = response.choices[0].message.content
    if not response_text:
        raise ValueError("Received empty response from the API.")
    return response_text
```

The preceding example will retry the `make_request` function up to three times, waiting two seconds between each attempt, if an exception is raised during execution (e.g., due to a failed request or an empty response). If the function succeeds without raising an exception, it returns the API response text. If all attempts fail, the last exception is raised.

Let's now shift our focus to the features of the DeepSeek API.

API features

In this final section about the DeepSeek API, we'll briefly cover some of the most interesting (current) features that it offers. We don't want to deep dive specifically into all of them, but we would like to give you a good initial grasp of each one. We will talk about reasoning, streaming, JSON output, function calling, and **fill-in-the-middle** (**FIM**) features.

Reasoning

The `deepseek-reasoner` model/endpoint has the capability to reason about a certain topic and return its reasoning traces. This can be very useful for more complicated topics, but it might also be overkill for others.

Here's how you can use it:

```
model = "deepseek-reasoner"
messages = [
    {"role": "user", "content": "What is the population of Copenhagen in 
2030?"}
]
response = CLIENT.chat.completions.create(
    model=model, messages=messages, temperature=TEMPERATURE
```

```
)
reasoning_content = response.choices[0].message.reasoning_content
content = response.choices[0].message.content
print("Reasoning Content:")
print(reasoning_content)
# Okay, the user is asking about Copenhagen's population in 2030...
print("\nFinal Answer:")
print(content)
# The projected population for **Copenhagen Municipality ...
```

Streaming

No user likes to wait around with a blank screen for the computer to answer a question. Streaming responses is a great way to make your LLM response seem snappy and responsive to the user, without actually accelerating it:

```
model = "deepseek-chat"
messages = [{"role": "user", "content": "What is the second largest city
in Portugal?"}]
response = CLIENT.chat.completions.create(
    model=model,
    messages=messages,
    stream=True,  # this is important!
    temperature=TEMPERATURE
)
for chunk in response:
    if chunk.choices[0].delta.content:
        print(chunk.choices[0].delta.content, end="", flush=True)

# prints: The second largest city in Portugal is \*\*Porto\*\* ..
```

Now the user will see the responses as they come.

JSON output

JSON structured output is a great way to enforce structured output on an LLM and ensure it integrates well with the rest of an application. This is especially useful since LLMs don't work in silos and traditionally should integrate with other applications.

Here's how to ask DeepSeek for a structured JSON response:

```
model = "deepseek-chat"
messages = [
    {
        "role": "system",
        "content": "Extract a JSON response with the keys 'name', 'age',
and 'city'.",
    },
    {"role": "user", "content": "Duarte is 31 years old and lives in
Copenhagen."},
]
response = CLIENT.chat.completions.create(
    model=model,
    messages=messages,
    response_format={"type": "json_object"},
    temperature=TEMPERATURE,
)
json_object = json.loads(response.choices[0].message.content) # convert to
json object
print("JSON Response:")
print(json_object)
# {'name': 'Duarte', 'age': 31, 'city': 'Copenhagen'}
print(json_object["name"])
# Duarte
```

The `json.loads()` method can help you structure the LLM response as a JSON object.

Function calling

When we want to give the capability to the LLM to interact with the outside world (call an API, scrape a web page, or interact with another system), function calls are a great way to do that. We have already covered this topic in *Chapter 6* (in the *Tools* section).

FIM

FIM completion allows us to define a prefix and a suffix on the model responses. Defining a prefix and a suffix allows the model to generate content specifically for the gap between them. For code, for example, you can provide a function, a loop, or a method where the beginning and end are already defined - effectively asking the model to fill only the content in the middle. This is how automated autocompletions with GitHub Copilot (`https://github.com/features/copilot`) effectively work! For a simple example, let's try to make the DeepSeek model give us the number of people who live in Lisbon. We can provide an input and an output and let the model fill in the rest:

```
prompt = "The population of Lisbon is exactly "
suffix = " million people."
response = BETA_CLIENT.completions.create(
    model="deepseek-chat",
    prompt=prompt,
    suffix=suffix,
    max_tokens=5,
    temperature=TEMPERATURE,
)
final_text = prompt + response.choices[0].text + suffix
print(final_text)
# The population of Lisbon is exactly 2,000,000 million people.
```

This is, of course, not limited to code. You can have models complete JSON, XML, or anything else, preventing them from going *off track* and generating text you might not be expecting.

Note that at the time of writing, FIM is only available in the Beta API (you need to set `base_url=https://api.deepseek.com/beta`).

You can also use DeepSeek models with third-party APIs. Let's take a look at how to use DeepSeek models with third-party providers.

Using common third-party APIs

As previously mentioned, all of DeepSeek's models are open source. Due to this, DeepSeek has proliferated across many different cloud providers: Google Cloud Platform, Azure, AWS, Fireworks, OpenRouter, and Cloudflare, to name a few.

Talking about all of them would be overkill, so we will highlight the three main ones in this section:

- **Cloudflare** (`https://www.cloudflare.com/`): A large provider that is globally available. Users familiar with frontend technologies might already know about Cloudflare. They are also a "middle-of-the-range" provider due to their size.
- **AWS** (`https://aws.amazon.com/`): Many users will be familiar with AWS or work in companies already leveraging it, hence we will focus on AWS for the sake of brevity. Azure and Google Cloud Platform are other popular options. The reason we selected AWS is due to its popularity with enterprise users.
- **OpenRouter** (`https://openrouter.ai/`): OpenRouter is a relatively new cloud provider, but it is extremely focused on serving LLMs. Start-ups or new projects might be interested in a provider that can also give them the flexibility to easily switch models as they get released.

Let's start with Cloudflare.

Cloudflare

Cloudflare is an American company famous for their **content-delivery network (CDN)** products. Currently, Cloudflare makes access to LLMs easy through their Workers AI product. Here are a few details you should know about Cloudflare before we get started:

- **Supported models**: `deepseek-r1-distill-qwen-32b`, a distilled version of DeepSeek-R1 released in January 2025 (`https://arxiv.org/pdf/2501.12948`), and `deepseek-math-7b-instruct`, an instruction-tuned model specialized in math released in April 2024 (`https://arxiv.org/pdf/2402.03300`).
- **Pricing**: $0.50 per million input tokens; $4.88 per million output tokens for the Qwen 32B distilled version. No pricing information for the `math-7b` version.
- **Region**: Cloudflare Workers AI runs globally at the edge.
- **Authentication**: Can be done through a Cloudflare auth token.
- **OpenAI-compatible endpoints**: Supported at `/v1/chat/completions` and `/v1/embeddings`.

Here's how you can set up Cloudflare Workers AI:

1. Go to `cloudflare.com`.
2. Log in or create an account.

3. On the left menu, click on **AI** and select **Workers AI** (*Figure A*).

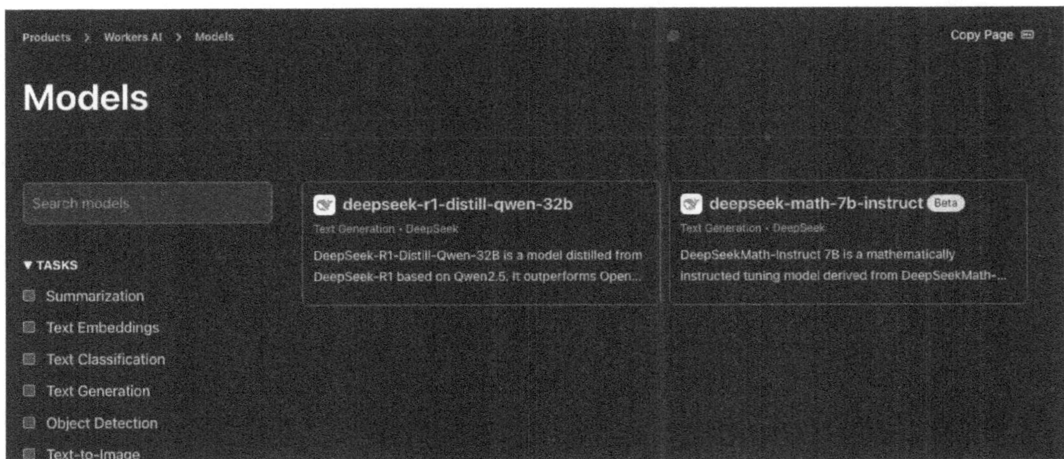

Figure A: The DeepSeek models supported by Cloudflare

1. Click on **{} Rest API**.
2. Click on **Create a Workers AI API Token.**
3. Save your account ID and token in a safe place.

Let's look at some sample API calls.

Here is an example of sending a request with `curl`. We start by exporting our environment variables and then issuing a request in the following format:

```
$ export CLOUDFLARE_ACCOUNT_ID=******
$ export CLOUDFLARE_AUTH_TOKEN=****
$ curl https://api.cloudflare.com/client/v4/accounts/$CLOUDFLARE_
ACCOUNT_ID/ai/run/@cf/deepseek-ai/deepseek-r1-distill-qwen-32b -X POST
-H "Authorization: Bearer $CLOUDFLARE_AUTH_TOKEN" -d '{ "messages": [{
"role": "system", "content": "You are a friendly assistant" }, { "role":
"user", "content": "Why is pizza so good" }]}'
```

If you want to use Python, here's an example Python call using the OpenAI-compatible endpoint provided by Cloudflare:

1. We start by setting our keys and defining our OpenAI client:

```
from openai import OpenAI

# setup keys and client
```

```
api_key = os.environ["CLOUDFLARE_AUTH_TOKEN"]
account_id = os.environ["CLOUDFLARE_ACCOUNT_ID"]
assert account_id, "Please set the CLOUDFLARE_ACCOUNT_ID environment
variable."
assert api_key, "Please set the CLOUDFLARE_API_KEY environment
variable."
model = "@cf/deepseek-ai/deepseek-r1-distill-qwen-32b"
client = OpenAI(
    base_url=f"https://api.cloudflare.com/client/v4/accounts/
{account_id}/ai/v1",
    api_key=api_key,
)
```

2. We then create a list of messages:

```
# create messages
messages = [
    {"role": "system", "content": "You are a helpful assistant."},
    {"role": "user", "content": "What is the most likely sky color
in Copenhagen?"},
]
```

3. Finally, we issue a request to the `@cf/deepseek-ai/deepseek-r1-distill-qwen-32b` model:

```
# make api call
response = client.chat.completions.create(
    model=model,
    messages=messages,
    max_tokens=1000,
    temperature=0.0,
)
```

4. The request includes both the thinking and the final response of the model in the `content` parameter. So, we use Python to extract the thinking portion, which is between the `<think>` tags:

```
# extract thinking content and final response text
raw_response = str(response.choices[0].message.content)
start = raw_response.index("<think>") + len("<think>")
```

```
end = raw_response.index("</think>")
thinking_content = raw_response[start:end]
response_text = raw_response[end + len("</think>") :].strip()

print("=" * 10, "Cloudflare Thinking", "=" * 10)
print(thinking_content)
# Okay, so I need to figure out what the most likely ...
print("=" * 10, "Cloudflare Response", "=" * 10)
print(response_text)
# The most likely sky color in Copenhagen is gray.
```

Now it's time for some quirks and tips while using Cloudflare.

Quirks and tips

- Function calling is not supported by any of the models that we tested in the Cloudflare platform.
- The format when calling the reasoning model does not break the reasoning content into a different `reasoning` component of the API. You'll notice that the thinking steps are included in an `xml` section inside two `<think>` tokens.
- Cloudflare does not support any of the models supported by the official DeepSeek API. Also important to note is that none of the models supported by Cloudflare are available in the official DeepSeek API.

Cloudflare is a good choice if you are looking for a straightforward provider that offers simple access to models. If you are already using Cloudflare, then it's a great choice. However, do note that the model availability, especially DeepSeek models, is limited.

Let's now look at AWS and how to use it.

AWS

If you've worked in technology, chances are that you've heard of **Amazon Web Services**, or **AWS**. They are currently the largest cloud provider (`https://www.statista.com/chart/18819/worldwide-market-share-of-leading-cloud-infrastructure-service-providers/`) in the world. AWS is known for quickly expanding and adopting new technologies in their cloud offering. Most of their AI products are offered under the **Bedrock** brand.

Here are some quick facts about using the AWS API for DeepSeek models in AWS:

- **Supported models**:
    - As a serverless deployment (runs without having to deploy it yourself), you can use the DeepSeek-R1 model. This might evolve in the future, so check `https://aws.amazon.com/bedrock/deepseek/` for up-to-date information.
    - You can also use most of the DeepSeek-R1 distilled models and the newest DeepSeek-R1-0528 model through Bedrock Marketplace. This means that you will need to manage the deployment yourself - and pay for it (even when not using it).
- **Pricing (on-demand)**: Please consult the AWS documentation at `https://aws.amazon.com/bedrock/pricing/` for up-to-date information on pricing. Keep in mind that serverless models are normally cheaper - since you only pay for the requests you make to the model. On the other hand, deploying models from Bedrock Marketplace means that you need to pay for the infrastructure yourself. We recommend going with the serverless offering as a starting point.
- **Region**: DeepSeek-R1 is available via a serverless offering in US East (N. Virginia), US East (Ohio), and US West (Oregon). Bedrock Marketplace models can be deployed in any AWS Region.
- **Authentication**: You can use your AWS account for IAM-based authentication and Bedrock service integration (`https://aws.amazon.com/iam/`).
- **OpenAI-compatible endpoints**: Not available out of the box, but it can be used with some open source projects from AWS (`http://github.com/aws-samples/bedrock-access-gateway`).

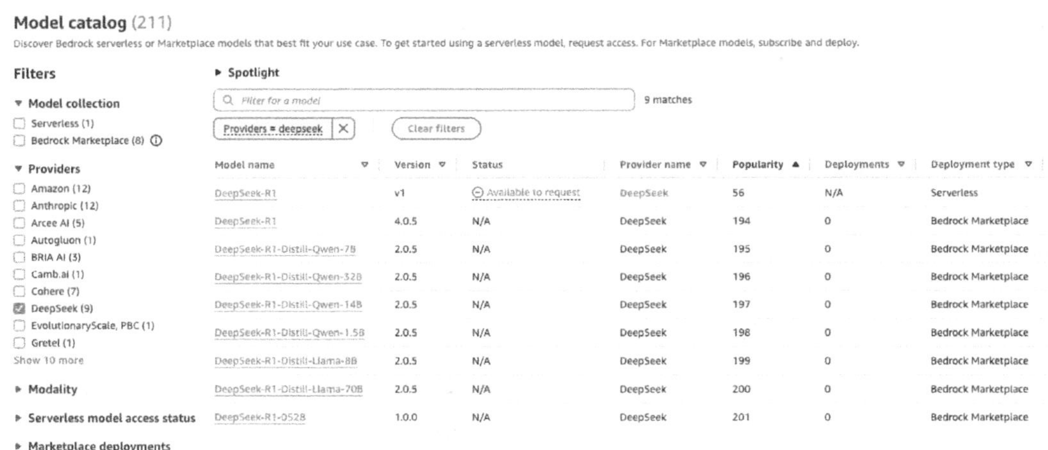

Figure B: List of available DeepSeek models in the AWS Bedrock model catalog

Let's get set up:

1. Create or set up an AWS account if you don't have one: `https://signin.aws.amazon.com/signup`.
2. In the AWS console, search for `Billing and Cost Management` and open the first result to set up billing.
3. Make sure you are in the correct Region - `us-east-1` is a good default choice since most models are available there first.
4. Search for `Amazon Bedrock` in the search bar at the top and go to the **Amazon Bedrock** service.
5. In the right-hand panel, go to **Model Catalog** under **Foundation models.**
6. Use the **Provider** filter and select **DeepSeek.**
7. Click on the model you're interested in (you may need to enable access in the console first; do this by clicking on a model in the console and then **Modify Access,** and then request access).
8. Install the AWS CLI using the guide here: `https://docs.aws.amazon.com/cli/latest/userguide/getting-started-quickstart.html`.
9. (Recommended) Configure the AWS CLI: `https://docs.aws.amazon.com/cli/`.

Once you've installed the AWS CLI, you can make a request to a model by running the following:

```
        --model-id us.deepseek.r1-v1:0 \
        --messages '[{"role": "user", "content": [{"text": "What is the
population of Ancona?"}]}]' \
        --region us-east-1
```

We can also use Python and the boto3 library to make a simple request to our model. The text and thinking content are separated by default from AWS. So, we can access both fields independently. Also notice that the Bedrock runtime (brt) has a slightly different API format:

```
import boto3

brt = boto3.client("bedrock-runtime")
model_id = "us.deepseek.r1-v1:0"

# create our messages
conversation = [
    {
        "role": "user",
        "content": [{"text": "What is the most likely sky color in
Copenhagen?"}],
    }
]

# request
response = brt.converse(
    modelId=model_id,
    messages=conversation,
    inferenceConfig={"maxTokens": 5000, "temperature": 0.0},
)

response_text = response["output"]["message"]["content"][0]["text"]
repsonse_reasoning = response["output"]["message"]["content"][1]
["reasoningContent"][
    "reasoningText"
]["text"]
print("=" * 10, "AWS Thinking", "=" * 10)
print(repsonse_reasoning)
```

```
# Okay, so I need to figure out the ..
print("=" * 10, "AWS Response", "=" * 10)
print(response_text)
# The most likely sky color in Copenhagen is **pale gray or overcast
white**...
```

Quirks and tips

- The AWS interface for invoking models can be confusing. There is an invoke and a converse API. Read more about their differences here: `https://dgallitelli95.medium.com/amazon-bedrock-explained-with-memes-converse-api-and-tool-usage-w-anthropic-claude-3-001c341347ca`.
- The documentation is very extensive. The following is a recommended read to learn about tool calling, prompt caching, compute usage, and more: `https://dgallitelli95.medium.com/amazon-bedrock-explained-with-memes-converse-api-and-tool-usage-w-anthropic-claude-3-001c341347ca`.
- If you are making many calls (for classification or other "batch" use cases), consider using AWS Batch inference. It's a great service to run models at a discounted price by trading off response time.
- You might need to tweak your permissions in the AWS IAM console to invoke models within AWS.
- Not all models are available in all Regions - check the AWS console to see what's available where.
- Most programmatic usage is done with the `boto3` Python library. For Bedrock, note the distinction between the `bedrock` and `bedrock-runtime` APIs:
    - `https://boto3.amazonaws.com/v1/documentation/api/latest/reference/services/bedrock.html`
    - `https://boto3.amazonaws.com/v1/documentation/api/latest/reference/services/bedrock-runtime.html`

AWS is an ever-evolving platform, adding support for models very quickly - and giving you possibilities to deploy models yourself (at a cost, of course). It can be overwhelming navigating the console and seeing all the possibilities, but it's a powerful tool to have under your belt.

Let's talk about a simpler, newer provider, OpenRouter, next.

OpenRouter

OpenRouter (`https://openrouter.ai/`) is a platform that acts as a universal gateway for accessing LLMs from various providers using a simple unified interface. More interestingly, for the case of open source models, OpenRouter will aggregate multiple providers under the same API, allowing users to query the best-performing provider. For example, for DeepSeek-V3, they support Deep Infra, Novita AI, Nebius AI Studio, and Fireworks as providers.

Here are some facts you should know about the OpenRouter API for DeepSeek:

- **Supported models:** At the time of writing, DeepSeek-R1, DeepSeek-R1-0528, DeepSeek-V2, DeepSeek-V3, and additional distilled or fine-tuned models.

Providers for DeepSeek V3

OpenRouter routes requests to the best providers that are able to handle your prompt size and parameters, with fallbacks to maximize uptime.

Sort by

Provider	Context	Max Output	Input	Output	Latency	Throughput	Uptime
DeepInfra (US, fp8)	164K	164K	$0.38	$0.89	0.57s	49.96tps	
NovitaAI (US)	64K	16K	$0.40	$1.30	1.09s	25.42tps	
Nebius AI Studio (DE, fp8)	164K	164K	$0.50	$1.50	0.37s	20.90tps	
Fireworks (US)	131K	131K	$0.90	$0.90	1.22s	63.72tps	

Figure C: Multiple providers for the same DeepSeek-V3 model

- **Pricing (on demand):** OpenRouter directs your request to the "best available providers" of the model you are requesting. They charge you when you purchase credits on the platform (5% + 0.35 USD fee). They also provide a wide range of free models (such as DeepSeek-R1-0528).
- **Region:** It does not support "regions" per se. It routes your request to the provider directly. Therefore, you should consider it a "global" region.

- **Authentication**: It uses an API key that you need to generate through the OpenRouter console.
- **OpenAI-compatible endpoints**: All endpoints from OpenRouter are compatible with the OpenAI format and SDK.

Here's how to get set up:

1. Go to `https://openrouter.ai`.
2. Log in or create an account.
3. Hover over the hamburger menu on the top right, and click **Credits**.
4. Add credits to your account.
5. Hover over the hamburger menu on the top right again and click **API Keys**.
6. Generate an API key and save it.

Here's how you can make an API call using `curl`:

```
curl https://openrouter.ai/api/v1/chat/completions \
  -H "Content-Type: application/json" \
  -H "Authorization: Bearer $OPENROUTER_API_KEY" \
  -d '{
  "model": "deepseek/deepseek-r1-0528",
  "messages": [
    {
      "role": "user",
      "content": "What is the most likely sky color in Copenhagen?"
    }
  ]

}'
```

As you can see, we define our list of messages and send them to the necessary endpoint.

Using Python, the request is very similar to other requests to the OpenAI SDK client:

```
from openai import OpenAI

client = OpenAI(
    base_url="https://openrouter.ai/api/v1",
    api_key=os.environ["OPENROUTER_API_KEY"],
)
```

```
response = client.chat.completions.create(
    model="deepseek/deepseek-r1-0528",
    messages=[
        {"role": "user", "content": "What is the most likely sky color in
Copenhagen?"}
    ],
)

response_reasoning = response.choices[0].message.reasoning
response_text = response.choices[0].message.content

print("=" * 10, "OpenRouter Thinking", "=" * 10)
print(response_reasoning)
# Okay, the user asked about the most likely sky col...
print("=" * 10, "OpenRouter Response", "=" * 10)
print(response_text)
```

You will notice that all we need to do is override the `base_url` parameter of the OpenAI client.

You should get an output similar to this:

```
# The **most statistically likely overall sky color in Copenha...
```

Here are some tips and specifics when you use OpenRouter.

Quirks and tips

- **Free models**: OpenRouter gives access to a large suite of models completely free of charge for you to test out. Simply visit their model dashboard (or `https://openrouter.ai/models?max_price=0`) and start making API calls! (This is not advised for production.)
- You can append `:nitro` to a provider to access the provider with the best throughput, or `:floor` for the provider with the best price. For example, to access the fastest DeepSeek-R1, query `deepseek/deepseek-r1-0528:nitro`.
- OpenRouter supports all the main features you might expect (tool calling, images and PDFs, structured outputs, and prompt caching on some providers). Visit their docs for implementation specifics: `https://openrouter.ai/docs/quickstart`.
- Keep in mind that you might receive different results between providers since OpenRouter does not control the hardware where the actual models run.

- OpenRouter provides a ranking page over at `https://openrouter.ai/rankings` where you can see which models are being used for which categories, and get a sense of what is trending. For example, at the time of writing, DeepSeek-R1-0528 was ranked #2 in the **Finance** category.

Working with Cursor's IDE for DeepSeek

We will demonstrate DeepSeek's capabilities using Cursor's IDE, a powerful AI-enhanced development environment that seamlessly integrates with DeepSeek's models. However, the principles and techniques we explore are adaptable to any development environment that supports DeepSeek integration, whether you prefer traditional IDEs, cloud-based platforms, or local web interfaces. The essential element is establishing a robust connection between your development workflow and DeepSeek-R1's advanced reasoning capabilities.

With the API access confirmed, we can proceed to establish the development environment that will serve as our laboratory for exploring DeepSeek's practical applications.

Setting up your development environment

Creating an environment for AI-assisted development requires carefully selecting tools that complement DeepSeek's capabilities while supporting the full development life cycle. Our recommended toolkit centers around Cursor's IDE, which you can download from `cursor.com`. This AI-native editor provides seamless integration with various language models, including DeepSeek-R1, making it an ideal choice for our demonstrations.

The foundation of our development stack includes Python 3.11 or higher, which serves as the primary language for our backend implementations due to its extensive AI and data processing libraries. Docker Desktop enables us to containerize our applications, ensuring consistent deployment environments and simplified distribution. Git provides essential version control capabilities, which is particularly important when collaborating with AI-generated code, where tracking changes and maintaining code history becomes crucial. Finally, Node.js 18 and higher support various frontend components and development tooling that we'll leverage in our more comprehensive examples.

Configuring DeepSeek in Cursor's IDE

The integration between Cursor's IDE and DeepSeek-R1 represents the cornerstone of our development approach, transforming traditional coding workflows into collaborative partnerships between human creativity and AI reasoning capabilities. This configuration process, while straightforward, establishes the foundation for all our subsequent demonstrations.

Direct integration: Connecting Cursor to DeepSeek

Begin by accessing Cursor's model configuration through the **Settings** menu. On macOS, you'll find this under **Cursor** | **Settings**, while Windows and Linux users can find it under **File** | **Settings**. Within the settings interface, the **Models** section in the left sidebar contains all the options for managing AI model integrations.

Cursor's IDE comes with built-in support for DeepSeek models, which you can enable by scrolling through the available models list and selecting **deepseek-r1**. Once enabled, the model appears in your available options, ready for configuration with your specific API credentials.

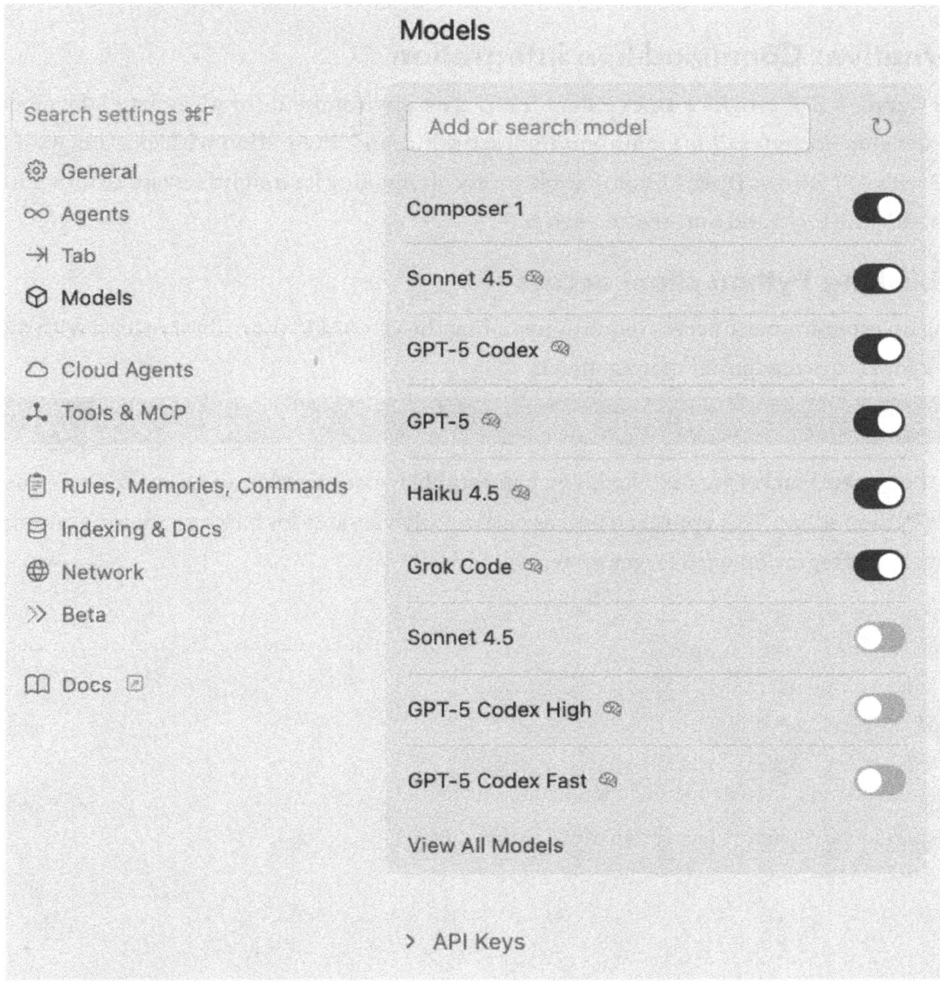

Figure D: Cursor IDE DeepSeek-R1 model selection interface

The configuration process requires entering your DeepSeek API credentials along with the appropriate connection settings. You'll specify `deepseek-r1` as the model name, provide your API key from the DeepSeek platform, set the base URL to `https://api.deepseek.com/v1`, and configure the provider as **OpenAI Compatible** to ensure proper API communication protocols.

To verify that your integration works correctly, open a new file in Cursor and invoke the AI command palette using *Cmd* + *K* on macOS or *Ctrl* + *K* on Windows and Linux. Select **DeepSeek-R1** from the model dropdown and test with a substantive prompt, such as "Explain the difference between microservices and monolithic architecture." A successful response confirms that your development environment is ready for the advanced use cases we'll explore.

Alternative: Command-line integration

While Cursor's IDE provides an excellent interactive environment for AI-assisted development, many developers prefer CLIs for automation, scripting, and integration with existing workflows. DeepSeek's API follows OpenAI-compatible protocols, making it straightforward to integrate into command-line tools and automation scripts.

Establishing Python client access

Setting up programmatic access requires installing the OpenAI Python library along with `python-dotenv` for secure credential management:

```
pip install openai python-dotenv
```

Once the dependencies are installed, you can establish a connection to DeepSeek's API using a simple Python script. This approach proves particularly valuable for batch processing, automated testing, and integration with larger systems:

```
import os
from openai import OpenAI
client = OpenAI(
 api_key=os.getenv("DEEPSEEK_API_KEY"),
 base_url="https://api.deepseek.com/v1"
)
response = client.chat.completions.create(
 model="deepseek-r1",
 messages=[{"role": "user", "content": "Hello DeepSeek!"}]
)
print(response.choices[0].message.content)
```

Running or deploying DeepSeek yourself

One interesting aspect of the DeepSeek models is that they are, in fact, open for anyone to interact with. In this section, we will go over some methods to interact with and deploy these models using your own infrastructure. Knowing that your data and application are completely controlled by you brings a variety of benefits; privacy and compliance are just two of them. Finally, it's worth noting that deploying and managing these models yourself (especially the larger variants) can be quite the undertaking.

Here, we'll cover some methods to use these models locally and also introduce you to ways of taking it further and deploying them yourself. We will be working with llama.cpp and Ollama to help you use DeepSeek locally.

Using llama.cpp

llama.cpp is a high-performance, open source C/C++ inference library designed to run LLMs efficiently on local hardware. It was started by Georgi Gerganov, and has a vibrant community and repo (`https://github.com/ggml-org/llama.cpp`). It allows users to execute models locally, without needing specialized GPUs or cloud infrastructure.

To install llama.cpp, please follow the installation instructions on the GitHub repo (`https://github.com/ggml-org/llama.cpp/blob/master/docs/install.md`). If you are on a Mac, installing llama.cpp is as easy as the following:

```
$ brew install llama.cpp
```

To verify your installation worked correctly, just run the following:

```
$ llama-cli --help
```

You should see some output explaining how to use the CLI tool:

```
----- common params -----
-h, --help, --usage print usage and exit --version show version and build
info --completion-bash print source-able bash completion script for llama.
cpp --verbose-prompt print a verbose prompt before generation (default:
false)
...
```

llama.cpp uses the GGUF file format (read more about it at `https://github.com/ggml-org/ggml/blob/master/docs/gguf.md`). **GGUF** stands for **GPT-Generated Unified Format** (`https://www.ibm.com/think/topics/gguf-versus-ggml`). In order to use models with the tool, you need to download the models in GGUF format or convert them from PyTorch into that format. Thankfully, the folks at Unsloth (`https://unsloth.ai/`) provide GGUF variants of the DeepSeek models for free on Hugging Face (`https://huggingface.co/collections/unsloth/deepseek-r1-all-versions`).

Chatting locally with the original DeepSeek-R1 model would be challenging. You would need several machines running with multiple GPUs in order to run it. Let's choose a simpler option and run one of the distilled versions of DeepSeek-R1. `DeepSeek-R1-Distill-Qwen-1.5B-GGUF:Q4_K_M` is a version of the Qwen 1.5 billion parameters model that was distilled from the DeepSeek-R1 model. In this case, we are running the quantized version, `Q4_K_M`, which means it's a small model and can probably run on our CPU:

```
$ llama-cli -hf unsloth/DeepSeek-R1-Distill-Qwen-1.5B-GGUF:Q4_K_M
```

This will automatically download the model from the Hugging Face repository and throw you into a chat interface right in your terminal.

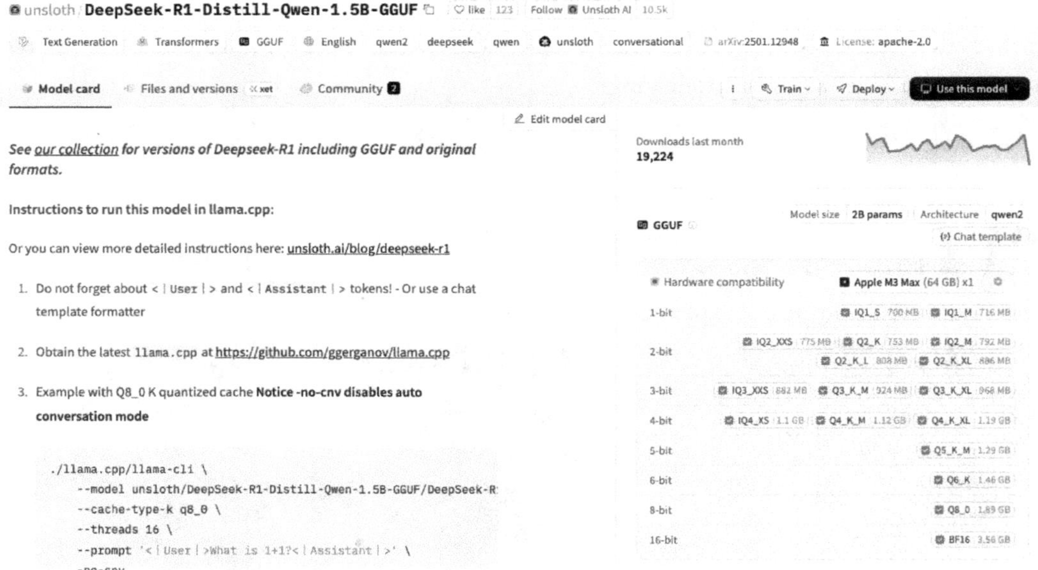

Figure E: Use the DeepSeek model locally with the Unsloth interface

Hugging Face also provides a convenient way for you to get started with any model you see while navigating by clicking the **Use this model** button and following the instructions.

If you are thinking of integrating with a wider application, you might be interested in running this model using Python or any other programming language. Fortunately, we can use llama-cpp-python (`https://github.com/abetlen/llama-cpp-python`), a Python library that offers Python bindings to the exact same CLI. Here's an example of using the model with Python. As you can see, we provide the same parameters as if we were using llama.cpp through the CLI, but now passing it into the library directly:

```
from llama_cpp import Llama

REPO_ID = "unsloth/DeepSeek-R1-Distill-Qwen-1.5B-GGUF"
MODEL_FILENAME = "DeepSeek-R1-Distill-Qwen-1.5B-Q4_K_M.gguf"

llm = Llama.from_pretrained(
    repo_id=REPO_ID,
    filename=MODEL_FILENAME,
    verbose=False,
)

response = llm.create_chat_completion(
    messages=[
        {
            "role": "user",
            "content": "What is the most likely sky color in Copenhagen?
Think hard and answer in one word.",
        },
    ],
)

text_response = response["choices"][0]["message"]["content"]

print(f"{MODEL_FILENAME} response:\n{text_response}")
```

If you are interested in deploying llama.cpp and using it as an OpenAI-compatible server, you can! Simply run the following:

```
$ llama-server -hf unsloth/DeepSeek-R1-Distill-Qwen-1.5B-GGUF:Q4_K_M
```

Now you can access the chat interface by visiting `http://localhost:8080`, which allows you to play with a completely local model.

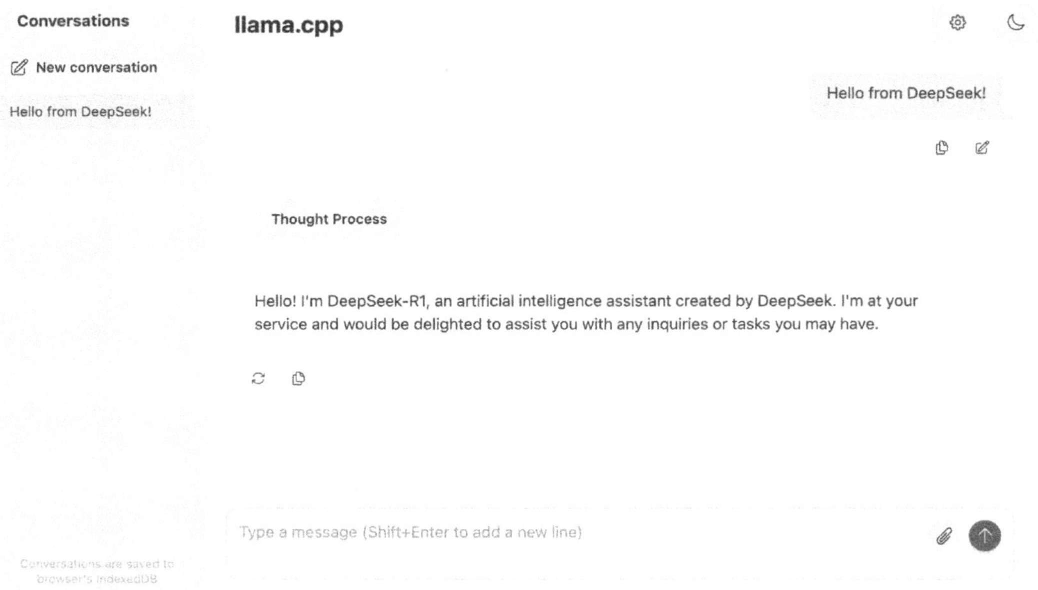
Conversations
llama.cpp
New conversation
Hello from DeepSeek!
Hello from DeepSeek!
Thought Process
Hello! I'm DeepSeek-R1, an artificial intelligence assistant created by DeepSeek. I'm at your service and would be delighted to assist you with any inquiries or tasks you may have.
Type a message (Shift+Enter to add a new line)

Figure F: Using DeepSeek through llama.cpp

Alternatively, you can query the OpenAI-compatible API at `http://localhost:8080/v1/chat/completions`. After starting your `llama-server` with the preceding command, open another terminal and send a `curl` request like so:

```
$ curl --request POST \
          --url http://localhost:8080/completion \
          --header "Content-Type: application/json" \
          --data '{"prompt": "What is the capital of Portugal?","n_
predict": 120}'
```

This will output a response straight from the model you are running the server with.

Now let's talk about another interesting tool that builds on top of llama.cpp, called Ollama.

Ollama

Ollama (`https://ollama.com/`) is a library and CLI tool first released in 2023. Its goal is to allow you to run LLMs locally on your machine, with minimal setup. Its backend is powered by llama.cpp, but it provides a more user-friendly experience. Ollama has a wide range of models that you can download by visiting `https://ollama.com/search`. This includes many open source models (including, of course, DeepSeek models).

To get up and running with Ollama, head to their downloads page at `https://ollama.com/download` and download the binary for your relevant platform. Once you're done, you can verify the installation worked correctly by running the following in your terminal:

```
$ ollama help
```

You should see a help message with the different options you can use to run Ollama.

To know what models you can run, start by visiting the library of models available at `https://ollama.com/library`.

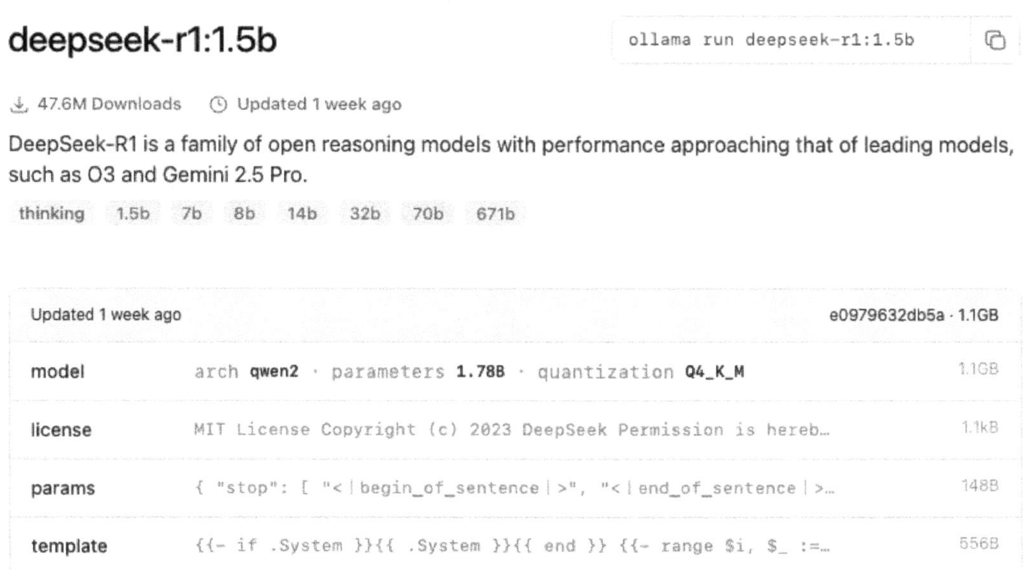

Figure G: DeepSeek-R1-1.5B on Ollama.com

Once you have selected the model (in our case, **deepseek-r1:1.5b**) you wish to run locally, you can simply pull it, as you would with a Docker image:

```
$ ollama run deepseek-r1:1.5b
```

You can now start chatting with the model on your local machine. An interesting tip you can use is turning thinking on and off (this only applies to reasoning models) by typing `/set nothink` or `/set think`, respectively. Here's an example of a terminal session and setting those modes dynamically:

```
➤ ollama run deepseek-r1:1.5b
>>> /set nothink
Set 'nothink' mode.
>>> What is the capital of the Le Marche Region in Italy?
The capital of the Le Marche Region in Italy is Rome

>>> /set think
Set 'think' mode.
>>> What is the capital of the Le Marche Region in Italy?
Thinking...
Alright, let's see. The user initially asked about the capital of the Le
Marche region and I...
```

Additionally, Ollama also provides a Python SDK called ollama-python, available at `https://github.com/ollama/ollama-python`, which you can use as follows:

```
from ollama import chat

messages = [
    {
        "role": "user",
        "content": "What is the capital of Le Marche region in Italy?",
    },
]

response = chat(
    "deepseek-r1:1.5b", messages=messages, think=True,
options={"temperature": 0.0}
)

print(f"Thinking:\n========\n\n{response.message.thinking}")
# Okay, so I need to figure out the capital of the Le Marche region in
Italy...
```

```
print(f"\nResponse:\n========\n\n{response.message.content}")
# The capital of the Le Marche region in Italy is
```

Finally, Ollama also provides an OpenAI-compatible API that you can use. Here's the same request as previously, using the API with `curl`:

```
$ curl --location 'http://localhost:11434/api/chat' \
      --header 'Content-Type: application/json' \
      --data '{
    "model": "deepseek-r1:1.5b",
    "options": { "temperature": 0.0 },
    "messages": [
      {
        "role": "user",
        "content": "What is the capital of Le Marche region in Italy?"
      }
    ],
    "think": true
  }'
```

You'll see the model response in your terminal as it comes in, as it is supposed to with streaming:

```
{"model":"deepseek-r1:1.5b","created_at":"2025-06-13T14:29:01.074249Z","
message":{"role":"assistant","content":"","thinking":"Okay"},"done":fal
se}...
{"model":"deepseek-r1:1.5b","created_at":"2025-06-13T14:29:01.084569Z","me
ssage":{"role":"assistant","content":"","thinking":","},"done":false}...
...
```

Ollama is a great tool for using and even deploying models locally. It's a very nice addition to what llama.cpp has to offer. It's really up to you which one you prefer to use. While llama.cpp offers a bit more power user features, such as setting sampling rates, chat templates, and tokenizers, Ollama tries to be as simple as possible and integrate with the world around it. Test both and decide which one you like best!

Deploying DeepSeek yourself

Depending on the size of the model, deploying an LLM yourself is no small feat. If you are deploying a 1 Gigabyte model that runs on a CPU, it's not a problem. If you are serving a 405 billion parameter model to multiple users, and have latency and throughput requirements, then things start to get more complicated.

Let's take an example. You would like to deploy the full DeepSeek-R1 model. The DeepSeek-R1 model at `https://huggingface.co/deepseek-ai/DeepSeek-R1` has a total of 671 billion parameters. In full precision, this would mean that your model will be approximately 1.5 TB in size. Remember, this is RAM size, not disk size. You would need approximately 16 A100 GPUs with 80 GB of RAM each. An alternative is to deploy a smaller model (the 7B parameter version, for example). If you decide to deploy a smaller model, a great place to start is AWS SageMaker, for example. Hugging Face has a great tutorial for deploying (pretty much) any model in their repo onto AWS over at `https://huggingface.co/docs/sagemaker/en/inference`.

If you think using an API or deploying a smaller model is not an option for you, then I ask you to seriously reconsider this. It's likely that deploying, managing, and paying for your own GPU cluster might actually be a bigger cost than using an API.

Let's now talk about how to create your own setup.

Building your own setup for DeepSeek

In the final section of this appendix, we will highlight some interesting libraries that you could add to your arsenal when building with DeepSeek models. We've found these to be particularly useful when building on top of models. These libraries offer you more flexibility, are agnostic to models and providers, and help you do structured outputs.

Remember that these libraries are forever evolving, so make sure to visit the documentation for each one for up-to-date information. Hopefully, the core of many of these isn't going to change anytime soon - which is the reason why we cover them here.

LiteLLM

LiteLLM (`https://www.litellm.ai/`) is a library and both a proxy server and an SDK focused on facilitating the use of LLMs when building with them. Here, we'll focus on the SDK, since that's what we use most for building with these models. It provides some good solutions to common problems:

- **Common interface**: Allows you to use the same API when building with models. Rather than figuring out how to use models with AWS, Azure, GCP, Cloudflare, or any other provider, with LiteLLM, you can use the same completion function.
- **Retries and fallbacks**: LLM APIs can be "flaky." They can be down, slow, or even refuse to complete your request. LiteLLM enables you to try a given request multiple times. Additionally, you can set a number of models to act as "fallbacks," using them instead if your primary model fails

- **Caching**: Caching is an important part of both serving and using LLMs. With caching, you can avoid calling an LLM twice when it's not needed. This makes both your costs go down and your requests much faster.

Let's take a look at a script to achieve caching:

1. We will first cache responses on disk and confirm that a DeepSeek API key is present:

```
from litellm import completion
from litellm.caching.caching import Cache
import litellm
import os

litellm.cache = Cache(type="disk")

env_var_name = "DEEPSEEK_API_KEY"
assert os.environ[env_var_name], f"Please set your {env_var_name}
environment variable."
```

2. Then we send a chat-completion request to the `deepseek-reasoner` model:

```
response = completion(
    model="deepseek/deepseek-reasoner",
    messages=[
        {
            "role": "user",
            "content": "What is the capital of region of Le Marche
in Italy?",
        }
    ],
```

3. It tells LiteLLM to retry the call up to two times and, if that model fails, fall back to `deepseek-chat`:

```
    num_retries=2,  # Number of retries
    fallbacks=["deepseek/deepseek-chat"],  # Fallback models
    caching=True,  # Enable caching
)
```

4. Since caching is enabled, an identical request will later be served from disk instead of hitting the model again:

```
if hasattr(response.choices[0].message, "reasoning_content"):
    reasoning = response.choices[0].message.reasoning_content
    print(f"Reasoning:\n{reasoning}\n")
# Okay, the user is asking about the capital o

final_msg = response.choices[0].message.content
print(f"Final Answer:\n{final_msg}\n")
# The capital of the region of \*\*Le Marche (...
```

It is now time to look at LangChain.

LangChain

LangChain (`https://python.langchain.com/docs/introduction/`) is one of the most popular open source frameworks that covers most aspects of building with LLMs: thousands of integrations with an increasing number of providers, components for building RAG systems, agents, and more. It's great for prototyping and to get something out there. However, when your application starts getting bigger, you might consider implementing some of the components yourself for added control. They could include:

- **Unified API**: Use the same code and interface for all the models and providers, including local models such as Ollama and llama.cpp.
- **RAG helpers**: Document loaders help you quickly load external data and pass that as context to the LLM. Document loaders, text splitters, and retrieval and generation workflows help make your RAG pipelines very easy to implement.
- **Structured outputs**: Integrations for you to get structured data out of the LLMs. Support JSON schemas, streaming, few-shot prompting, and many more features.

Let's look at the following script to see how we can use LangChain:

1. A `ChatDeepSeek` LLM wrapper from `langchain_deepseek` is created first:

```
from langchain_deepseek import ChatDeepSeek
from pydantic import BaseModel, Field
from typing import Optional
from enum import Enum
```

```
llm = ChatDeepSeek(
    model="deepseek-chat",
    temperature=0,
    max_tokens=None,
    timeout=None,
    max_retries=2,
)
```

2. Then we create a Pydantic model (`SkyColor`), which defines the expected structured output:

```
class SkyColorEnum(str, Enum):
    BLUE = "blue"
    GRAY = "gray"
    WHITE = "white"
    CLOUDY = "cloudy"
    OVERCAST = "overcast"
    CLEAR = "clear"


class SkyColor(BaseModel):
    """Sky color prediction for Copenhagen."""

    color: SkyColorEnum = Field(description="The primary color of
the sky")
    description: str = Field(description="Detailed description of
the sky appearance")
    confidence: Optional[int] = Field(
        default=None, description="Confidence level of the
prediction, from 1 to 10"
    )
```

3. The `with_structured_output` method wraps the LLM so that any reply is automatically parsed and validated against that schema. The code calls the model with a prompt and receives a fully validated `SkyColor` object:

```
structured_llm = llm.with_structured_output(SkyColor)
result: SkyColor = structured_llm.invoke(
    "What color is the sky likely to be in Copenhagen today?"
```

```
)

print(result.color)

# prints SkyColorEnum.GRAY
```

Instructor

Instructor (`https://python.useinstructor.com/`) is the most popular Python library for extracting structured data from LLMs. It's built on top of Pydantic and provides type-safe data extraction with automatic validation, retries, and streaming support. It supports most major platforms and models. The best thing about Instructor is actually their documentation, which provides great guides, cookbooks, and other great gems!

- **Structured outputs**: Pass a Pydantic model as a response model and get a Pydantic model back. You can also use open source or self-hosted models, and Instructor will support it.
- **Automatic retries and self-correction**: Failed validations trigger retries that inject the error message into the model context. This works great so that the model patches its own answer.
- **Streaming validated chunks**: Instructor also supports streaming of partially validated objects. That means that you don't have to wait for the full model response to show something to users. Read more about it here: `https://python.useinstructor.com/blog/2023/11/26/python-generators-and-llm-streaming/#stream-processing`.

We will now look at the use of the Instructor library in the following script. The resulting object is typed, validated, and ready for use:

1. Instructor wraps the OpenAI-compatible DeepSeek endpoint:

```
import os
from openai import OpenAI
import instructor

from pydantic import BaseModel, Field

client = instructor.from_openai(
    OpenAI(api_key=os.getenv("DEEPSEEK_API_KEY"), base_url="https://
api.deepseek.com"),
    mode=instructor.Mode.MD_JSON,  # because this is a reasoning
```

```
    model..
)
```

2. We then add two Pydantic classes (`City` and `CitiesResponse`), which describe the structure of the desired response:

```
class City(BaseModel):
    name: str = Field(description="The name of the city")
    population: int = Field(description="The population of the
city")
    notable_landmarks: list[str] = Field(
        description="List of notable landmarks in the city"
    )


class CitiesResponse(BaseModel):
    cities: list[City] = Field(description="List of interesting
cities")
```

3. We then make a call to `deepseek-reasoner`, asking for three interesting Portuguese cities:

```
cities: CitiesResponse = client.chat.completions.create(
    model="deepseek-reasoner",
    messages=[
        {
            "role": "user",
            "content": "Top 3 most interesting cities in Portugal",
        },
    ],
    response_model=CitiesResponse,
    temperature=0.0,
)
```

4. Instructor will ensure the reply *exactly* matches the schema (the base model), retrying if the validation fails, giving the validation error to the LLM:

```
for city in cities.cities:
    print(f"City: {city.name}")
    print(f"Population: {city.population}")
    print(f"Notable Landmarks: {', '.join(city.notable_landmarks)}")
```

You will observe the following output:

```
# City: Lisbon
# Population: 545796
# Notable Landmarks: Belém Tower, Jerónimos Monastery, São Jorge Castle,
Alfama District
# City: Porto
# Population: 237584
# ...
```

Now that we have covered a few essential libraries, we would like to mention some more that might be useful in your journey.

Other interesting libraries and resources

- **llm** (`https://github.com/simonw/llm`) is a CLI + Python library that speaks to OpenAI, Anthropic, Gemini, Llama, and other models while logging every prompt/response and embedding to SQLite for later analysis. Its plugin system and Unix-style piping let you automate tasks such as summarizing web pages, generating shell commands, or comparing models straight from the terminal.
- **Pydantic AI** (`https://ai.pydantic.dev`) is a type-safe agent framework from the Pydantic team that validates LLM outputs against Pydantic schemas while supporting providers such as OpenAI, Anthropic, Gemini, and Groq. It features dependency injection, streaming, and graph-based control flow and adds built-in monitoring to move GenAI projects into production with minimal boilerplate.
- **Outlines** (`https://dottxt-ai.github.io/outlines/latest`) guides a model to emit output that matches a regex, JSON schema, grammar, or enum so downstream code can parse it without fuss. It runs with proprietary or open source backends and adds almost no latency, which is why many teams rely on it for reliable structured generation in production.

We've now covered a lot of different libraries that you can add to your toolbelt when building DeepSeek.

By using DeepSeek models, you have a lot of options and can effectively build where it suits you ranging from the official API or third-party providers, such as AWS or OpenRouter. If control matters, you can also run models locally with llama.cpp or Ollama. We also provided a good guide on where to go if you need to deploy in GPU clusters (if you have the means).

We also covered libraries such as LiteLLM, LangChain, and Instructor, which will help you take the most juice possible out of DeepSeek models, while keeping your logic and code sane.

11

Unlock Your Exclusive Benefits

Your copy of this book includes the following exclusive benefits:

- Next-gen Packt Reader
- DRM-free PDF/ePub downloads

Follow the guide below to unlock them. The process takes only a few minutes and needs to be completed once.

Unlock this Book's Free Benefits in 3 Easy Steps

Step 1

Keep your purchase invoice ready for *Step 3*. If you have a physical copy, scan it using your phone and save it as a PDF, JPG, or PNG.

For more help on finding your invoice, visit `https://www.packtpub.com/unlock-benefits/help`.

Note: If you bought this book directly from Packt, no invoice is required. After *Step 2*, you can access your exclusive content right away.

Step 2

Scan the QR code or go to `packtpub.com/unlock`.

On the page that opens (similar to *Figure 11.1* on desktop), search for this book by name and select the correct edition.

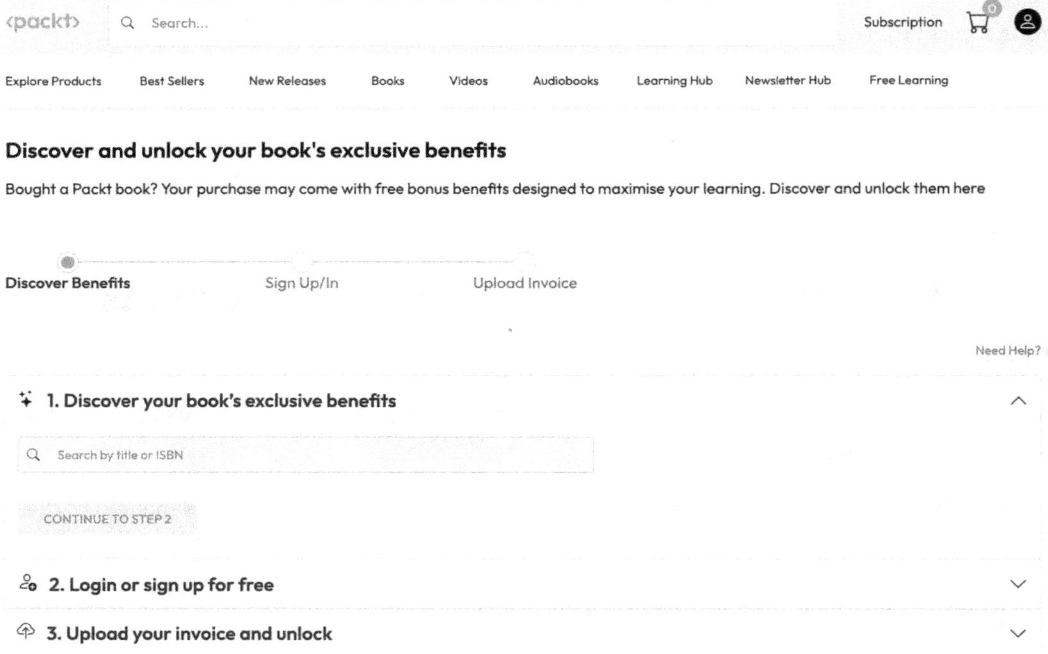

Figure 11.1: Packt unlock landing page on desktop

Step 3

After selecting your book, sign in to your Packt account or create one for free. Then upload your invoice (PDF, PNG, or JPG, up to 10 MB). Follow the on-screen instructions to finish the process.

Need help?

If you get stuck and need help, visit `https://www.packtpub.com/unlock-benefits/help` for a detailed FAQ on how to find your invoices and more. This QR code will take you to the help page.

Note: If you are still facing issues, reach out to `customercare@packt.com`.

packtpub.com

Subscribe to our online digital library for full access to over 7,000 books and videos, as well as industry leading tools to help you plan your personal development and advance your career. For more information, please visit our website.

Why subscribe?

- Spend less time learning and more time coding with practical eBooks and Videos from over 4,000 industry professionals
- Improve your learning with Skill Plans built especially for you
- Get a free eBook or video every month
- Fully searchable for easy access to vital information
- Copy and paste, print, and bookmark content

At www.packtpub.com, you can also read a collection of free technical articles, sign up for a range of free newsletters, and receive exclusive discounts and offers on Packt books and eBooks.

Other Books You May Enjoy

If you enjoyed this book, you may be interested in these other books by Packt:

EXPERT INSIGHTS
Building
Agentic AI Systems
Create intelligent, autonomous AI agents that can reason, plan, and adapt
Anjanava Biswas | Wrick Talukdar
packt

Building Agentic AI Systems

Anjanava Biswas, Wrick Talukdar

ISBN: 9781803238753

- Master the core principles of GenAI and agentic systems
- Understand how AI agents operate, reason, and adapt in dynamic environments
- Enable AI agents to analyze their own actions and improvise
- Implement systems where AI agents can leverage external tools and plan complex tasks
- Apply methods to enhance transparency, accountability, and reliability in AI
- Explore real-world implementations of AI agents across industries

LLMs in Enterprise

Ahmed Menshawy, Mahmoud Fahmy

ISBN: 9781836203070

- Apply design patterns to integrate LLMs into enterprise applications for efficiency and scalability
- Overcome common challenges in scaling and deploying LLMs
- Use fine-tuning techniques and RAG approaches to enhance LLM efficiency
- Stay ahead of the curve with insights into emerging trends and advancements, including multimodality
- Optimize LLM performance through customized contextual models, advanced inferencing engines, and evaluation patterns
- Ensure fairness, transparency, and accountability in AI applications

Packt is searching for authors like you

If you're interested in becoming an author for Packt, please visit `authors.packtpub.com` and apply today. We have worked with thousands of developers and tech professionals, just like you, to help them share their insight with the global tech community. You can make a general application, apply for a specific hot topic that we are recruiting an author for, or submit your own idea.

Share your thoughts

Now you've finished *DeepSeek in Practice*, we'd love to hear your thoughts! Scan the QR code below to go straight to the Amazon review page for this book and share your feedback or leave a review on the site that you purchased it from.

`https://packt.link/r/180602084X`

Your review is important to us and the tech community and will help us make sure we're delivering excellent quality content.

Index

A

B

L

M

N

O

P

Q

R

S

W

X

Z

www.ingramcontent.com/pod-product-compliance
Lightning Source LLC
Chambersburg PA
CBHW081221220326
41598CB00037B/6858

* 9 7 8 1 8 0 6 0 2 0 8 5 0 *